Published by Fiery Studios, PO Box 51595, Kalamazoo, Michigan 49005.
fierystudios@hotmail.com • http://www.fierystudios.com.
First printing, December 2013. Printed in the USA by Edwards Brothers Malloy. ISBN 978-0-9743110-2-9

CLOCKWORK·GAME

THE ILLUSTRIOUS CAREER OF A CHESS-PLAYING AUTOMATON

A GRAPHIC NOVEL BY

JANE·IRWIN

Foreword by Nisi Shawl

Fiery Studios

For Paul
for everything

INTO THE CANNY VALLEY

The truth is right there in a word balloon on page 165. "People believe stories, not facts," says Johann Maelzel, one in a series of owners of "The Turk," the figure at the center of the real-life, 85-year conspiracy depicted in *Clockwork Game*. Telling The Turk's strange story through expressive drawings and apt words, Jane Irwin makes us believe everything, from its first appearance before eighteenth-century Vienna's royal court up to its blazing finale in nineteenth-century Philadelphia. There's the supposed chess-playing automaton's match against Benjamin Franklin, Napoleon's pragmatic skepticism when presented with The Turk in the wake of his Austrian victories, and Edgar Allan Poe's article debunking the claim that its prowess was that of a pure machine. The Turk rubbed elbows with Beethoven and shared an exhibit hall with P.T. Barnum's Joice Heth, who the fledgling impresario said was the 161-year-old former nurse of President George Washington.

Clockwork Game is true. It's also, unlike Barnum's showman's patter, mostly facts. Though not entirely.

But to paraphrase Maelzel's lead-up sentence to the aphorism above, the story's telling is what Jane Irwin gets right.

The Ottoman Empire had a long and glorious tradition of engineering marvels and expanding scientific knowledge. Irwin makes this tradition concrete in the book's opening pages with a charming sequence showing Al-Jazari's elephant clock in operation, complete with dragon heads and drummer. In nineteenth-century Philadelphia, Turkish-American doctor Yusuf bin Ibrahim provides another lens on the racially-charged lampoon its inventor created in his ostensible automaton. Again and again Irwin challenges herself to question comfortable assumptions, looking at The Turk's career through the eyes of those so often classified as "others": workers, women, people of color, the physically disabled. Again and again she enriches the telling of this fascinating tale by doing so; *Clockwork Game* is simultaneously funnier and more tragic than readers may expect.

In the field of human aesthetics, the "uncanny valley" is the dip in the graph of our tolerance of human simulacra. We react with rising positivity to dolls and robots as they become more and more like us—up to a certain point. At that point there's a drop-off in acceptance, a sinking into revulsion. Too lifelike, yet not alive, inhabitants of this figurative valley are uncanny in appearance. If their similarity to us is developed further and continues to grow, the positive reaction reasserts itself and the graph line trends upward again.

Wolfgang von Kempelen, The Turk's inventor, despised what he'd created as a fraud, "base trickery." Discussing one of his "serious" devices he bemoans the way audiences focus on the odd appearance of his Speaking Machine, explaining that he'd frequently begin demonstrations with its wheezing bellow and nostril-simulating tubes covered by a sheet. He tells a sympathetic visitor that he hopes eventually to hide the apparatus inside the dummy of a young girl's body. I think doing this would have been a mistake; a human-looking doll that spoke would have been far too disturbing to people of that time. The Turk was saved from inhabiting in the uncanny valley by several factors: the clockwork noises made during its operation; the standing invitation to inspect its inner workings and thus disregard its outward appearance; and its likeness to an exoticized other, which allowed the intended viewers to distance themselves from it rather than identify with it. These dehumanizing elements kept The Turk on the valley's far side.

What I call the canny valley—without any experiments or charts to back my theory up—is the sweet spot authors aim for between data and whimsy. *Clockwork Game* sits in the canny valley's exact center. Here the dip represents a fall in resistance to the unfamiliar. Beginning with sheer nonsense, what writers and artists offer becomes more captivating as it encompasses more verifiable facts—but not too many. There is a place on this imaginary graph where, suddenly, facts take on the allure of fantasy and speculation the weight of certainty. *Clockwork Game*'s dramatic framing and quick pace make it easy for the book to fulfill our innate biological hunger for narratives, and Irwin's art—particularly her characters' enchantingly expressive faces—fleshes out the mere names and dates that would have comprised her initial research. And that research was both broad and deep, as can be ascertained by referring to her twelve pages of notes and four of bibliography. It included books, videos, websites, and consultations with people knowledgeable in areas such as Turkish culture and the representation of diversity in fiction.

Composer and comedian Neil Innes once famously said, "I've suffered for my music. Now it's your turn." It was a joke, but other creative artists have sometimes had to strive to avoid meaning something similar—especially when they do lots research to support their projects. They're drawn to the far side of the canny valley, the dry and tortuously infertile terrain of facts for facts sake. A book filled with nothing but the poorly presented results of research will beguile very few of us to spend our precious time struggling through its pages. Resistance will be high.

Irwin's motto might well be "I've been suffused with pleasure for my work's sake. Now it's your turn." Though she carefully describes when, where, how, and why she departed from what's known about The Turk and its many adventures, she keeps these notes out of the story's way, confining them to *Clockwork Game*'s after matter, where they rightfully belong. This leaves us free to luxuriate in the delightful greenery where the story proper grows—to speed through it or linger, to return to the canny valley as often as we like.

—Nisi Shawl
Tiptree-Award winning author of *Filter House*

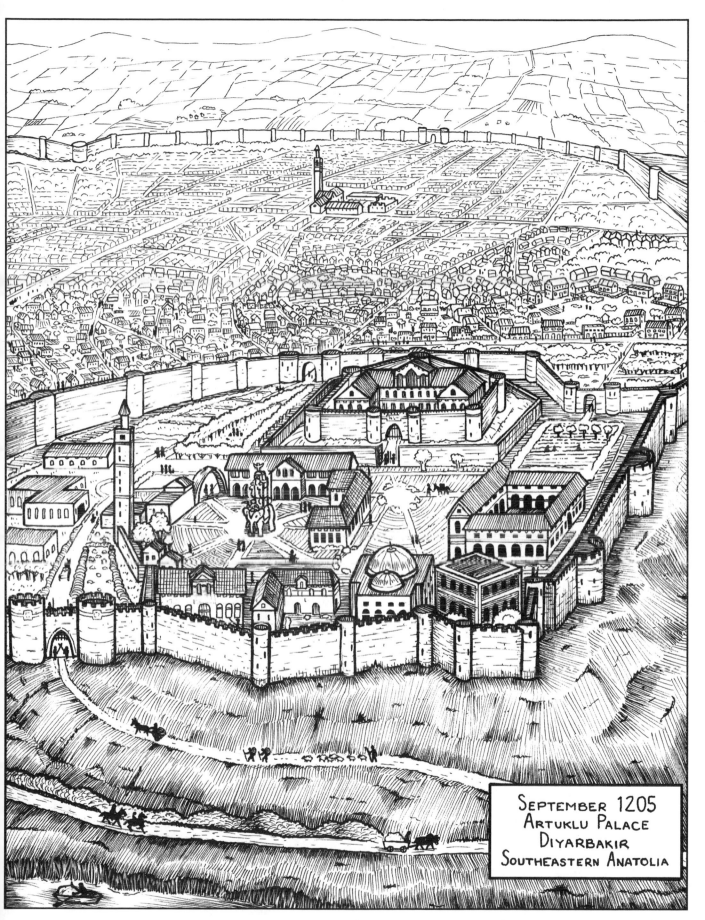

September 1205
Artuklu Palace
Diyarbakir
Southeastern Anatolia

11

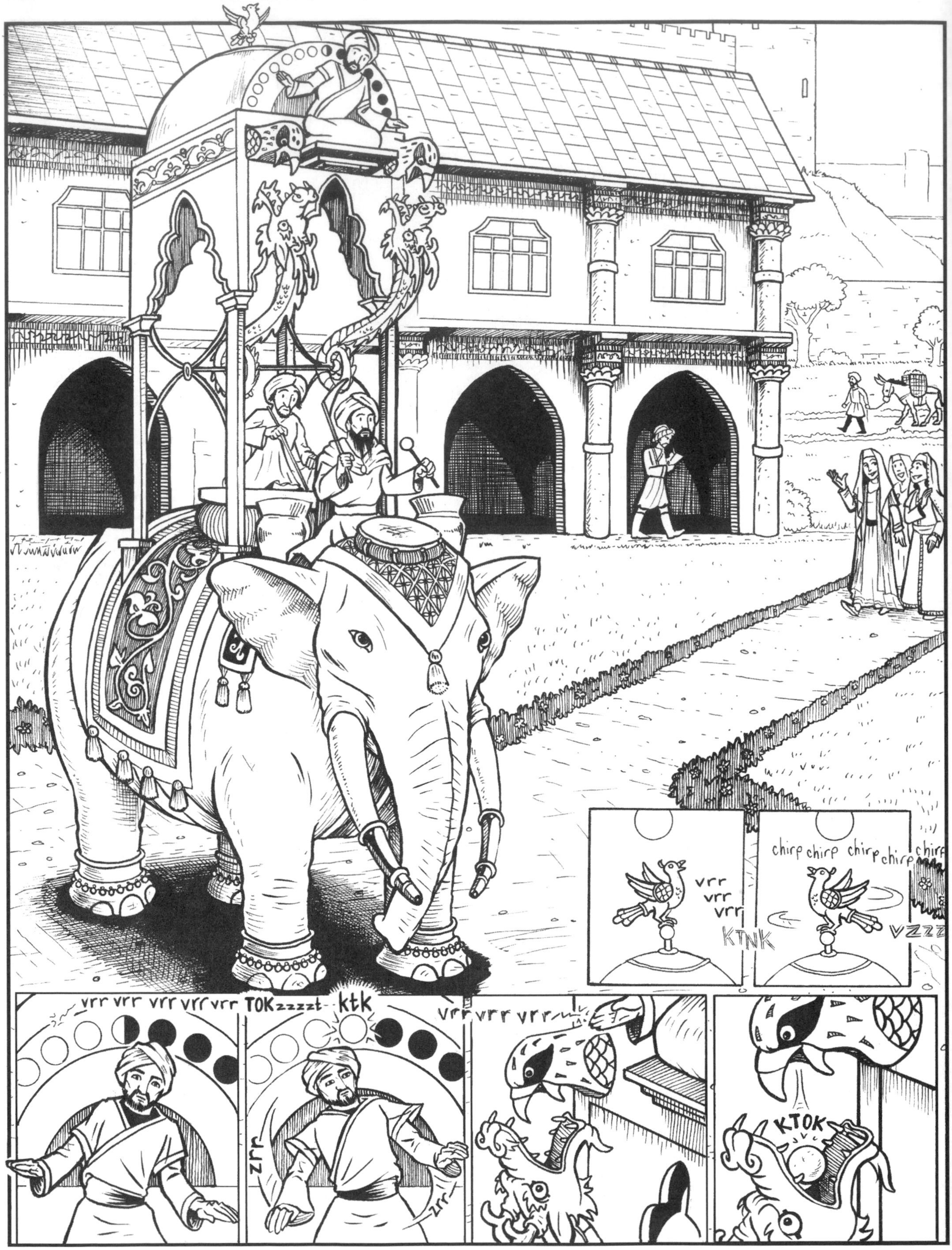
vrr
vrr
vrr
KTNK
chirp chirp chirp chirp chirp
vzzz
vrr vrr vrr vrr vrr
TOKzzzzt
ktk
zrr
zrr
vrr vrr vrr
KTOK

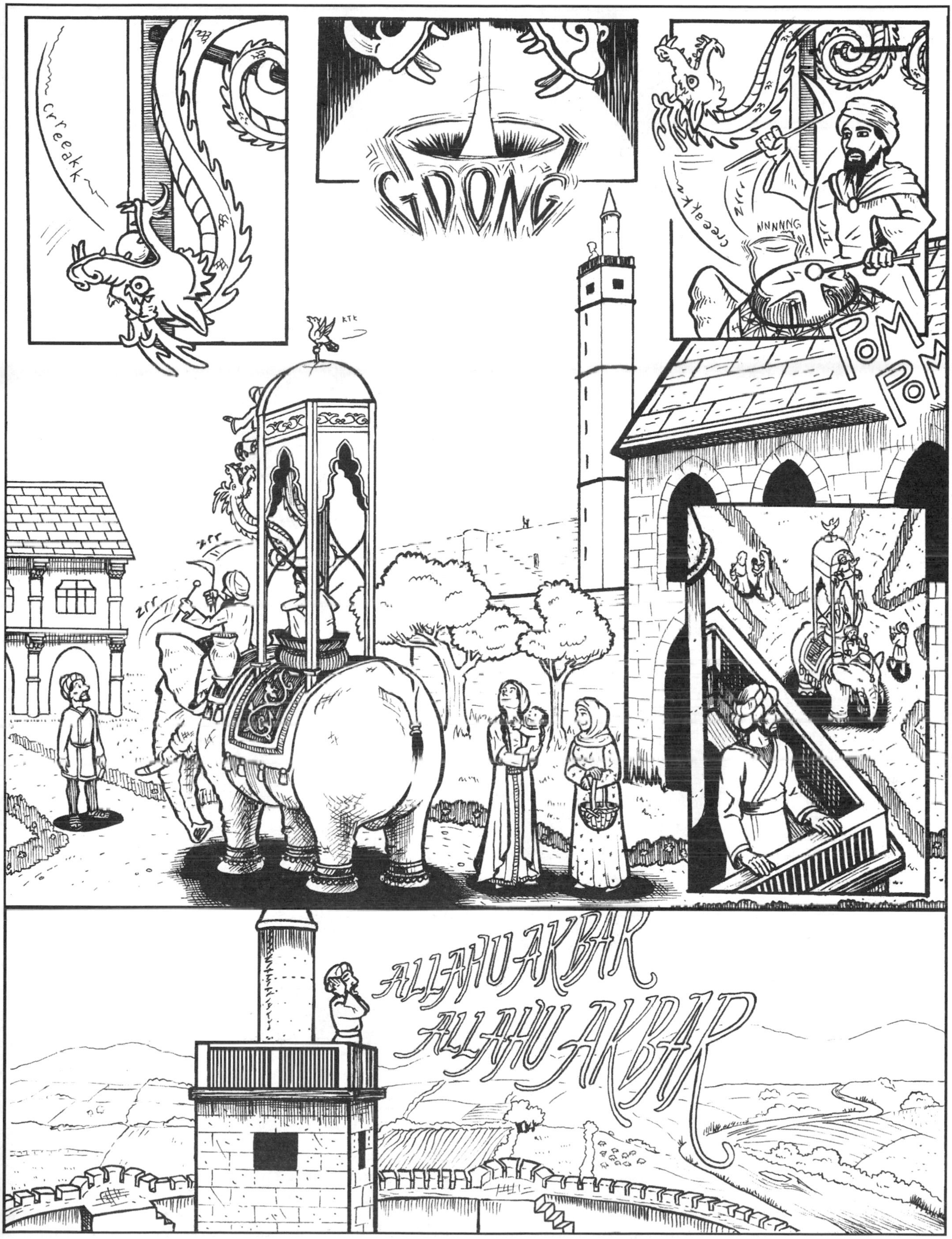
crreeakk
GDONG
creeakk
NNNNG
POM
POM
KTK
zrr
zrr
ALLAHU AKBAR
ALLAHU AKBAR

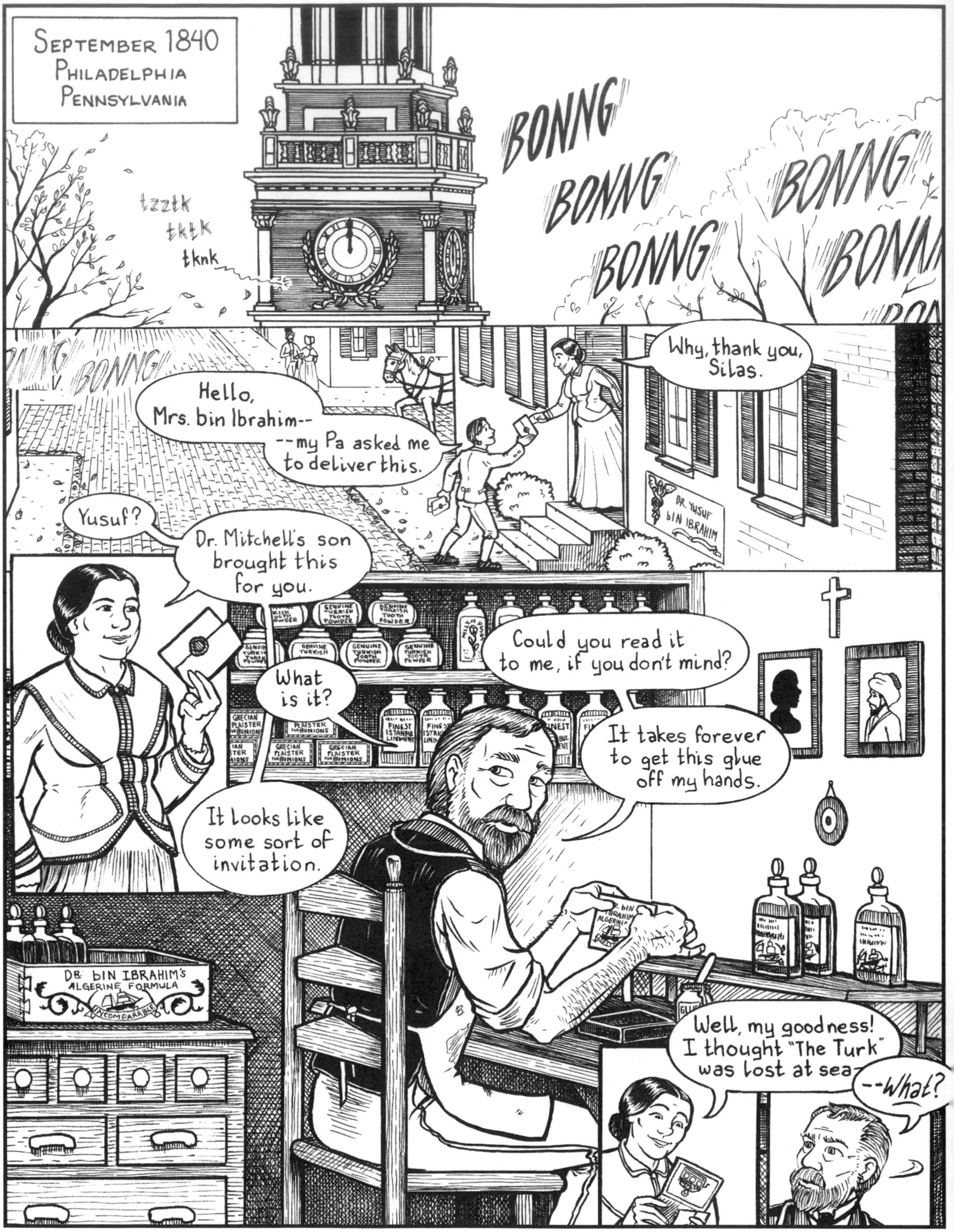

September 1840
Philadelphia
Pennsylvania
tzztk
tktk
tknk
BONNG
BONNG
BONNG
BONNG
BONNG
BONNG
Hello, Mrs. bin Ibrahim--
--my Pa asked me to deliver this.
Why, thank you, Silas.
Dr. Yusuf bin Ibrahim
Yusuf?
Dr. Mitchell's son brought this for you.
Genuine Turkish Tooth Powder
Grecian Plaister for Bunions
Finest Istanbul Liniment
What is it?
It looks like some sort of invitation.
Could you read it to me, if you don't mind?
It takes forever to get this glue off my hands.
Dr. bin Ibrahim's Algerine Formula
Incomparable
Glue
Well, my goodness! I thought "The Turk" was lost at sea--
--What?

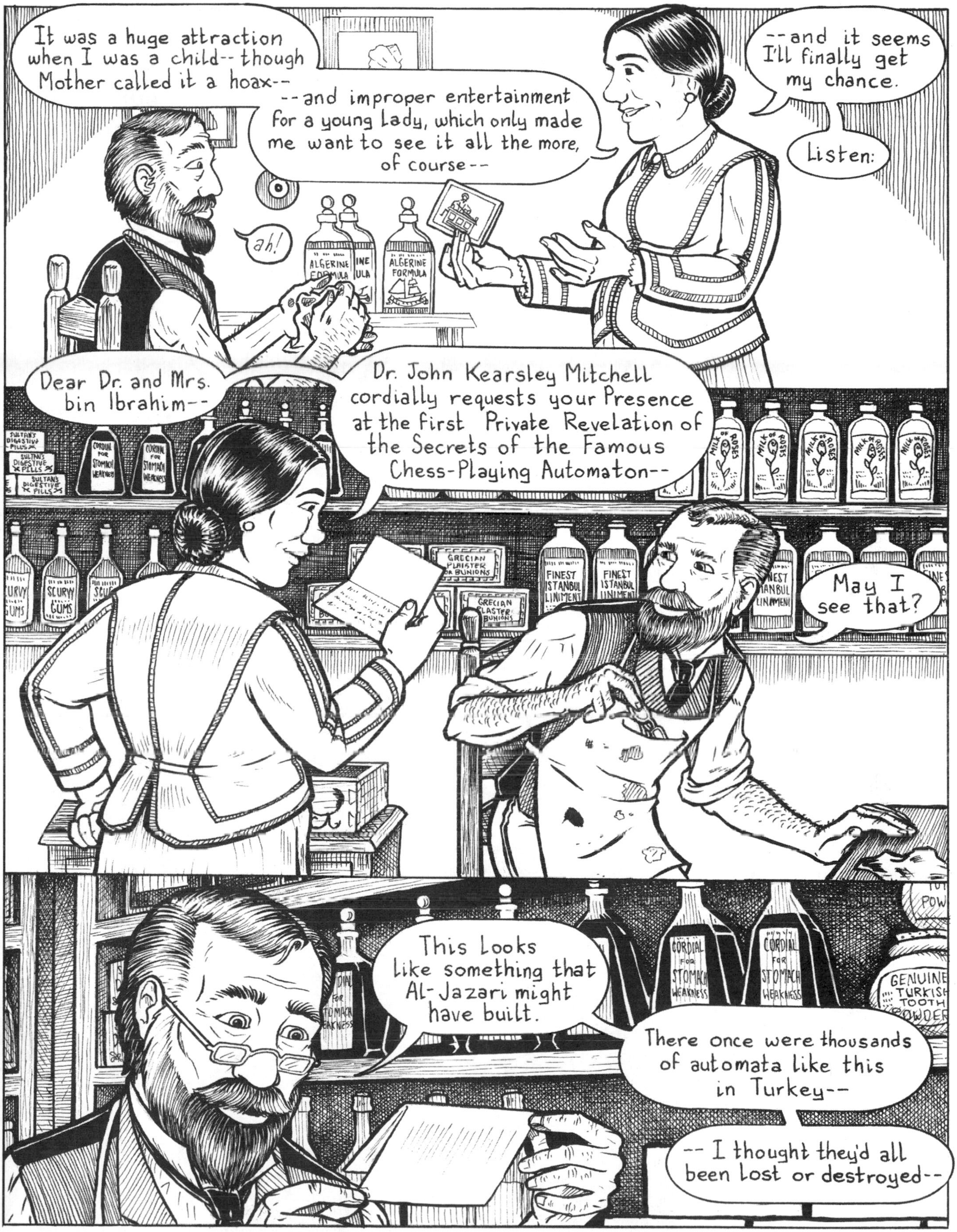
It was a huge attraction when I was a child-- though Mother called it a hoax--
--and improper entertainment for a young lady, which only made me want to see it all the more, of course--
ah!
--and it seems I'll finally get my chance.
Listen:
ALGERINE FORMULA
Dear Dr. and Mrs. bin Ibrahim--
Dr. John Kearsley Mitchell cordially requests your Presence at the first Private Revelation of the Secrets of the Famous Chess-Playing Automaton--
May I see that?
SULTAN'S DIGESTIVE PILLS
CORDIAL FOR STOMACH WEAKNESS
MILK OF ROSES
SCURVY GUMS
GRECIAN PLAISTER for BUNIONS
FINEST ISTANBUL LINIMENT
This looks like something that Al-Jazari might have built.
There once were thousands of automata like this in Turkey--
-- I thought they'd all been lost or destroyed--
GENUINE TURKISH TOOTH POWDER

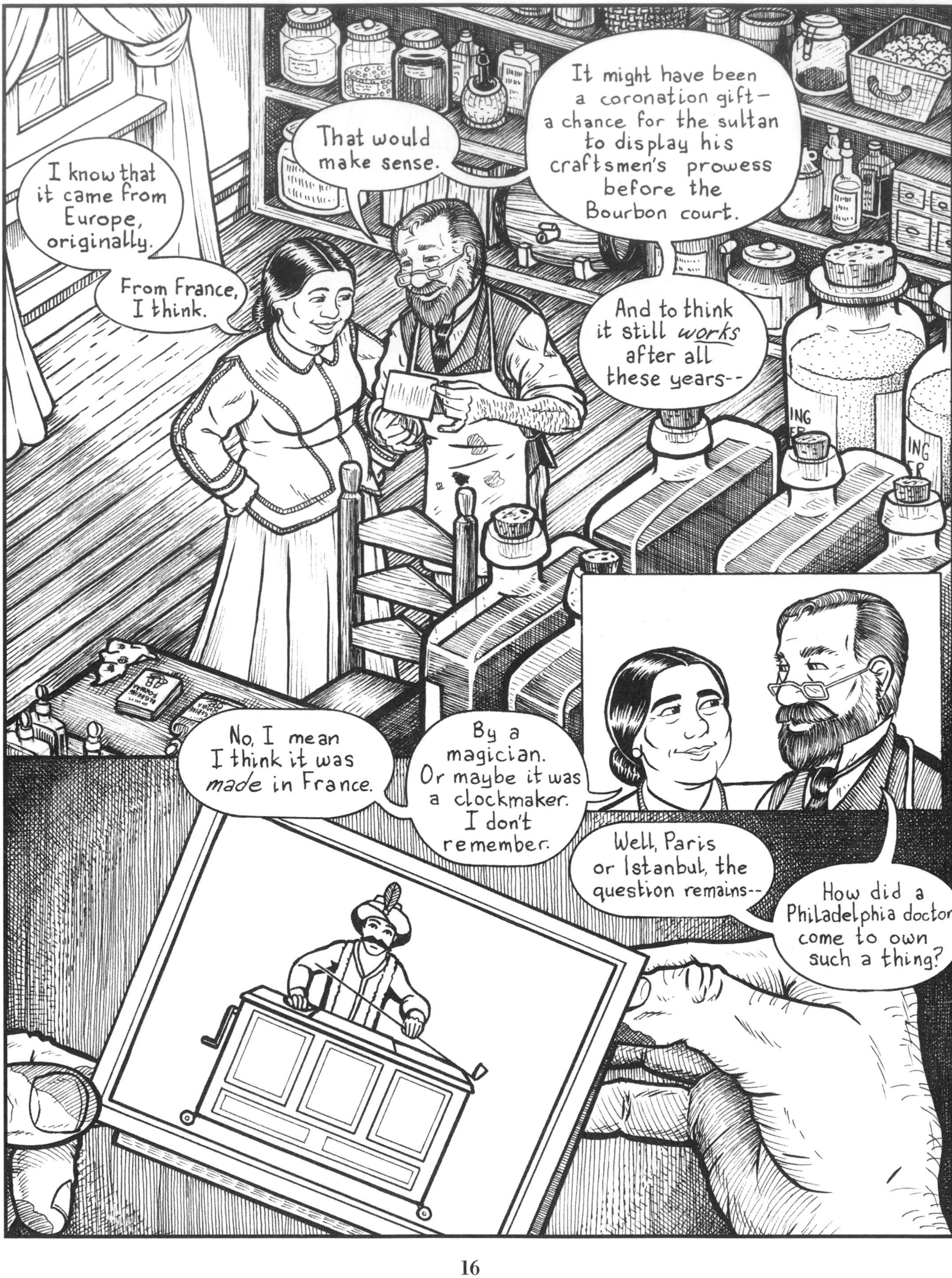
I know that it came from Europe, originally.
From France, I think.
That would make sense.
It might have been a coronation gift— a chance for the sultan to display his craftsmen's prowess before the Bourbon court.
And to think it still *works* after all these years--
No, I mean I think it was *made* in France.
By a magician. Or maybe it was a clockmaker. I don't remember.
Well, Paris or Istanbul, the question remains--
How did a Philadelphia doctor come to own such a thing?

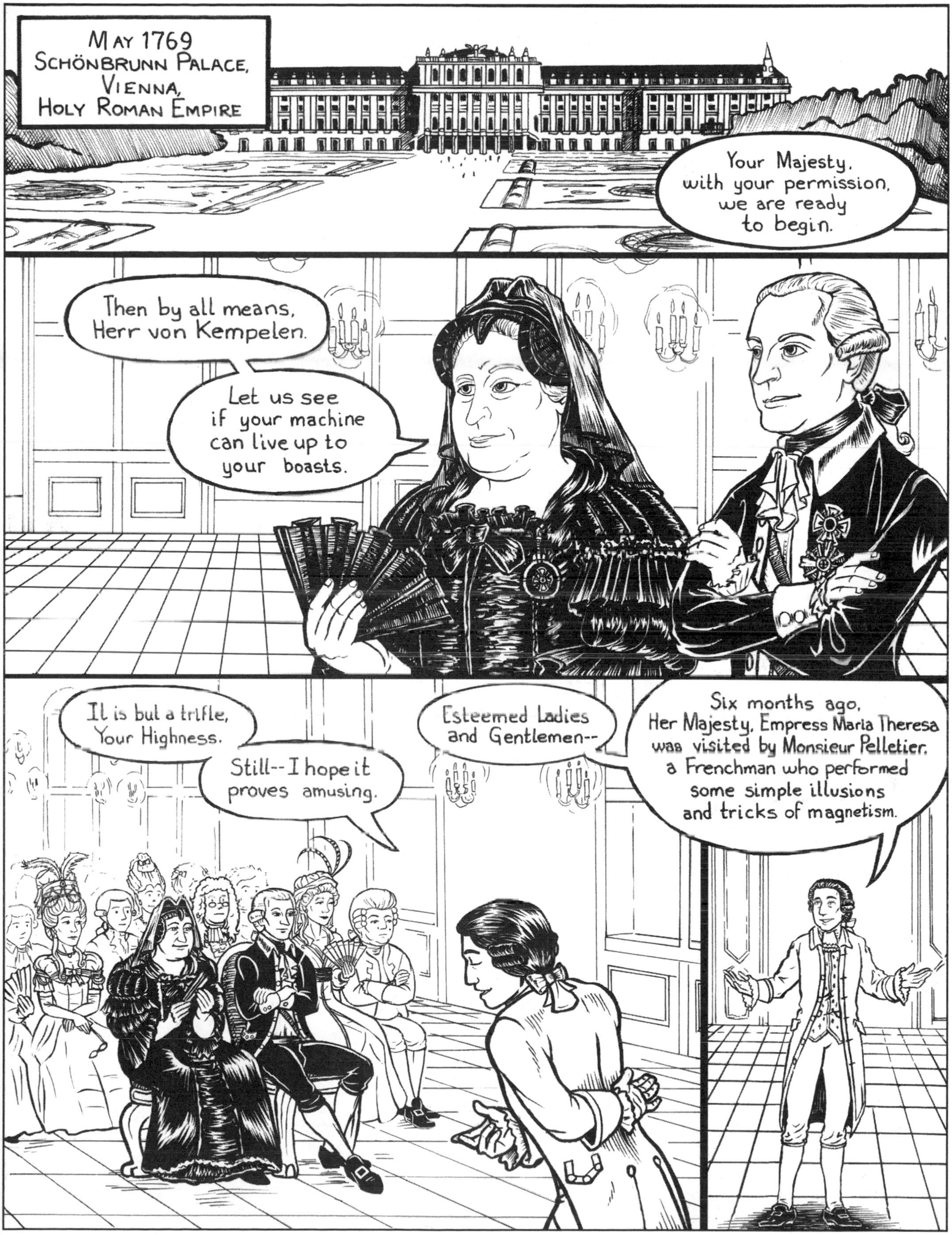
May 1769
Schönbrunn Palace,
Vienna,
Holy Roman Empire
Your Majesty, with your permission, we are ready to begin.
Then by all means, Herr von Kempelen.
Let us see if your machine can live up to your boasts.
It is but a trifle, Your Highness.
Still--I hope it proves amusing.
Esteemed Ladies and Gentlemen--
Six months ago, Her Majesty, Empress Maria Theresa was visited by Monsieur Pelletier, a Frenchman who performed some simple illusions and tricks of magnetism.

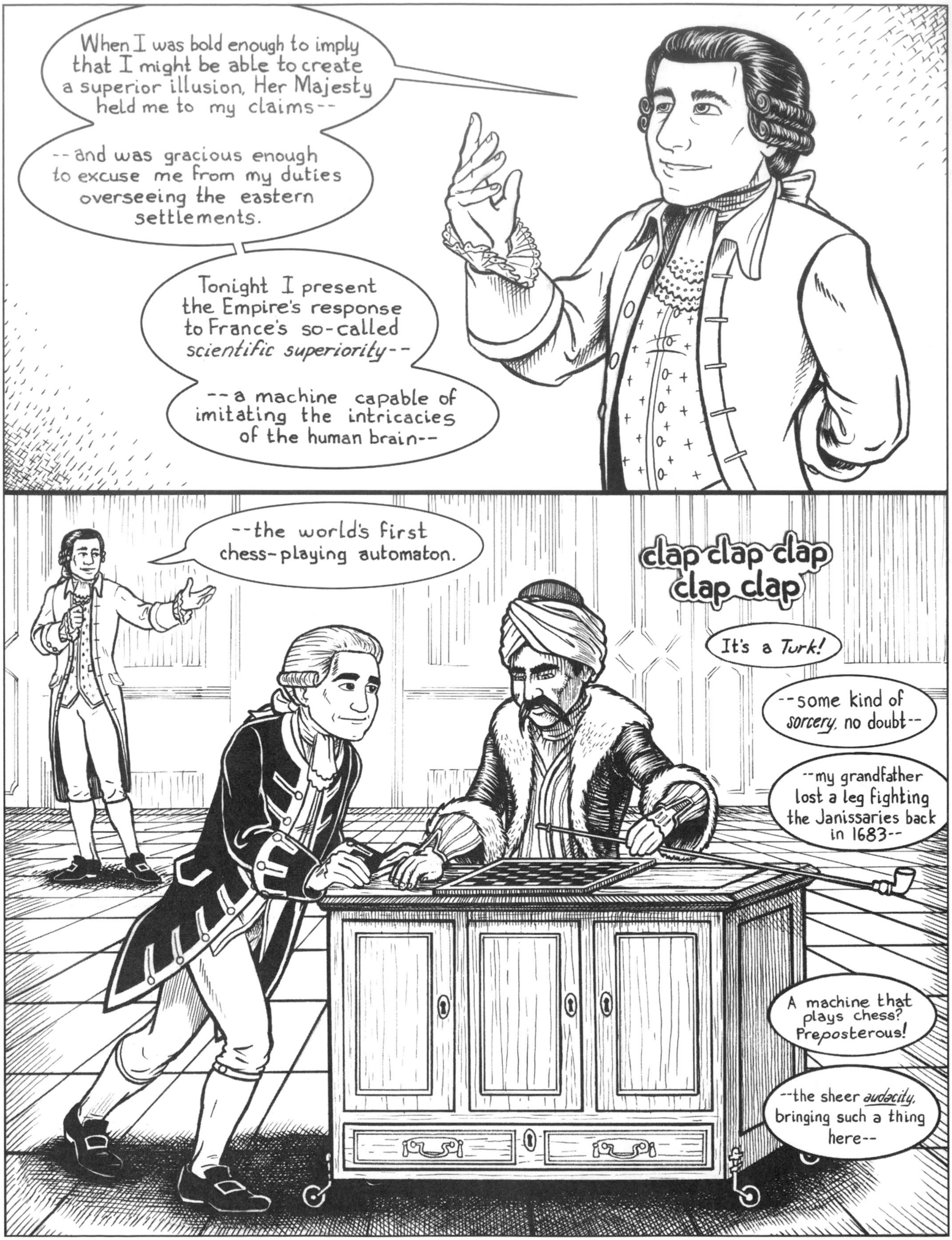
When I was bold enough to imply that I might be able to create a superior illusion, Her Majesty held me to my claims--
--and was gracious enough to excuse me from my duties overseeing the eastern settlements.
Tonight I present the Empire's response to France's so-called *scientific superiority*--
--a machine capable of imitating the intricacies of the human brain--
--the world's first chess-playing automaton.
clap clap clap clap clap
It's a *Turk!*
--some kind of *sorcery,* no doubt--
--my grandfather lost a leg fighting the Janissaries back in 1683--
A machine that plays chess? Preposterous!
--the sheer *audacity,* bringing such a thing here--

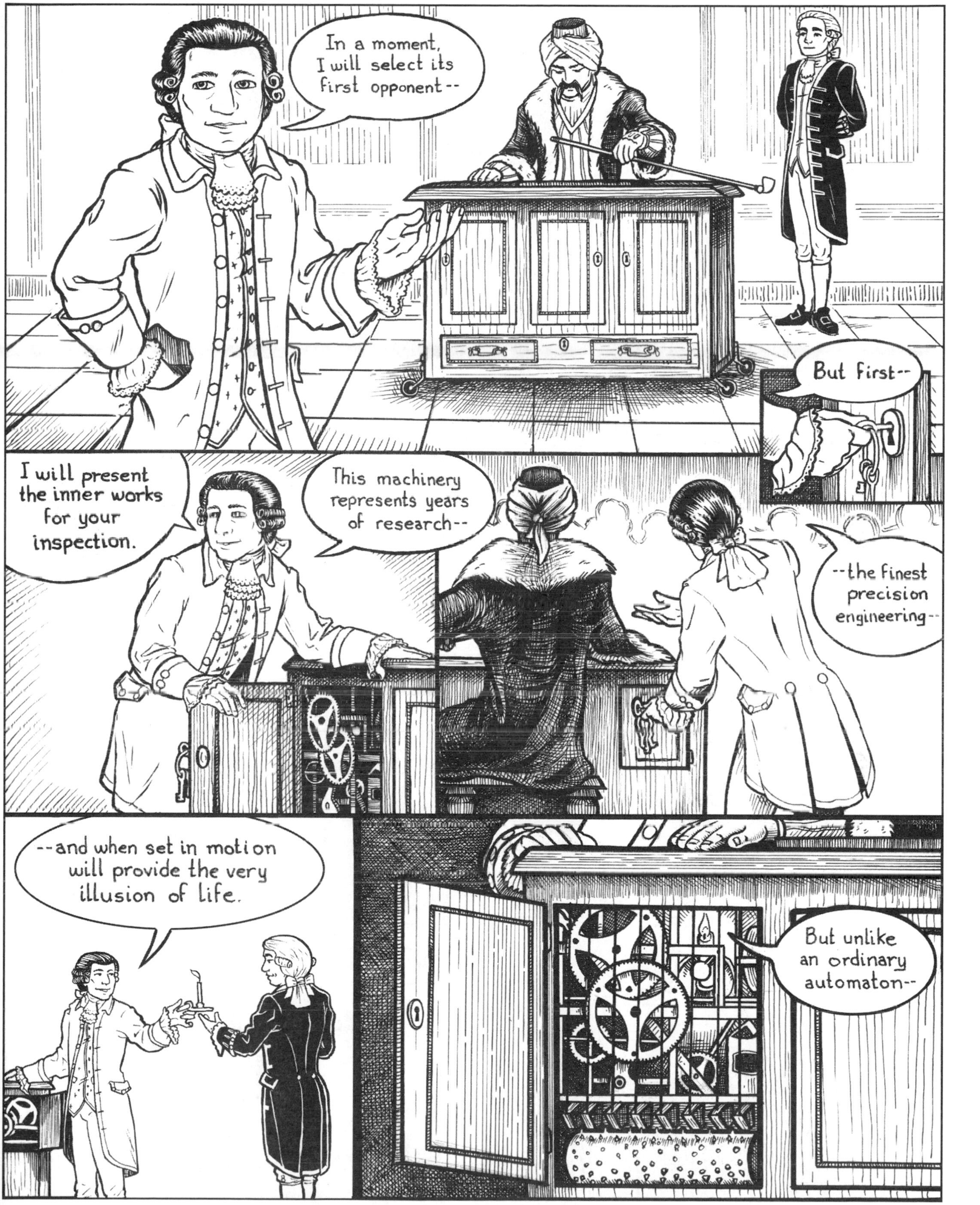
In a moment, I will select its first opponent--
But first--
I will present the inner works for your inspection.
This machinery represents years of research--
--the finest precision engineering--
--and when set in motion will provide the very illusion of life.
But unlike an ordinary automaton--

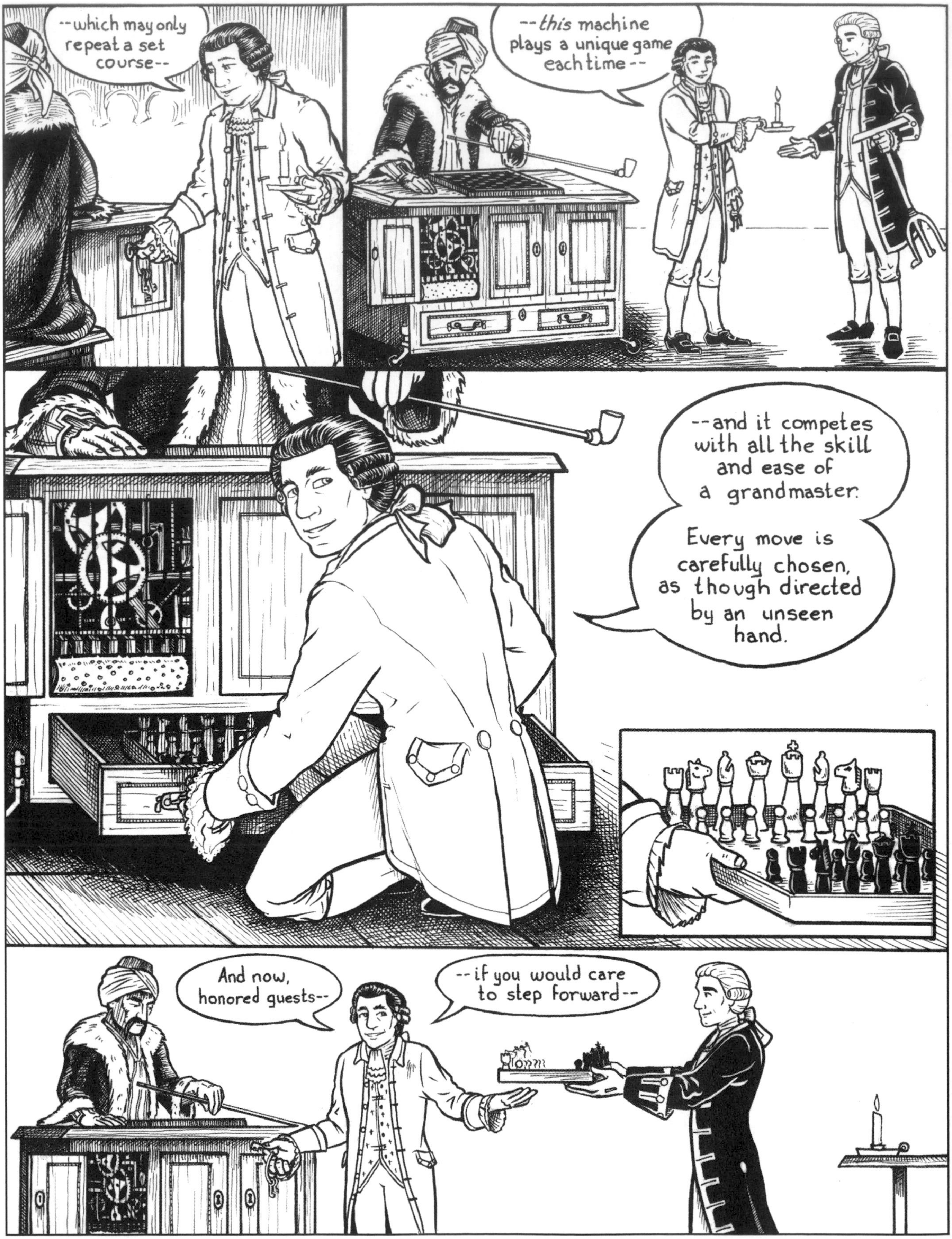

--which may only repeat a set course--
--*this* machine plays a unique game each time--
--and it competes with all the skill and ease of a grandmaster.
Every move is carefully chosen, as though directed by an unseen hand.
And now, honored guests--
--if you would care to step forward--

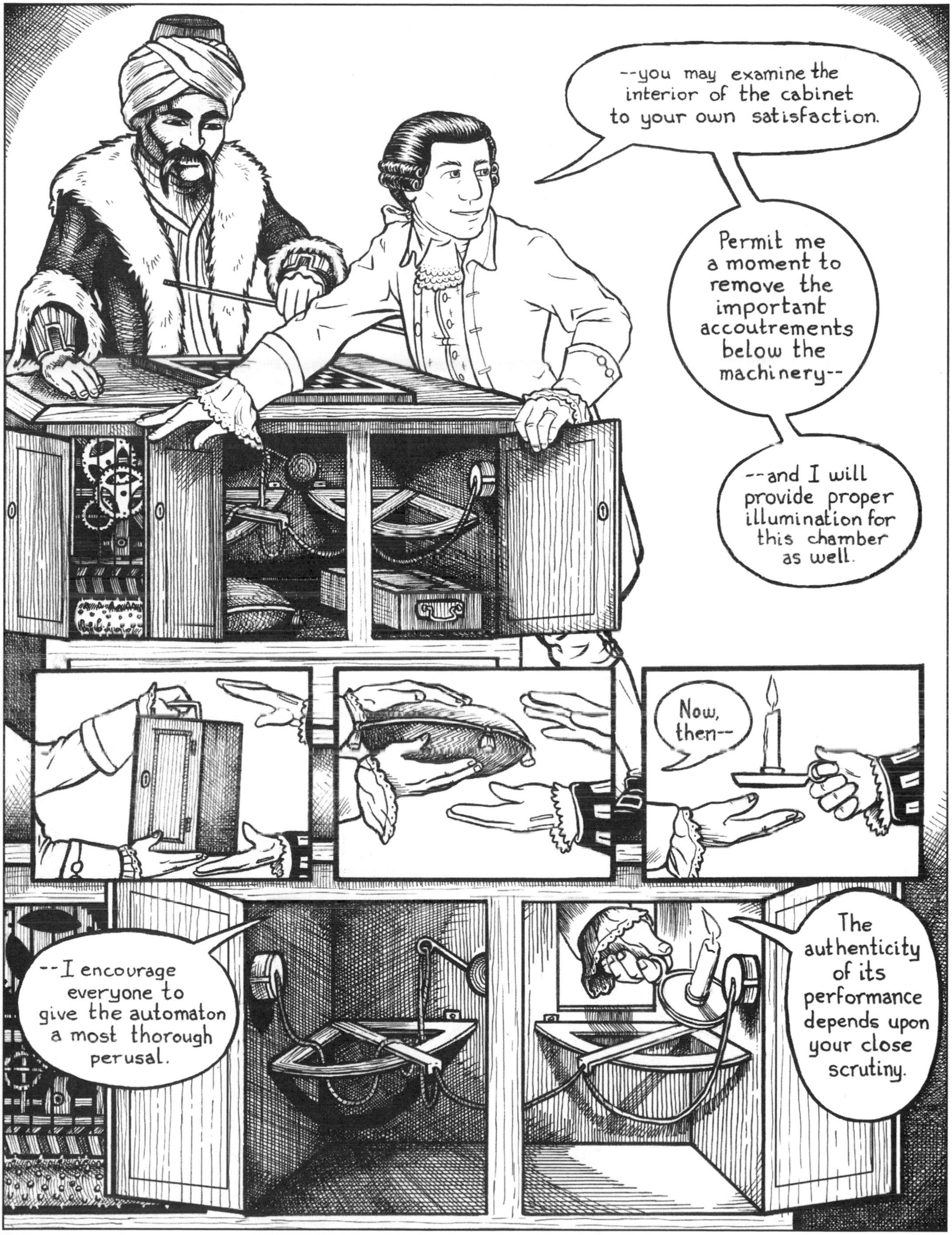
--you may examine the interior of the cabinet to your own satisfaction.
Permit me a moment to remove the important accoutrements below the machinery--
--and I will provide proper illumination for this chamber as well.
Now, then--
--I encourage everyone to give the automaton a most thorough perusal.
The authenticity of its performance depends upon your close scrutiny.

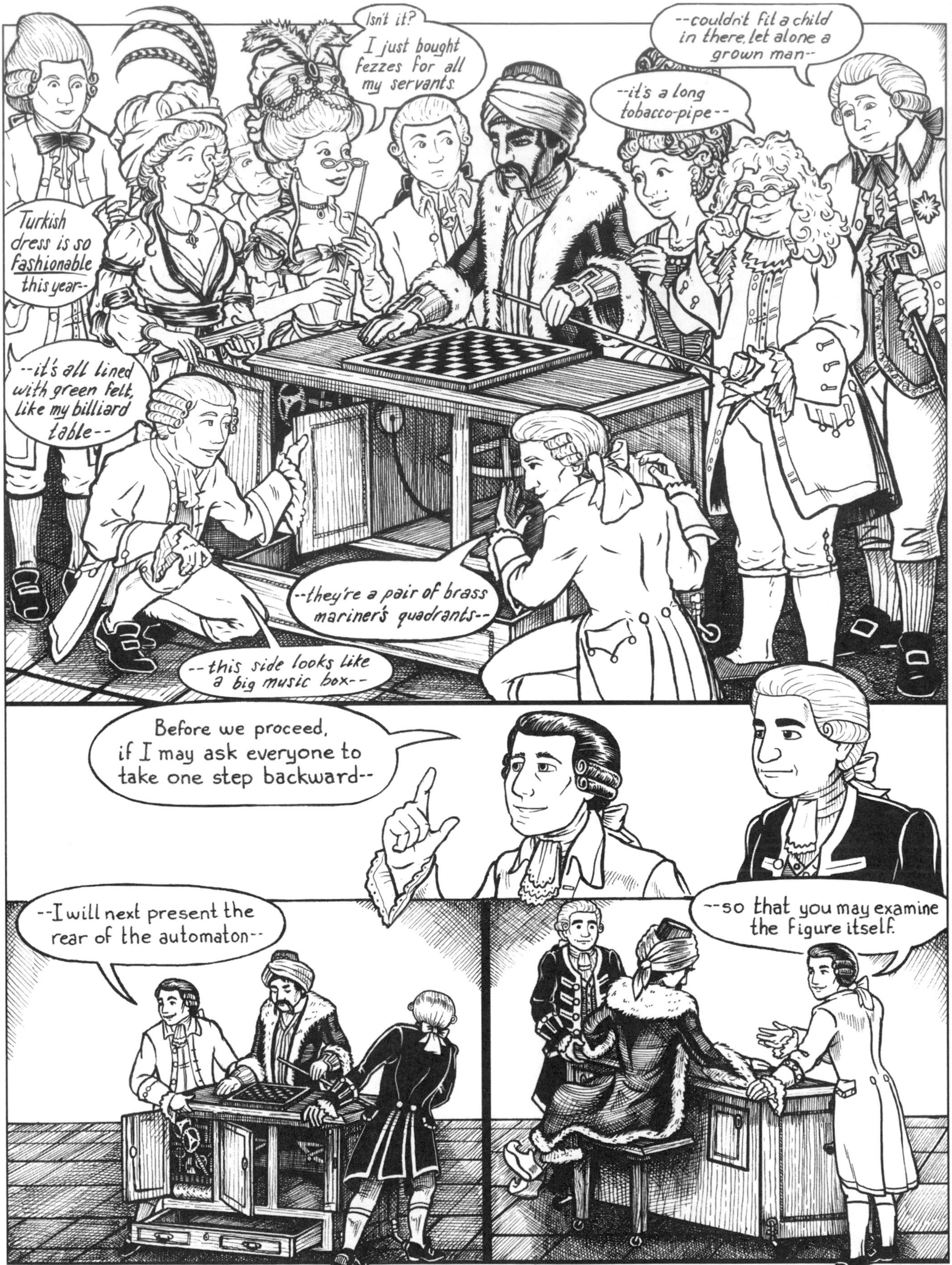
Turkish dress is so fashionable this year--
Isn't it? I just bought fezzes for all my servants.
--it's a long tobacco-pipe--
--couldn't fit a child in there, let alone a grown man--
--it's all lined with green felt, like my billiard table--
--they're a pair of brass mariner's quadrants--
--this side looks like a big music box--
Before we proceed, if I may ask everyone to take one step backward--
--I will next present the rear of the automaton--
--so that you may examine the figure itself.

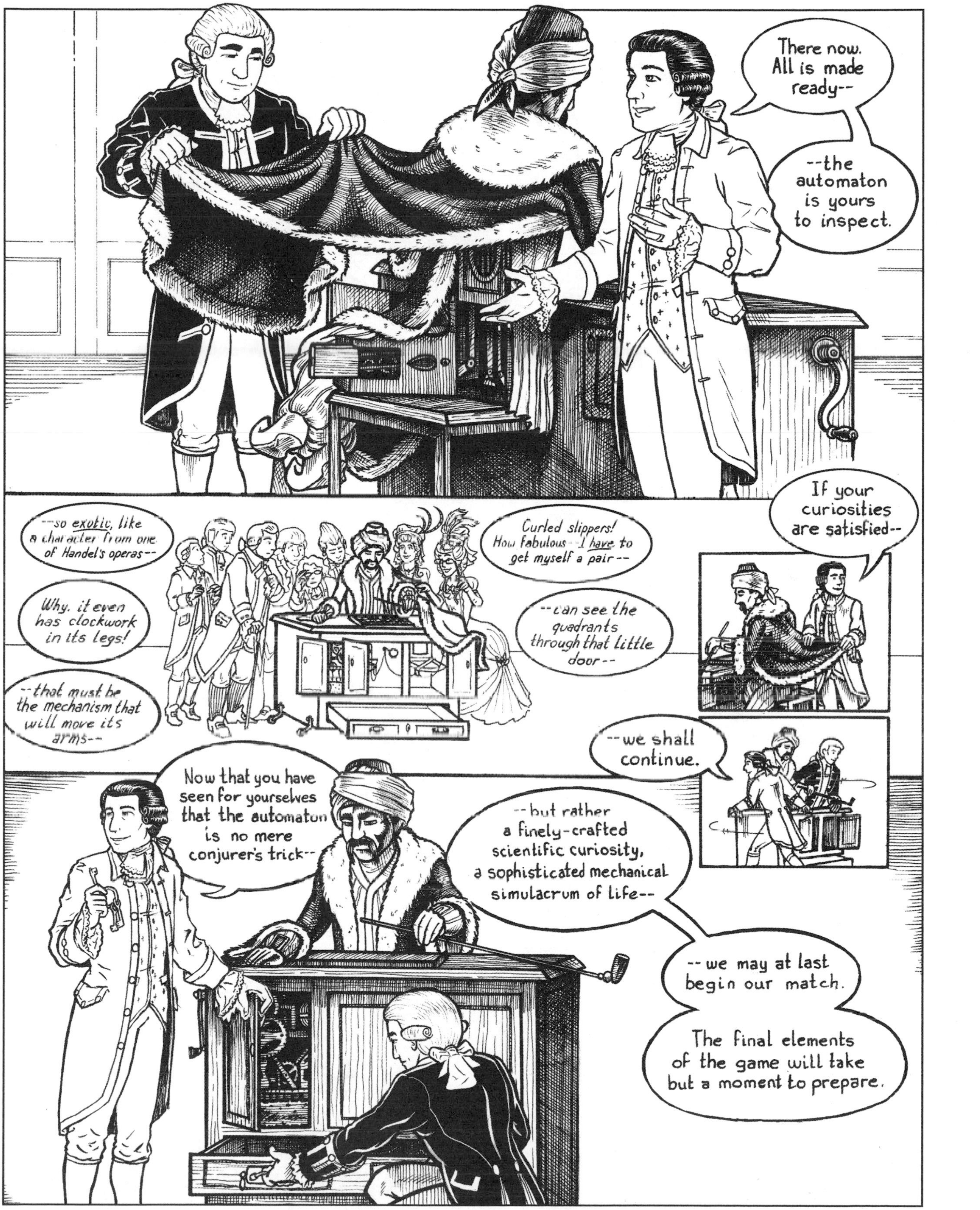
There now. All is made ready--
--the automaton is yours to inspect.
--so exotic, like a character from one of Handel's operas--
Why, it even has clockwork in its legs!
--that must be the mechanism that will move its arms--
Curled slippers! How fabulous--I have to get myself a pair--
--can see the quadrants through that little door--
If your curiosities are satisfied--
--we shall continue.
Now that you have seen for yourselves that the automaton is no mere conjurer's trick--
--but rather a finely-crafted scientific curiosity, a sophisticated mechanical simulacrum of life--
--we may at last begin our match.
The final elements of the game will take but a moment to prepare.

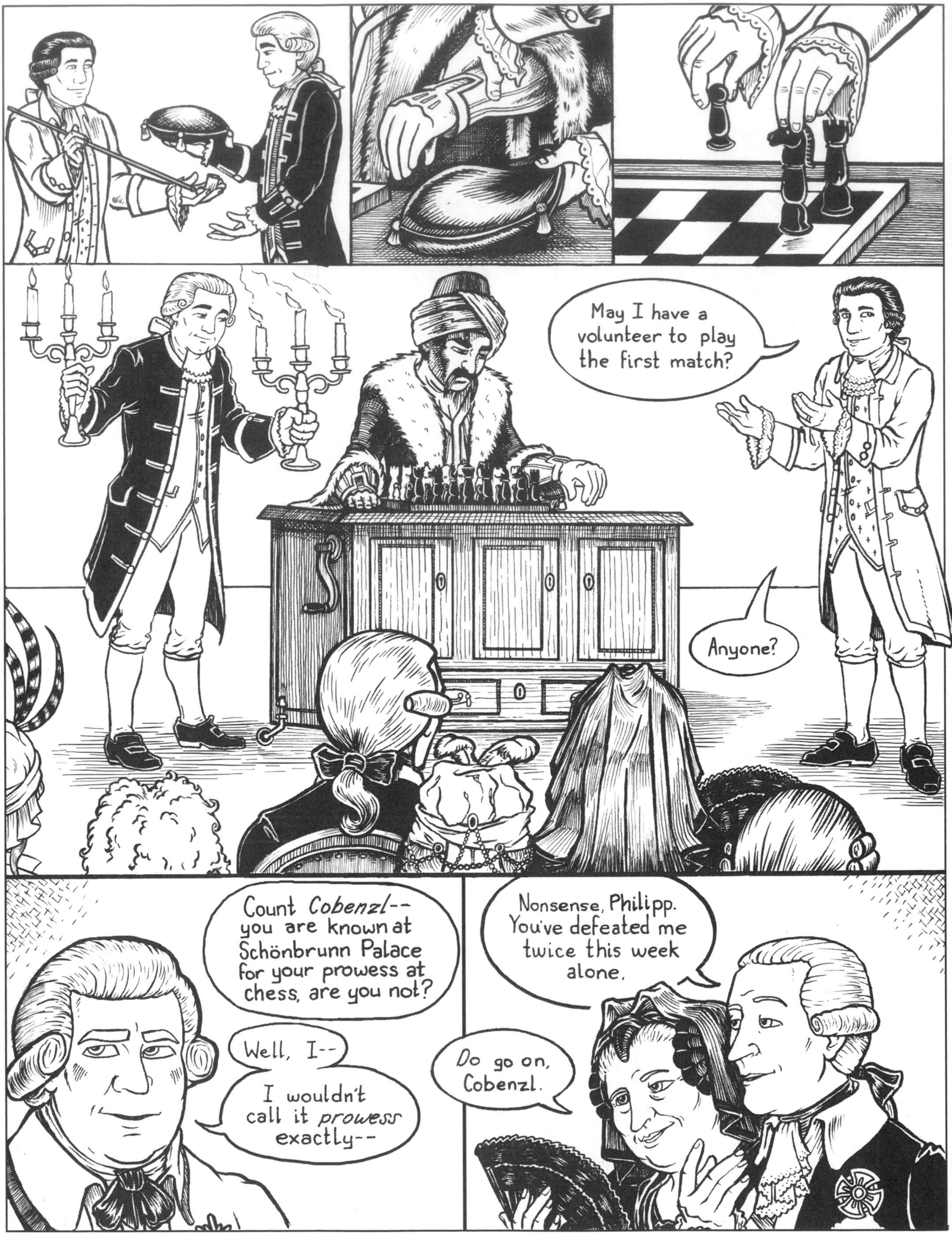
May I have a volunteer to play the first match?
Anyone?
Count *Cobenzl*-- you are known at Schönbrunn Palace for your prowess at chess, are you not?
Well, I--
I wouldn't call it *prowess* exactly--
Nonsense, Philipp. You've defeated me twice this week alone.
Do go on, Cobenzl.

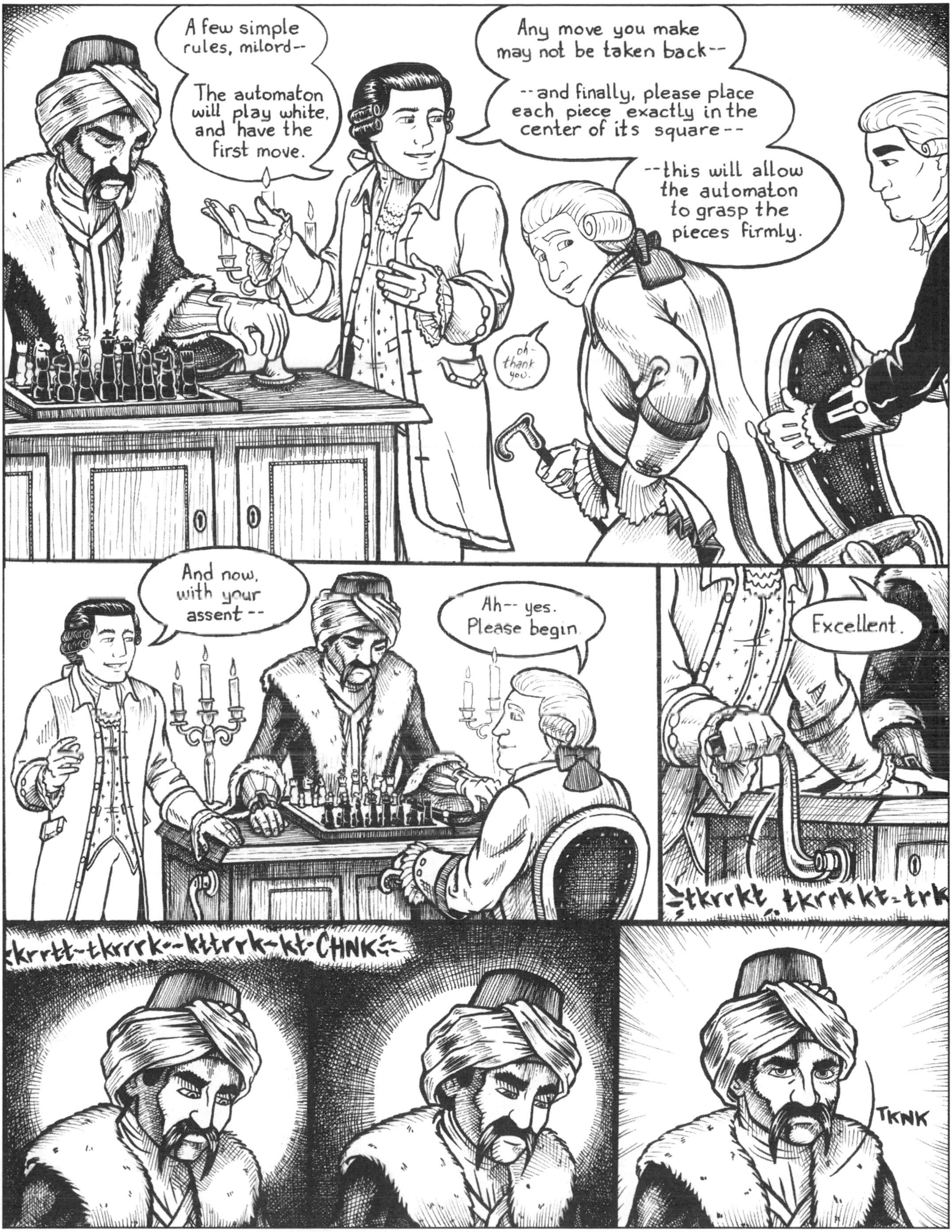
A few simple rules, milord--
The automaton will play white, and have the first move.
Any move you make may not be taken back--
--and finally, please place each piece exactly in the center of its square--
--this will allow the automaton to grasp the pieces firmly.
oh- thank you.
And now, with your assent--
Ah-- yes. Please begin.
Excellent.
tkrrkt tkrrkkt-trk
tkrrtt-tkrrrk--kttrrk-kt-CHNK
TKNK

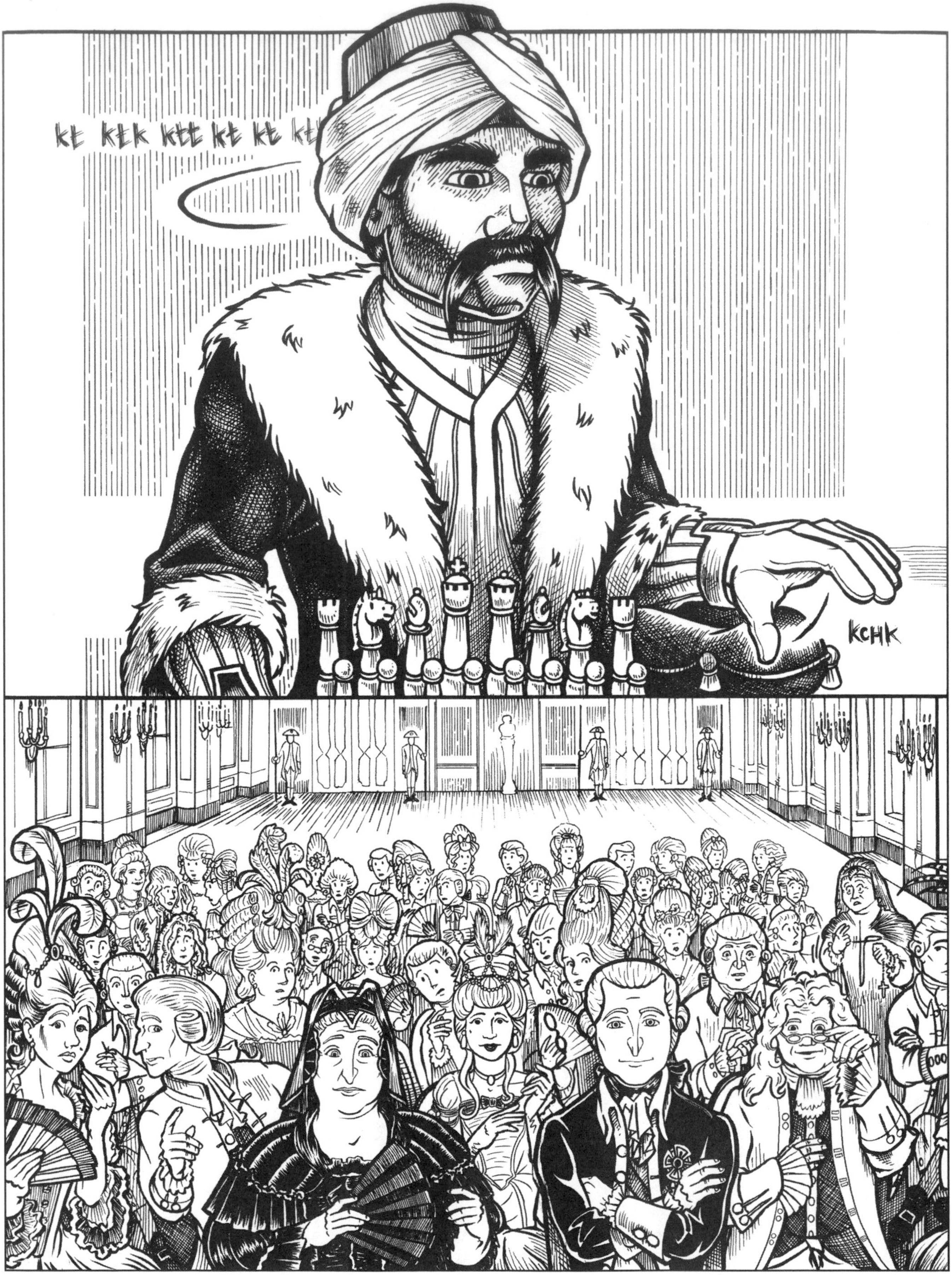
kt ktk ktt kt kt kt
KCHK

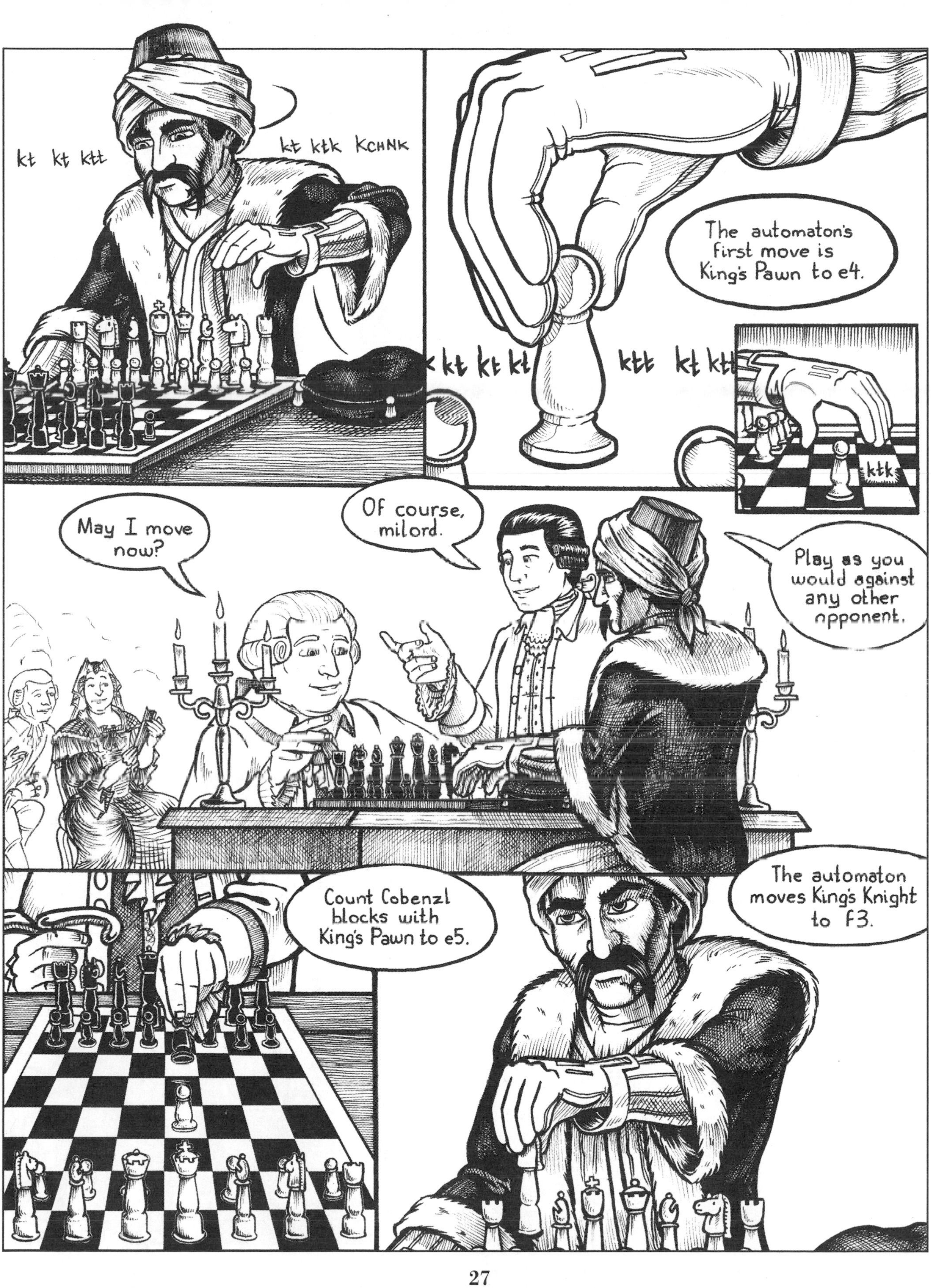
kt kt ktt
kt ktk KCHNK
The automaton's first move is King's Pawn to e4.
kt kt kt
ktt kt ktt
ktk
May I move now?
Of course, milord.
Play as you would against any other opponent.
Count Cobenzl blocks with King's Pawn to e5.
The automaton moves King's Knight to f3.

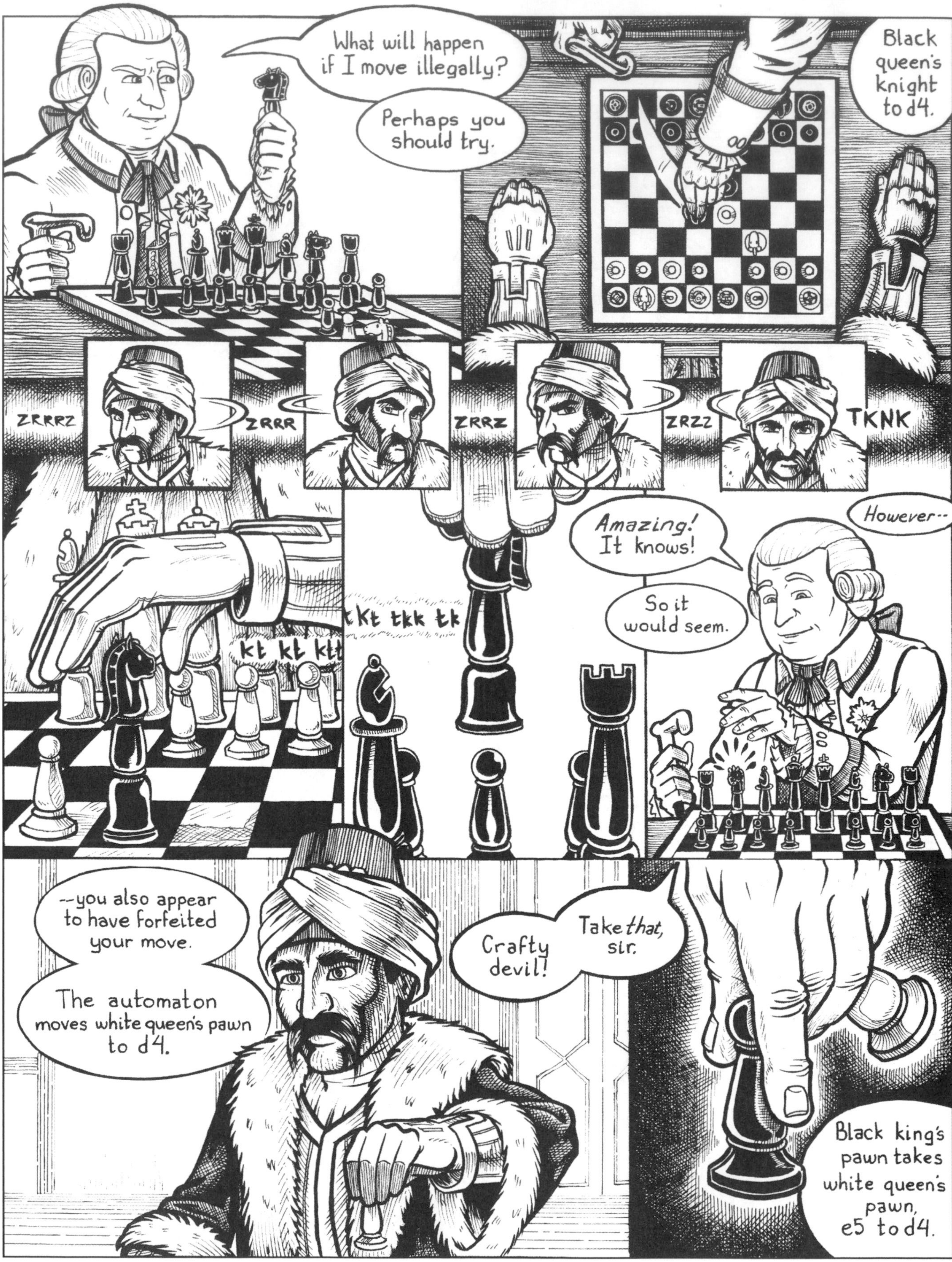

What will happen if I move illegally?
Perhaps you should try.
Black queen's knight to d4.
ZRRRZ
ZRRR
ZRRZ
ZRZZ
TKNK
tkt tkk tk
kt kt kt
Amazing! It knows!
So it would seem.
However--
--you also appear to have forfeited your move.
The automaton moves white queen's pawn to d4.
Crafty devil!
Take *that*, sir.
Black king's pawn takes white queen's pawn, e5 to d4.

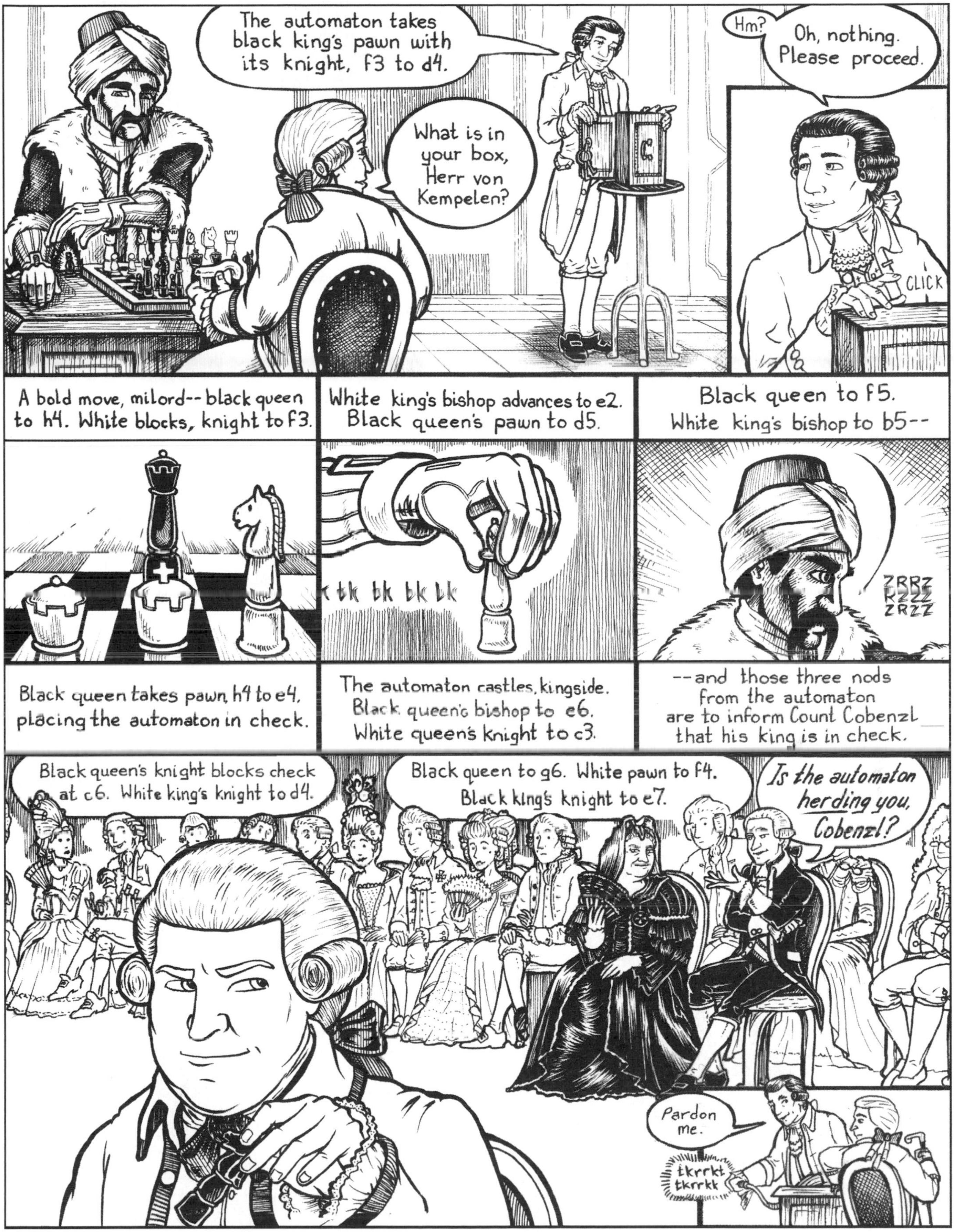

The automaton takes black king's pawn with its knight, f3 to d4.
What is in your box, Herr von Kempelen?
Hm?
Oh, nothing. Please proceed.
CLICK
A bold move, milord-- black queen to h4. White blocks, knight to f3.
White king's bishop advances to e2. Black queen's pawn to d5.
Black queen to f5. White king's bishop to b5--
tk tk tk tk
ZRRZ RZZZ ZRZZ
Black queen takes pawn, h4 to e4, placing the automaton in check.
The automaton castles, kingside. Black queen's bishop to e6. White queen's knight to c3.
--and those three nods from the automaton are to inform Count Cobenzl that his king is in check.
Black queen's knight blocks check at c6. White king's knight to d4.
Black queen to g6. White pawn to f4. Black king's knight to e7.
Is the automaton herding you, Cobenzl?
Pardon me.
tkrrkt tkrrkk

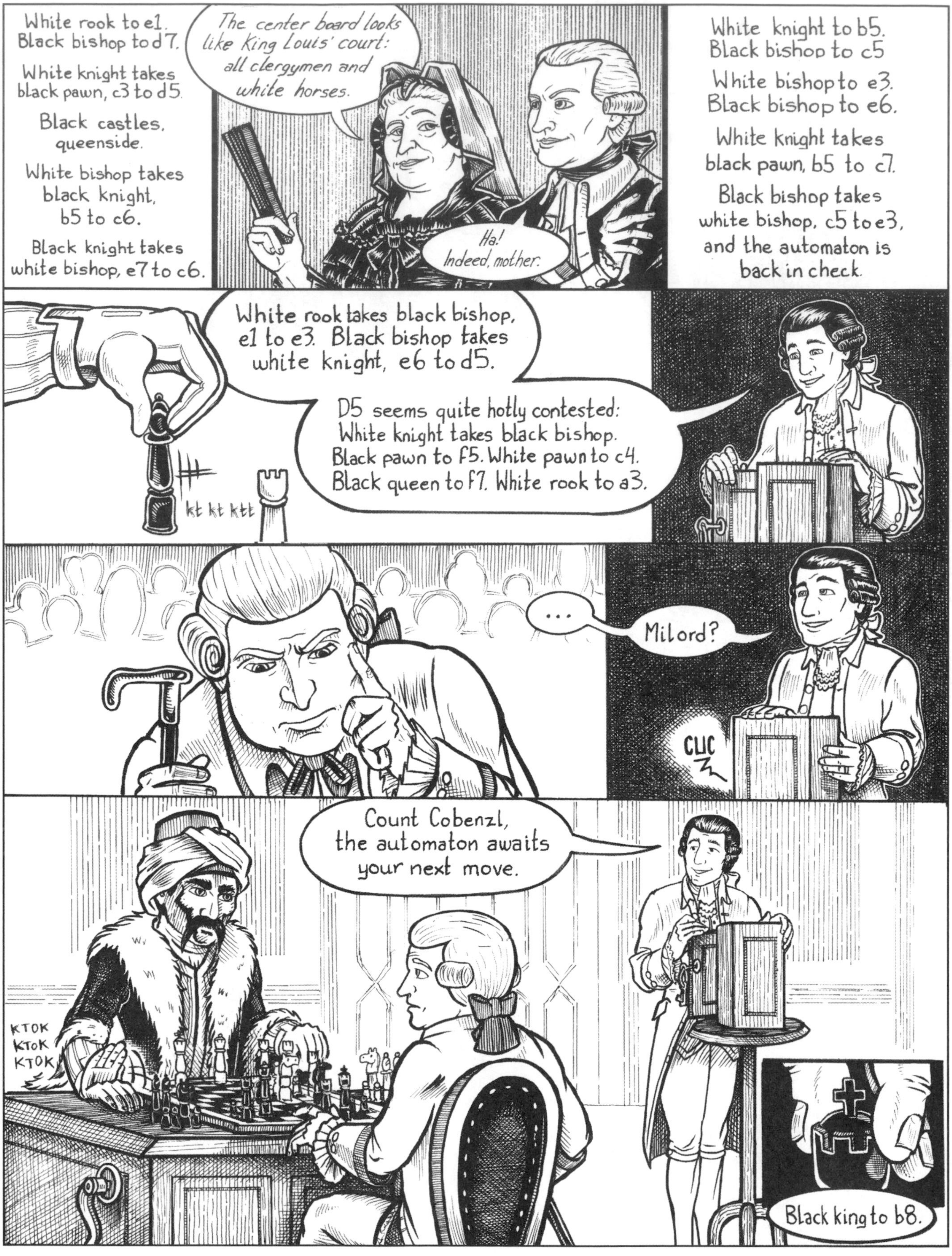
White rook to e1. Black bishop to d7.
White knight takes black pawn, c3 to d5.
Black castles, queenside.
White bishop takes black knight, b5 to c6.
Black knight takes white bishop, e7 to c6.
The center board looks like King Louis' court: all clergymen and white horses.
Ha! Indeed, mother.
White knight to b5. Black bishop to c5
White bishop to e3. Black bishop to e6.
White knight takes black pawn, b5 to c7.
Black bishop takes white bishop, c5 to e3, and the automaton is back in check.
White rook takes black bishop, e1 to e3. Black bishop takes white knight, e6 to d5.
kt kt ktt
D5 seems quite hotly contested: White knight takes black bishop. Black pawn to f5. White pawn to c4. Black queen to f7. White rook to a3.
...
Milord?
CLIC
Count Cobenzl, the automaton awaits your next move.
KTOK KTOK KTOK
Black king to b8.

White rook to b1.

Black queen to f8.

White pawn to b4.

Black knight takes white pawn, c6 to b4.

White queen to d4.

Black knight retreats, b4 to c6.

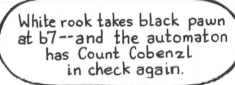
White rook takes black pawn at b7 -- and the automaton has Count Cobenzl in check again.

It shan't have my king quite yet, the cheeky knave.

King takes rook, b8 to b7.

zrrz rzrr

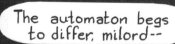
The automaton begs to differ, milord --

White rook takes black pawn at a7 -- and that puts black back in check.

Are *you* making it roll its eyes at me, von Kempelen?

Nothing of the sort, milord.

rzzr zrzz

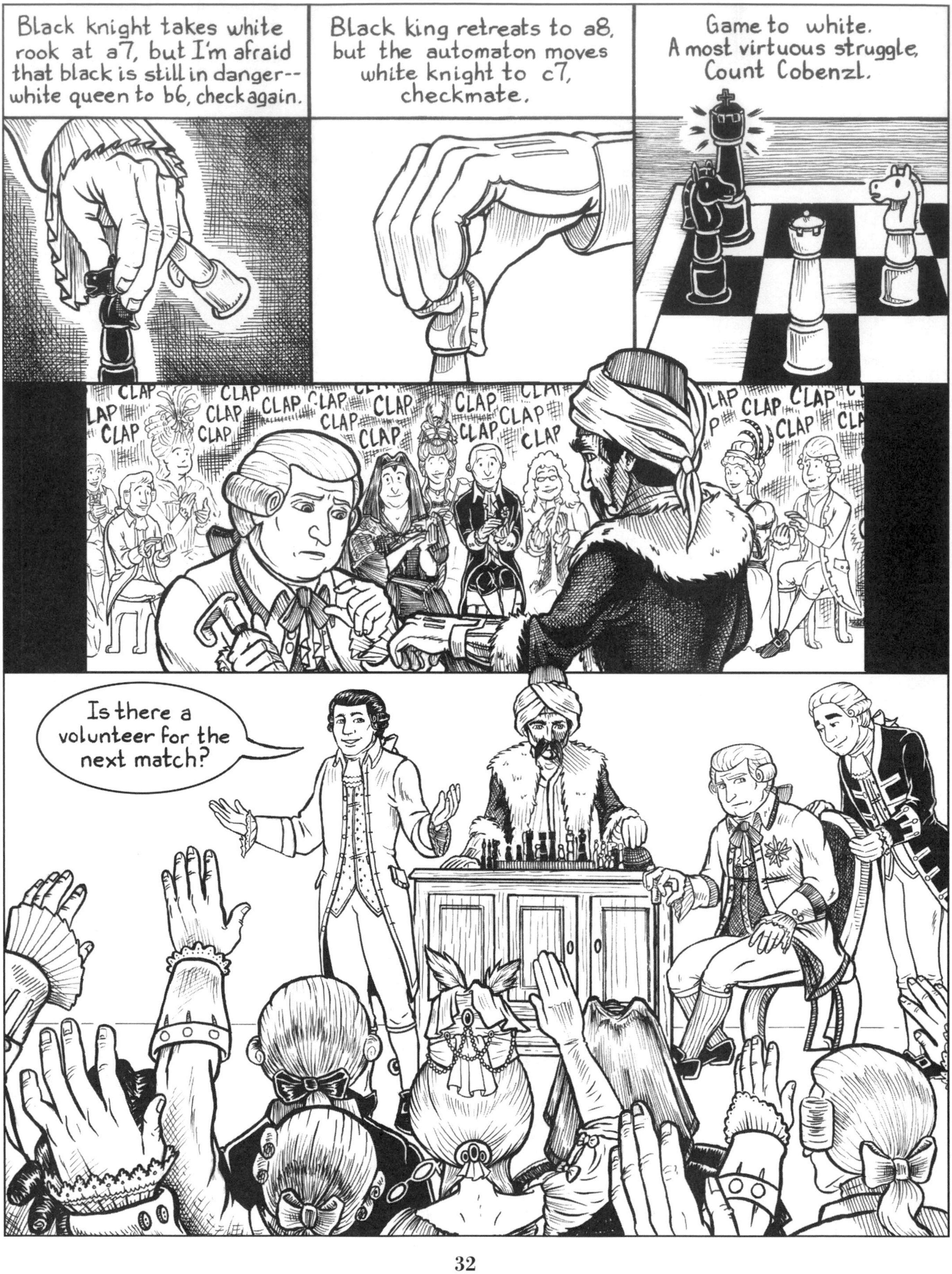
Black knight takes white rook at a7, but I'm afraid that black is still in danger-- white queen to b6, check again.
Black king retreats to a8, but the automaton moves white knight to c7, checkmate.
Game to white. A most virtuous struggle, Count Cobenzl.
CLAP CLAP CLAP CLAP CLAP CLAP CLAP CLAP CLAP CLAP CLAP CLAP CLAP CLAP CLAP
Is there a volunteer for the next match?

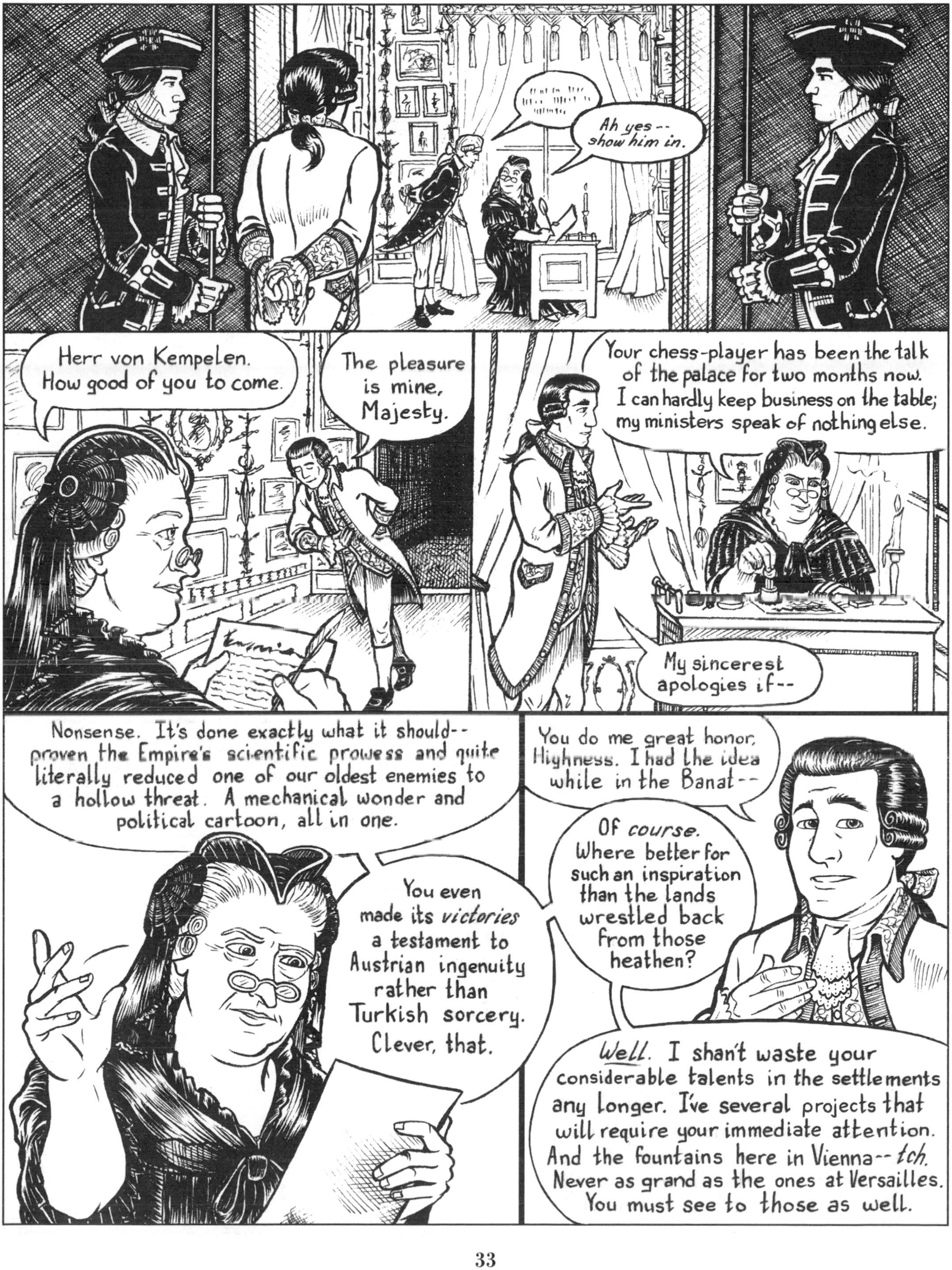
Ah yes--
show him in.
Herr von Kempelen. How good of you to come.
The pleasure is mine, Majesty.
Your chess-player has been the talk of the palace for two months now. I can hardly keep business on the table; my ministers speak of nothing else.
My sincerest apologies if--
Nonsense. It's done exactly what it should--proven the Empire's scientific prowess and quite literally reduced one of our oldest enemies to a hollow threat. A mechanical wonder and political cartoon, all in one.
You even made its victories a testament to Austrian ingenuity rather than Turkish sorcery. Clever, that.
You do me great honor, Highness. I had the idea while in the Banat--
Of course. Where better for such an inspiration than the lands wrestled back from those heathen?
Well. I shan't waste your considerable talents in the settlements any longer. I've several projects that will require your immediate attention. And the fountains here in Vienna--tch. Never as grand as the ones at Versailles. You must see to those as well.

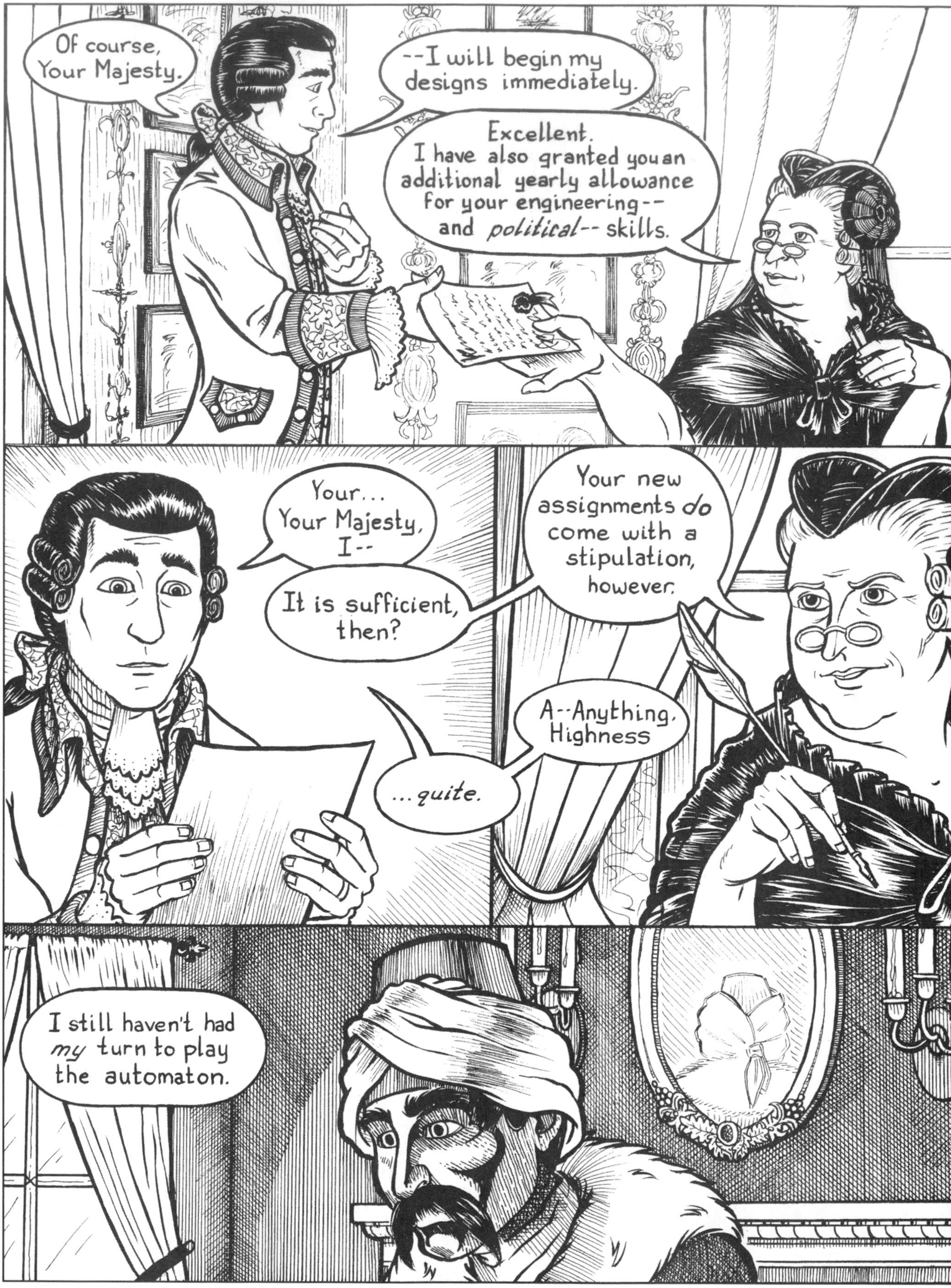

Of course, Your Majesty.
--I will begin my designs immediately.
Excellent. I have also granted you an additional yearly allowance for your engineering-- and *political*-- skills.
Your... Your Majesty, I--
It is sufficient, then?
...*quite*.
Your new assignments *do* come with a stipulation, however.
A--Anything, Highness
I still haven't had *my* turn to play the automaton.

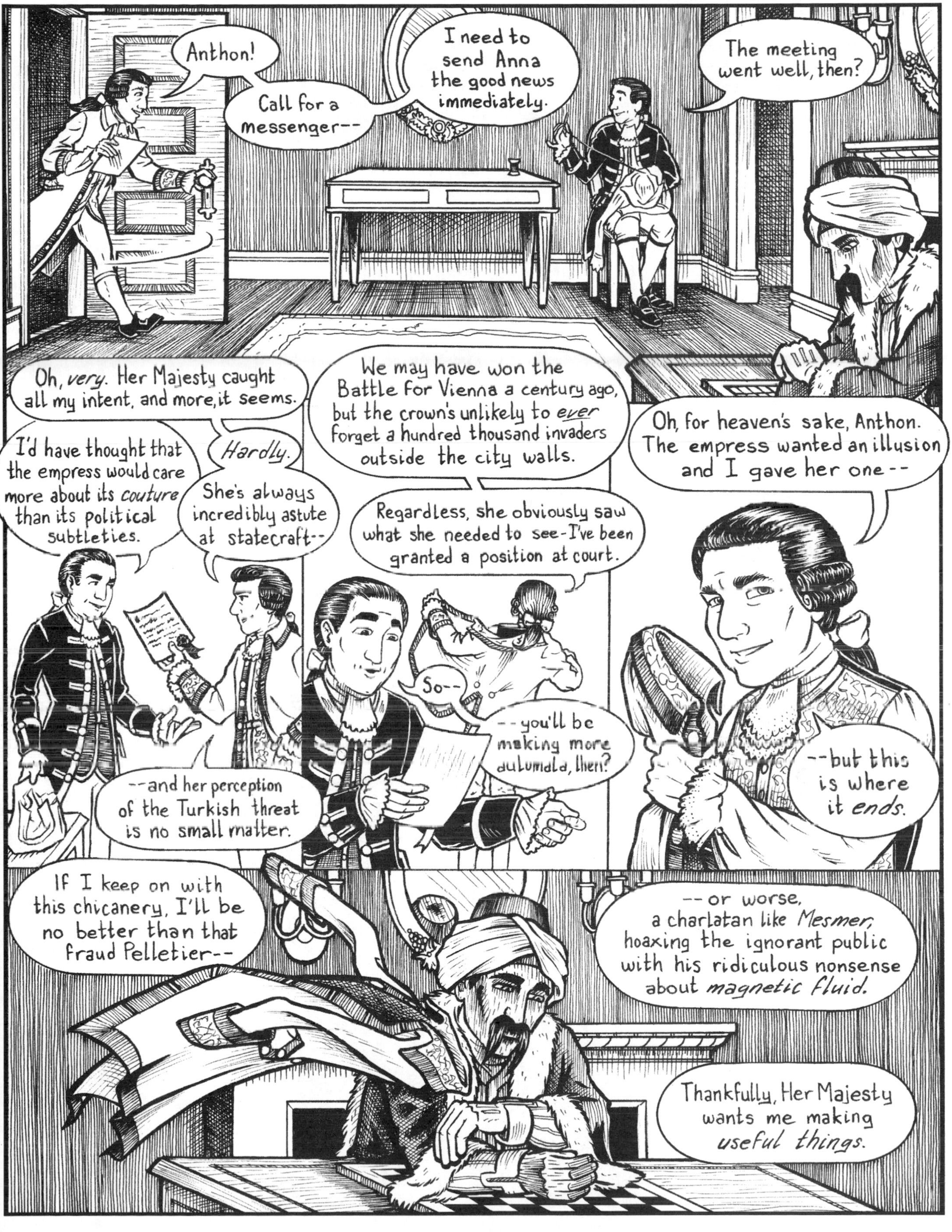

Anthon!
Call for a messenger--
I need to send Anna the good news immediately.
The meeting went well, then?
Oh, *very*. Her Majesty caught all my intent, and more, it seems.
I'd have thought that the empress would care more about its *couture* than its political subtleties.
Hardly.
She's always incredibly astute at statecraft--
--and her perception of the Turkish threat is no small matter.
We may have won the Battle for Vienna a century ago, but the crown's unlikely to *ever* forget a hundred thousand invaders outside the city walls.
Regardless, she obviously saw what she needed to see-I've been granted a position at court.
So--
--you'll be making more automata, then?
Oh, for heaven's sake, Anthon. The empress wanted an illusion and I gave her one--
--but this is where it *ends*.
If I keep on with this chicanery, I'll be no better than that fraud Pelletier--
--or worse, a charlatan like *Mesmer*, hoaxing the ignorant public with his ridiculous nonsense about *magnetic fluid*.
Thankfully, Her Majesty wants me making *useful things*.

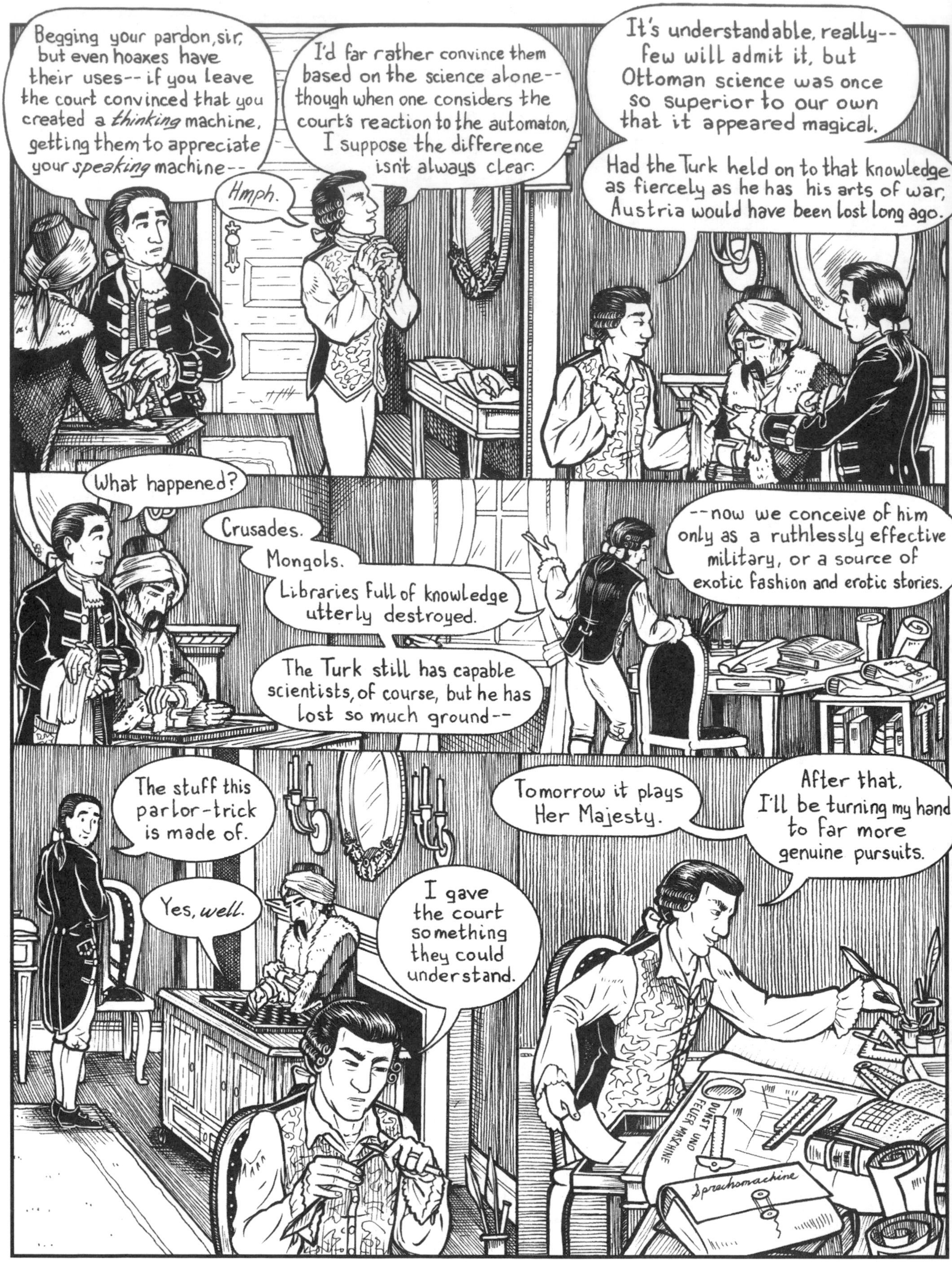
Begging your pardon, sir, but even hoaxes have their uses-- if you leave the court convinced that you created a *thinking* machine, getting them to appreciate your *speaking* machine--
Hmph.
I'd far rather convince them based on the science alone-- though when one considers the court's reaction to the automaton, I suppose the difference isn't always clear.
It's understandable, really-- few will admit it, but Ottoman science was once so superior to our own that it appeared magical.
Had the Turk held on to that knowledge as fiercely as he has his arts of war, Austria would have been lost long ago.
What happened?
Crusades.
Mongols.
Libraries full of knowledge utterly destroyed.
The Turk still has capable scientists, of course, but he has lost so much ground--
--now we conceive of him only as a ruthlessly effective military, or a source of exotic fashion and erotic stories.
The stuff this parlor-trick is made of.
Yes, *well*.
I gave the court something they could understand.
Tomorrow it plays Her Majesty.
After that, I'll be turning my hand to far more genuine pursuits.
DUNST UND FEUER MASCHINE
Sprechmaschine

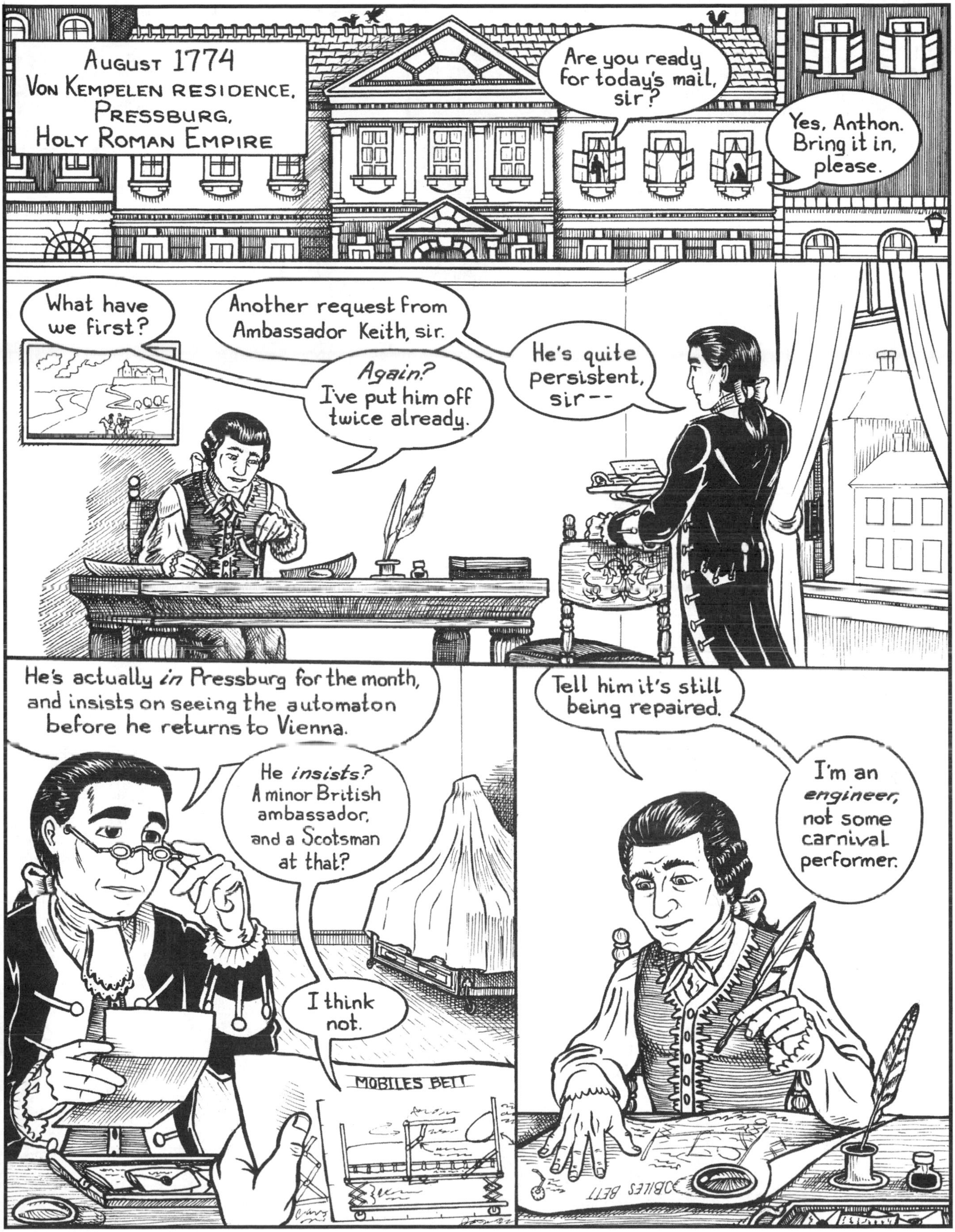
August 1774
Von Kempelen residence,
Pressburg,
Holy Roman Empire
Are you ready for today's mail, sir?
Yes, Anthon. Bring it in, please.
What have we first?
Another request from Ambassador Keith, sir.
Again? I've put him off twice already.
He's quite persistent, sir--
He's actually in Pressburg for the month, and insists on seeing the automaton before he returns to Vienna.
He insists? A minor British ambassador, and a Scotsman at that?
I think not.
MOBILES BETT
Tell him it's still being repaired.
I'm an engineer, not some carnival performer.

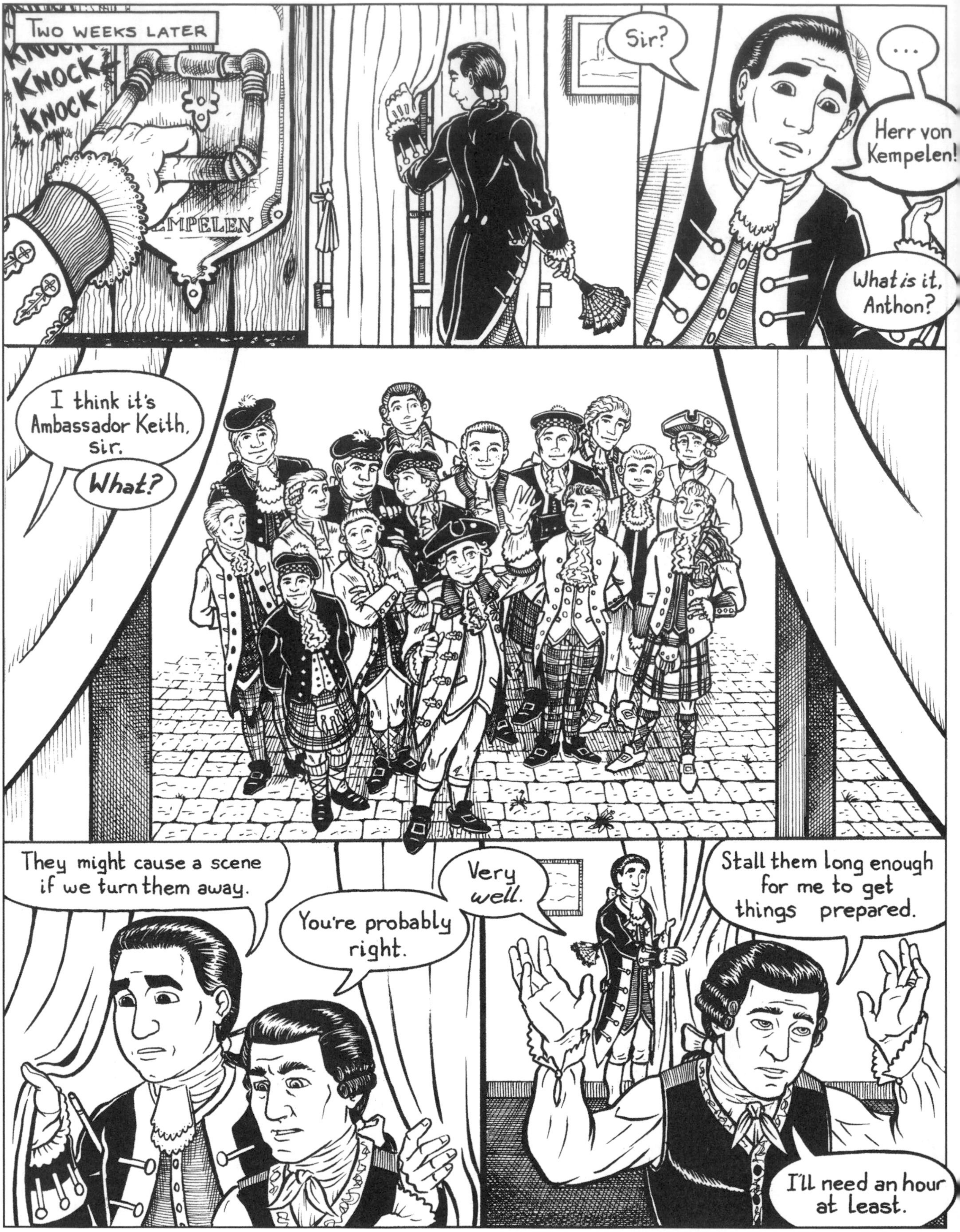

TWO WEEKS LATER
KNOCK KNOCK KNOCK
KEMPELEN
Sir?
...
Herr von Kempelen!
What is it, Anthon?
I think it's Ambassador Keith, sir.
What?
They might cause a scene if we turn them away.
You're probably right.
Very well.
Stall them long enough for me to get things prepared.
I'll need an hour at least.

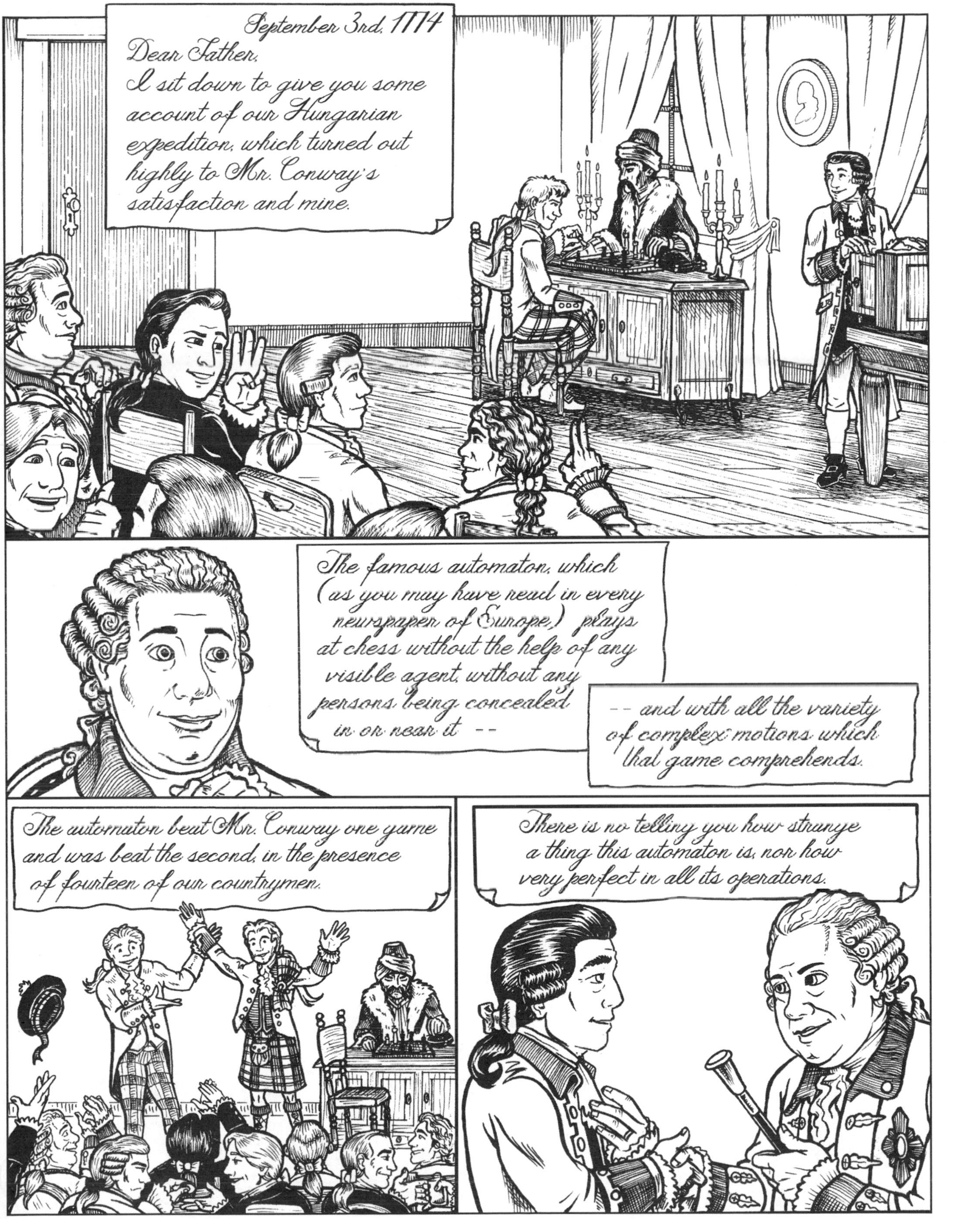
September 3rd, 1774
Dear Father,
I sit down to give you some account of our Hungarian expedition, which turned out highly to Mr. Conway's satisfaction and mine.
The famous automaton, which (as you may have read in every newspaper of Europe) plays at chess without the help of any visible agent, without any persons being concealed in or near it --
-- and with all the variety of complex motions which that game comprehends.
The automaton beat Mr. Conway one game and was beat the second, in the presence of fourteen of our countrymen.
There is no telling you how strange a thing this automaton is, nor how very perfect in all its operations.

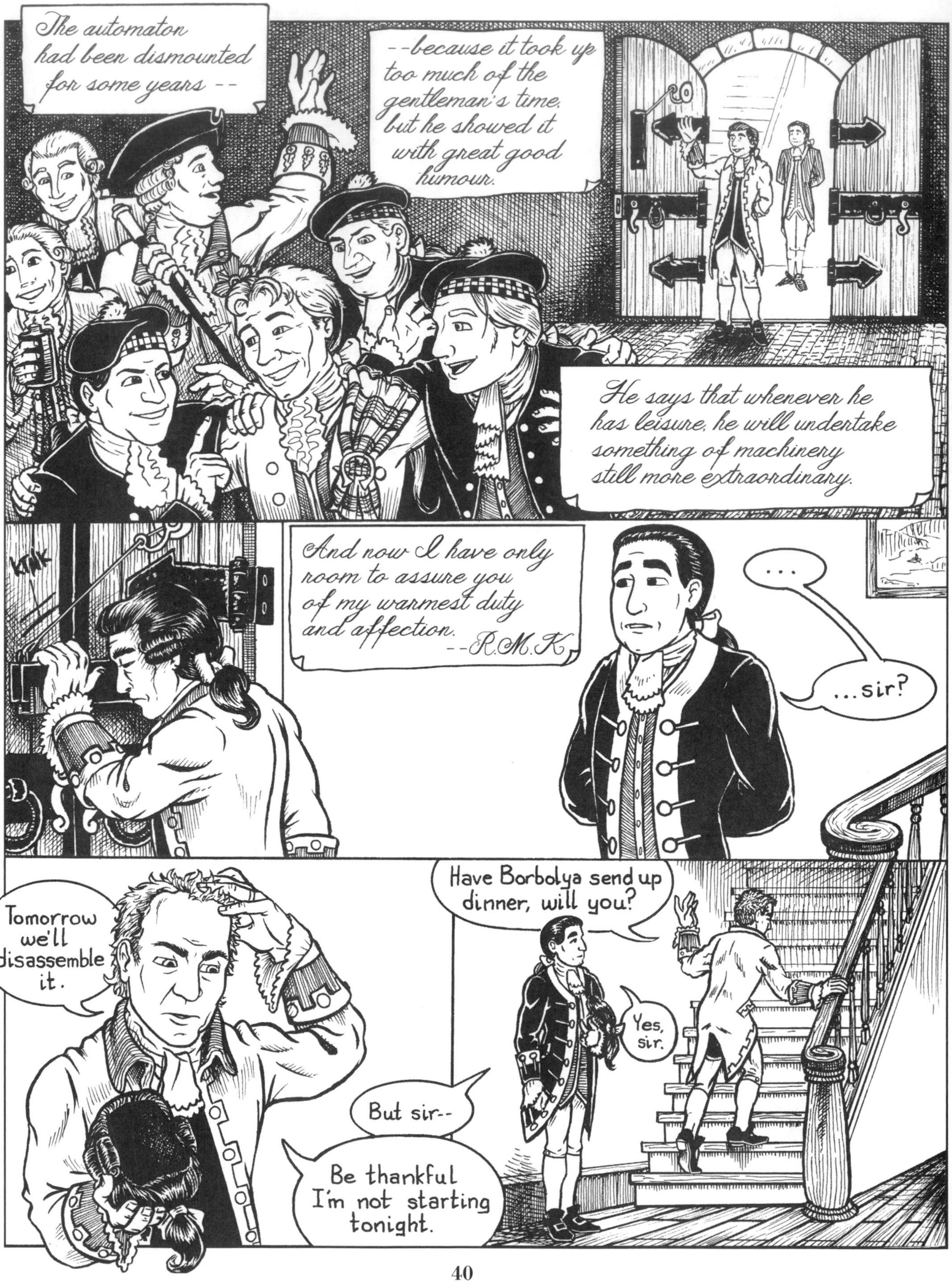
The automaton had been dismounted for some years --
--because it took up too much of the gentleman's time, but he showed it with great good humour.
He says that whenever he has leisure, he will undertake something of machinery still more extraordinary.
KTNK
And now I have only room to assure you of my warmest duty and affection. --R.M.K
...
...sir?
Tomorrow we'll disassemble it.
But sir--
Be thankful I'm not starting tonight.
Have Borbolya send up dinner, will you?
Yes, sir.

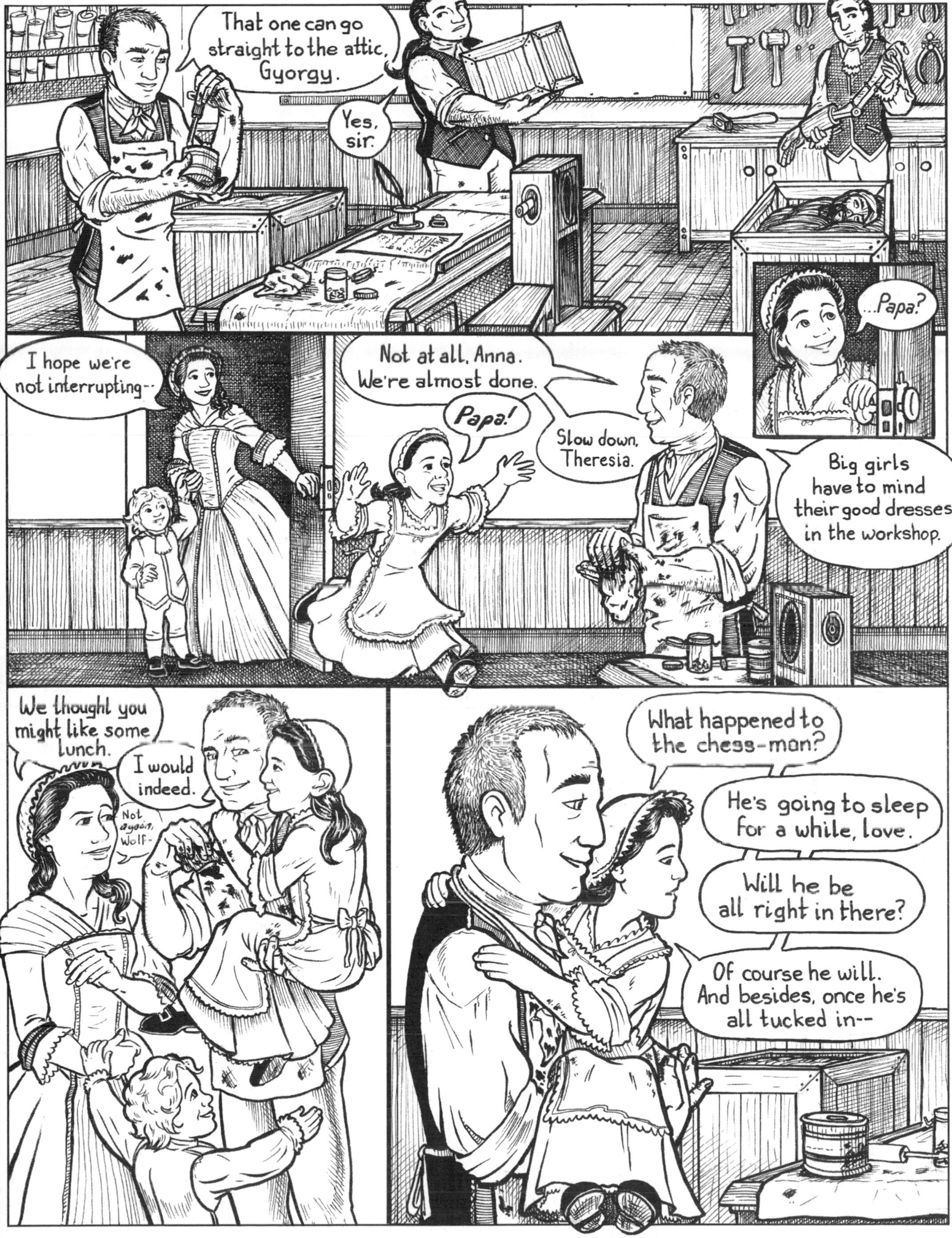
That one can go straight to the attic, Gyorgy.
Yes, sir.
...Papa?
I hope we're not interrupting--
Not at all, Anna. We're almost done.
Papa!
Slow down, Theresia.
Big girls have to mind their good dresses in the workshop.
We thought you might like some lunch.
I would indeed.
Not again, Wolf-
What happened to the chess-man?
He's going to sleep for a while, love.
Will he be all right in there?
Of course he will. And besides, once he's all tucked in--

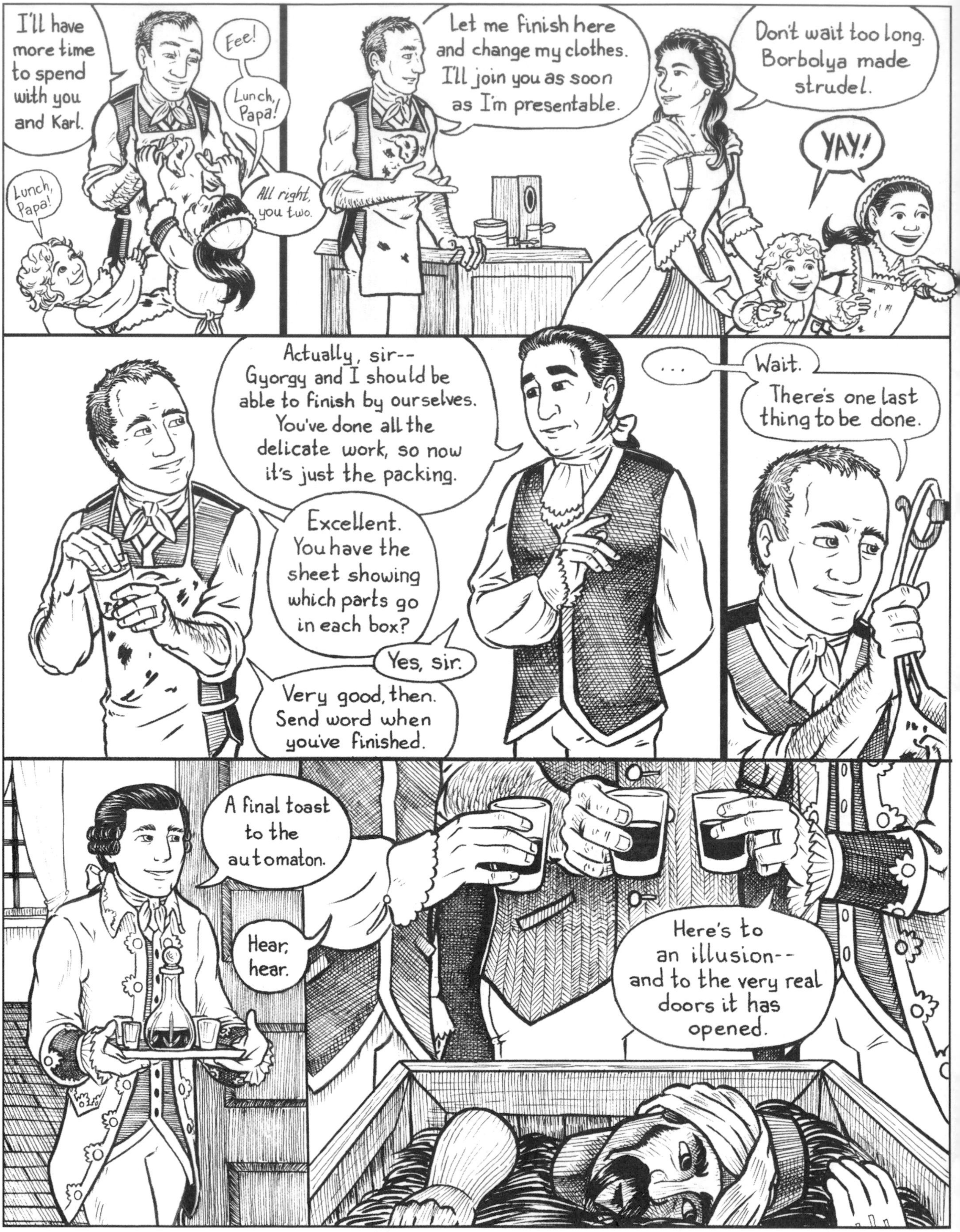
I'll have more time to spend with you and Karl.
Eee!
Lunch, Papa!
Lunch, Papa!
All right, you two.
Let me finish here and change my clothes. I'll join you as soon as I'm presentable.
Don't wait too long. Borbolya made strudel.
YAY!
Actually, sir-- Gyorgy and I should be able to finish by ourselves. You've done all the delicate work, so now it's just the packing.
Excellent. You have the sheet showing which parts go in each box?
Yes, sir.
Very good, then. Send word when you've finished.
. . .
Wait.
There's one last thing to be done.
A final toast to the automaton.
Hear, hear.
Here's to an illusion-- and to the very real doors it has opened.

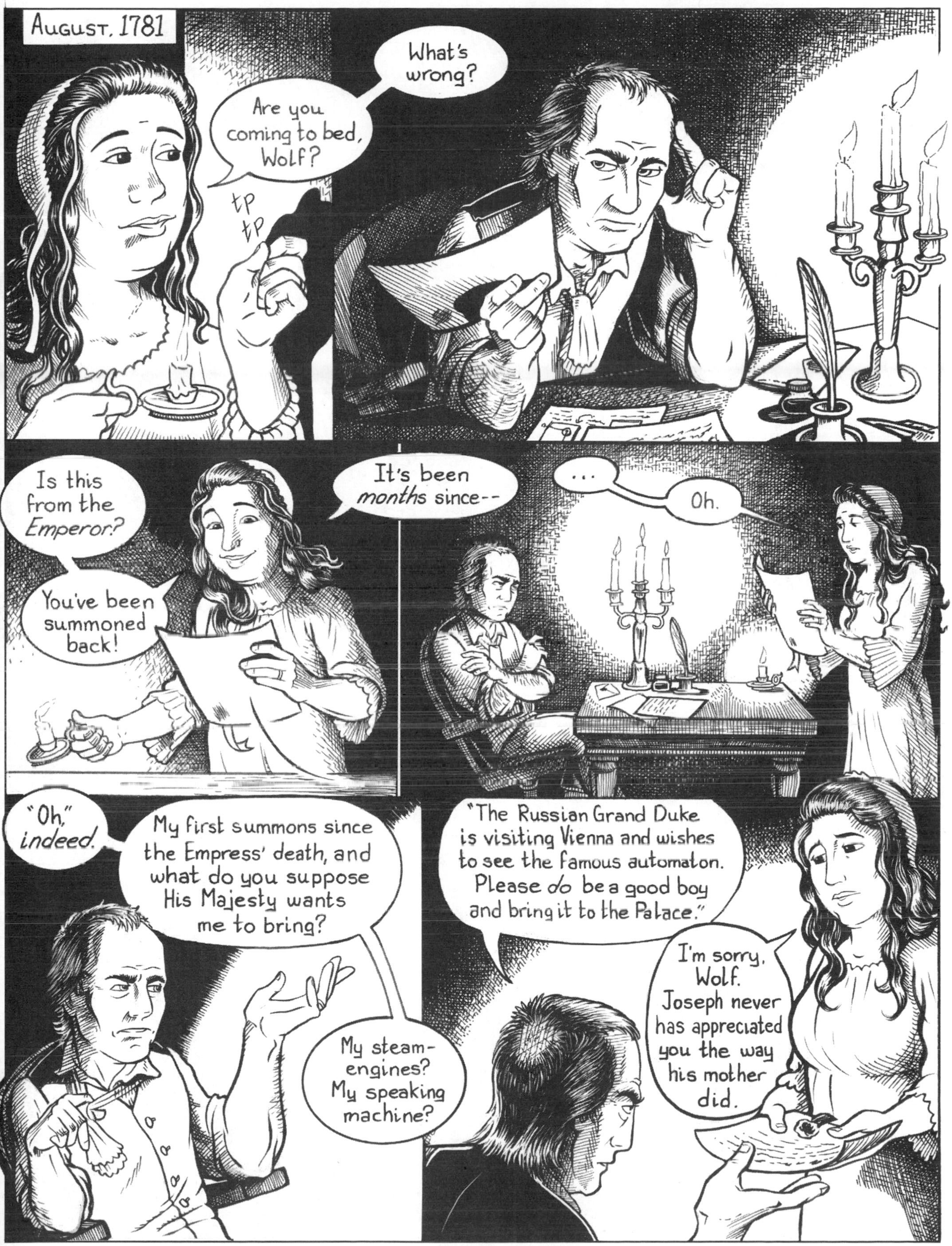

August, 1781
Are you coming to bed, Wolf?
tp tp
What's wrong?
Is this from the *Emperor?*
You've been summoned back!
It's been *months* since--
...
Oh.
"Oh," *indeed.*
My first summons since the Empress' death, and what do you suppose His Majesty wants me to bring?
My steam-engines? My speaking machine?
"The Russian Grand Duke is visiting Vienna and wishes to see the famous automaton. Please *do* be a good boy and bring it to the Palace."
I'm sorry, Wolf. Joseph never has appreciated you the way his mother did.

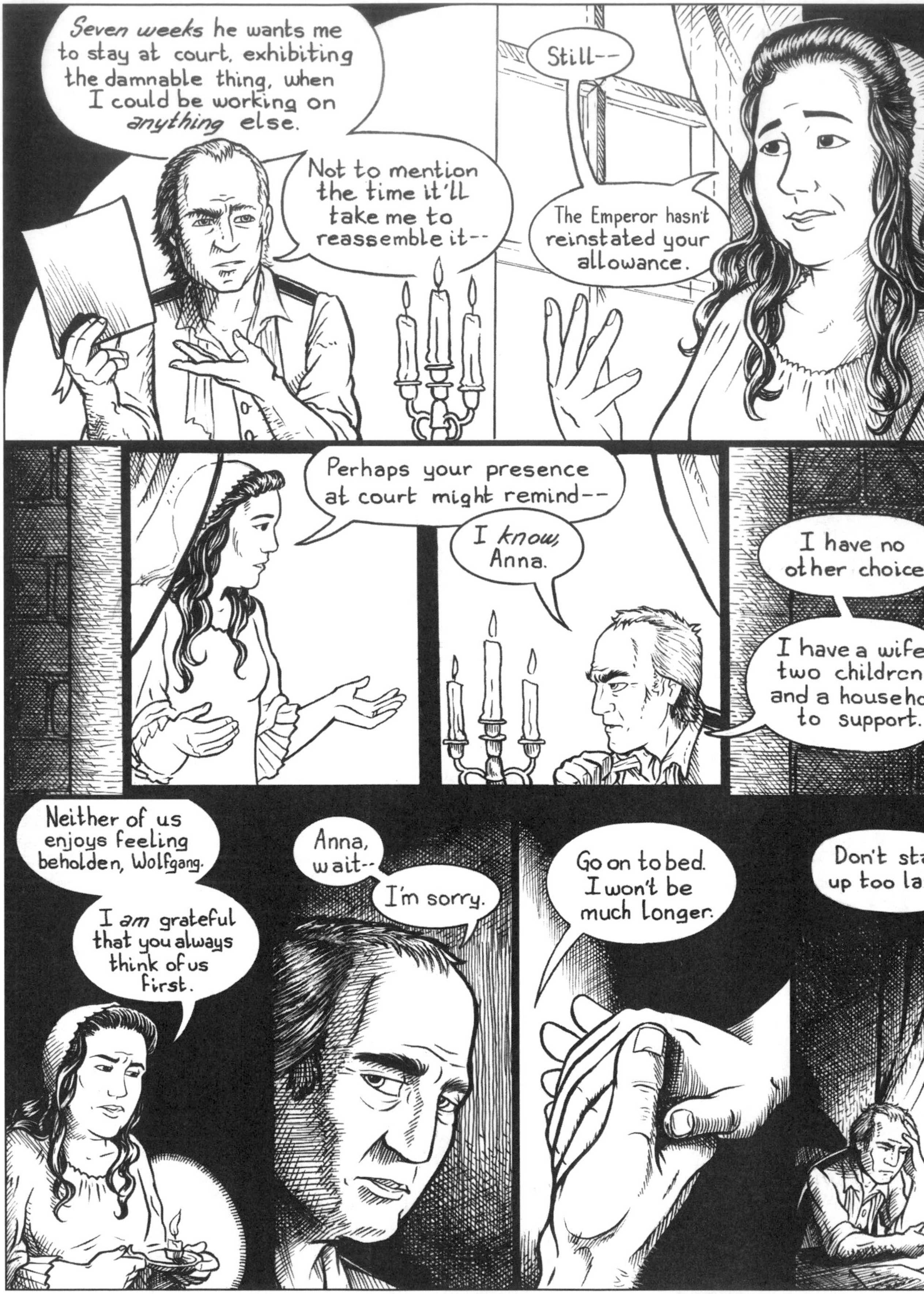
Seven weeks he wants me to stay at court, exhibiting the damnable thing, when I could be working on anything else.
Not to mention the time it'll take me to reassemble it--
Still--
The Emperor hasn't reinstated your allowance.
Perhaps your presence at court might remind--
I know, Anna.
I have no other choice.
I have a wife, two children and a household to support.
Neither of us enjoys feeling beholden, Wolfgang.
I am grateful that you always think of us first.
Anna, wait--
I'm sorry.
Go on to bed. I won't be much longer.
Don't stay up too late--

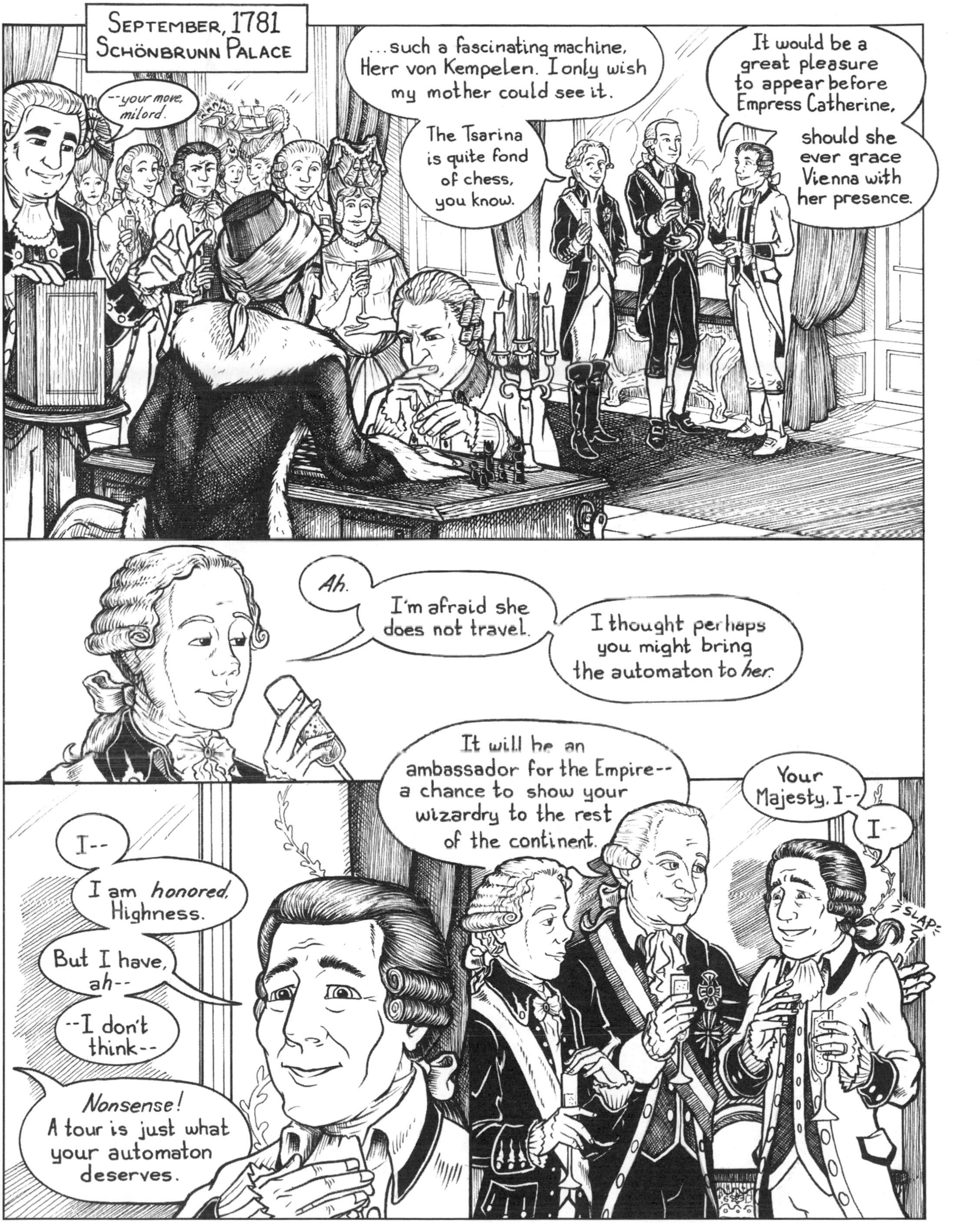

September, 1781
Schönbrunn Palace
--your move, milord.
...such a fascinating machine, Herr von Kempelen. I only wish my mother could see it.
The Tsarina is quite fond of chess, you know.
It would be a great pleasure to appear before Empress Catherine,
should she ever grace Vienna with her presence.
Ah.
I'm afraid she does not travel.
I thought perhaps you might bring the automaton to *her*.
It will be an ambassador for the Empire--a chance to show your wizardry to the rest of the continent.
Your Majesty, I--
I--
I--
I am *honored*, Highness.
But I have, ah--
--I don't think--
Nonsense! A tour is just what your automaton deserves.
SLAP

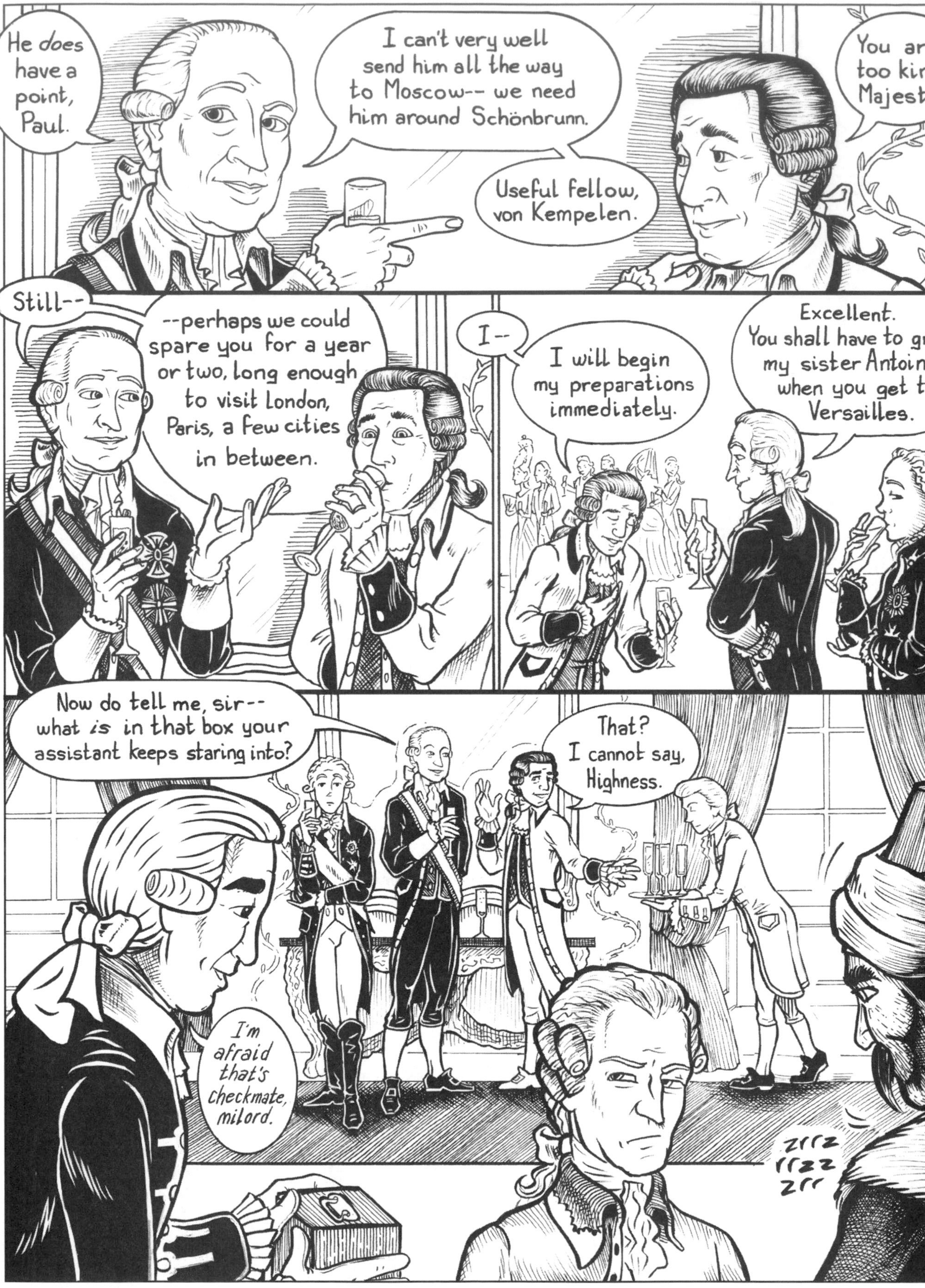

He *does* have a point, Paul.
I can't very well send him all the way to Moscow-- we need him around Schönbrunn.
Useful fellow, von Kempelen.
You are too kind, Majesty.
Still--
--perhaps we could spare you for a year or two, long enough to visit London, Paris, a few cities in between.
I--
I will begin my preparations immediately.
Excellent. You shall have to greet my sister Antoine when you get to Versailles.
Now do tell me, sir-- what *is* in that box your assistant keeps staring into?
That? I cannot say, Highness.
I'm afraid that's checkmate, milord.
zrrz rrzz zrr

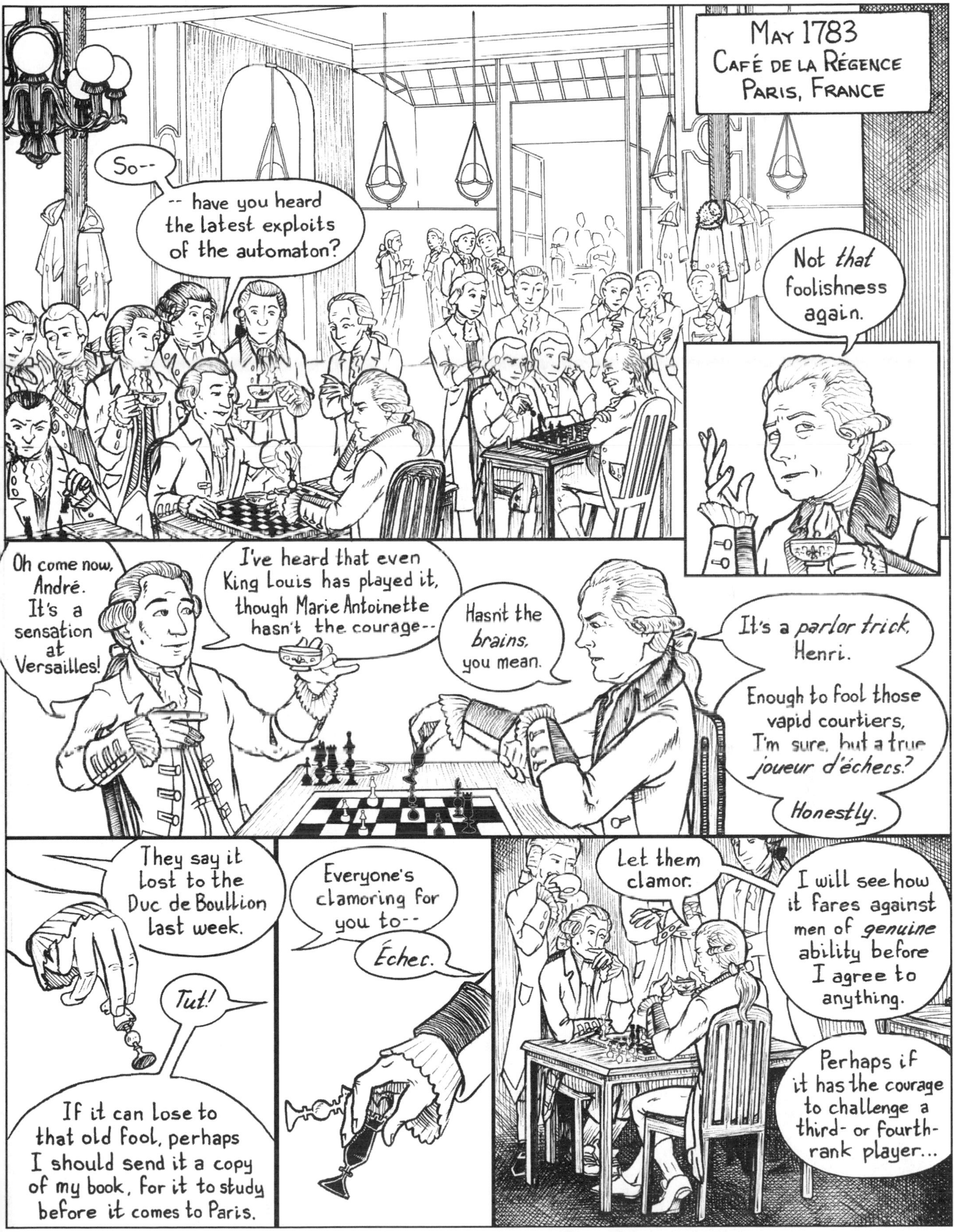
May 1783
Café de la Régence
Paris, France
So--
-- have you heard the latest exploits of the automaton?
Not *that* foolishness again.
Oh come now, André. It's a sensation at Versailles!
I've heard that even King Louis has played it, though Marie Antoinette hasn't the courage--
Hasn't the *brains,* you mean.
It's a *parlor trick,* Henri.
Enough to fool those vapid courtiers, I'm sure, but a true *joueur d'échecs?*
Honestly.
They say it lost to the Duc de Boullion last week.
Tut!
If it can lose to that old fool, perhaps I should send it a copy of my book, for it to study before it comes to Paris.
Everyone's clamoring for you to--
Échec.
Let them clamor.
I will see how it fares against men of *genuine* ability before I agree to anything.
Perhaps if it has the courage to challenge a third- or fourth-rank player...

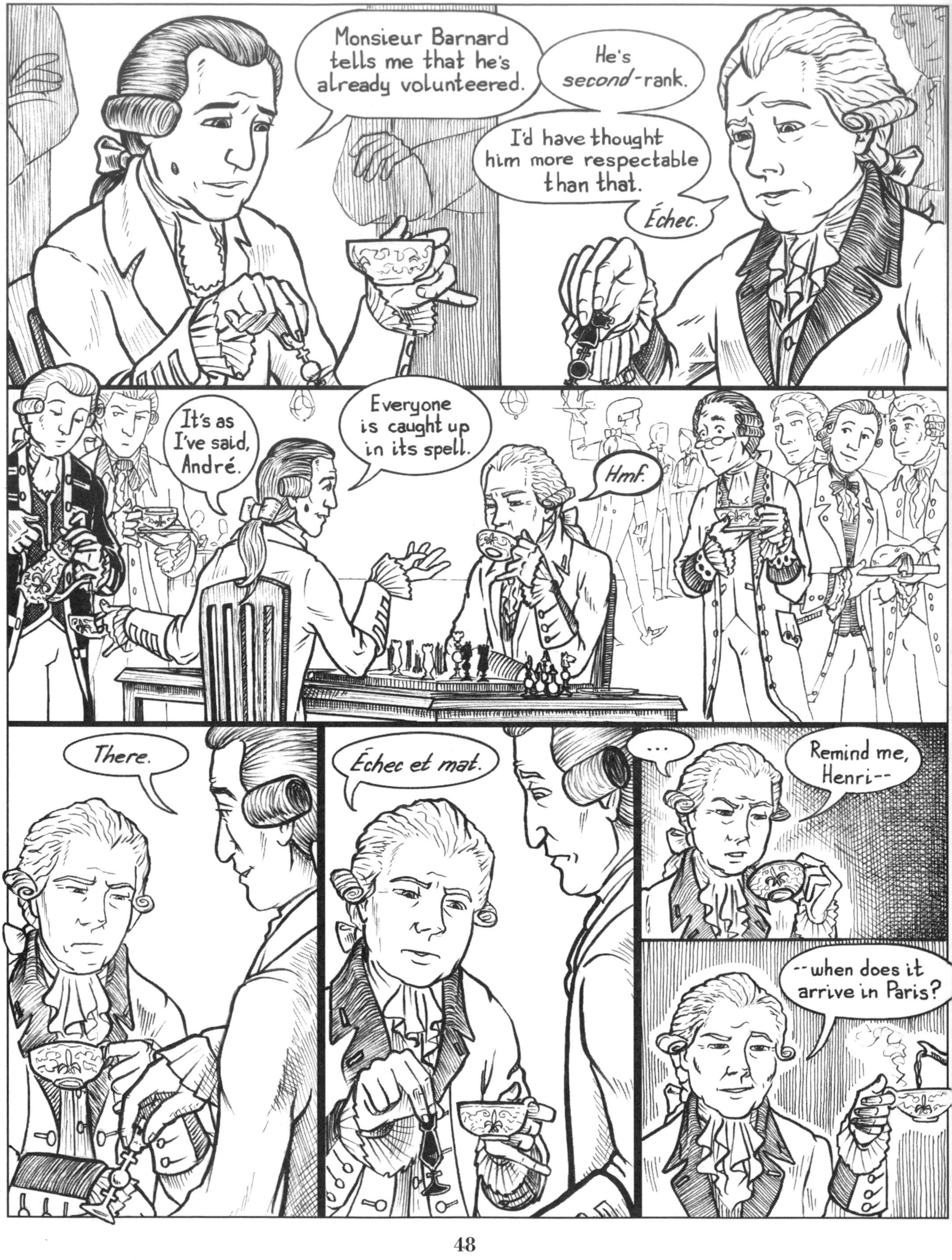
Monsieur Barnard tells me that he's already volunteered.
He's *second*-rank.
I'd have thought him more respectable than that.
Échec.
It's as I've said, André.
Everyone is caught up in its spell.
Hmf.
There.
Échec et mat.
...
Remind me, Henri--
--when does it arrive in Paris?

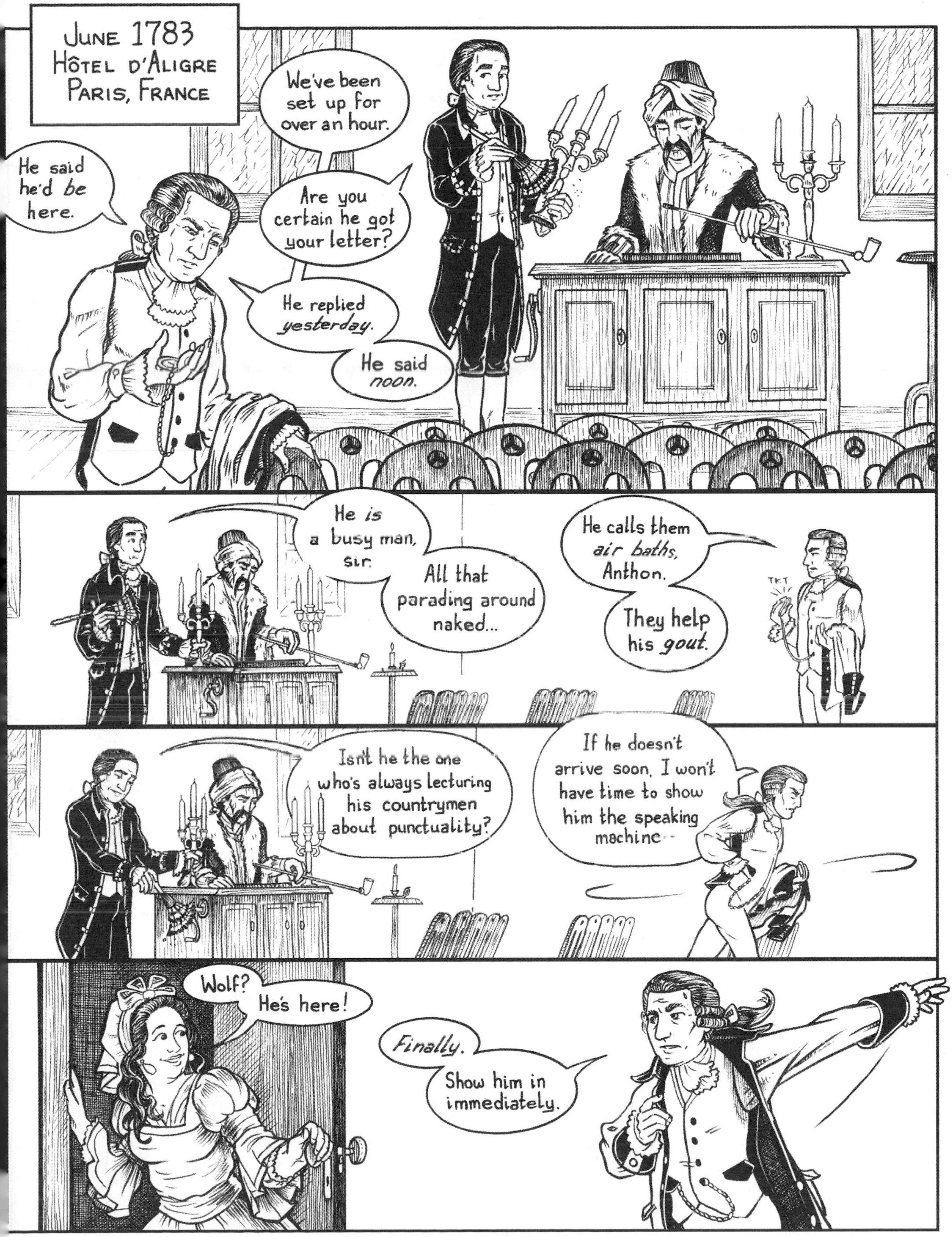
June 1783
Hôtel d'Aligre
Paris, France
He said he'd *be* here.
We've been set up for over an hour.
Are you certain he got your letter?
He replied *yesterday*.
He said *noon*.
He *is* a busy man, sir.
All that parading around naked...
He calls them *air baths*, Anthon.
They help his *gout*.
TKT
Isn't he the one who's always lecturing his countrymen about punctuality?
If he doesn't arrive soon, I won't have time to show him the speaking machine--
Wolf? He's here!
Finally.
Show him in immediately.

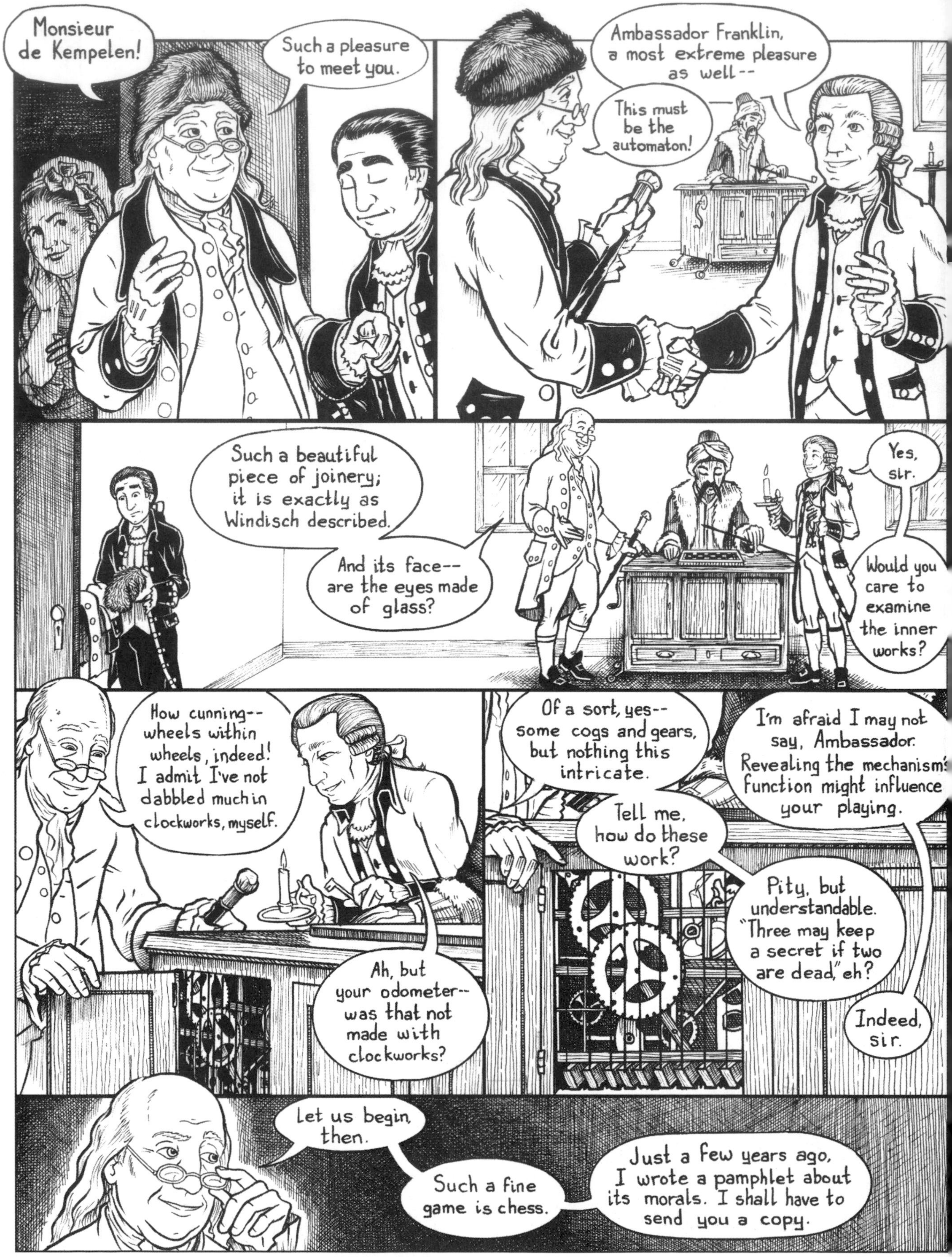

Monsieur de Kempelen!
Such a pleasure to meet you.
Ambassador Franklin, a most extreme pleasure as well--
This must be the automaton!
Such a beautiful piece of joinery; it is exactly as Windisch described.
And its face-- are the eyes made of glass?
Yes, sir.
Would you care to examine the inner works?
How cunning-- wheels within wheels, indeed! I admit I've not dabbled much in clockworks, myself.
Ah, but your odometer-- was that not made with clockworks?
Of a sort, yes-- some cogs and gears, but nothing this intricate.
Tell me, how do these work?
I'm afraid I may not say, Ambassador. Revealing the mechanism's function might influence your playing.
Pity, but understandable. "Three may keep a secret if two are dead," eh?
Indeed, sir.
Let us begin, then.
Such a fine game is chess.
Just a few years ago, I wrote a pamphlet about its morals. I shall have to send you a copy.

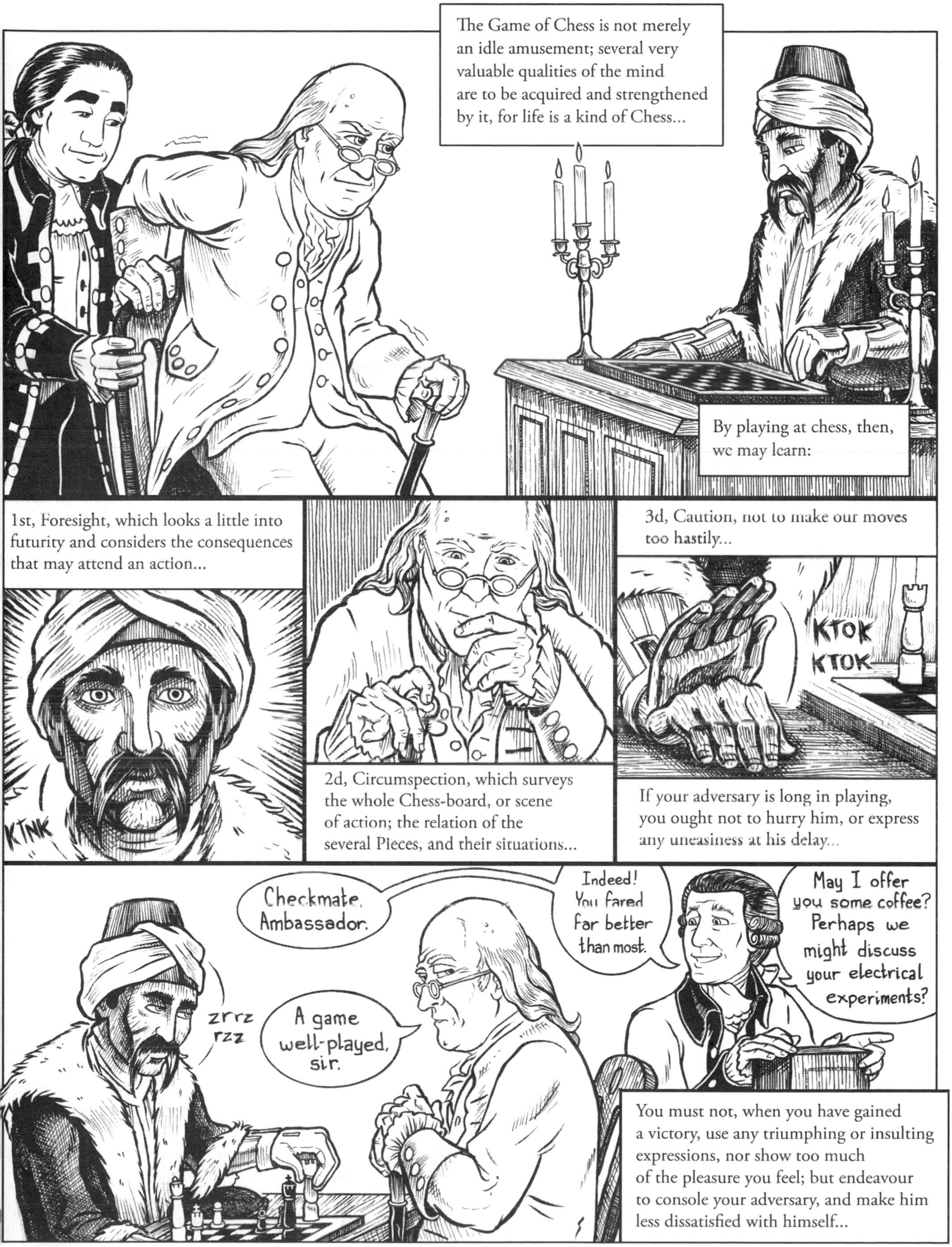
The Game of Chess is not merely an idle amusement; several very valuable qualities of the mind are to be acquired and strengthened by it, for life is a kind of Chess...
By playing at chess, then, we may learn:
1st, Foresight, which looks a little into futurity and considers the consequences that may attend an action...
KTNK
2d, Circumspection, which surveys the whole Chess-board, or scene of action; the relation of the several Pieces, and their situations...
3d, Caution, not to make our moves too hastily...
KTOK
KTOK
If your adversary is long in playing, you ought not to hurry him, or express any uneasiness at his delay...
Checkmate, Ambassador.
zrrz
rzz
A game well-played, sir.
Indeed! You fared far better than most.
May I offer you some coffee? Perhaps we might discuss your electrical experiments?
You must not, when you have gained a victory, use any triumphing or insulting expressions, nor show too much of the pleasure you feel; but endeavour to console your adversary, and make him less dissatisfied with himself...

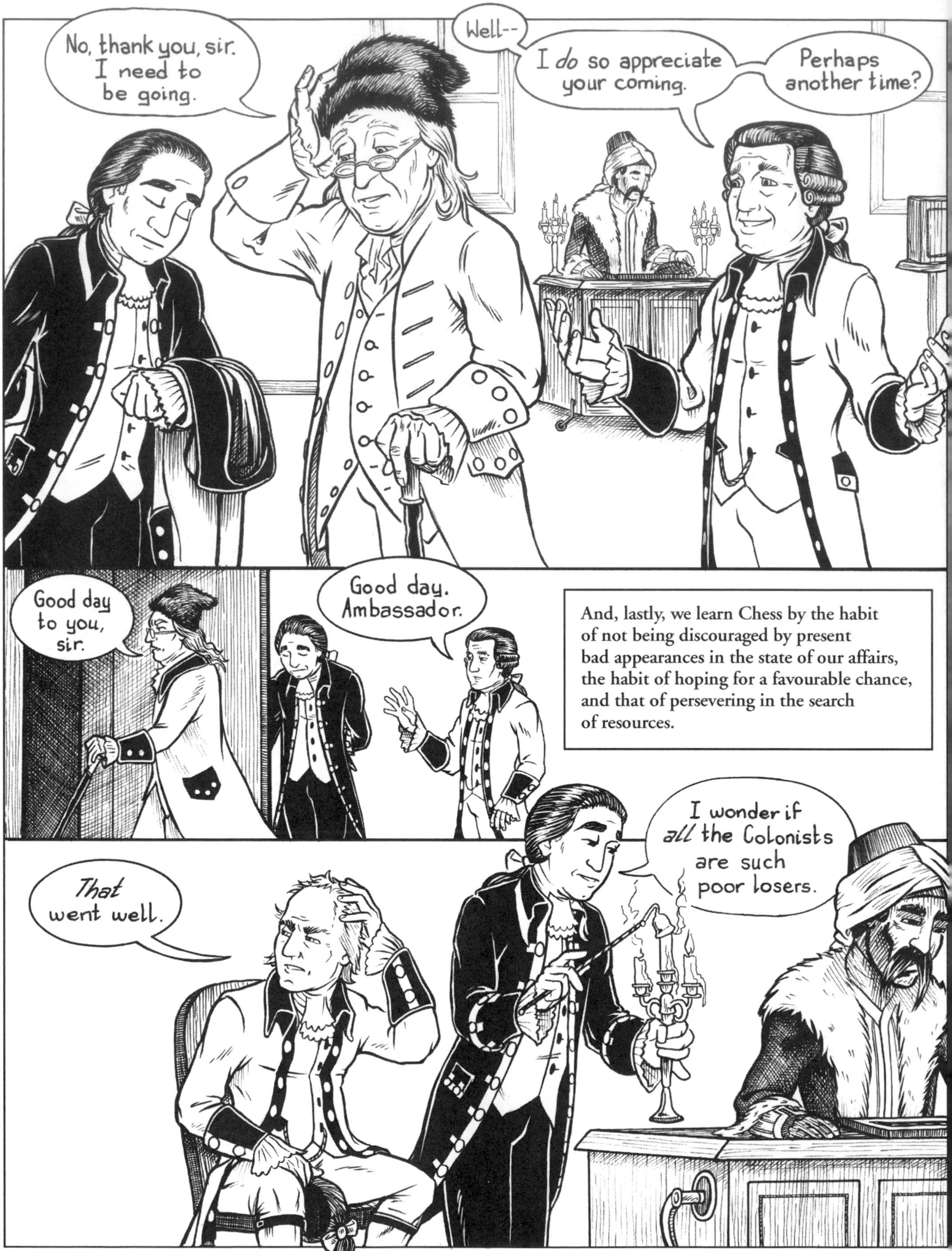

No, thank you, sir. I need to be going.
Well--
I *do* so appreciate your coming.
Perhaps another time?
Good day to you, sir.
Good day. Ambassador.
And, lastly, we learn Chess by the habit of not being discouraged by present bad appearances in the state of our affairs, the habit of hoping for a favourable chance, and that of persevering in the search of resources.
That went well.
I wonder if *all* the Colonists are such poor losers.

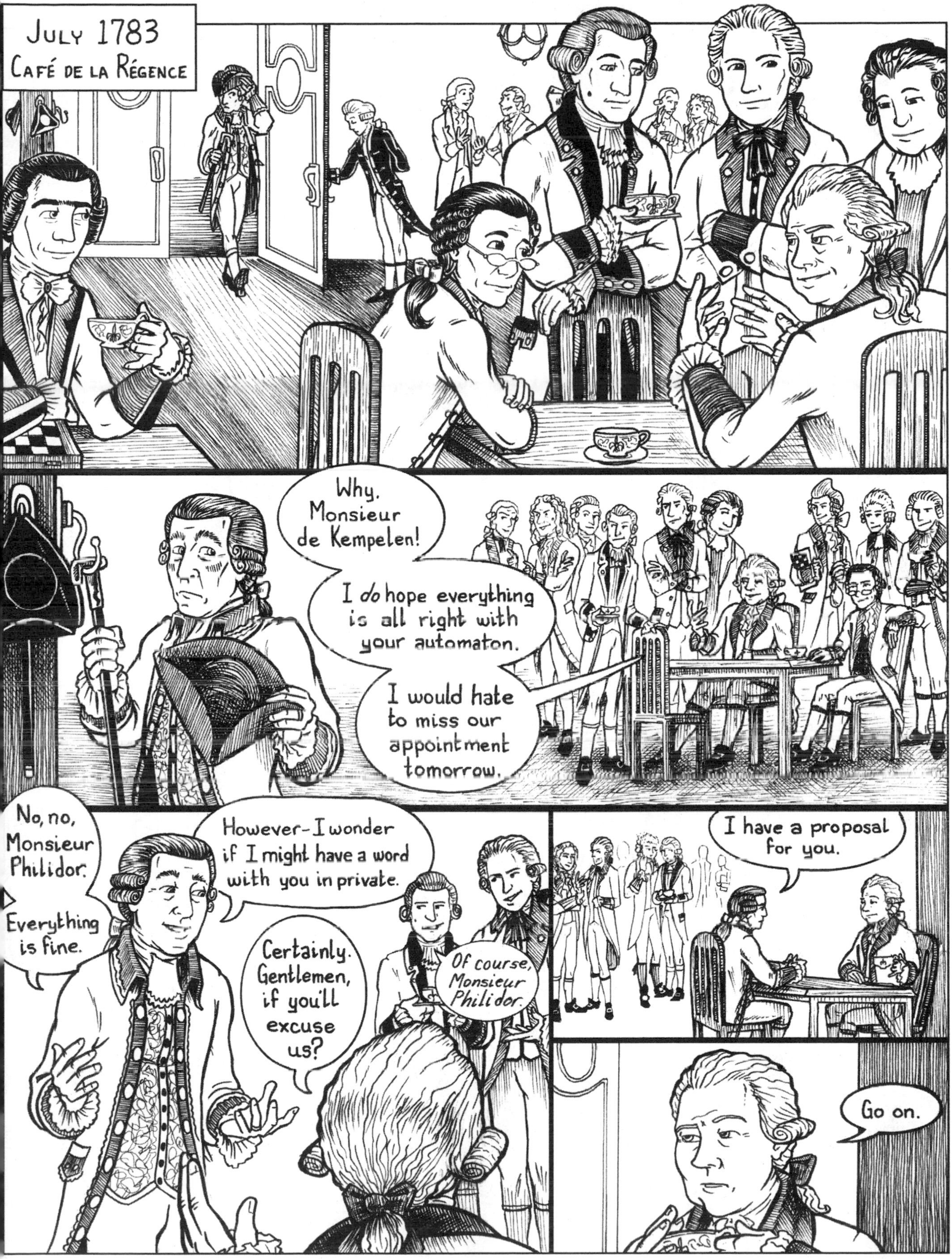
July 1783
Café de la Régence
Why. Monsieur de Kempelen!
I *do* hope everything is all right with your automaton.
I would hate to miss our appointment tomorrow.
No, no, Monsieur Philidor.
Everything is fine.
However-I wonder if I might have a word with you in private.
Certainly. Gentlemen, if you'll excuse us?
Of course, Monsieur Philidor.
I have a proposal for you.
Go on.

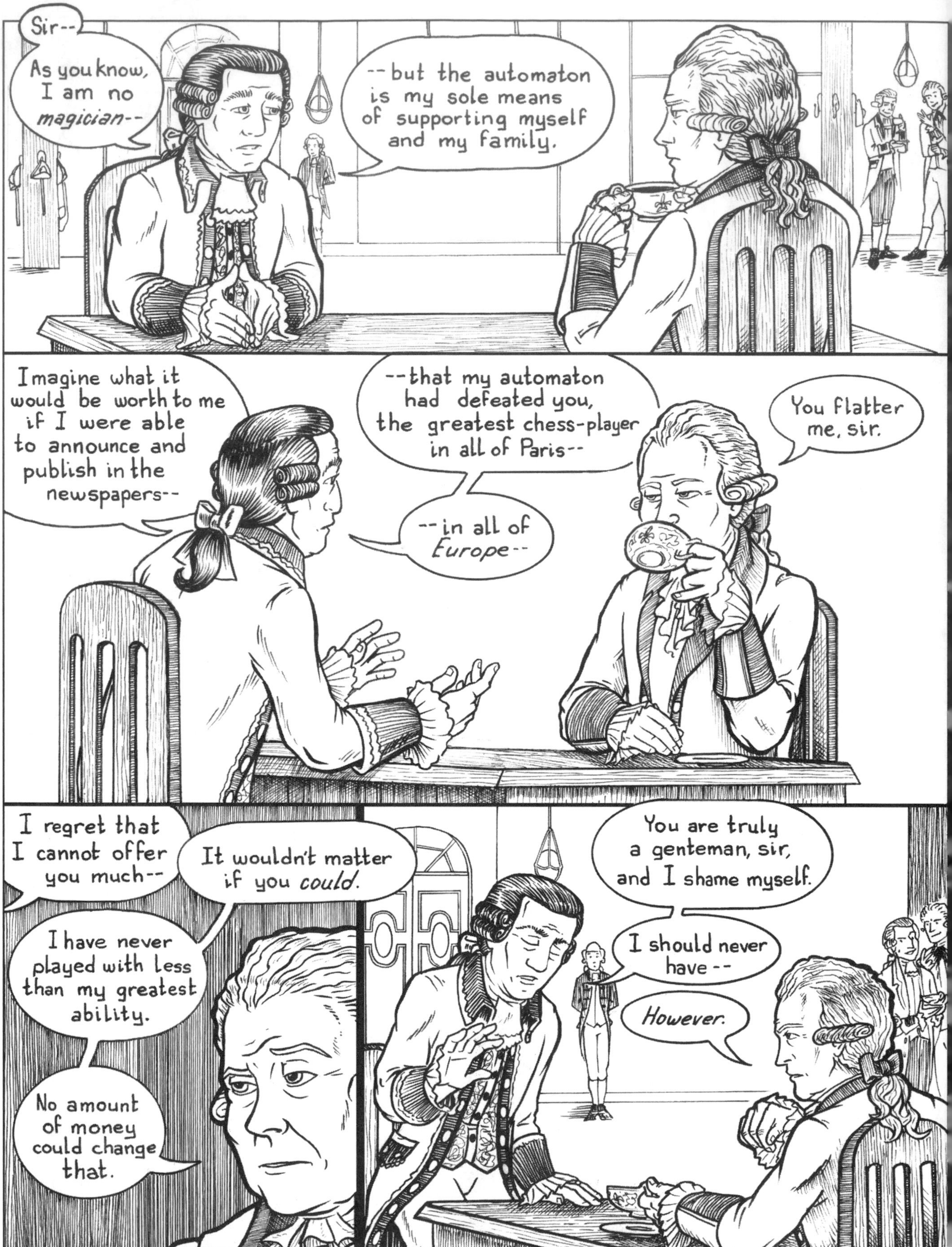
Sir--
As you know, I am no *magician*--
--but the automaton is my sole means of supporting myself and my family.
Imagine what it would be worth to me if I were able to announce and publish in the newspapers--
--that my automaton had defeated you, the greatest chess-player in all of Paris--
--in all of *Europe*--
You flatter me, sir.
I regret that I cannot offer you much--
It wouldn't matter if you *could*.
I have never played with less than my greatest ability.
No amount of money could change that.
You are truly a genteman, sir, and I shame myself.
I should never have--
However.

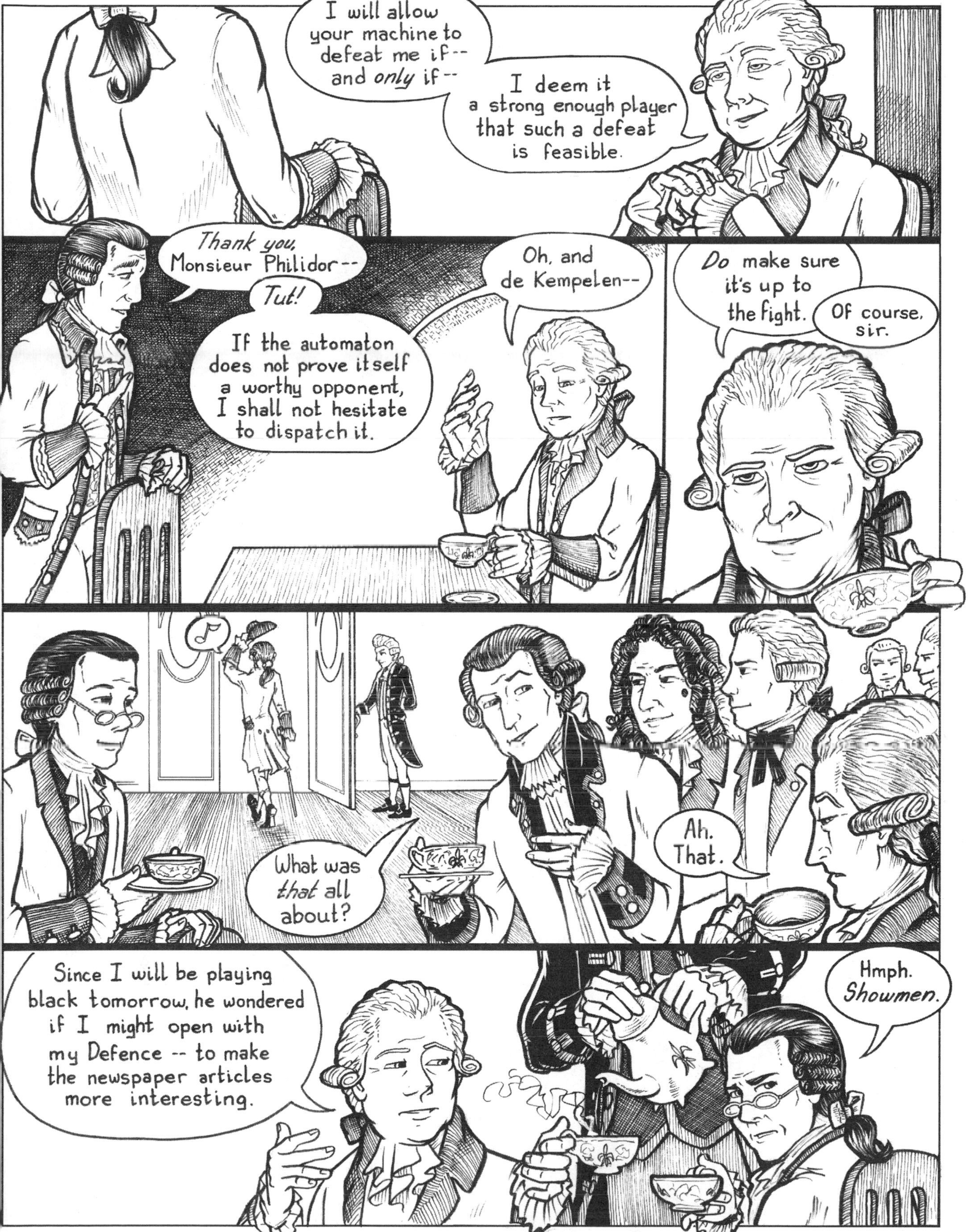

I will allow your machine to defeat me if -- and *only* if --
I deem it a strong enough player that such a defeat is feasible.
Thank you, Monsieur Philidor --
Tut!
If the automaton does not prove itself a worthy opponent, I shall not hesitate to dispatch it.
Oh, and de Kempelen --
Do make sure it's up to the fight.
Of course, sir.
What was *that* all about?
Ah. That.
Since I will be playing black tomorrow, he wondered if I might open with my Defence -- to make the newspaper articles more interesting.
Hmph. *Showmen.*

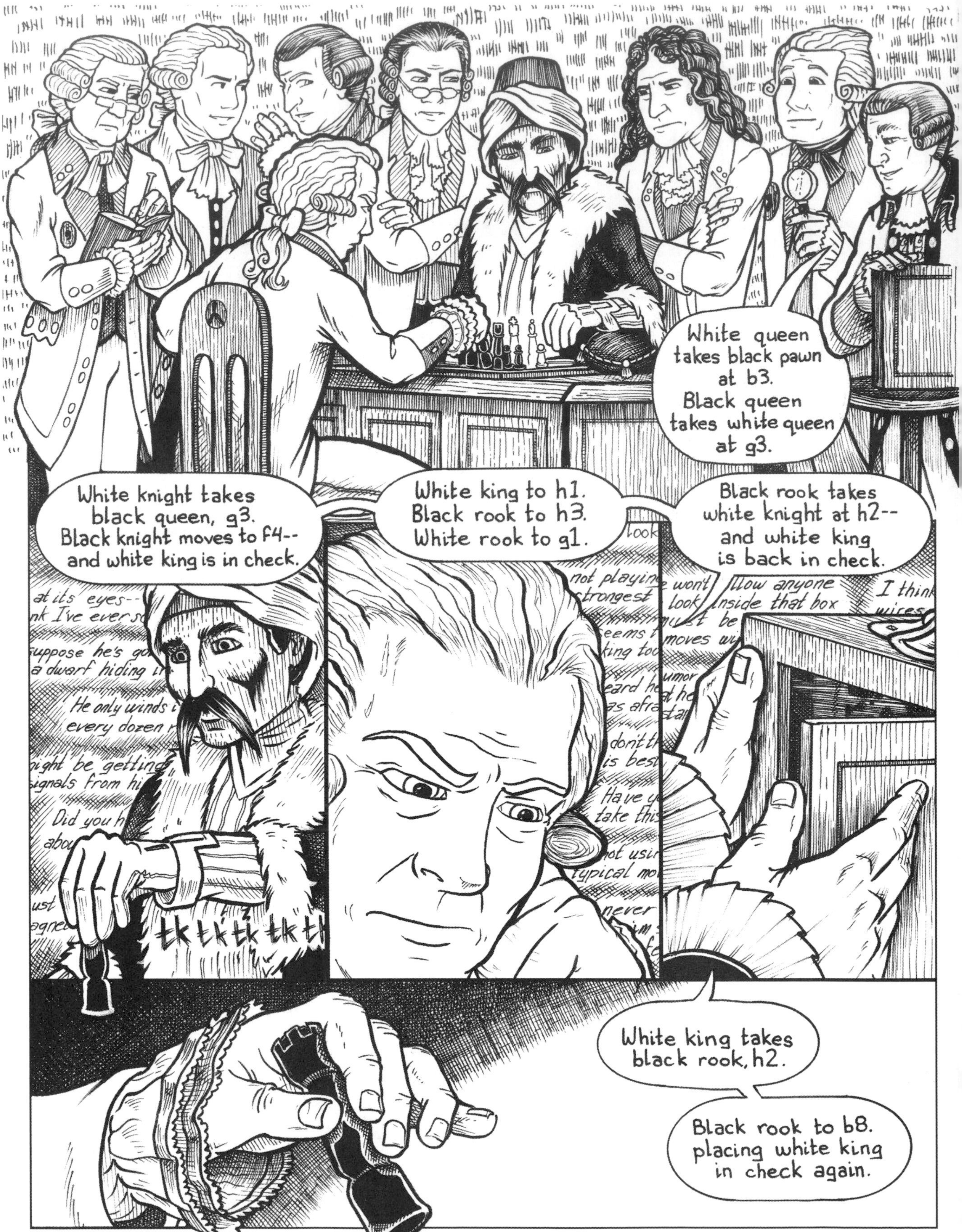
White queen takes black pawn at b3. Black queen takes white queen at g3.
White knight takes black queen, g3. Black knight moves to f4-- and white king is in check.
White king to h1. Black rook to h3. White rook to g1.
Black rook takes white knight at h2-- and white king is back in check.
White king takes black rook, h2.
Black rook to b8. placing white king in check again.

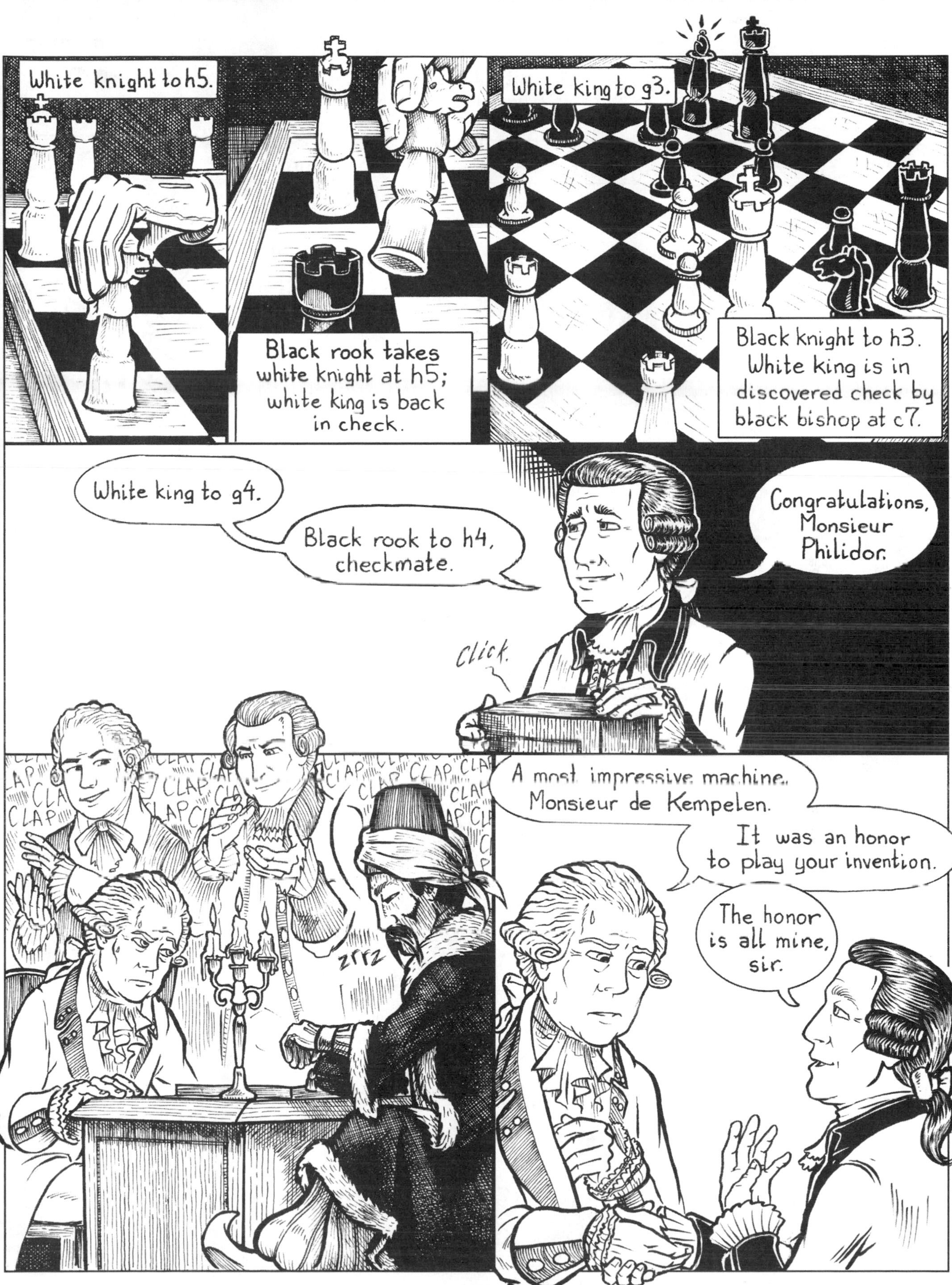
White knight to h5.
Black rook takes white knight at h5; white king is back in check.
White king to g3.
Black knight to h3. White king is in discovered check by black bishop at c7.
White king to g4.
Black rook to h4, checkmate.
Congratulations, Monsieur Philidor.
Click.
CLAP CLAP CLAP
zrrz
A most impressive machine, Monsieur de Kempelen.
It was an honor to play your invention.
The honor is all mine, sir.

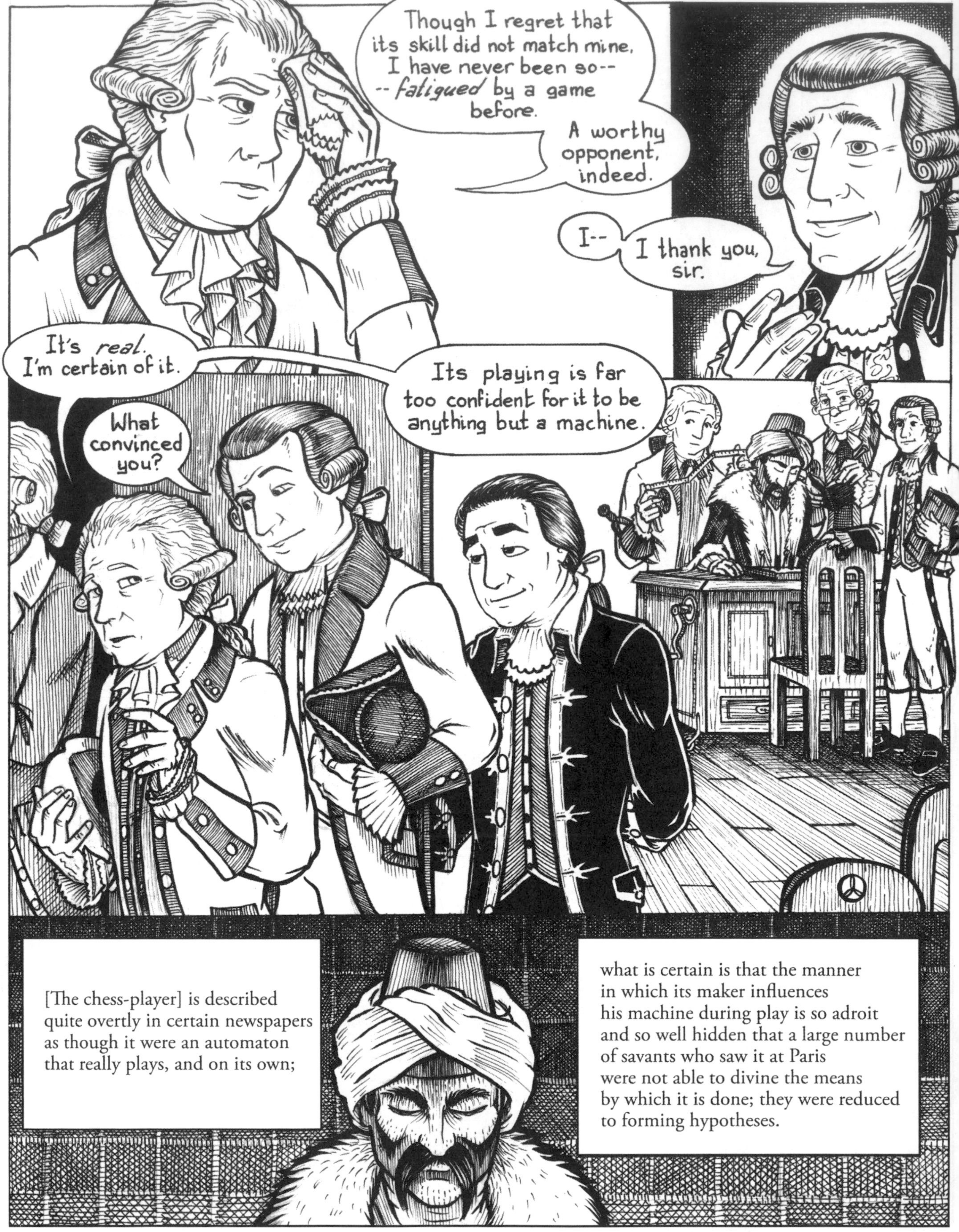
Though I regret that its skill did not match mine, I have never been so-- --*fatigued* by a game before.
A worthy opponent, indeed.
I--
I thank you, sir.
It's *real.* I'm certain of it.
What convinced you?
Its playing is far too confident for it to be anything but a machine.
[The chess-player] is described quite overtly in certain newspapers as though it were an automaton that really plays, and on its own;
what is certain is that the manner in which its maker influences his machine during play is so adroit and so well hidden that a large number of savants who saw it at Paris were not able to divine the means by which it is done; they were reduced to forming hypotheses.

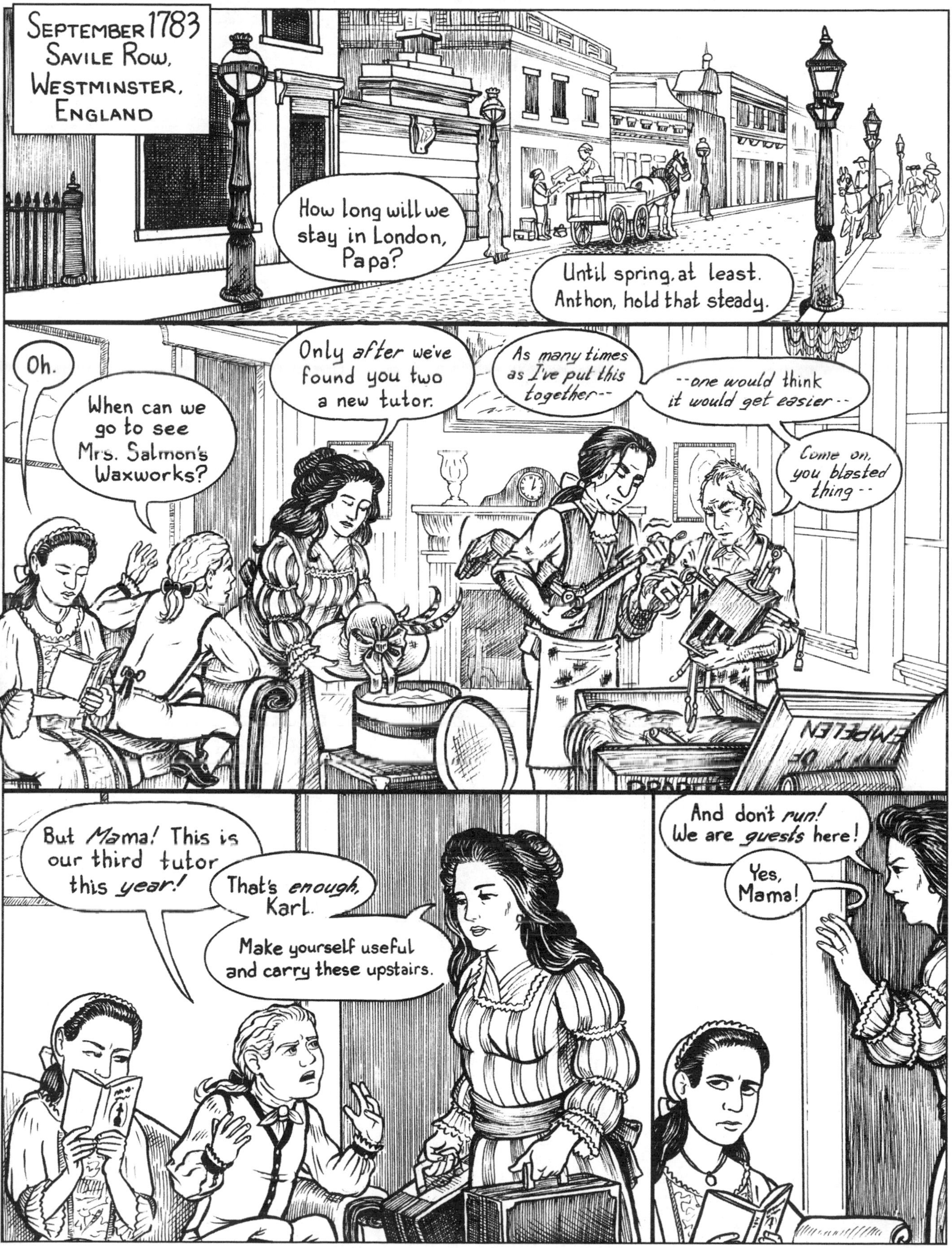
September 1783
Savile Row, Westminster, England
How long will we stay in London, Papa?
Until spring, at least. Anthon, hold that steady.
Oh.
When can we go to see Mrs. Salmon's Waxworks?
Only *after* we've found you two a new tutor.
As *many times* as *I've put this together*--
--*one would think it would get easier*--
Come on, you blasted thing--
But *Mama!* This is our third tutor this *year!*
That's *enough,* Karl.
Make yourself useful and carry these upstairs.
And don't *run!* We are *guests* here!
Yes, Mama!

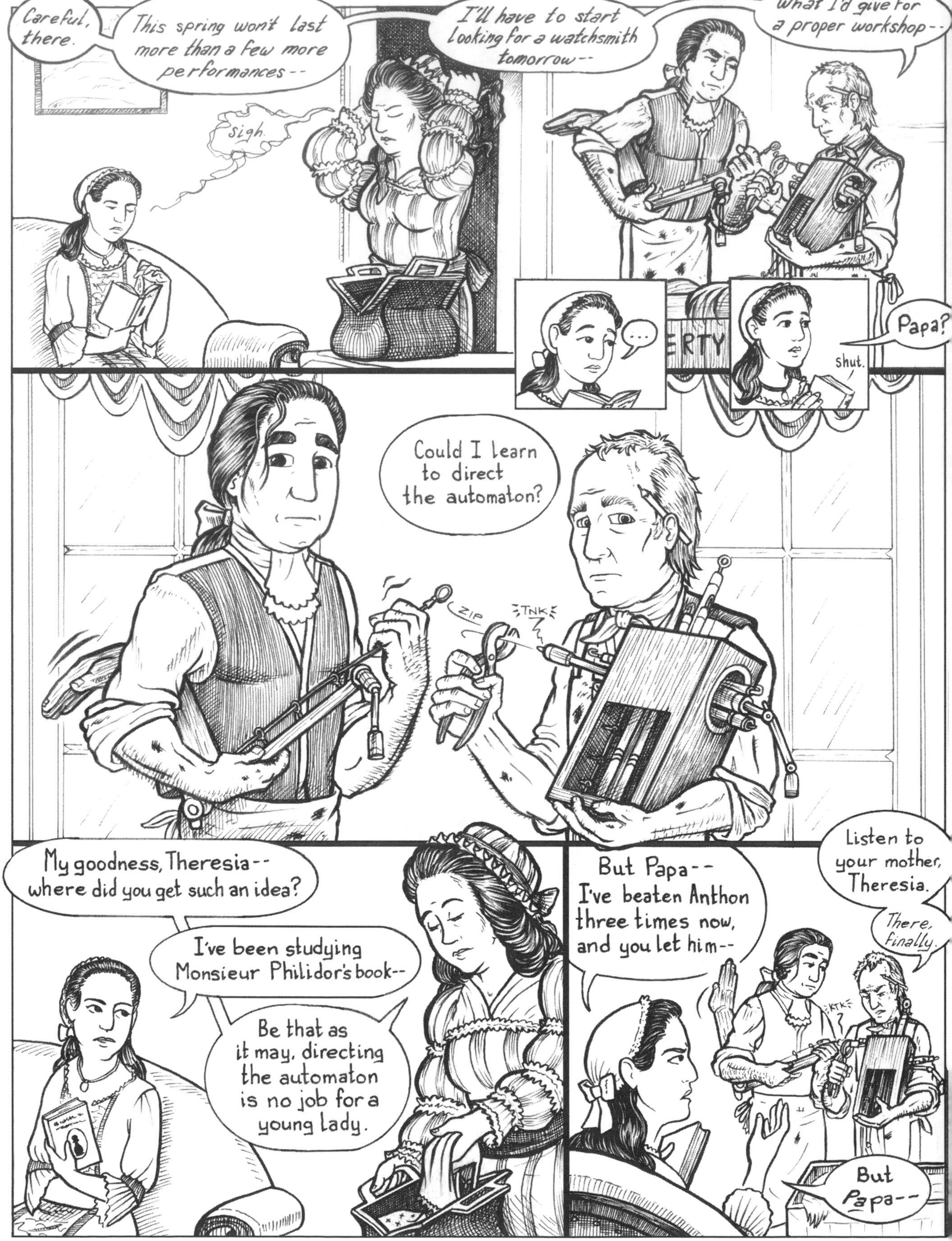
Careful, there.
This spring won't last more than a few more performances--
sigh.
I'll have to start looking for a watchsmith tomorrow--
What I'd give for a proper workshop--
...
ERTY
Papa?
shut.
Could I learn to direct the automaton?
ZIP
TNK
My goodness, Theresia-- where did you get such an idea?
I've been studying Monsieur Philidor's book--
Be that as it may, directing the automaton is no job for a young lady.
But Papa-- I've beaten Anthon three times now, and you let him--
Listen to your mother, Theresia.
There, finally.
KTK
But Papa--

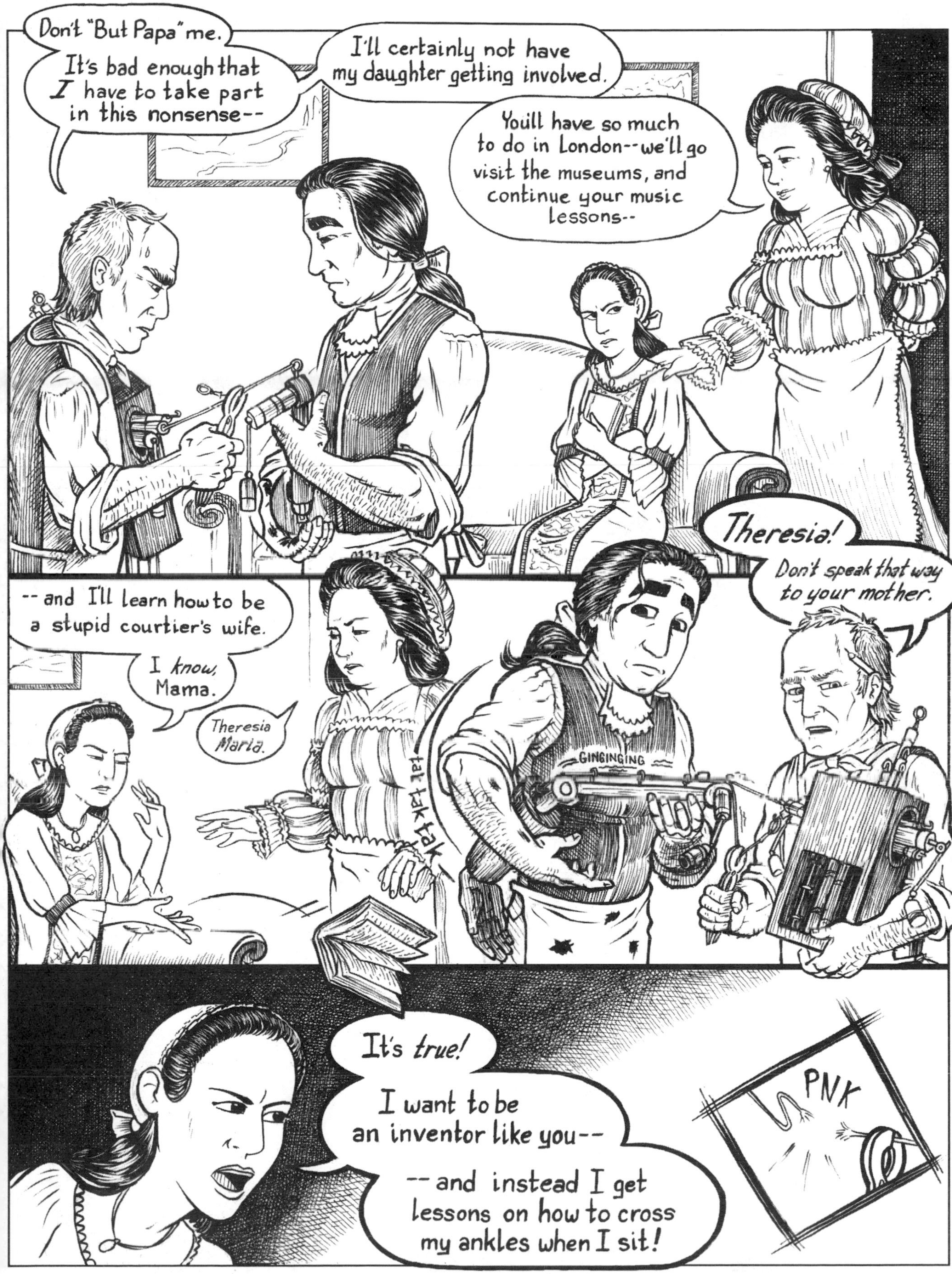
Don't "But Papa" me.
It's bad enough that I have to take part in this nonsense--
I'll certainly not have my daughter getting involved.
You'll have so much to do in London--we'll go visit the museums, and continue your music lessons--
-- and I'll learn how to be a stupid courtier's wife.
I know, Mama.
Theresia Maria.
Theresia!
Don't speak that way to your mother.
tak tak tak
GINGINGING
It's true!
I want to be an inventor like you--
-- and instead I get lessons on how to cross my ankles when I sit!
PNK

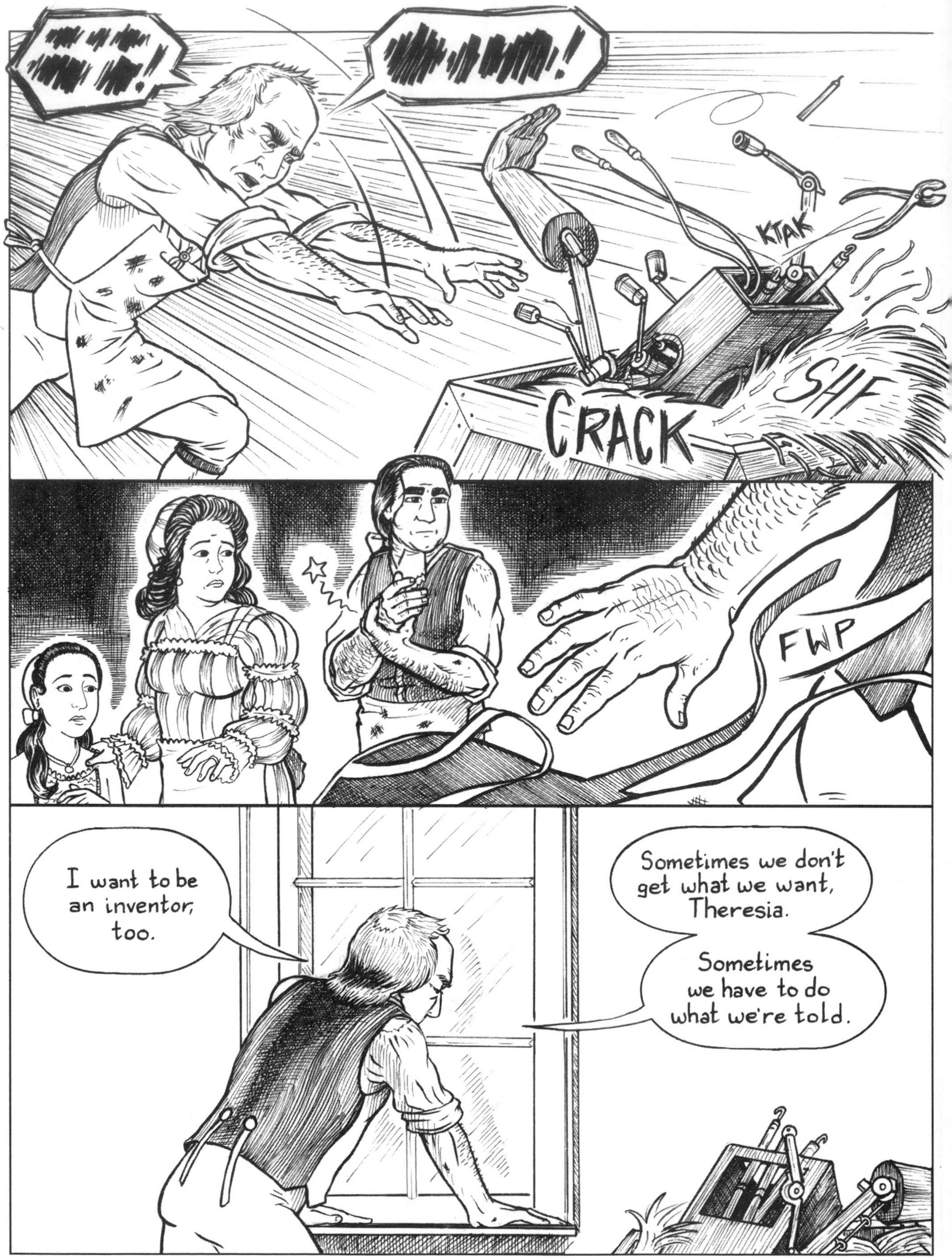
KTAK
CRACK
SHF
FWP
I want to be an inventor, too.
Sometimes we don't get what we want, Theresia.
Sometimes we have to do what we're told.

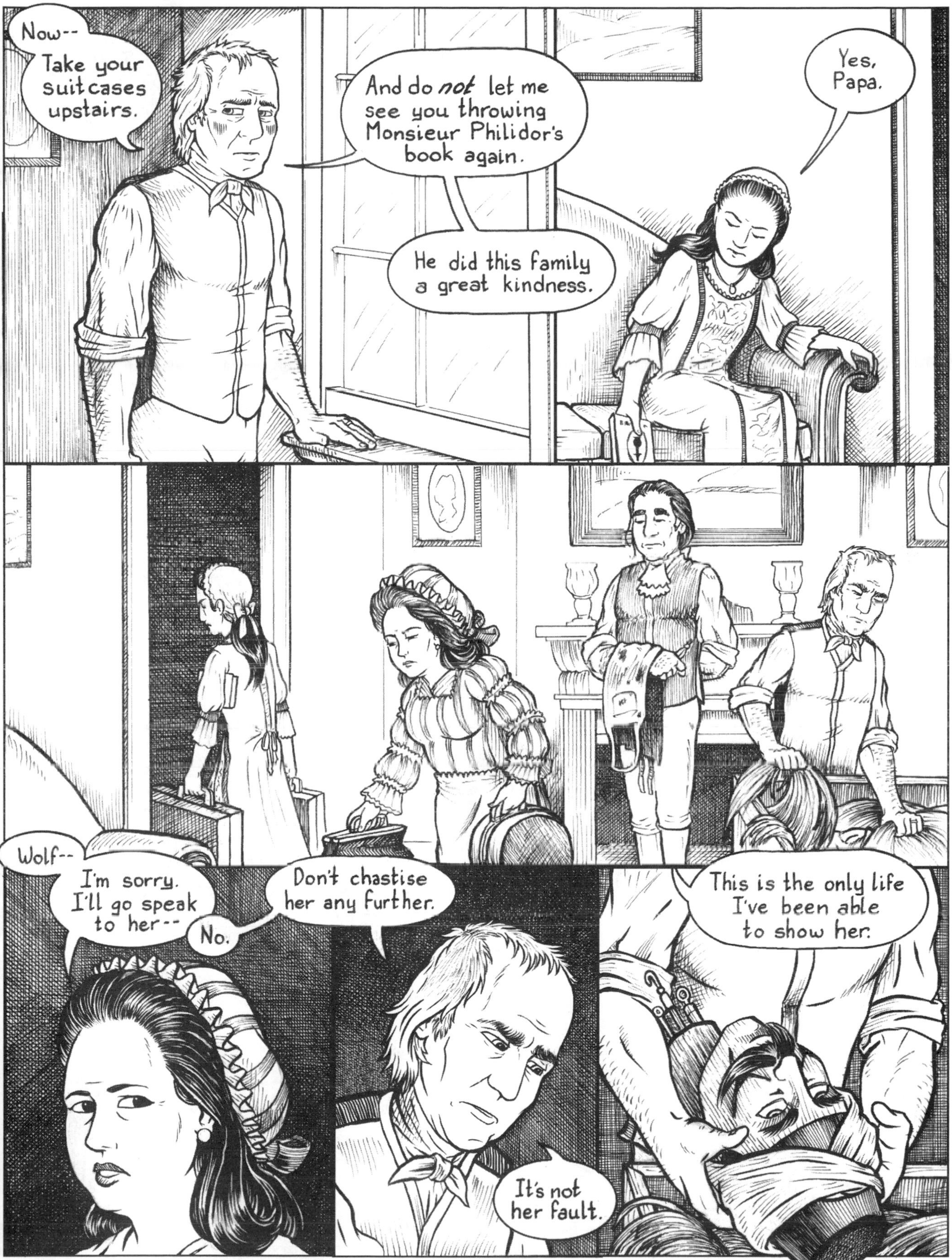
Now--
Take your suitcases upstairs.
And do *not* let me see you throwing Monsieur Philidor's book again.
He did this family a great kindness.
Yes, Papa.
Wolf--
I'm sorry. I'll go speak to her--
No.
Don't chastise her any further.
It's not her fault.
This is the only life I've been able to show her.

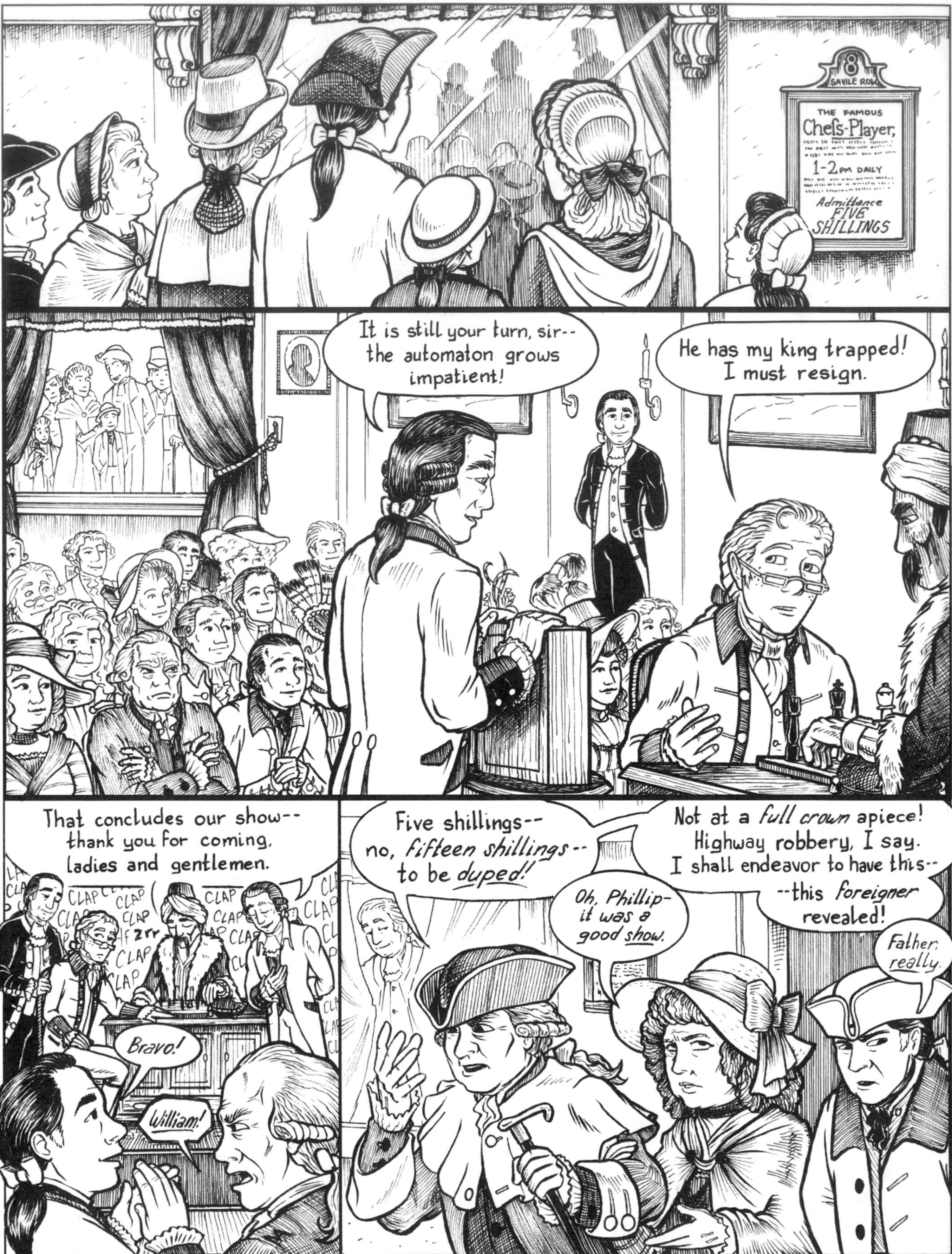

8
SAVILE ROW
THE FAMOUS
Chefs-Player,
1-2PM DAILY
Admittance FIVE SHILLINGS
It is still your turn, sir-- the automaton grows impatient!
He has my king trapped! I must resign.
That concludes our show-- thank you for coming, ladies and gentlemen.
CLAP CLAP CLAP CLAP CLAP CLAP CLAP
zrr
Bravo!
William!
Five shillings-- no, fifteen shillings-- to be duped!
Not at a full crown apiece! Highway robbery, I say. I shall endeavor to have this--
--this foreigner revealed!
Oh, Phillip- it was a good show.
Father, really.

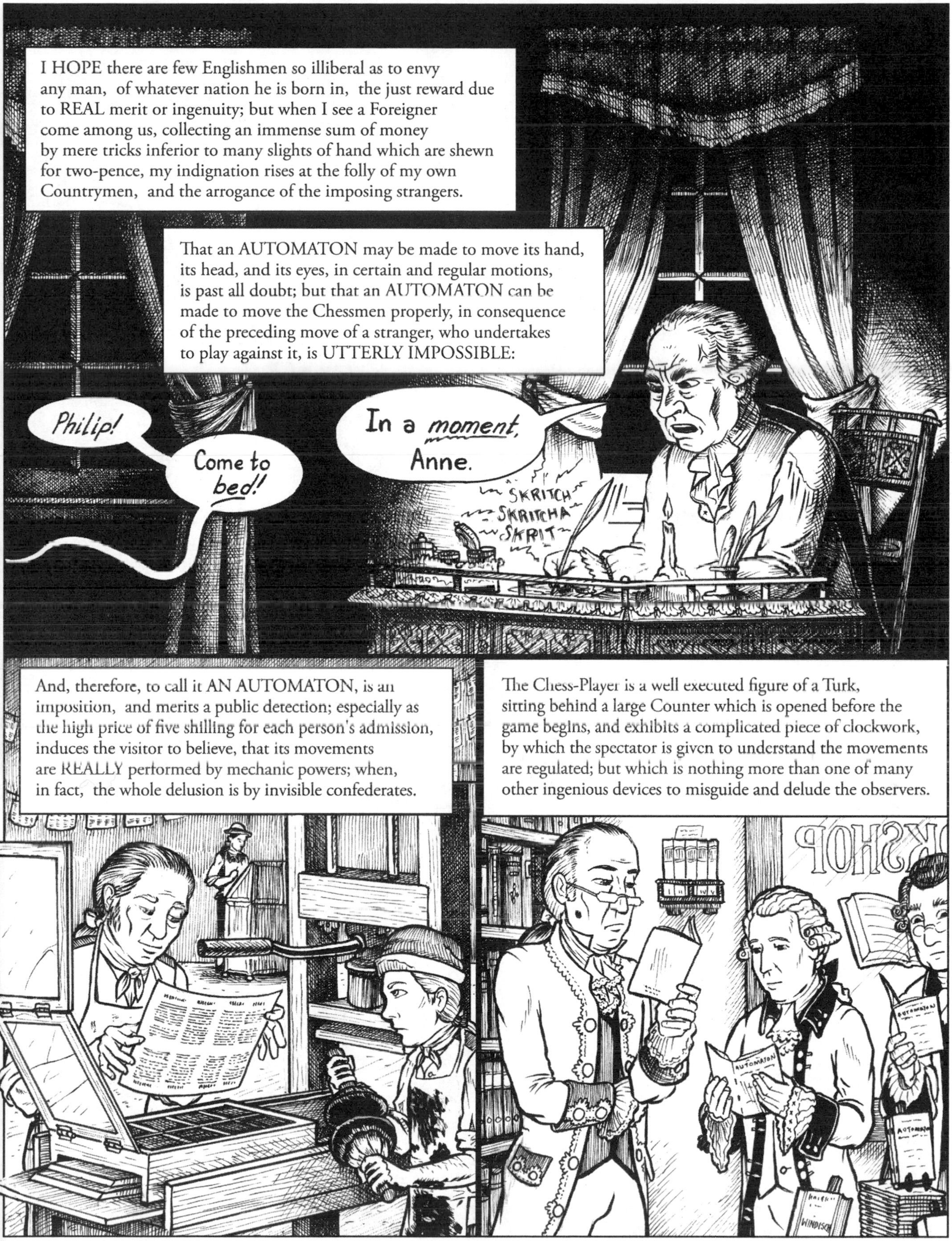
I HOPE there are few Englishmen so illiberal as to envy any man, of whatever nation he is born in, the just reward due to REAL merit or ingenuity; but when I see a Foreigner come among us, collecting an immense sum of money by mere tricks inferior to many slights of hand which are shewn for two-pence, my indignation rises at the folly of my own Countrymen, and the arrogance of the imposing strangers.
That an AUTOMATON may be made to move its hand, its head, and its eyes, in certain and regular motions, is past all doubt; but that an AUTOMATON can be made to move the Chessmen properly, in consequence of the preceding move of a stranger, who undertakes to play against it, is UTTERLY IMPOSSIBLE:
Philip!
Come to bed!
In a moment, Anne.
SKRITCH
SKRITCHA
SKRIT
And, therefore, to call it AN AUTOMATON, is an imposition, and merits a public detection; especially as the high price of five shilling for each person's admission, induces the visitor to believe, that its movements are REALLY performed by mechanic powers; when, in fact, the whole delusion is by invisible confederates.
The Chess-Player is a well executed figure of a Turk, sitting behind a large Counter which is opened before the game begins, and exhibits a complicated piece of clockwork, by which the spectator is given to understand the movements are regulated; but which is nothing more than one of many other ingenious devices to misguide and delude the observers.

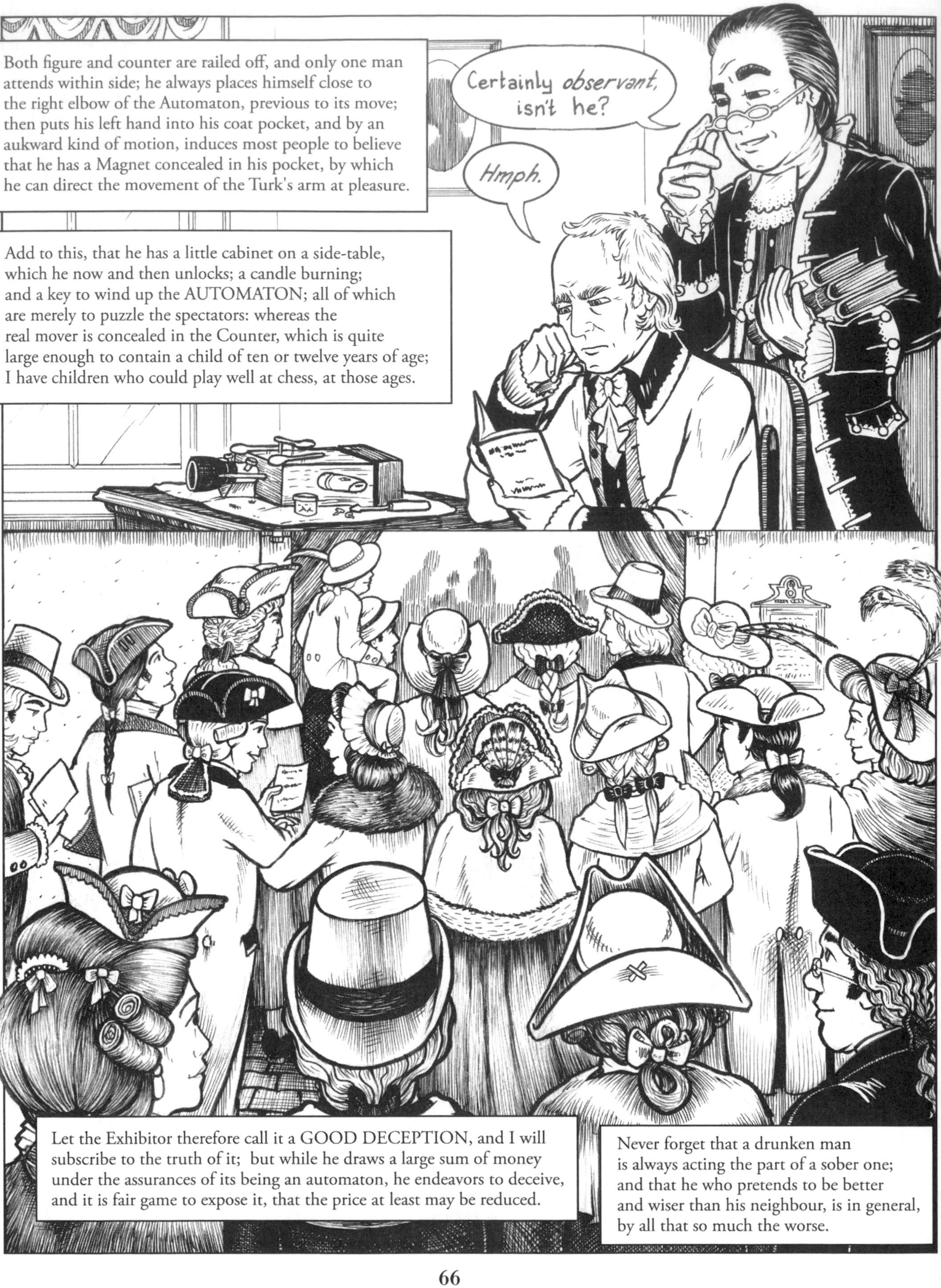
Both figure and counter are railed off, and only one man attends within side; he always places himself close to the right elbow of the Automaton, previous to its move; then puts his left hand into his coat pocket, and by an aukward kind of motion, induces most people to believe that he has a Magnet concealed in his pocket, by which he can direct the movement of the Turk's arm at pleasure.
Certainly *observant*, isn't he?
Hmph.
Add to this, that he has a little cabinet on a side-table, which he now and then unlocks; a candle burning; and a key to wind up the AUTOMATON; all of which are merely to puzzle the spectators: whereas the real mover is concealed in the Counter, which is quite large enough to contain a child of ten or twelve years of age; I have children who could play well at chess, at those ages.
Let the Exhibitor therefore call it a GOOD DECEPTION, and I will subscribe to the truth of it; but while he draws a large sum of money under the assurances of its being an automaton, he endeavors to deceive, and it is fair game to expose it, that the price at least may be reduced.
Never forget that a drunken man is always acting the part of a sober one; and that he who pretends to be better and wiser than his neighbour, is in general, by all that so much the worse.

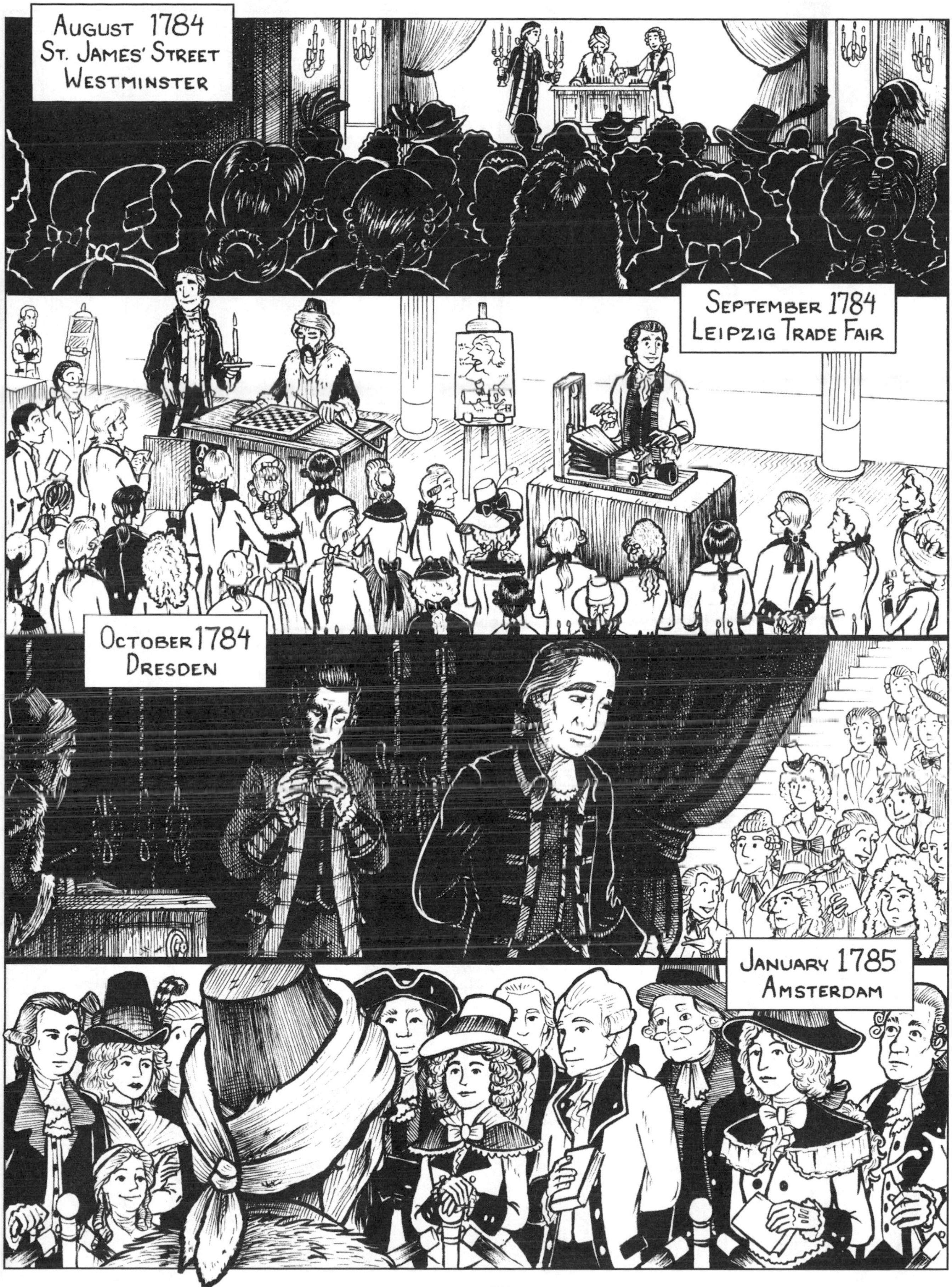
August 1784
St. James' Street
Westminster
September 1784
Leipzig Trade Fair
October 1784
Dresden
January 1785
Amsterdam

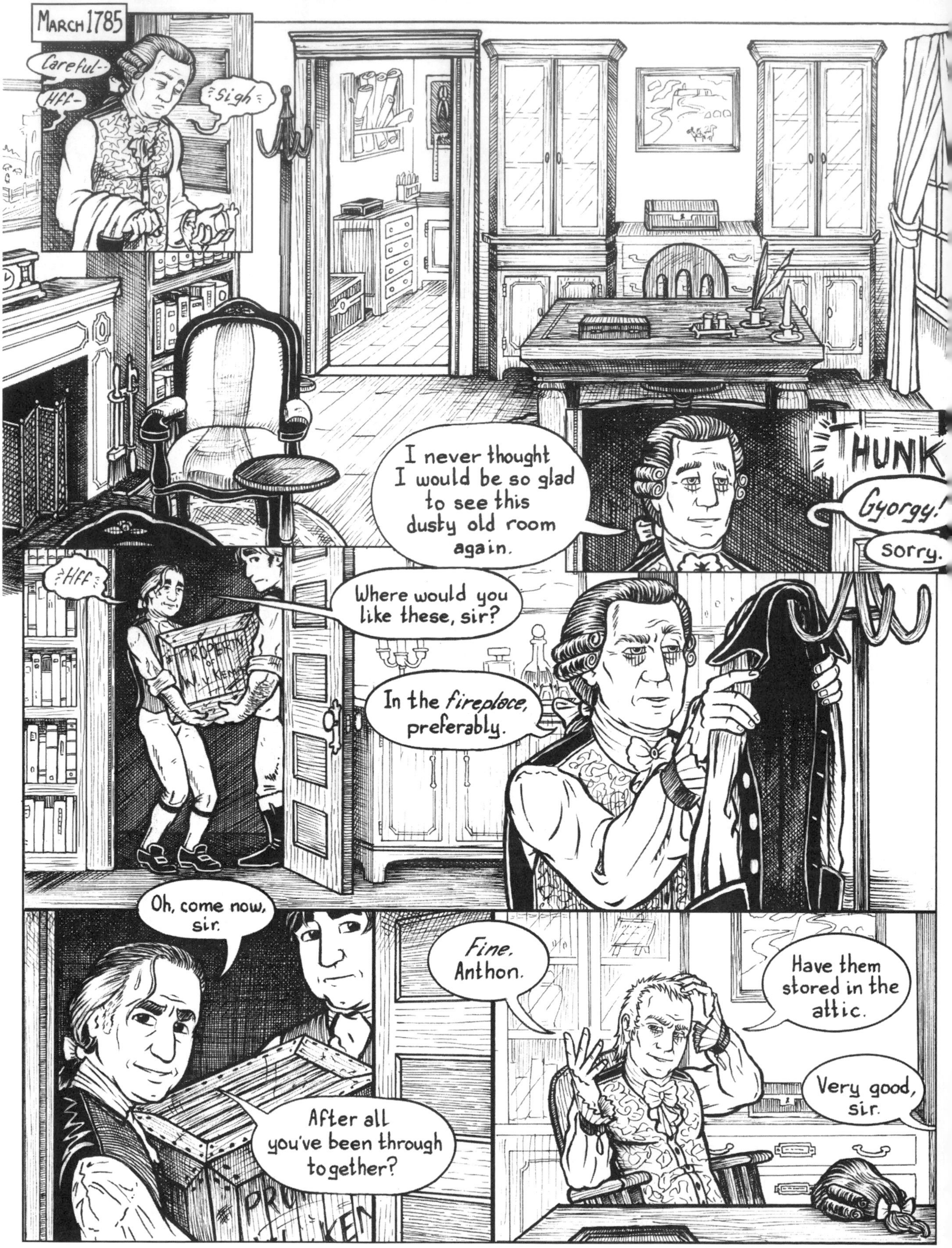
March 1785
Careful--
Hff-
Sigh
I never thought I would be so glad to see this dusty old room again.
THUNK
Gyorgy!
Sorry.
Hff
Where would you like these, sir?
In the *fireplace*, preferably.
Oh, come now, sir.
After all you've been through together?
Fine. Anthon.
Have them stored in the attic.
Very good, sir.

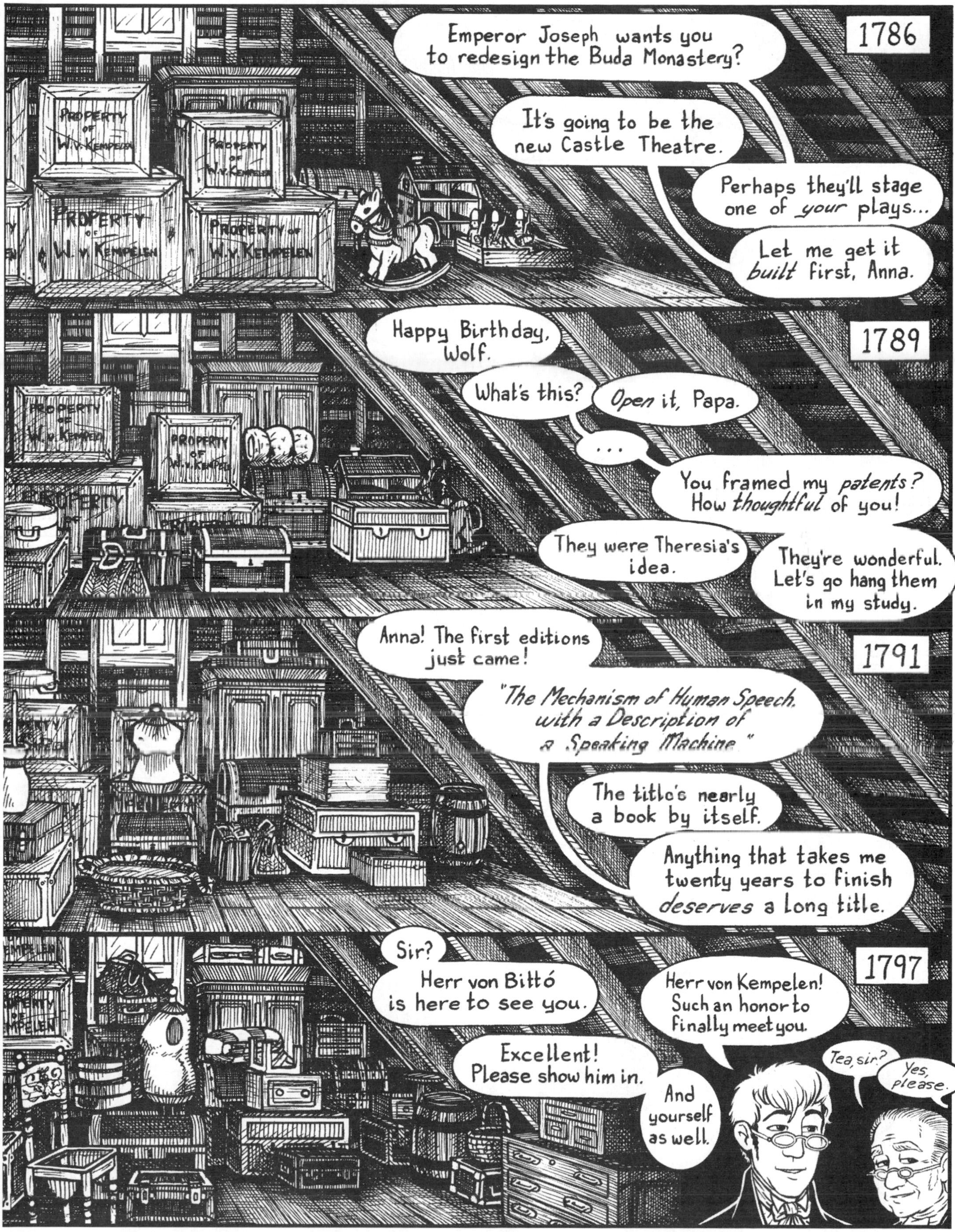
1786
Emperor Joseph wants you to redesign the Buda Monastery?
It's going to be the new Castle Theatre.
Perhaps they'll stage one of *your* plays...
Let me get it *built* first, Anna.
PROPERTY OF W.v. KEMPELEN
1789
Happy Birthday, Wolf.
What's this?
Open it, Papa.
...
You framed my *patents*? How *thoughtful* of you!
They were Theresia's idea.
They're wonderful. Let's go hang them in my study.
1791
Anna! The first editions just came!
"The Mechanism of Human Speech, with a Description of a Speaking Machine."
The title's nearly a book by itself.
Anything that takes me twenty years to finish *deserves* a long title.
1797
Sir?
Herr von Bittó is here to see you.
Herr von Kempelen! Such an honor to finally meet you.
Excellent! Please show him in.
And yourself as well.
Tea, sir?
Yes, please.

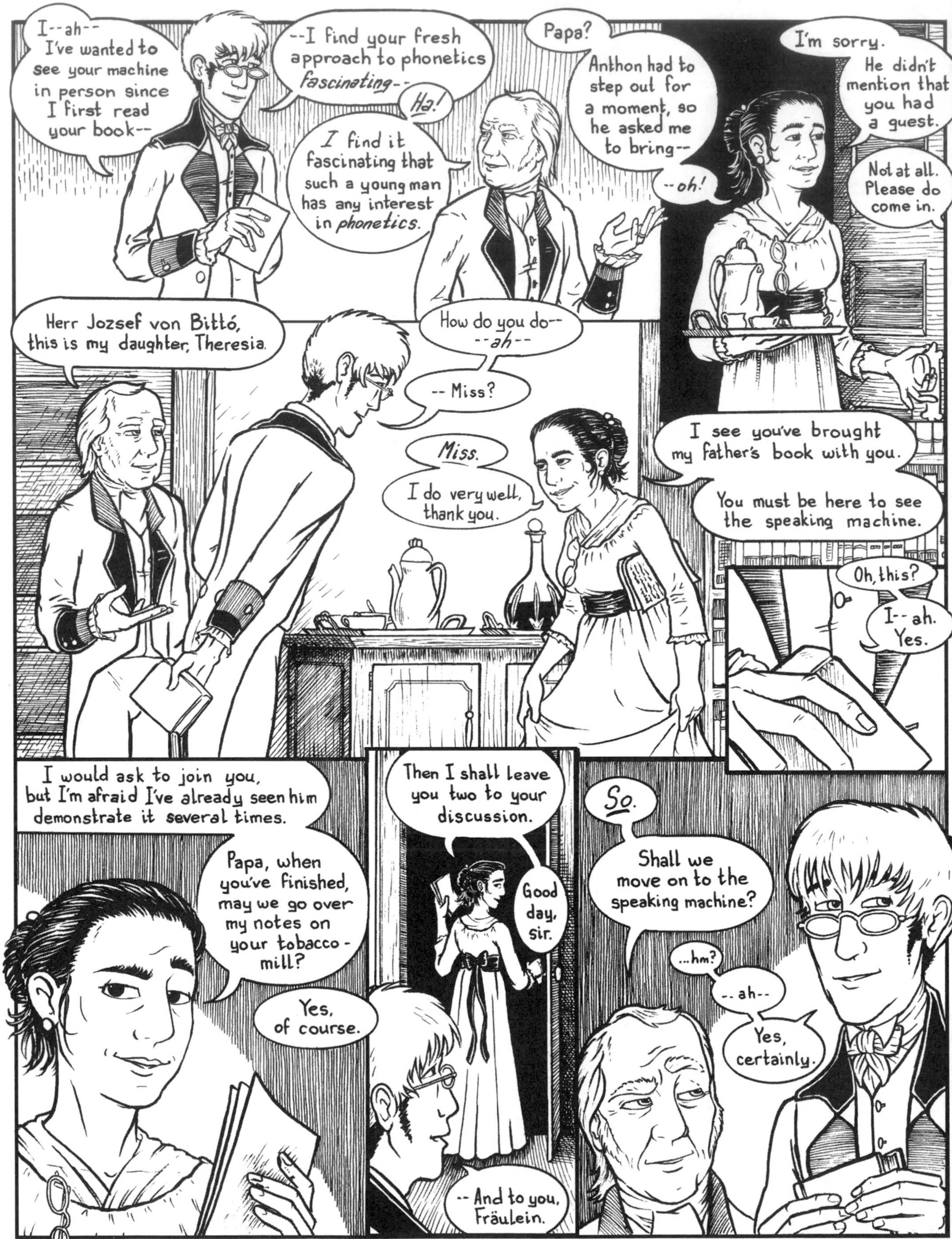

I--ah-- I've wanted to see your machine in person since I first read your book--
--I find your fresh approach to phonetics *fascinating*--
Ha!
I find it fascinating that such a young man has any interest in *phonetics*.
Papa?
Anthon had to step out for a moment, so he asked me to bring--
--*oh!*
I'm sorry.
He didn't mention that you had a guest.
Not at all. Please do come in.
Herr Jozsef von Bittó, this is my daughter, Theresia.
How do you do-- --*ah*--
-- Miss?
Miss.
I do very well, thank you.
I see you've brought my father's book with you.
You must be here to see the speaking machine.
Oh, this?
I--ah. Yes.
I would ask to join you, but I'm afraid I've already seen him demonstrate it several times.
Papa, when you've finished, may we go over my notes on your tobacco-mill?
Yes, of course.
Then I shall leave you two to your discussion.
Good day, sir.
--And to you, Fräulein.
So.
Shall we move on to the speaking machine?
...hm?
--ah--
Yes, certainly.

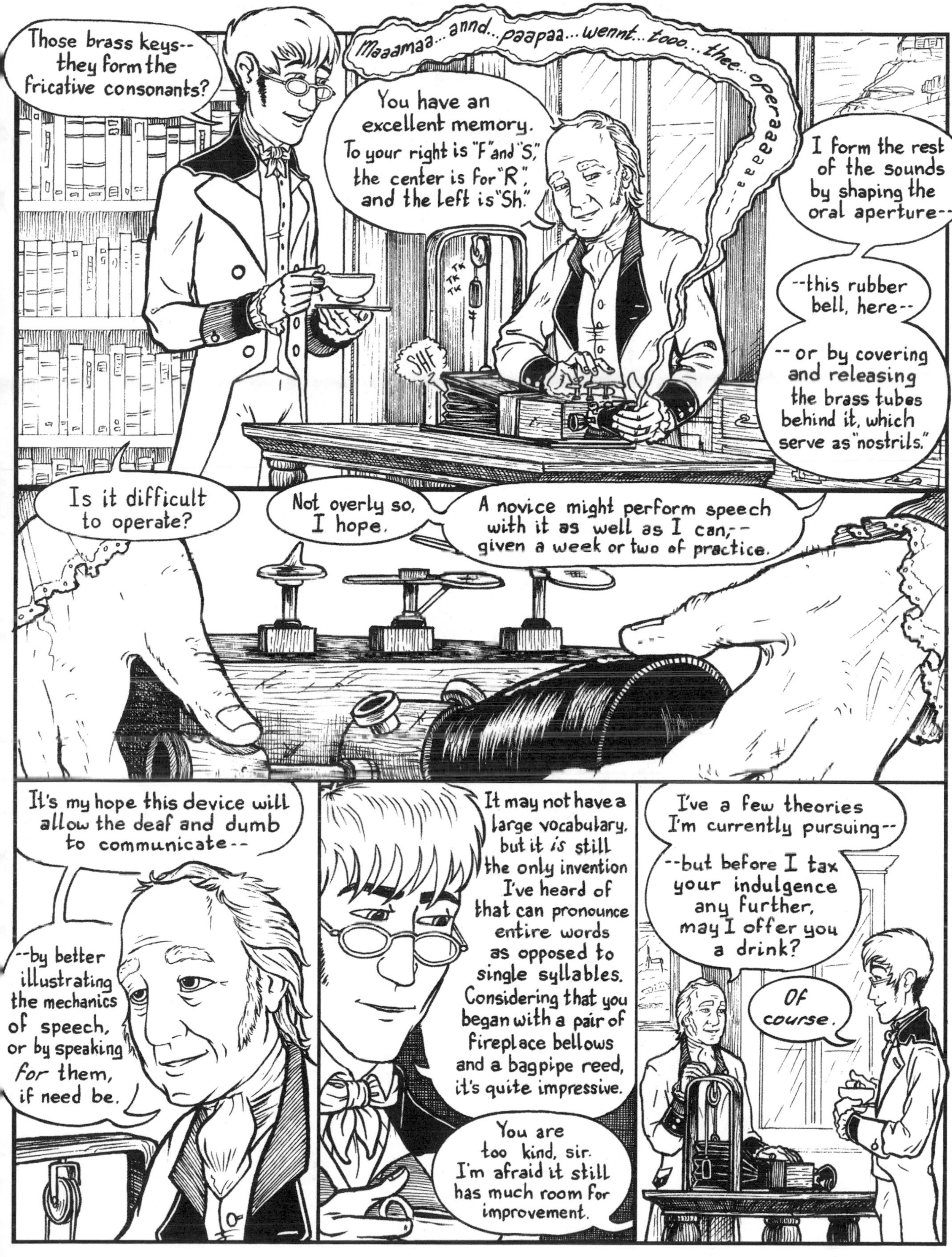

Those brass keys-- they form the fricative consonants?
Maaamaa...annd...paapaa...wennt...tooo...thee...operaaaaa...
You have an excellent memory. To your right is "F" and "S," the center is for "R", and the left is "Sh."
TK TK TK
SHF
I form the rest of the sounds by shaping the oral aperture--
--this rubber bell, here--
--or by covering and releasing the brass tubes behind it, which serve as "nostrils."
Is it difficult to operate?
Not overly so, I hope.
A novice might perform speech with it as well as I can,-- given a week or two of practice.
It's my hope this device will allow the deaf and dumb to communicate--
--by better illustrating the mechanics of speech, or by speaking *for* them, if need be.
It may not have a large vocabulary, but it *is* still the only invention I've heard of that can pronounce entire words as opposed to single syllables. Considering that you began with a pair of fireplace bellows and a bagpipe reed, it's quite impressive.
You are too kind, sir. I'm afraid it still has much room for improvement.
I've a few theories I'm currently pursuing--
--but before I tax your indulgence any further, may I offer you a drink?
Of course.

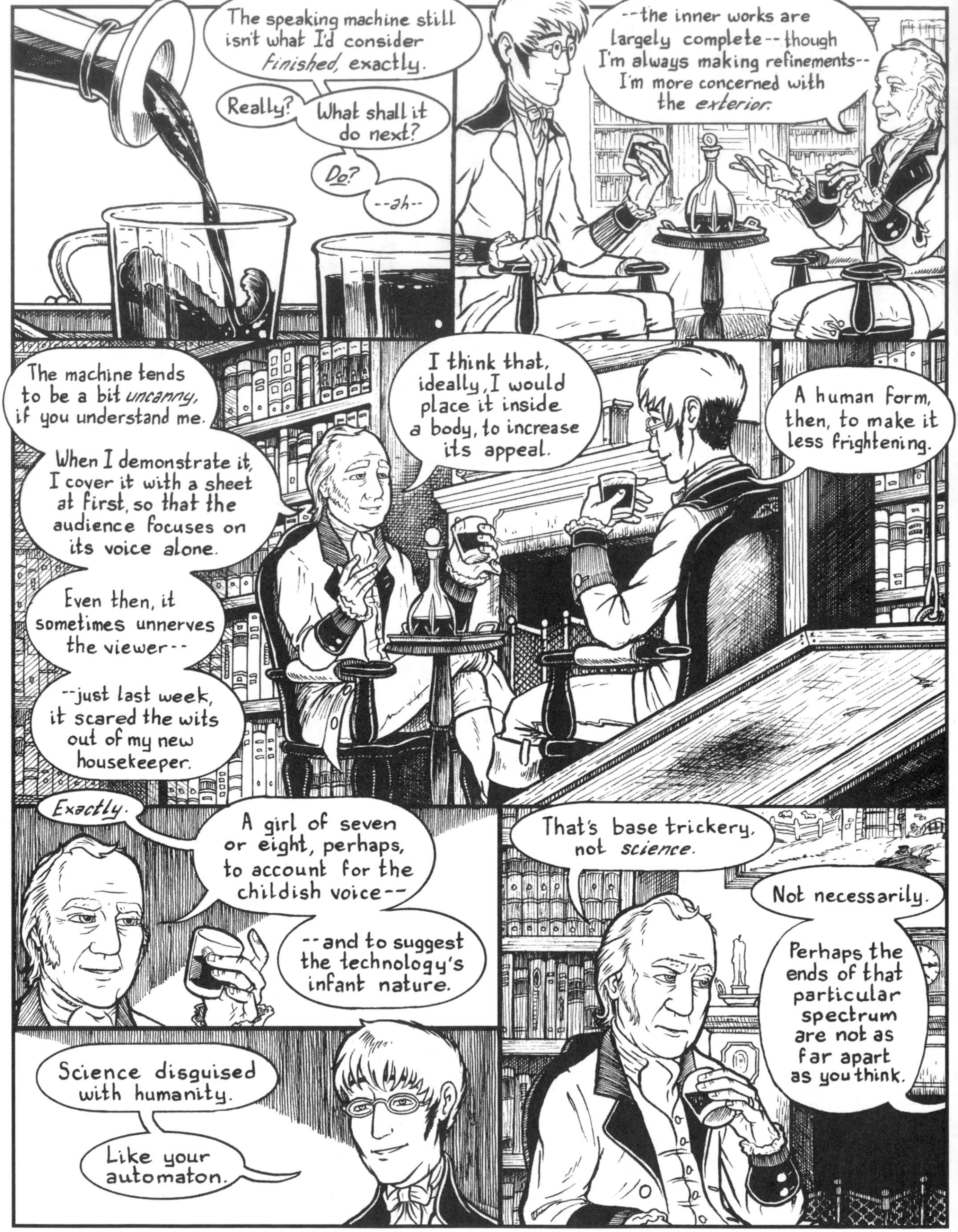

The speaking machine still isn't what I'd consider *finished*, exactly.
Really?
What shall it do next?
Do?
--ah--
--the inner works are largely complete--though I'm always making refinements--I'm more concerned with the *exterior*.
The machine tends to be a bit *uncanny*, if you understand me.
When I demonstrate it, I cover it with a sheet at first, so that the audience focuses on its voice alone.
Even then, it sometimes unnerves the viewer--
--just last week, it scared the wits out of my new housekeeper.
I think that, ideally, I would place it inside a body, to increase its appeal.
A human form, then, to make it less frightening.
Exactly.
A girl of seven or eight, perhaps, to account for the childish voice--
--and to suggest the technology's infant nature.
Science disguised with humanity.
Like your automaton.
That's base trickery, not *science*.
Not necessarily.
Perhaps the ends of that particular spectrum are not as far apart as you think.

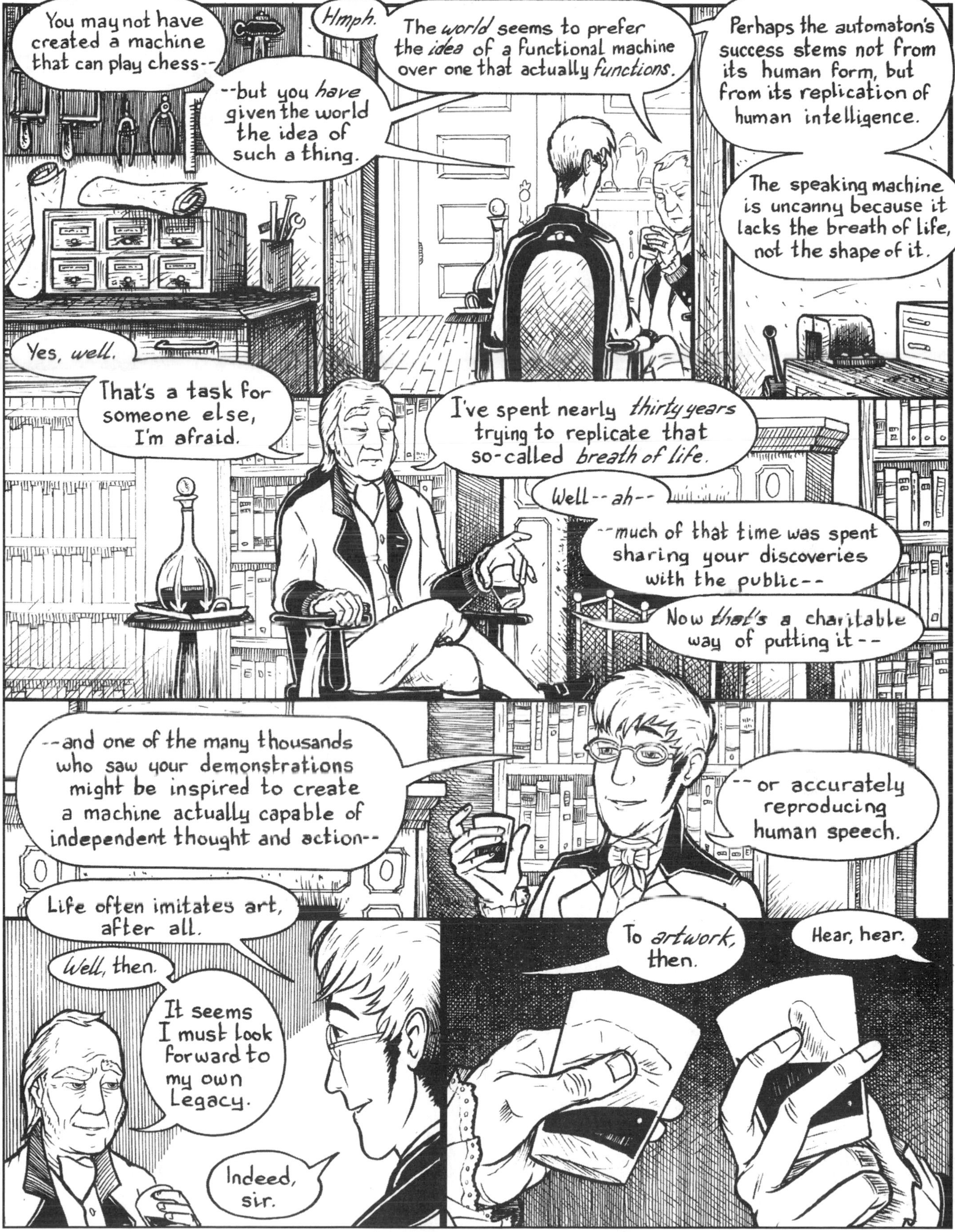
You may not have created a machine that can play chess--
--but you *have* given the world the idea of such a thing.
Hmph.
The *world* seems to prefer the *idea* of a functional machine over one that actually *functions*.
Perhaps the automaton's success stems not from its human form, but from its replication of human intelligence.
The speaking machine is uncanny because it lacks the breath of life, not the shape of it.
Yes, *well.*
That's a task for someone else, I'm afraid.
I've spent nearly *thirty years* trying to replicate that so-called *breath of life*.
Well--ah--
--*much of that time was spent* sharing your discoveries with the public--
Now *that's* a charitable way of putting it--
--and one of the many thousands who saw your demonstrations might be inspired to create a machine actually capable of independent thought and action--
--or accurately reproducing human speech.
Life often imitates art, after all.
Well, then.
It seems I must look forward to my own legacy.
Indeed, sir.
To *artwork,* then.
Hear, hear.

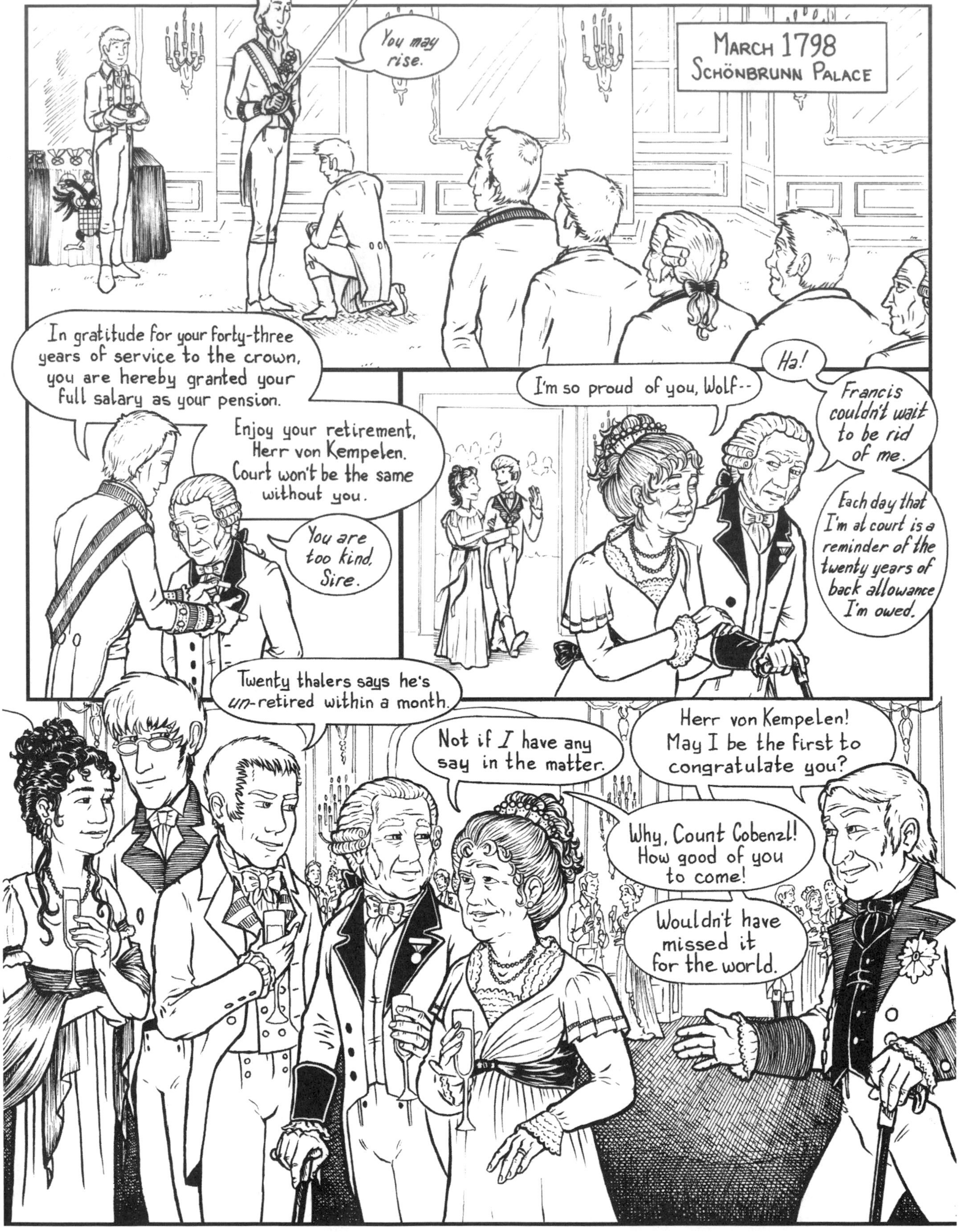
March 1798
Schönbrunn Palace
You may rise.
In gratitude for your forty-three years of service to the crown, you are hereby granted your full salary as your pension.
Enjoy your retirement, Herr von Kempelen. Court won't be the same without you.
You are too kind, Sire.
I'm so proud of you, Wolf--
Ha!
Francis couldn't wait to be rid of me.
Each day that I'm at court is a reminder of the twenty years of back allowance I'm owed.
Twenty thalers says he's *un*-retired within a month.
Not if *I* have any say in the matter.
Herr von Kempelen! May I be the first to congratulate you?
Why, Count Cobenzl! How good of you to come!
Wouldn't have missed it for the world.

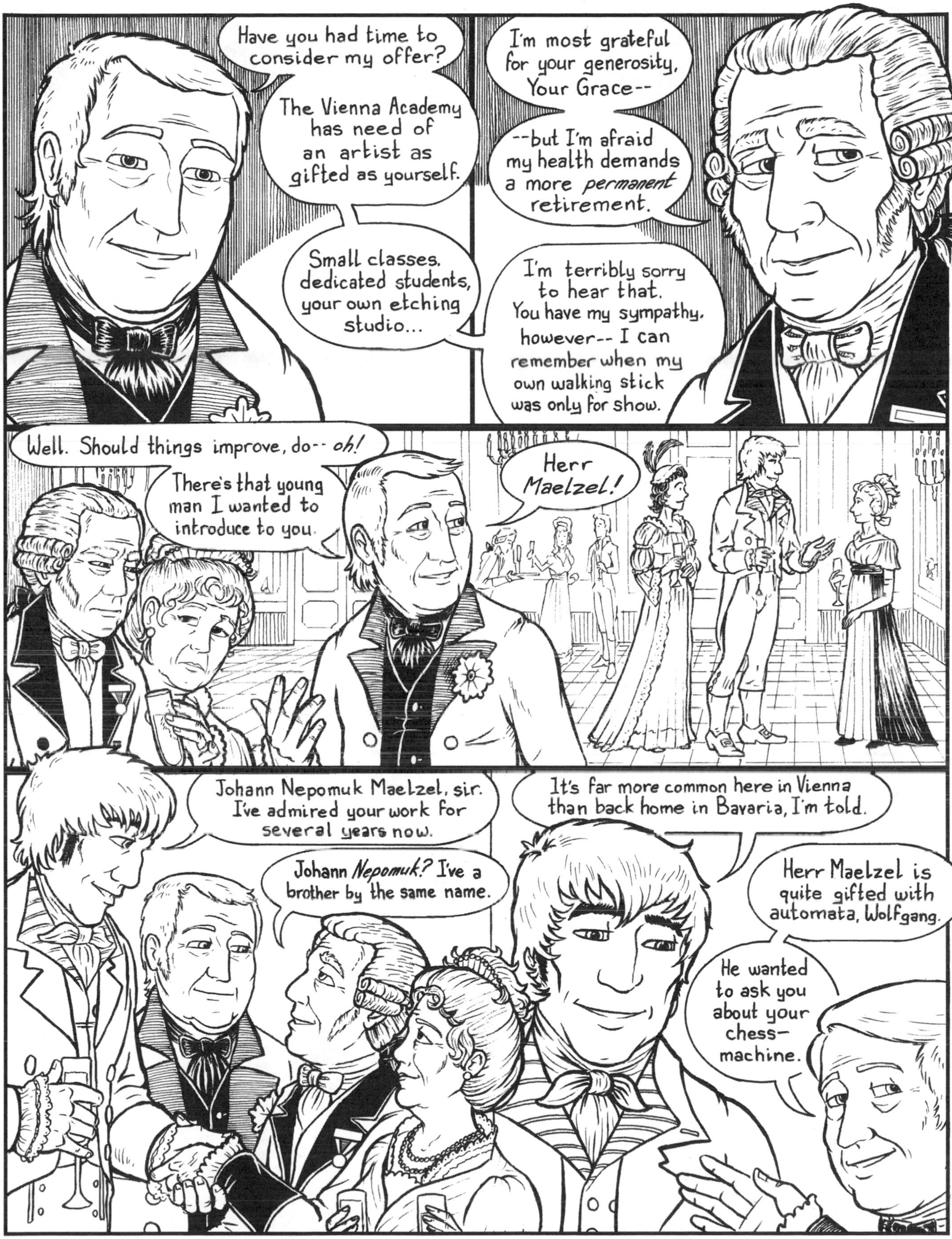
Have you had time to consider my offer?
The Vienna Academy has need of an artist as gifted as yourself.
Small classes, dedicated students, your own etching studio...
I'm most grateful for your generosity, Your Grace--
--but I'm afraid my health demands a more *permanent* retirement.
I'm terribly sorry to hear that. You have my sympathy, however-- I can remember when my own walking stick was only for show.
Well. Should things improve, do-- *oh!*
There's that young man I wanted to introduce to you.
Herr Maelzel!
Johann Nepomuk Maelzel, sir. I've admired your work for several years now.
Johann *Nepomuk?* I've a brother by the same name.
It's far more common here in Vienna than back home in Bavaria, I'm told.
Herr Maelzel is quite gifted with automata, Wolfgang.
He wanted to ask you about your chess-machine.

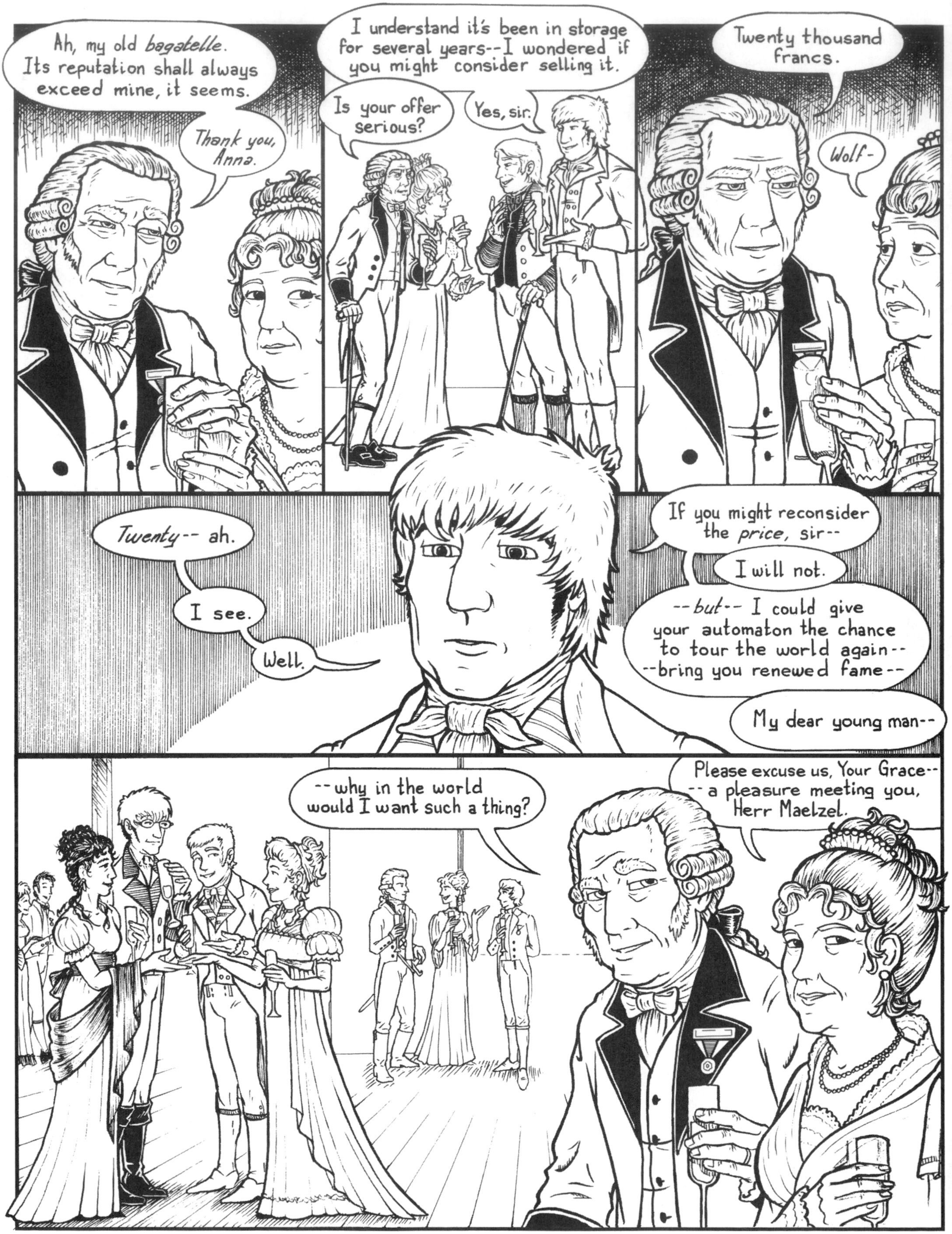

Ah, my old *bagatelle*. Its reputation shall always exceed mine, it seems.
Thank you, Anna.
I understand it's been in storage for several years--I wondered if you might consider selling it.
Is your offer serious?
Yes, sir.
Twenty thousand francs.
Wolf-
Twenty-- ah.
I see.
Well.
If you might reconsider the *price*, sir--
I will not.
--*but*-- I could give your automaton the chance to tour the world again--
--bring you renewed fame--
My dear young man--
--why in the world would I want such a thing?
Please excuse us, Your Grace--
--a pleasure meeting you, Herr Maelzel.

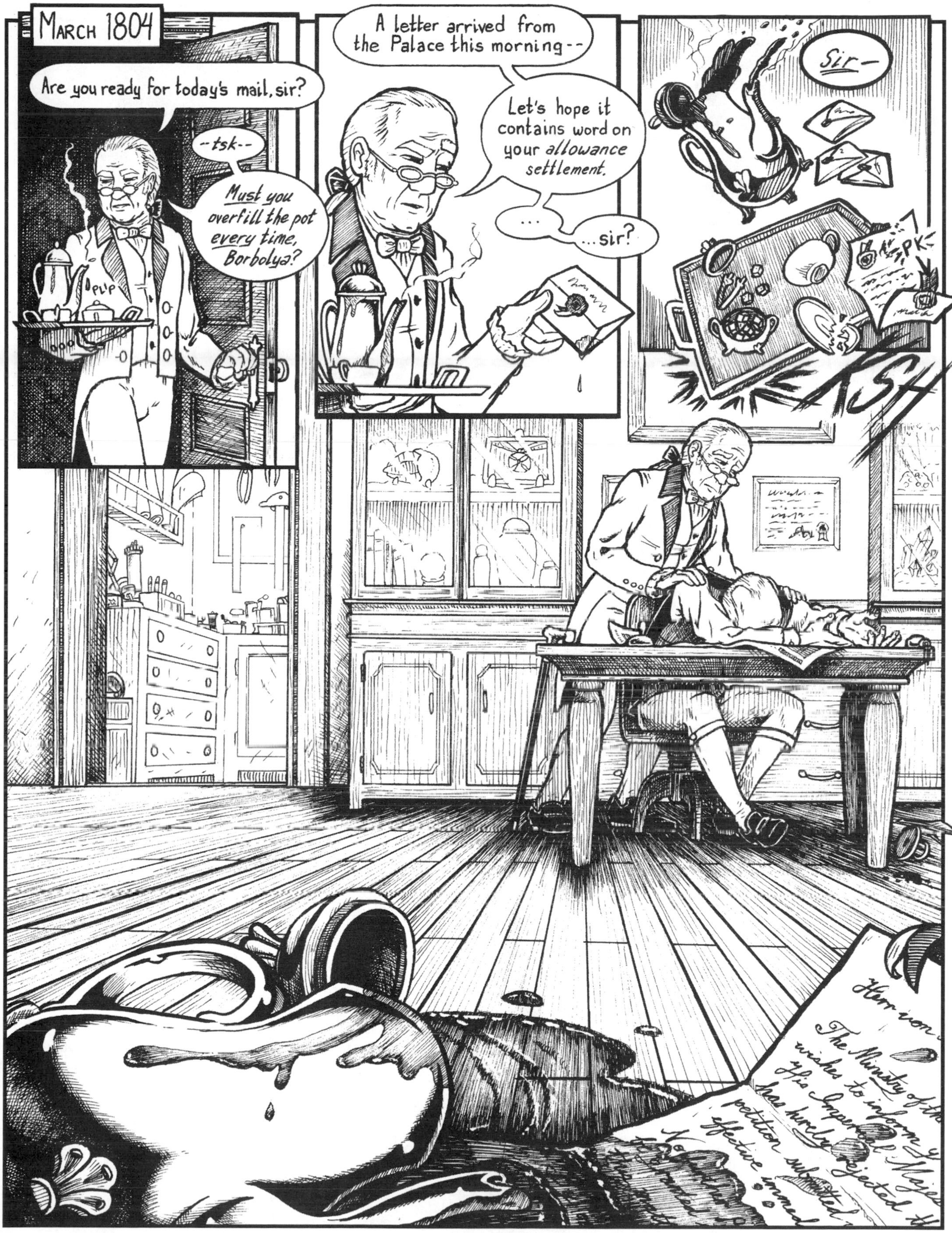
March 1804
Are you ready for today's mail, sir?
PLIP
--tsk--
Must you overfill the pot every time, Borbolya?
A letter arrived from the Palace this morning--
Let's hope it contains word on your allowance settlement.
...
...sir?
Sir-
PK
KSH
Herr von
The Ministry of th
wishes to inform
His Imperial
has hereby rejected
petition submitted
effective immed

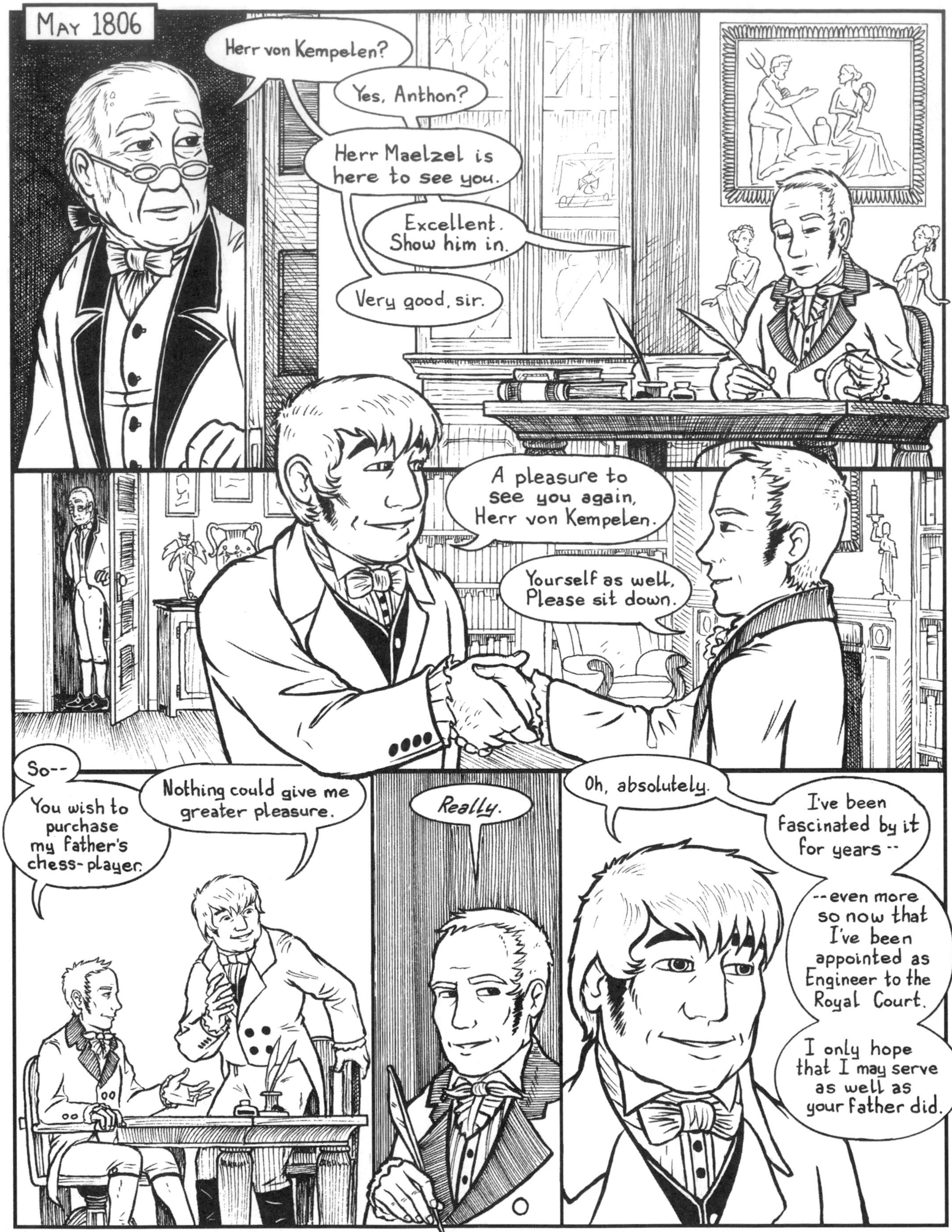
May 1806
Herr von Kempelen?
Yes, Anthon?
Herr Maelzel is here to see you.
Excellent. Show him in.
Very good, sir.
A pleasure to see you again, Herr von Kempelen.
Yourself as well, Please sit down.
So--
You wish to purchase my father's chess-player.
Nothing could give me greater pleasure.
Really.
Oh, absolutely.
I've been fascinated by it for years --
--even more so now that I've been appointed as Engineer to the Royal Court.
I only hope that I may serve as well as your father did.

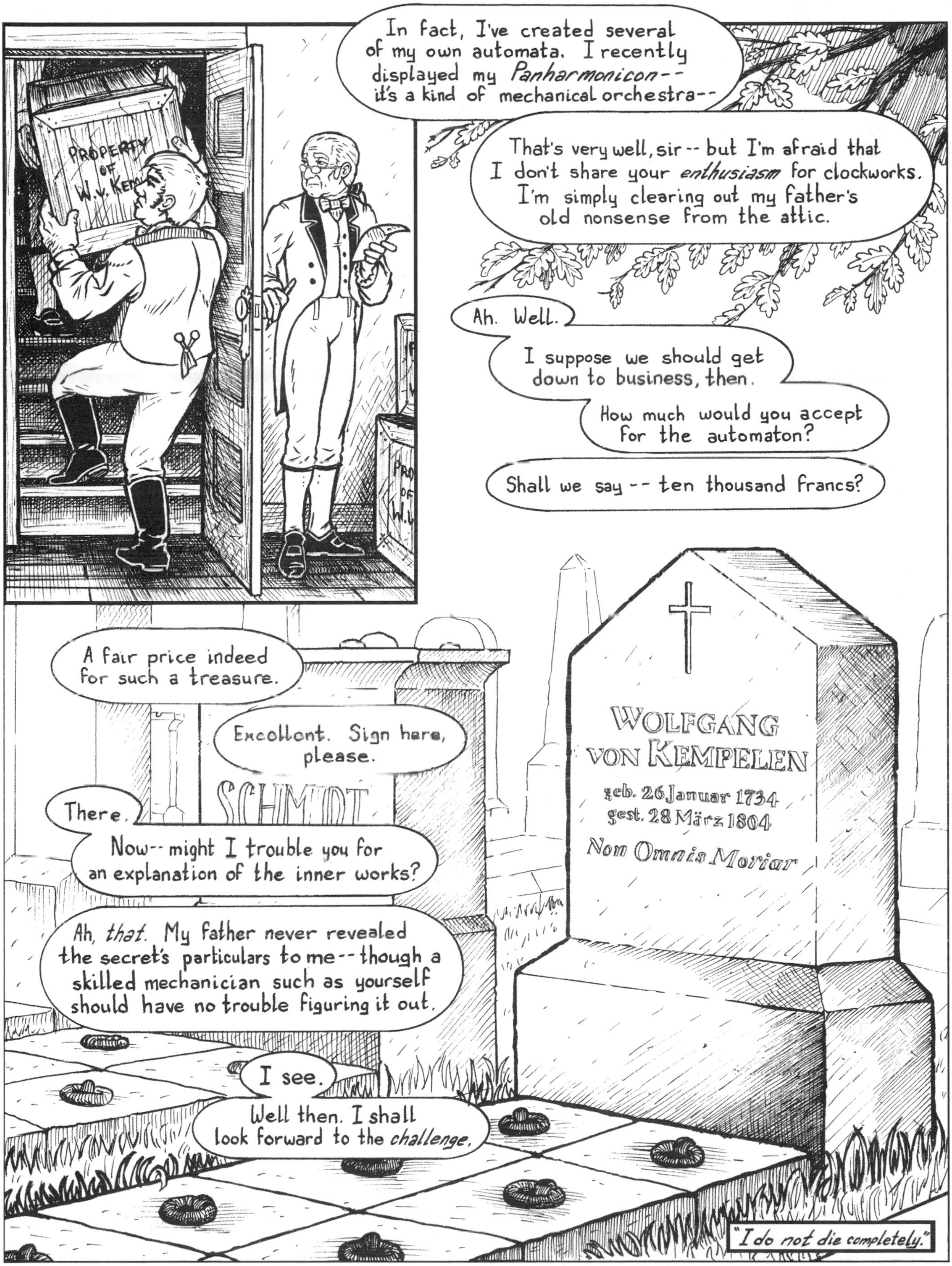
In fact, I've created several of my own automata. I recently displayed my *Panharmonicon*-- it's a kind of mechanical orchestra--
PROPERTY OF W.V. KEMP
That's very well, sir -- but I'm afraid that I don't share your *enthusiasm* for clockworks. I'm simply clearing out my father's old nonsense from the attic.
Ah. Well.
I suppose we should get down to business, then.
How much would you accept for the automaton?
Shall we say -- ten thousand francs?
A fair price indeed for such a treasure.
Excellent. Sign here, please.
SCHMIDT
There.
Now-- might I trouble you for an explanation of the inner works?
WOLFGANG VON KEMPELEN
geb. 26 Januar 1734
gest. 28 März 1804
Non Omnis Moriar
Ah, *that*. My father never revealed the secret's particulars to me-- though a skilled mechanician such as yourself should have no trouble figuring it out.
I see.
Well then. I shall look forward to the *challenge*.
"*I do not die completely.*"

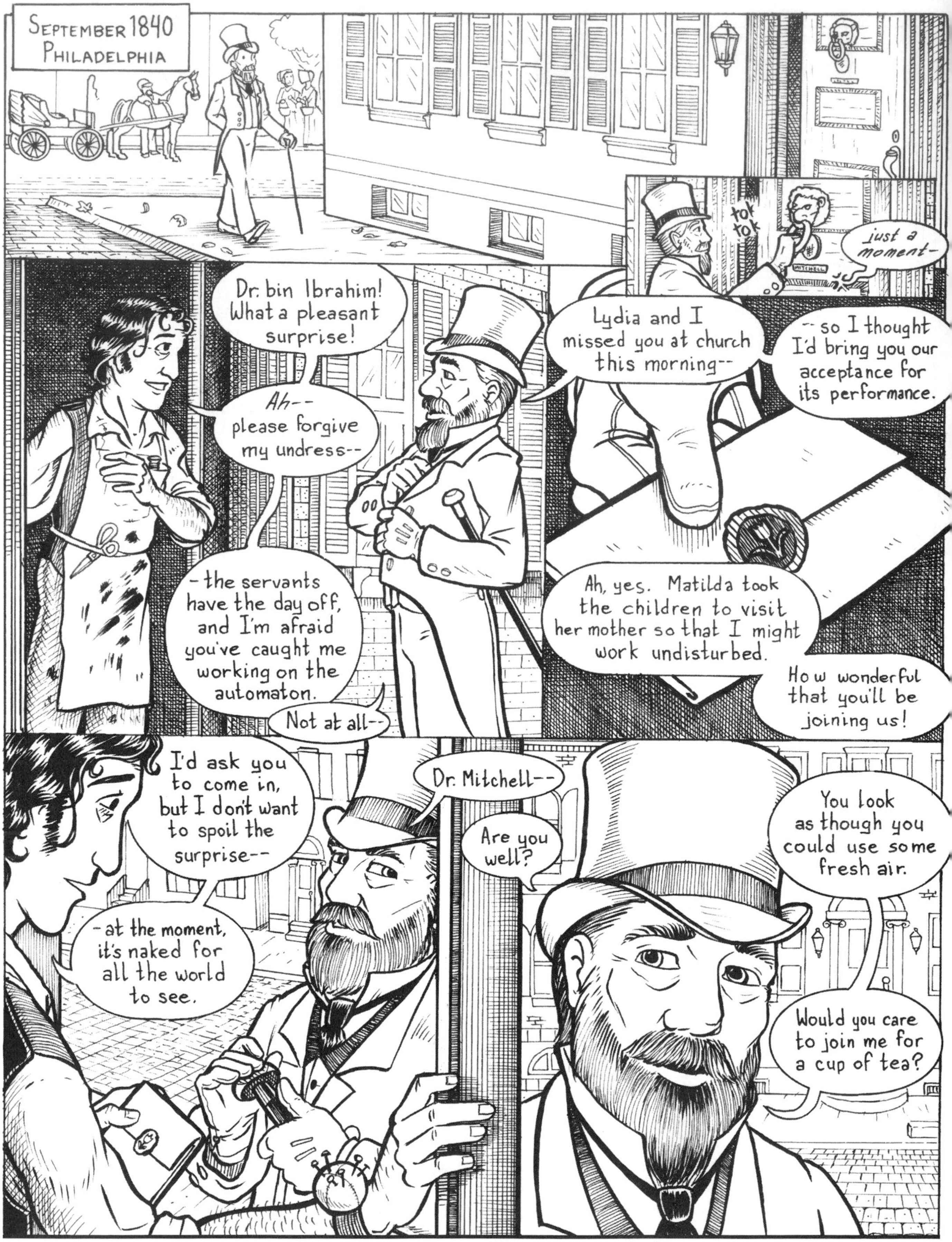

September 1840
Philadelphia
tok tok
MITCHELL
just a moment-
Dr. bin Ibrahim! What a pleasant surprise!
Ah-- please forgive my undress--
-the servants have the day off, and I'm afraid you've caught me working on the automaton.
Not at all--
Lydia and I missed you at church this morning--
--so I thought I'd bring you our acceptance for its performance.
Ah, yes. Matilda took the children to visit her mother so that I might work undisturbed.
How wonderful that you'll be joining us!
I'd ask you to come in, but I don't want to spoil the surprise--
-at the moment, it's naked for all the world to see.
Dr. Mitchell--
Are you well?
You look as though you could use some fresh air.
Would you care to join me for a cup of tea?

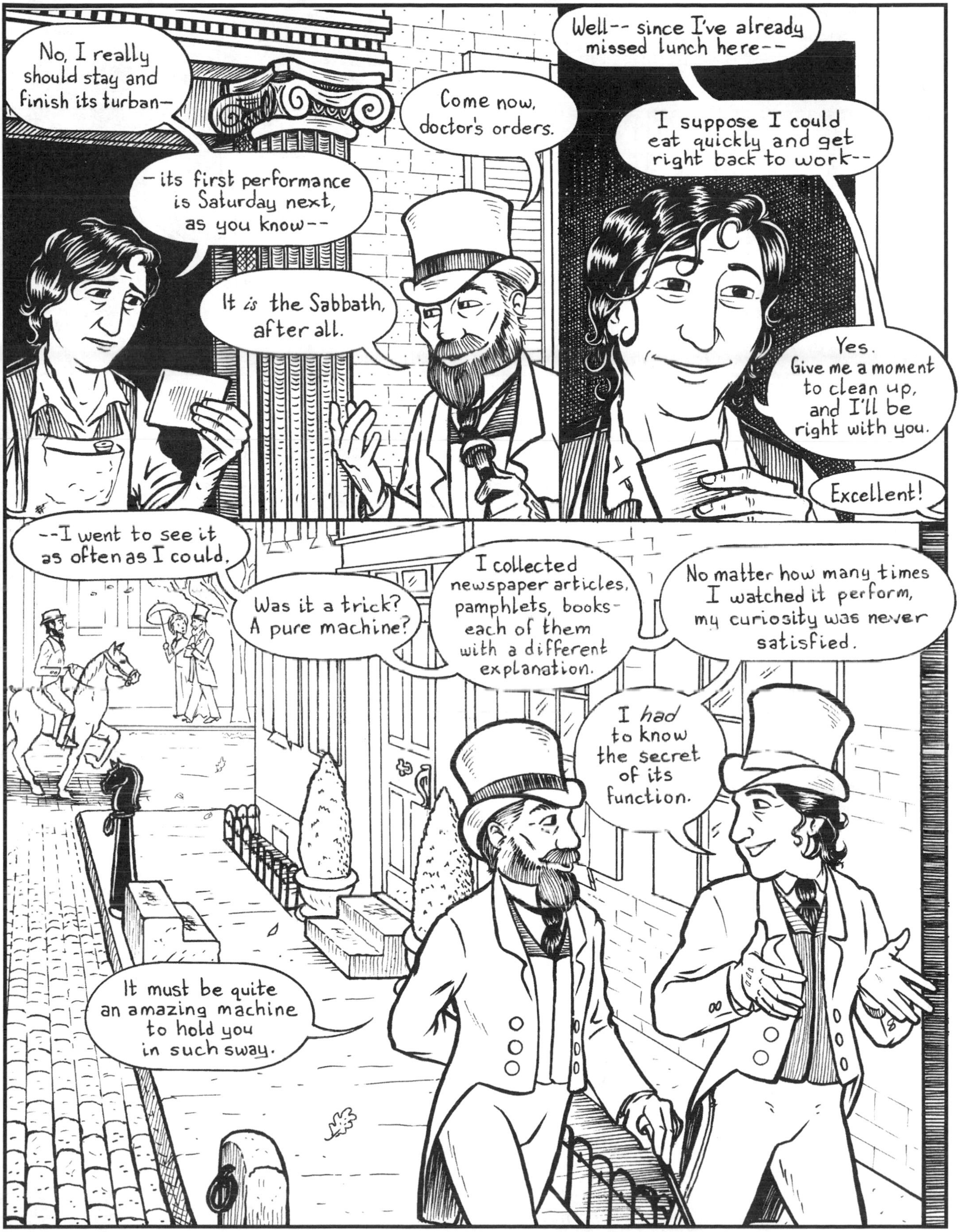
No, I really should stay and finish its turban–
Come now, doctor's orders.
–its first performance is Saturday next, as you know--
It *is* the Sabbath, after all.
Well-- since I've already missed lunch here--
I suppose I could eat quickly and get right back to work--
Yes. Give me a moment to clean up, and I'll be right with you.
Excellent!
--I went to see it as often as I could.
Was it a trick? A pure machine?
I collected newspaper articles, pamphlets, books-each of them with a different explanation.
No matter how many times I watched it perform, my curiosity was never satisfied.
I *had* to know the secret of its function.
It must be quite an amazing machine to hold you in such sway.

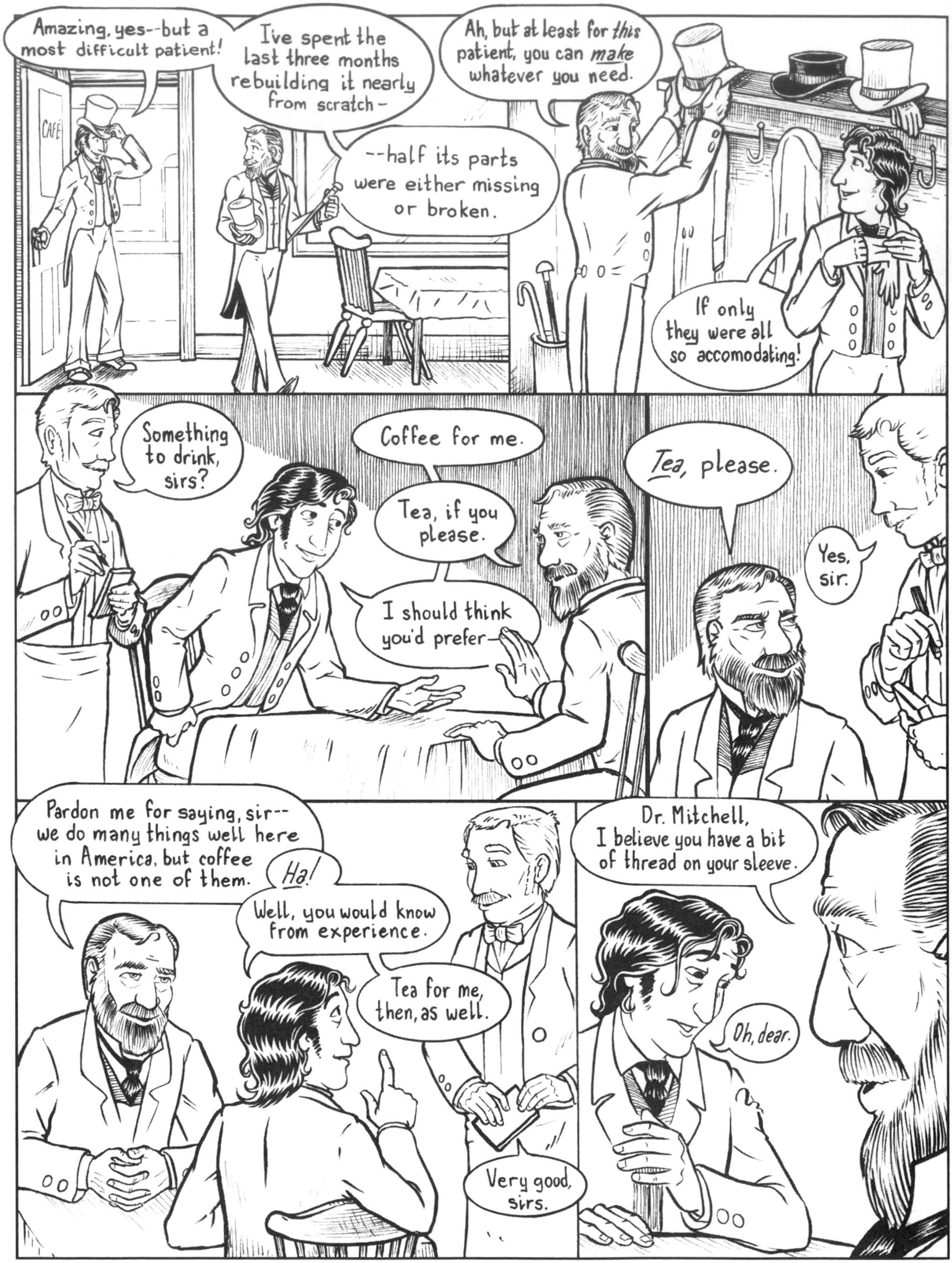
CAFÉ
Amazing, yes--but a most difficult patient!
I've spent the last three months rebuilding it nearly from scratch-
--half its parts were either missing or broken.
Ah, but at least for *this* patient, you can *make* whatever you need.
If only they were all so accomodating!
Something to drink, sirs?
Coffee for me.
Tea, if you please.
I should think you'd prefer-
Tea, please.
Yes, sir.
Pardon me for saying, sir-- we do many things well here in America, but coffee is not one of them.
Ha!
Well, you would know from experience.
Tea for me, then, as well.
Very good, sirs.
Dr. Mitchell, I believe you have a bit of thread on your sleeve.
Oh, dear.

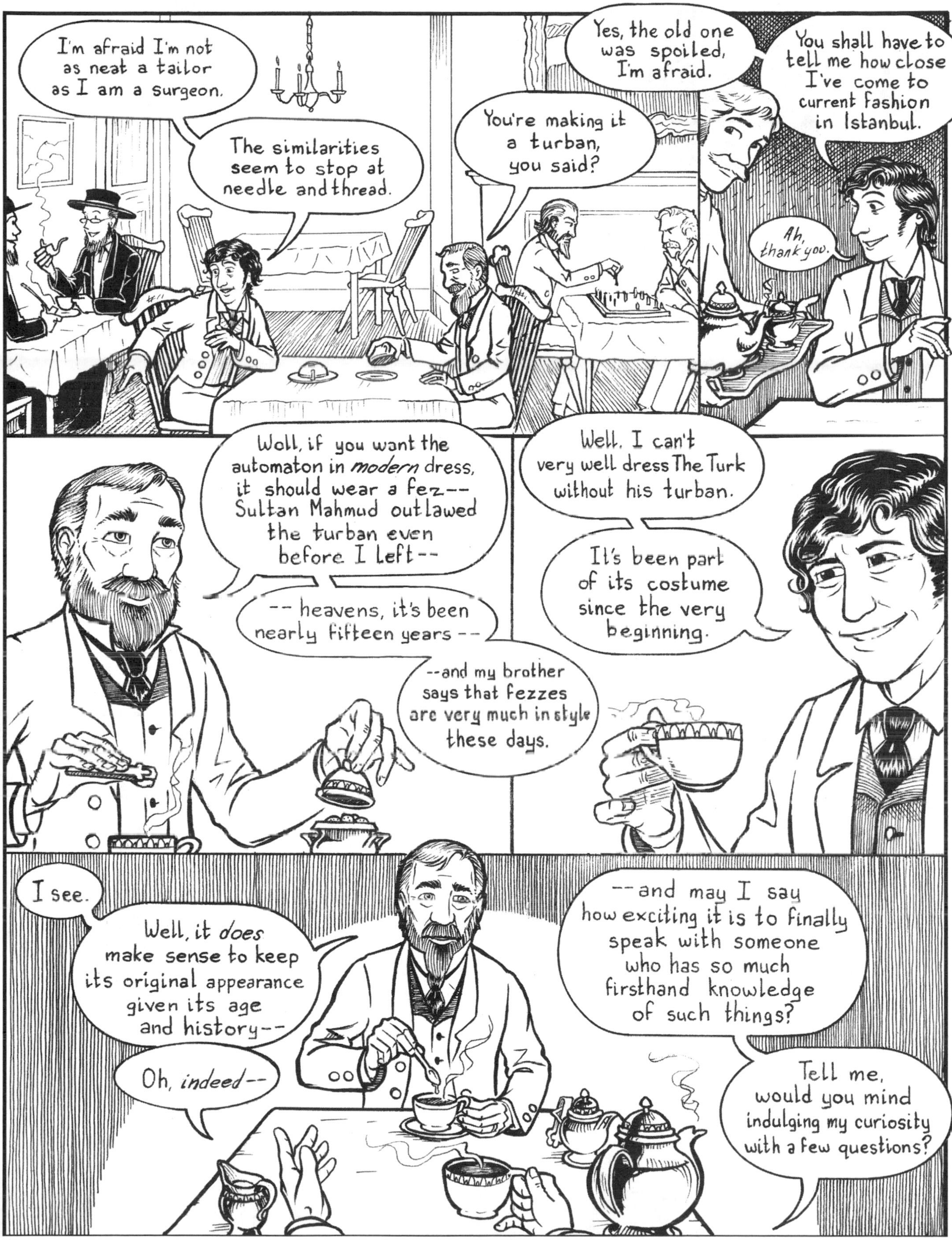
I'm afraid I'm not as neat a tailor as I am a surgeon.
The similarities seem to stop at needle and thread.
You're making it a turban, you said?
Yes, the old one was spoiled, I'm afraid.
You shall have to tell me how close I've come to current fashion in Istanbul.
Ah, thank you.
Well, if you want the automaton in *modern* dress, it should wear a fez-- Sultan Mahmud outlawed the turban even before I left--
-- heavens, it's been nearly fifteen years --
--and my brother says that fezzes are very much in style these days.
Well, I can't very well dress The Turk without his turban.
It's been part of its costume since the very beginning.
I see.
Well, it *does* make sense to keep its original appearance given its age and history--
Oh, *indeed*--
--and may I say how exciting it is to finally speak with someone who has so much firsthand knowledge of such things?
Tell me, would you mind indulging my curiosity with a few questions?

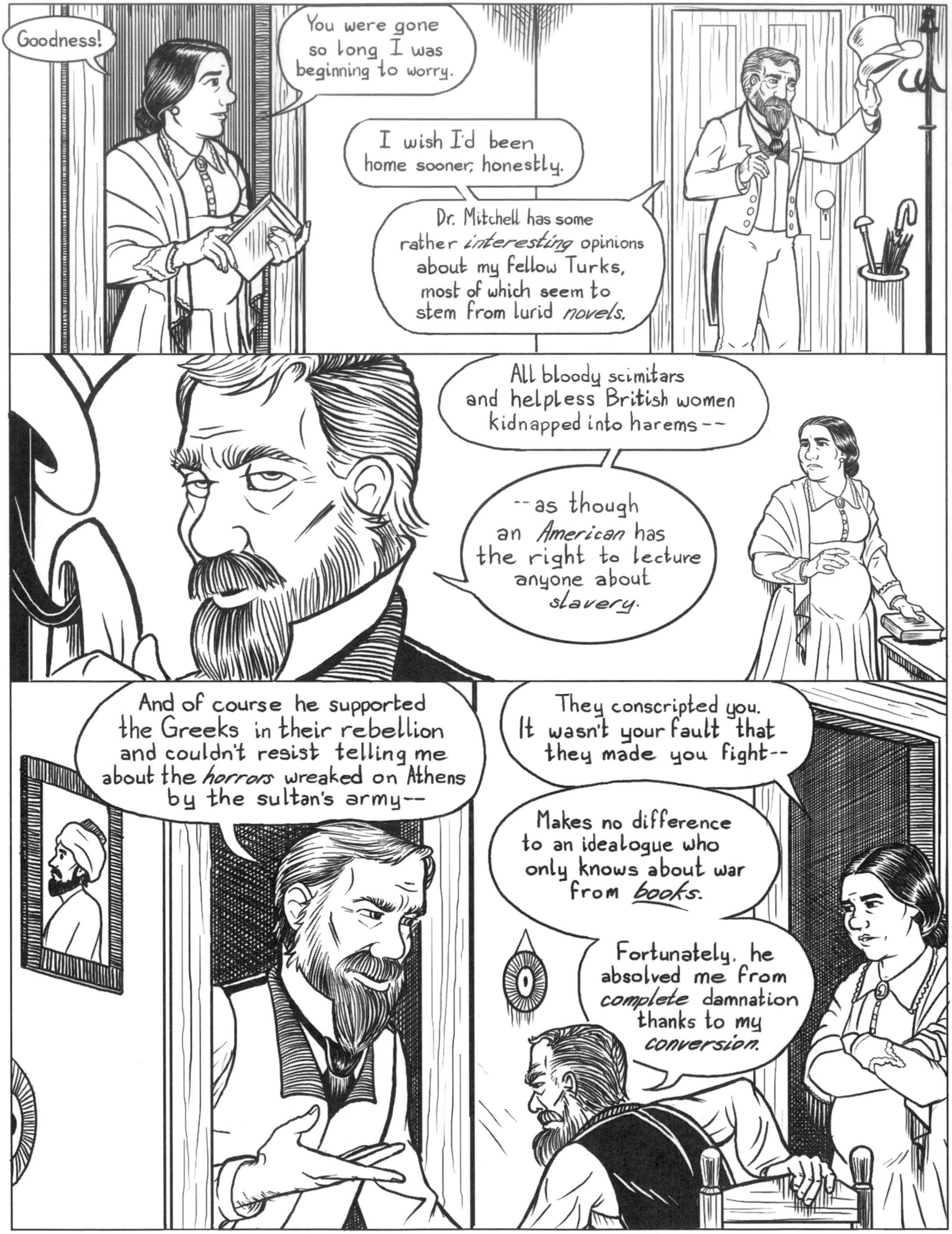
Goodness!
You were gone so long I was beginning to worry.
I wish I'd been home sooner, honestly.
Dr. Mitchell has some rather *interesting* opinions about my fellow Turks, most of which seem to stem from lurid *novels.*
All bloody scimitars and helpless British women kidnapped into harems --
-- as though an *American* has the right to lecture anyone about *slavery.*
And of course he supported the Greeks in their rebellion and couldn't resist telling me about the *horrors* wreaked on Athens by the sultan's army--
They conscripted you. It wasn't your fault that they made you fight--
Makes no difference to an idealogue who only knows about war from *books.*
Fortunately, he absolved me from *complete* damnation thanks to my *conversion.*

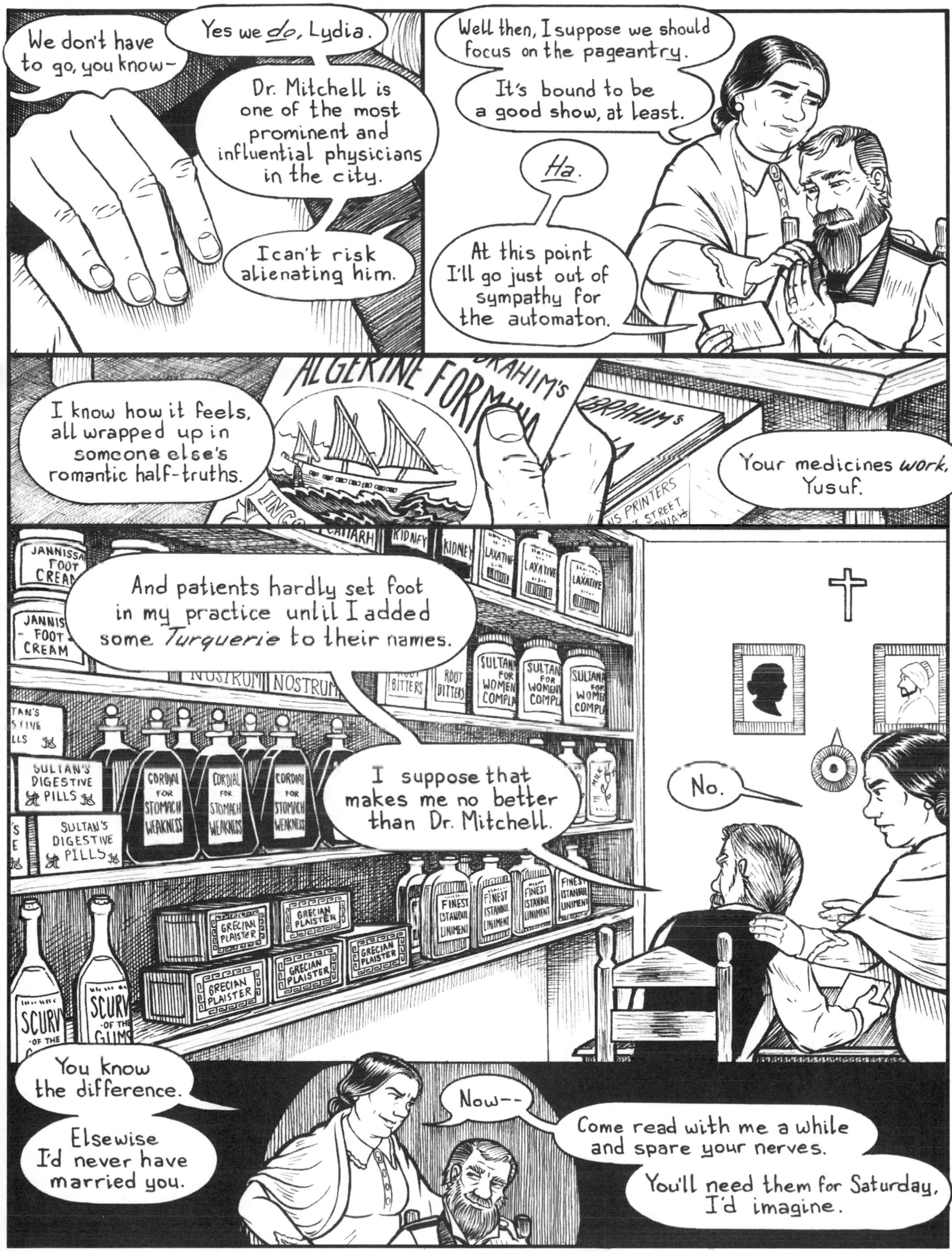
We don't have to go, you know–
Yes we *do*, Lydia.
Dr. Mitchell is one of the most prominent and influential physicians in the city.
I can't risk alienating him.
Well then, I suppose we should focus on the pageantry.
It's bound to be a good show, at least.
Ha.
At this point I'll go just out of sympathy for the automaton.
I know how it feels, all wrapped up in someone else's romantic half-truths.
Your medicines *work*, Yusuf.
And patients hardly set foot in my practice until I added some *Turquerie* to their names.
I suppose that makes me no better than Dr. Mitchell.
No.
SULTAN'S DIGESTIVE PILLS
CORDIAL FOR STOMACH WEAKNESS
GRECIAN PLAISTER
FINEST ISTANBUL LINIMENT
You know the difference.
Elsewise I'd never have married you.
Now--
Come read with me a while and spare your nerves.
You'll need them for Saturday, I'd imagine.

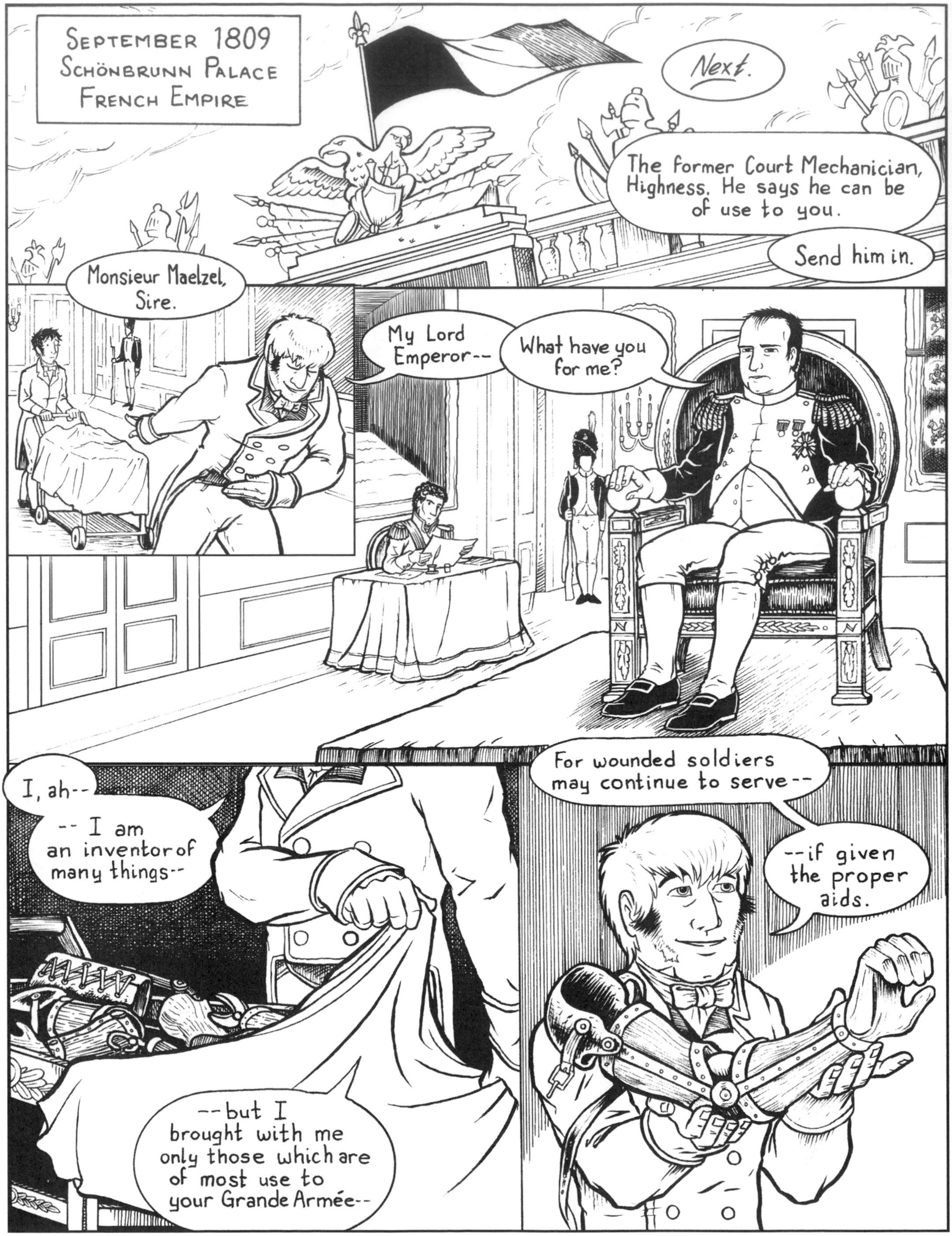
September 1809
Schönbrunn Palace
French Empire
Next.
The former Court Mechanician, Highness. He says he can be of use to you.
Send him in.
Monsieur Maelzel, Sire.
My Lord Emperor--
What have you for me?
I, ah--
-- I am an inventor of many things--
--but I brought with me only those which are of most use to your Grande Armée--
For wounded soldiers may continue to serve--
--if given the proper aids.

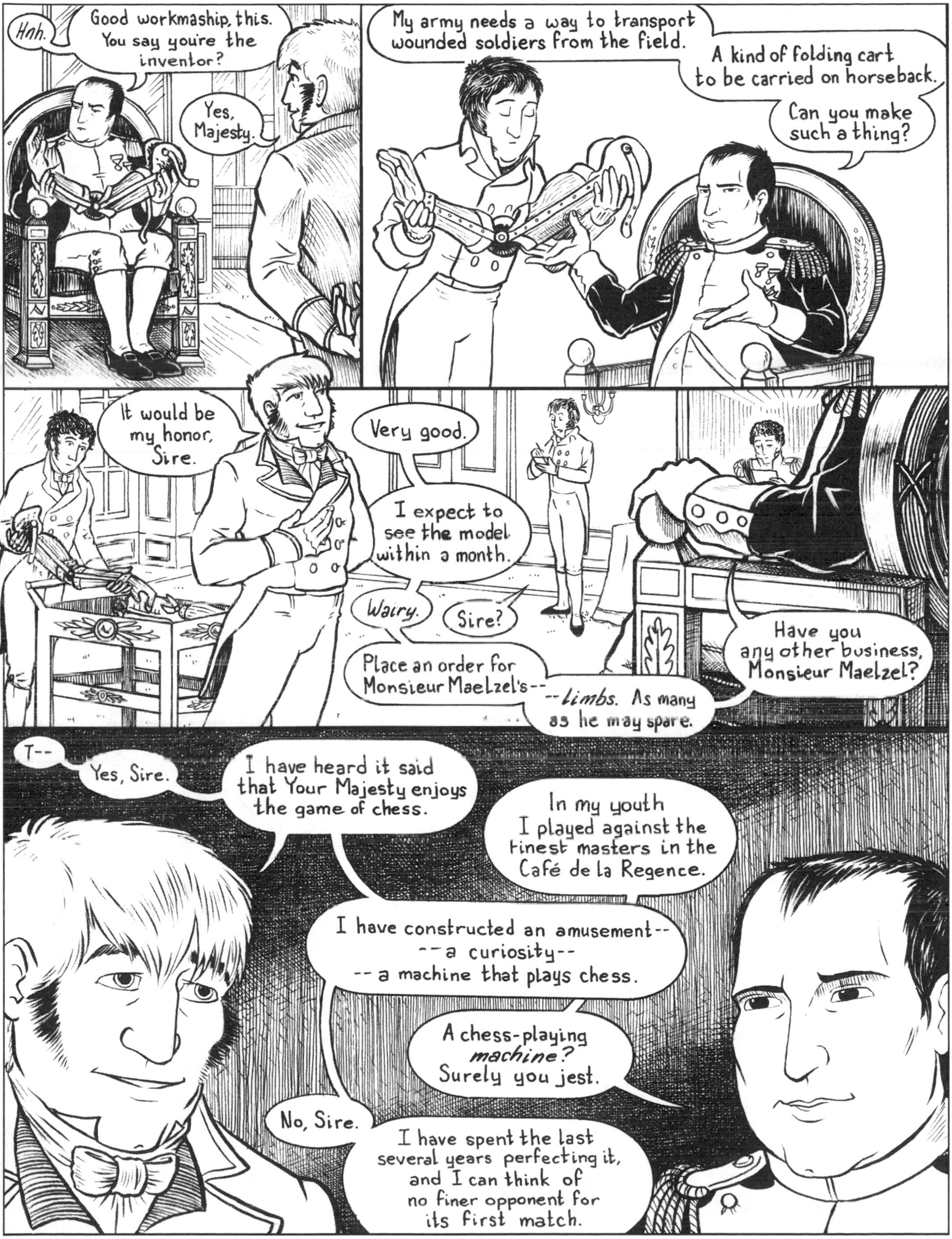

Hnh.
Good workmaship, this. You say you're the inventor?
Yes, Majesty.
My army needs a way to transport wounded soldiers from the field.
A kind of folding cart to be carried on horseback.
Can you make such a thing?
It would be my honor, Sire.
Very good.
I expect to see the model within a month.
Wairy.
Sire?
Place an order for Monsieur Maelzel's--
--*limbs.* As many as he may spare.
Have you any other business, Monsieur Maelzel?
T--
Yes, Sire.
I have heard it said that Your Majesty enjoys the game of chess.
In my youth I played against the finest masters in the Café de la Regence.
I have constructed an amusement-- --a curiosity-- --a machine that plays chess.
A chess-playing *machine?* Surely you jest.
No, Sire.
I have spent the last several years perfecting it, and I can think of no finer opponent for its first match.

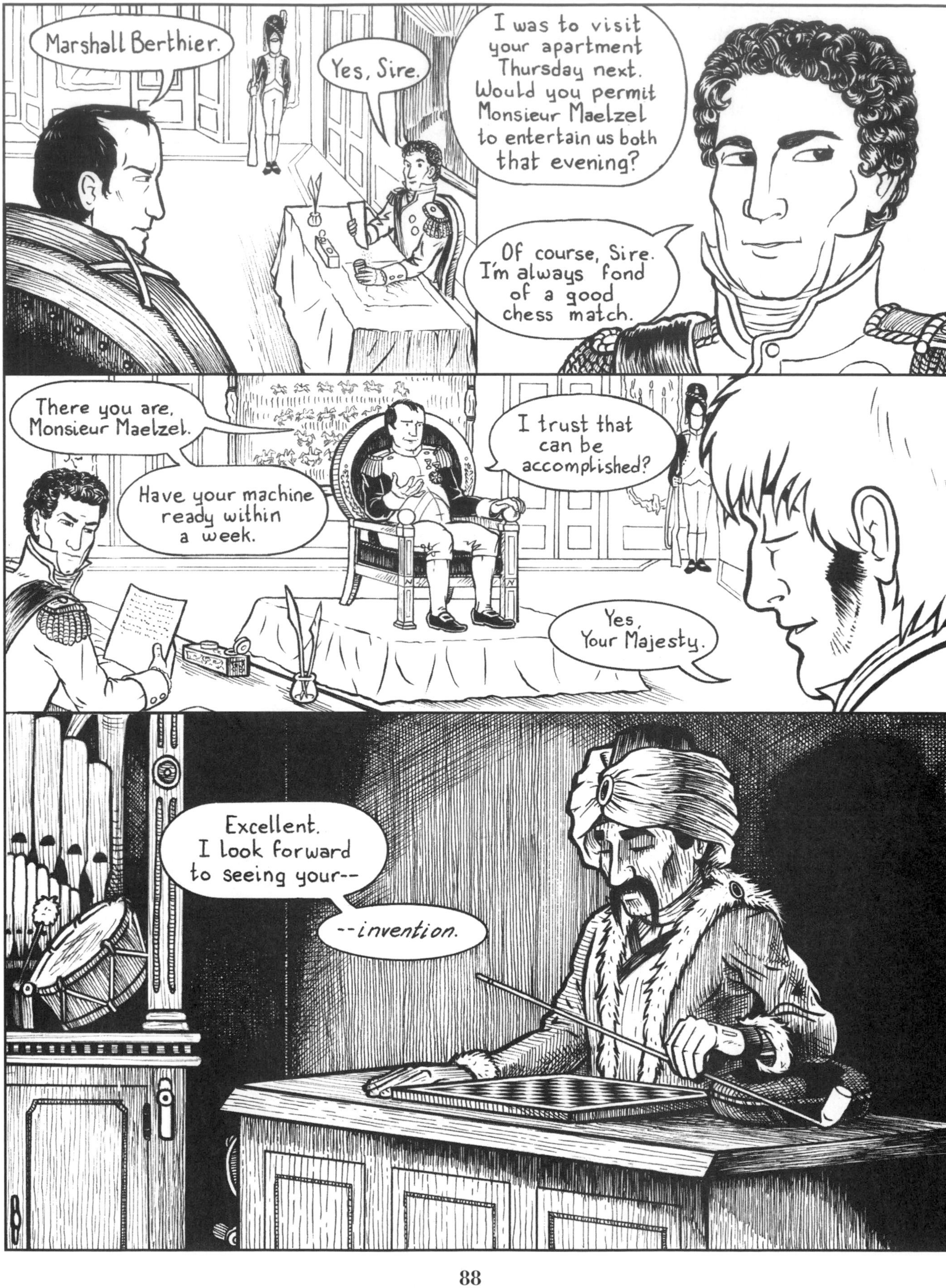
Marshall Berthier.
Yes, Sire.
I was to visit your apartment Thursday next. Would you permit Monsieur Maelzel to entertain us both that evening?
Of course, Sire. I'm always fond of a good chess match.
There you are, Monsieur Maelzel.
Have your machine ready within a week.
I trust that can be accomplished?
Yes, Your Majesty.
Excellent. I look forward to seeing your--
--*invention.*

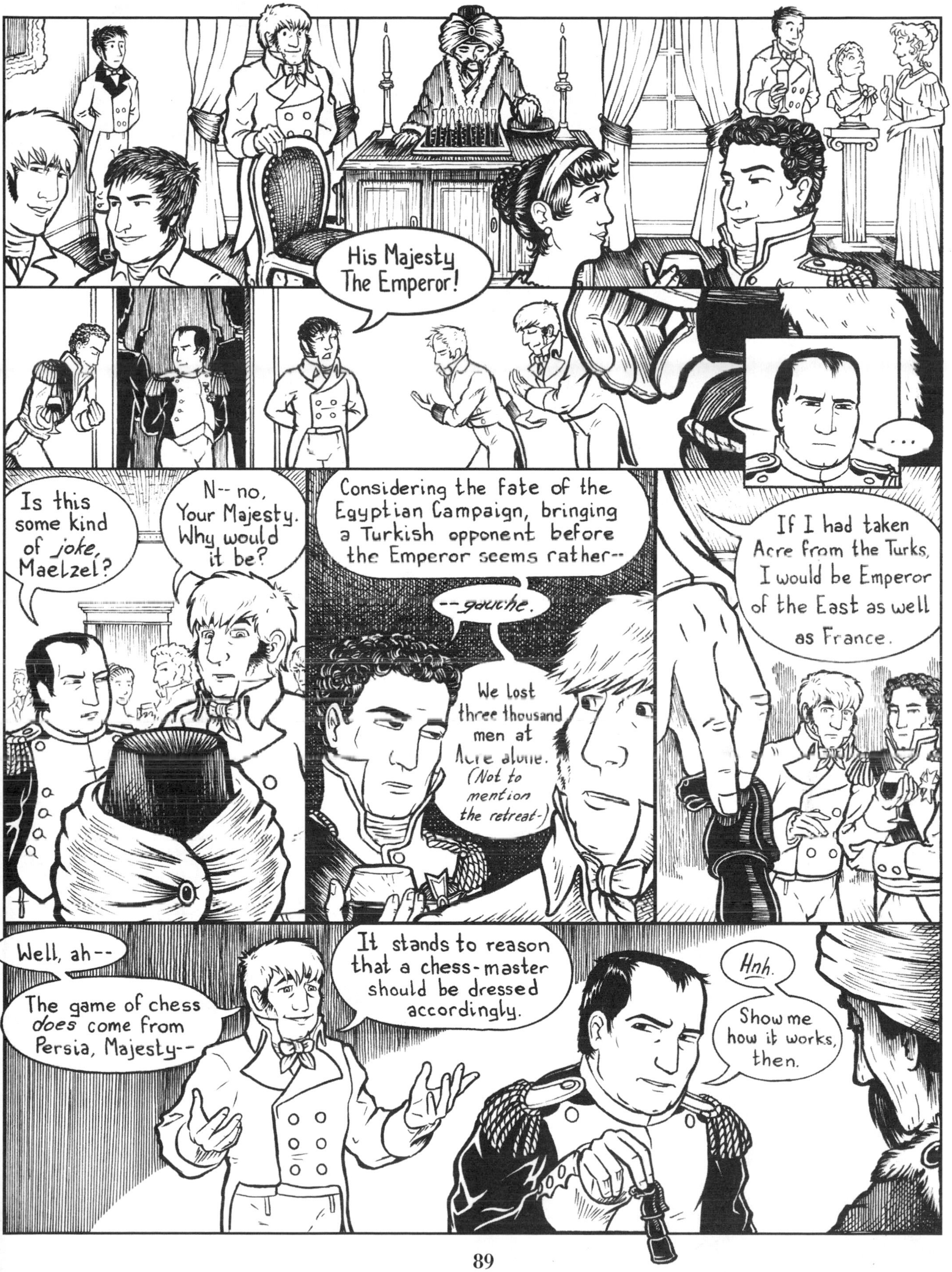
His Majesty The Emperor!
...
Is this some kind of *joke*, Maelzel?
N-- no, Your Majesty. Why would it be?
Considering the fate of the Egyptian Campaign, bringing a Turkish opponent before the Emperor seems rather--
--*gauche*.
We lost three thousand men at Acre alone. (*Not to mention the retreat*-)
If I had taken Acre from the Turks, I would be Emperor of the East as well as France.
Well, ah--
The game of chess *does* come from Persia, Majesty--
It stands to reason that a chess-master should be dressed accordingly.
Hnh.
Show me how it works, then.

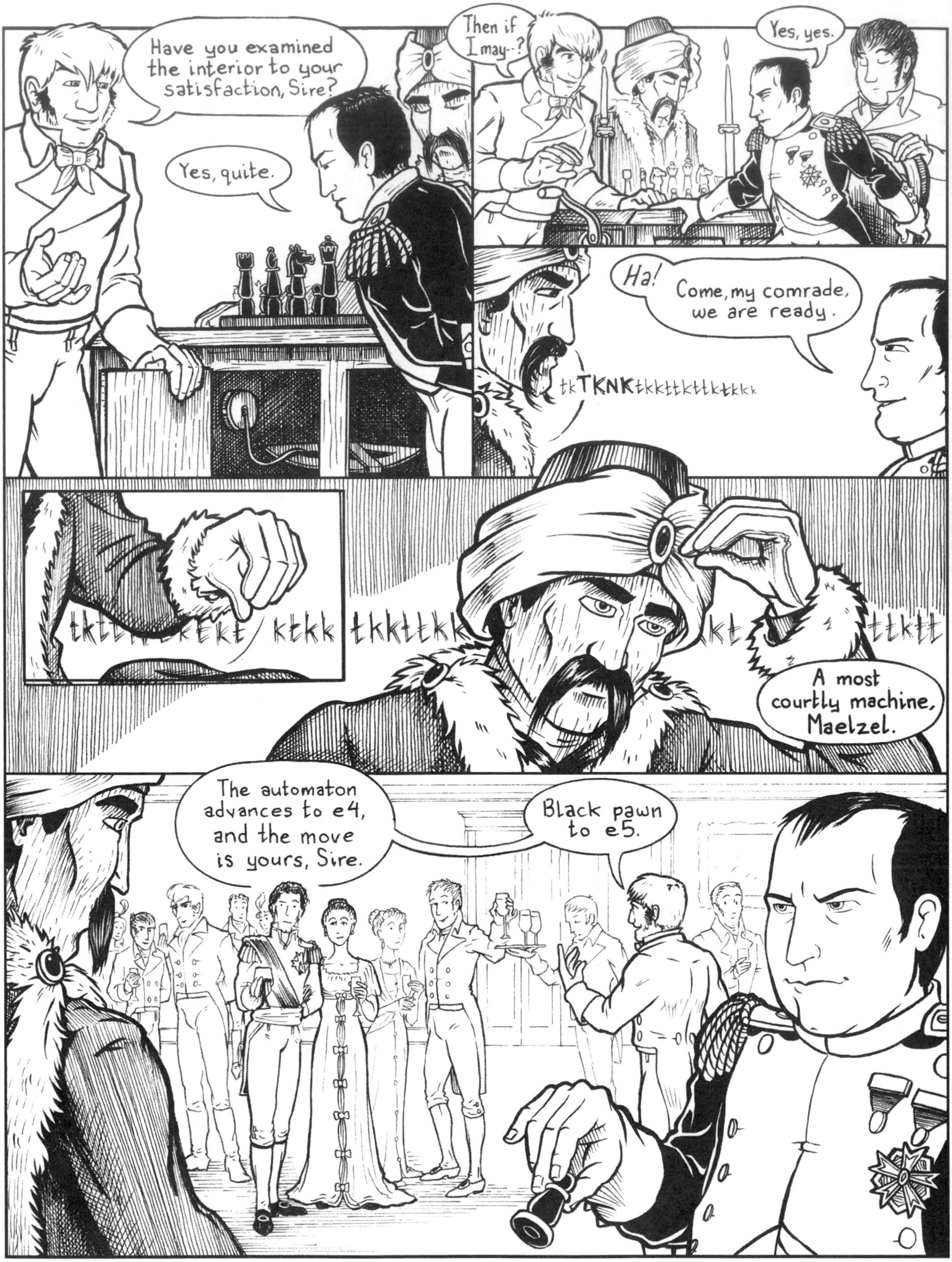
Have you examined the interior to your satisfaction, Sire?
Yes, quite.
Then if I may..?
Yes, yes.
Ha!
Come, my comrade, we are ready.
tkTKNKtkktktktktkkk
A most courtly machine, Maelzel.
The automaton advances to e4, and the move is yours, Sire.
Black pawn to e5.

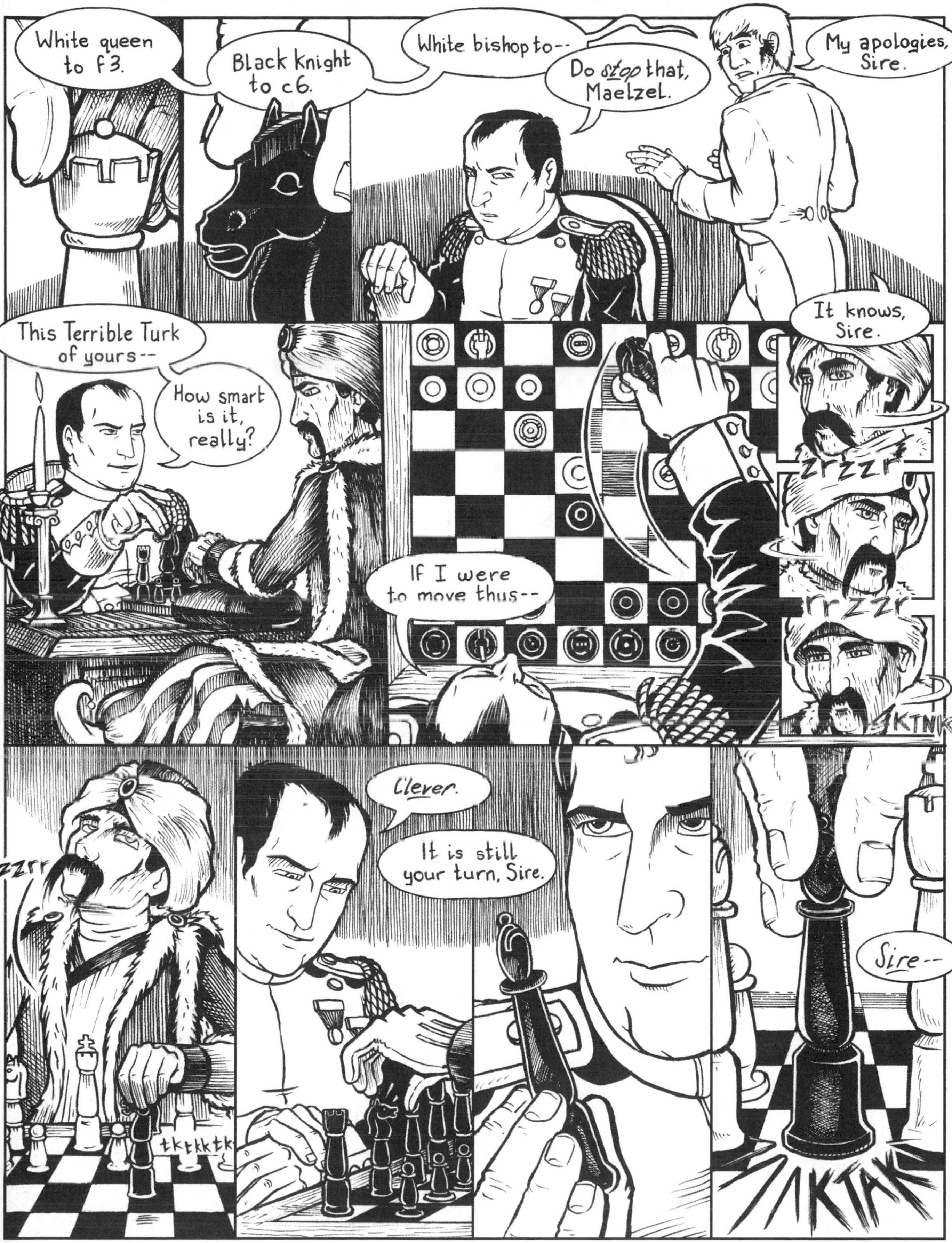
White queen to f3.
Black knight to c6.
White bishop to--
Do stop that, Maelzel.
My apologies, Sire.
This Terrible Turk of yours--
How smart is it, really?
If I were to move thus--
It knows, Sire.
zrzzr
rrzzr
KTNK
zzrr
tktkktk
Clever.
It is still your turn, Sire.
Sire--
KTAK

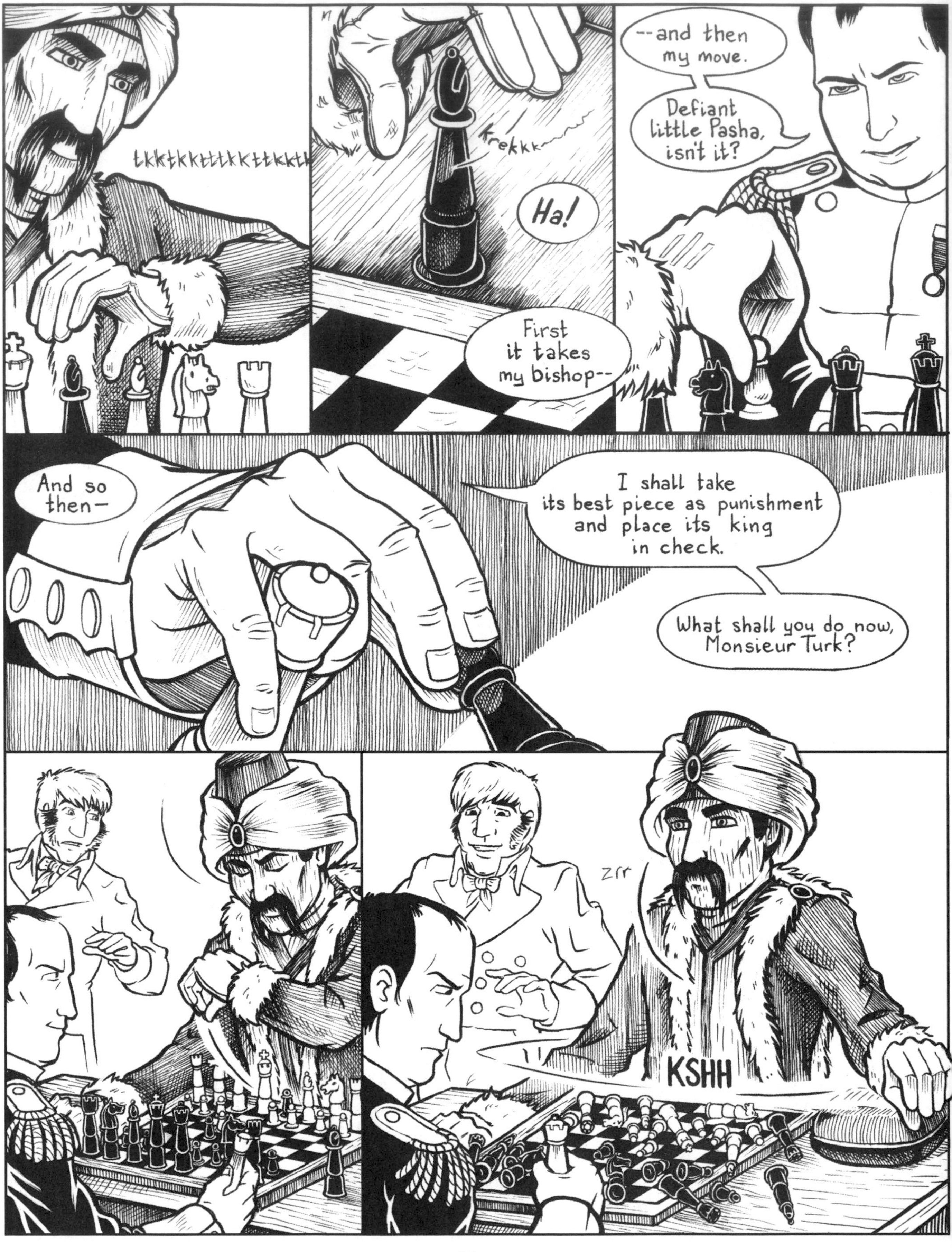
tkktkktttkkttkktk
Krekkk
Ha!
First it takes my bishop--
--and then my move.
Defiant little Pasha, isn't it?
And so then-
I shall take its best piece as punishment and place its king in check.
What shall you do now, Monsieur Turk?
zrr
KSHH

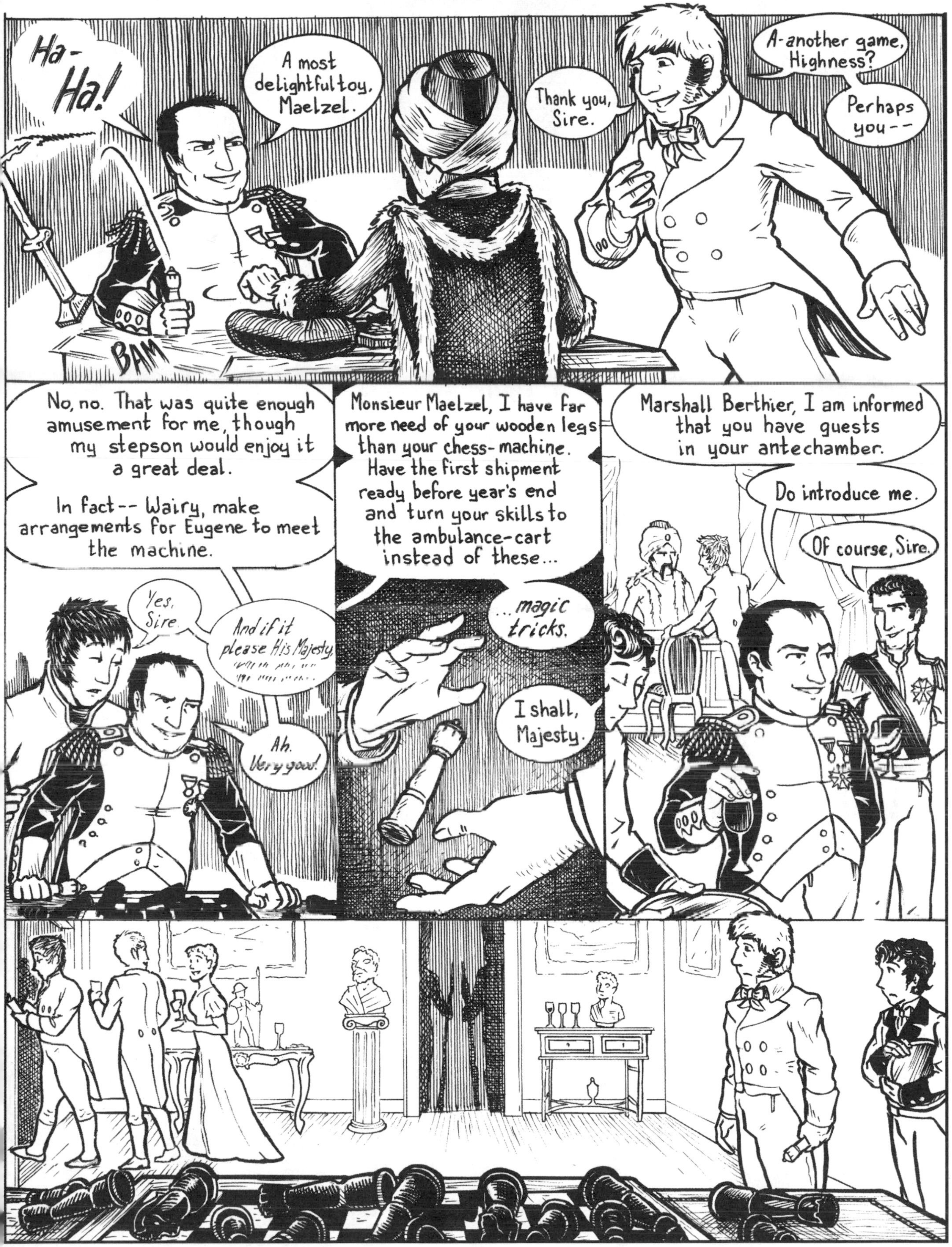
Ha-Ha!
A most delightful toy, Maelzel.
BAM
Thank you, Sire.
A-another game, Highness?
Perhaps you--
No, no. That was quite enough amusement for me, though my stepson would enjoy it a great deal.
In fact-- Wairy, make arrangements for Eugene to meet the machine.
Yes, Sire.
And if it please His Majesty,
Ah. Very good!
Monsieur Maelzel, I have far more need of your wooden legs than your chess-machine. Have the first shipment ready before year's end and turn your skills to the ambulance-cart instead of these...
...magic tricks.
I shall, Majesty.
Marshall Berthier, I am informed that you have guests in your antechamber.
Do introduce me.
Of course, Sire.

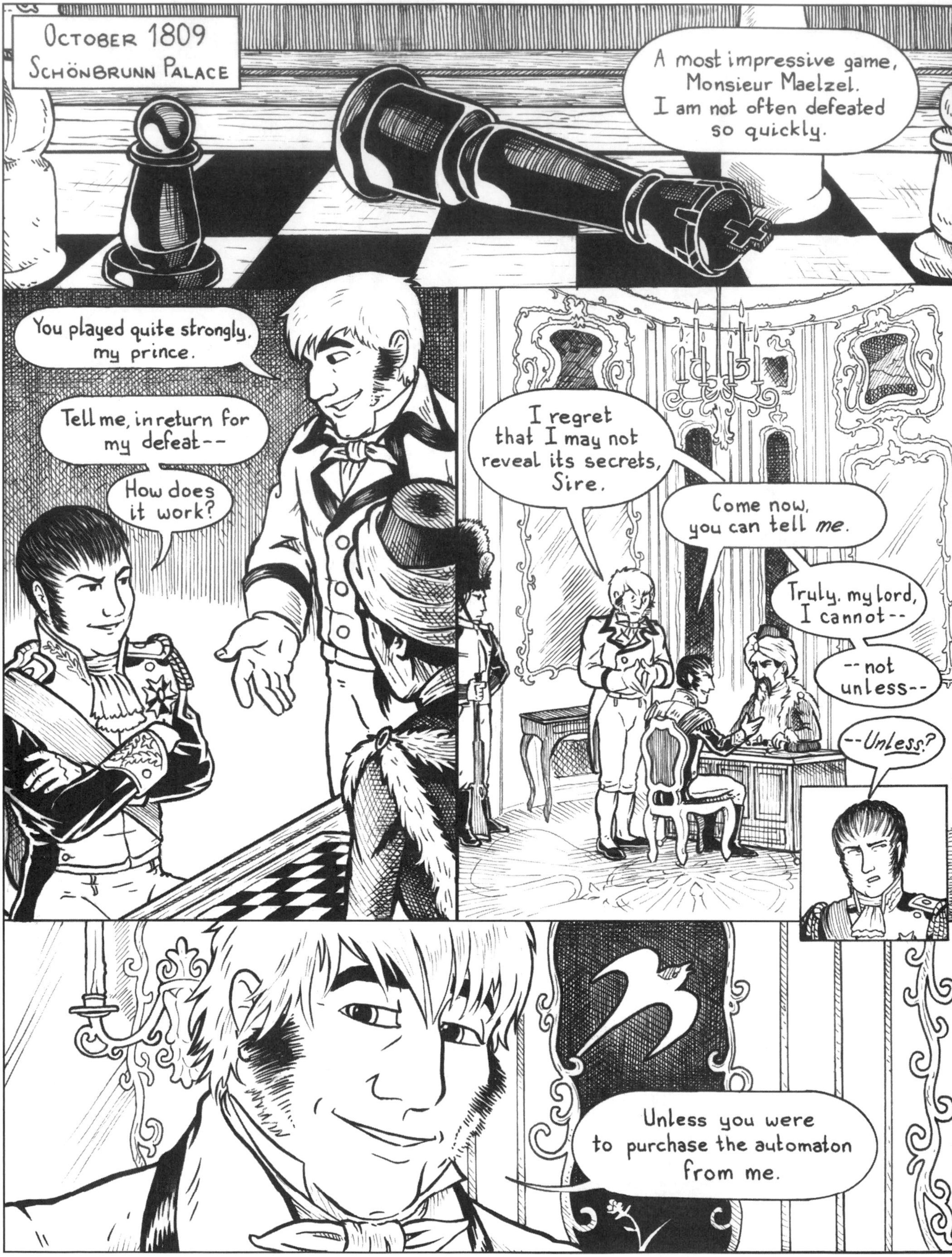
October 1809
Schönbrunn Palace
A most impressive game, Monsieur Maelzel. I am not often defeated so quickly.
You played quite strongly, my prince.
Tell me, in return for my defeat--
How does it work?
I regret that I may not reveal its secrets, Sire.
Come now, you can tell *me*.
Truly, my lord, I cannot--
--not unless--
--*Unless*?
Unless you were to purchase the automaton from me.

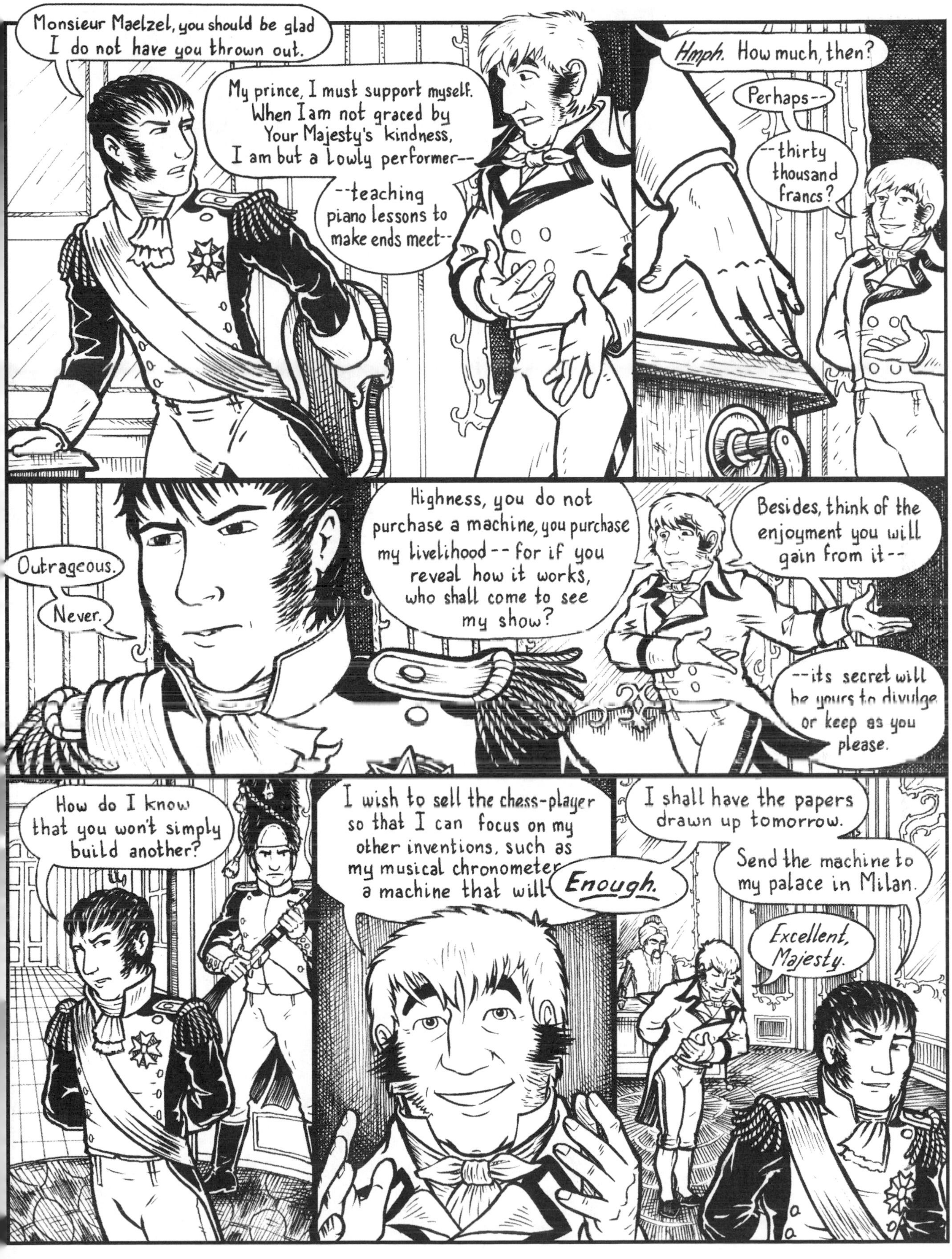
Monsieur Maelzel, you should be glad I do not have you thrown out.
My prince, I must support myself. When I am not graced by Your Majesty's kindness, I am but a lowly performer--
--teaching piano lessons to make ends meet--
Hmph. How much, then?
Perhaps--
--thirty thousand francs?
Outrageous.
Never.
Highness, you do not purchase a machine, you purchase my livelihood -- for if you reveal how it works, who shall come to see my show?
Besides, think of the enjoyment you will gain from it--
--its secret will be yours to divulge or keep as you please.
How do I know that you won't simply build another?
I wish to sell the chess-player so that I can focus on my other inventions, such as my musical chronometer, a machine that will-
Enough.
I shall have the papers drawn up tomorrow.
Send the machine to my palace in Milan.
Excellent, Majesty.

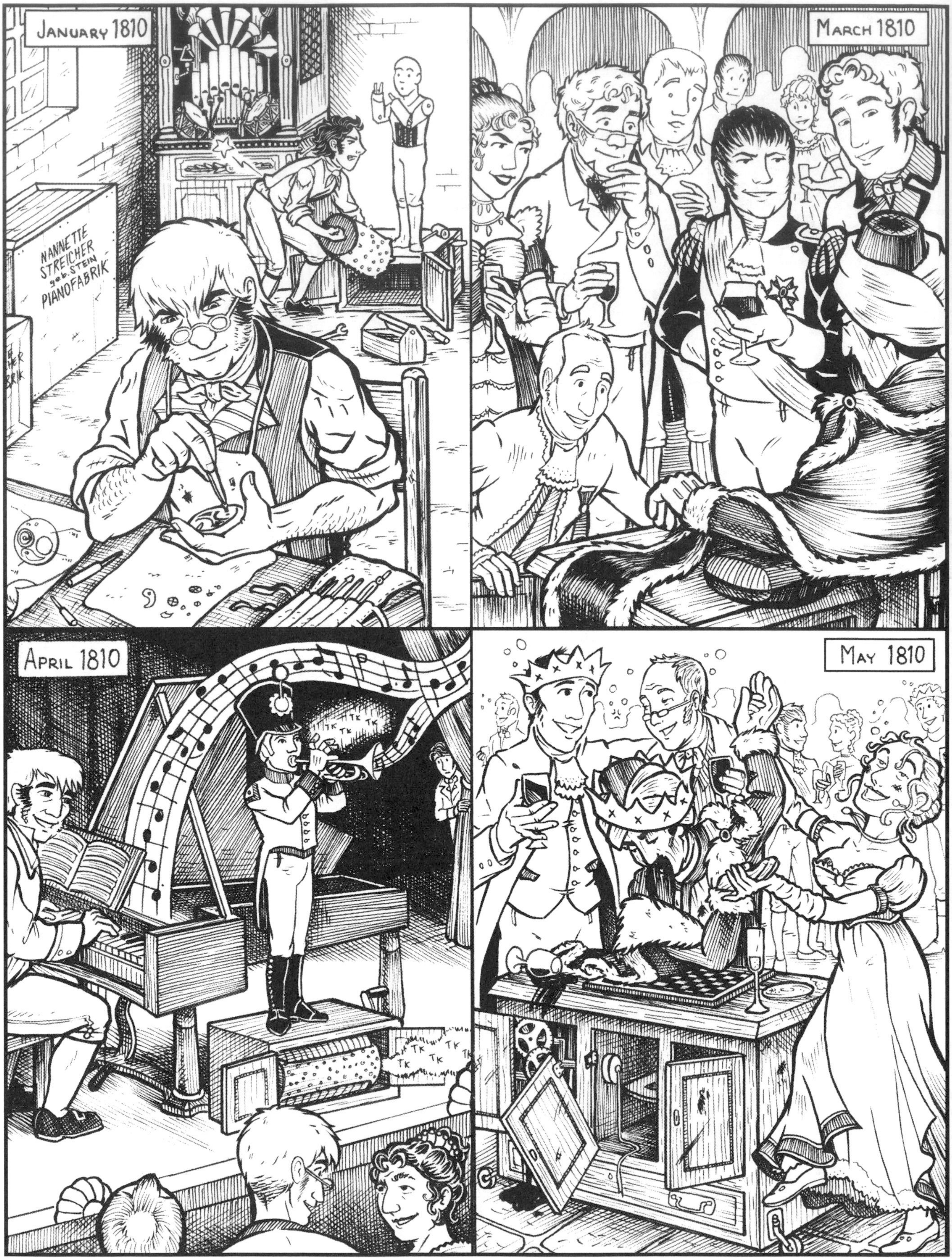
January 1810
NANNETTE STREICHER geb. STEIN PIANOFABRIK
March 1810
April 1810
TK TK TK TK TK
TK TK TK TK
May 1810

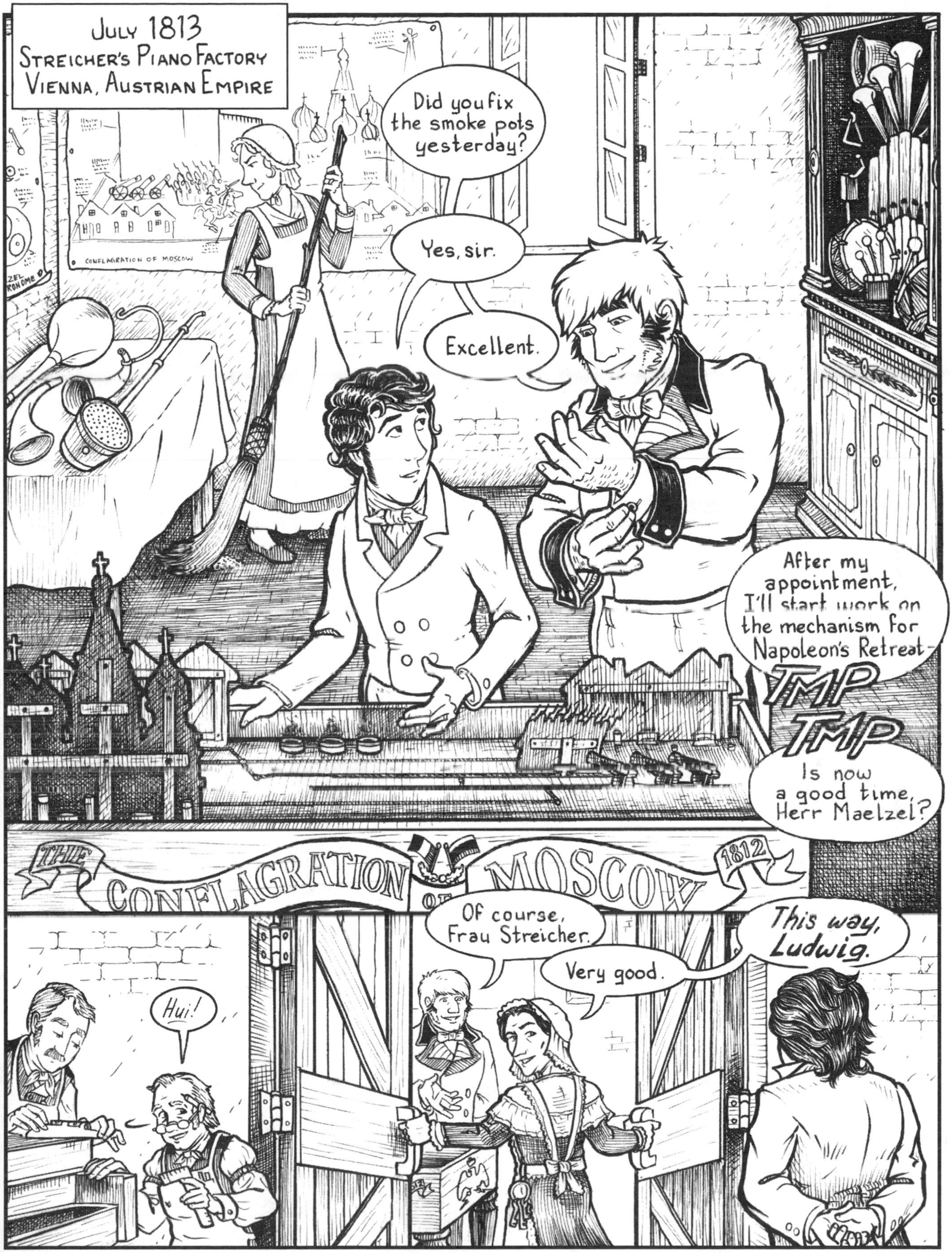
July 1813
Streicher's Piano Factory
Vienna, Austrian Empire
Did you fix the smoke pots yesterday?
Yes, sir.
Excellent.
After my appointment, I'll start work on the mechanism for Napoleon's Retreat-
TMP TMP
Is now a good time, Herr Maelzel?
CONFLAGRATION OF MOSCOW
THE CONFLAGRATION OF MOSCOW 1812
Hui!
Of course, Frau Streicher.
Very good.
This way, Ludwig.

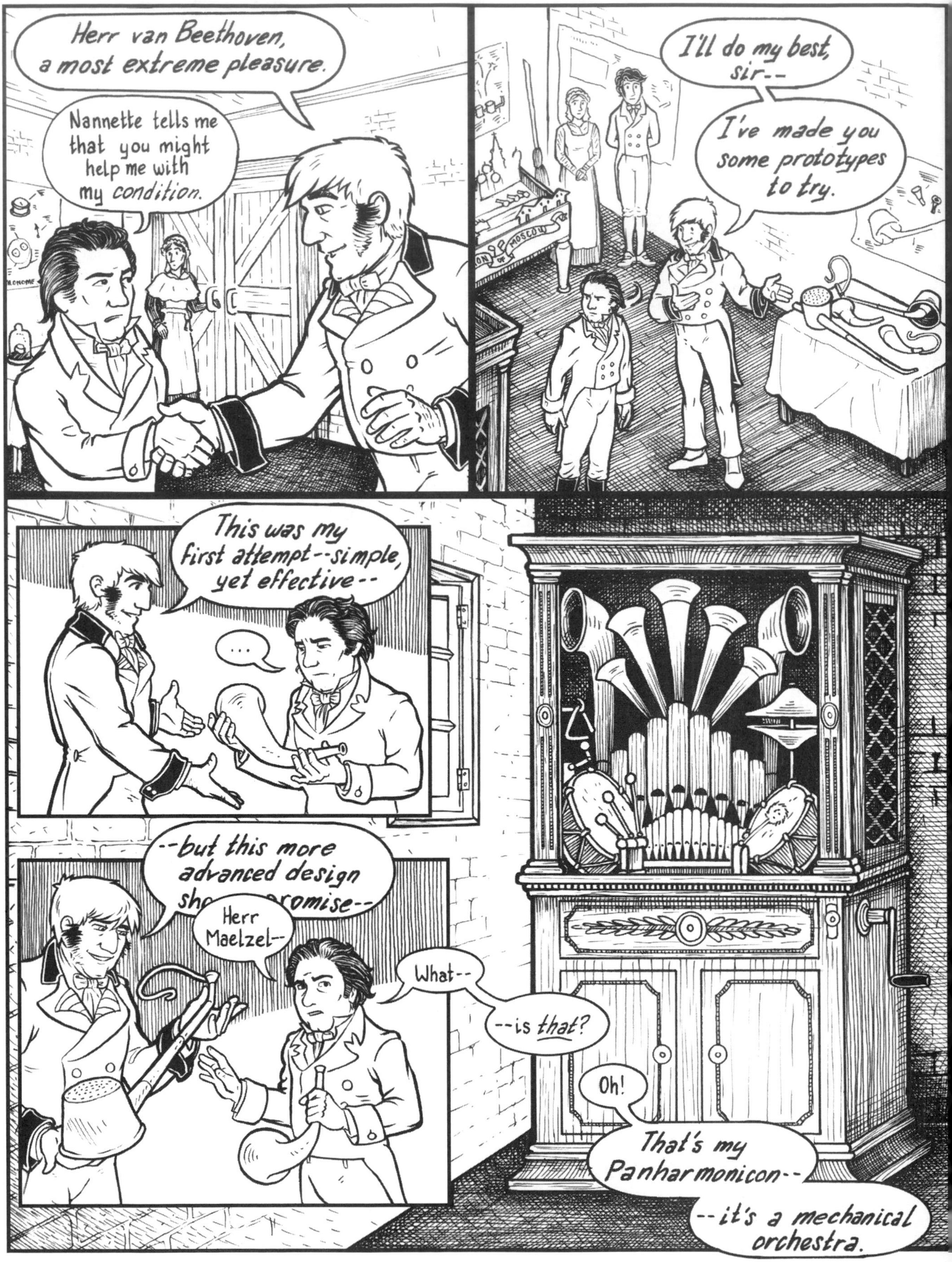

Herr van Beethoven, a most extreme pleasure.
Nannette tells me that you might help me with my *condition.*
I'll do my best, sir--
I've made you some prototypes to try.
This was my first attempt--simple, yet effective--
...
--but this more advanced design
Herr Maelzel--
What--
--is *that*?
Oh!
That's my Panharmonicon--
--it's a mechanical orchestra.

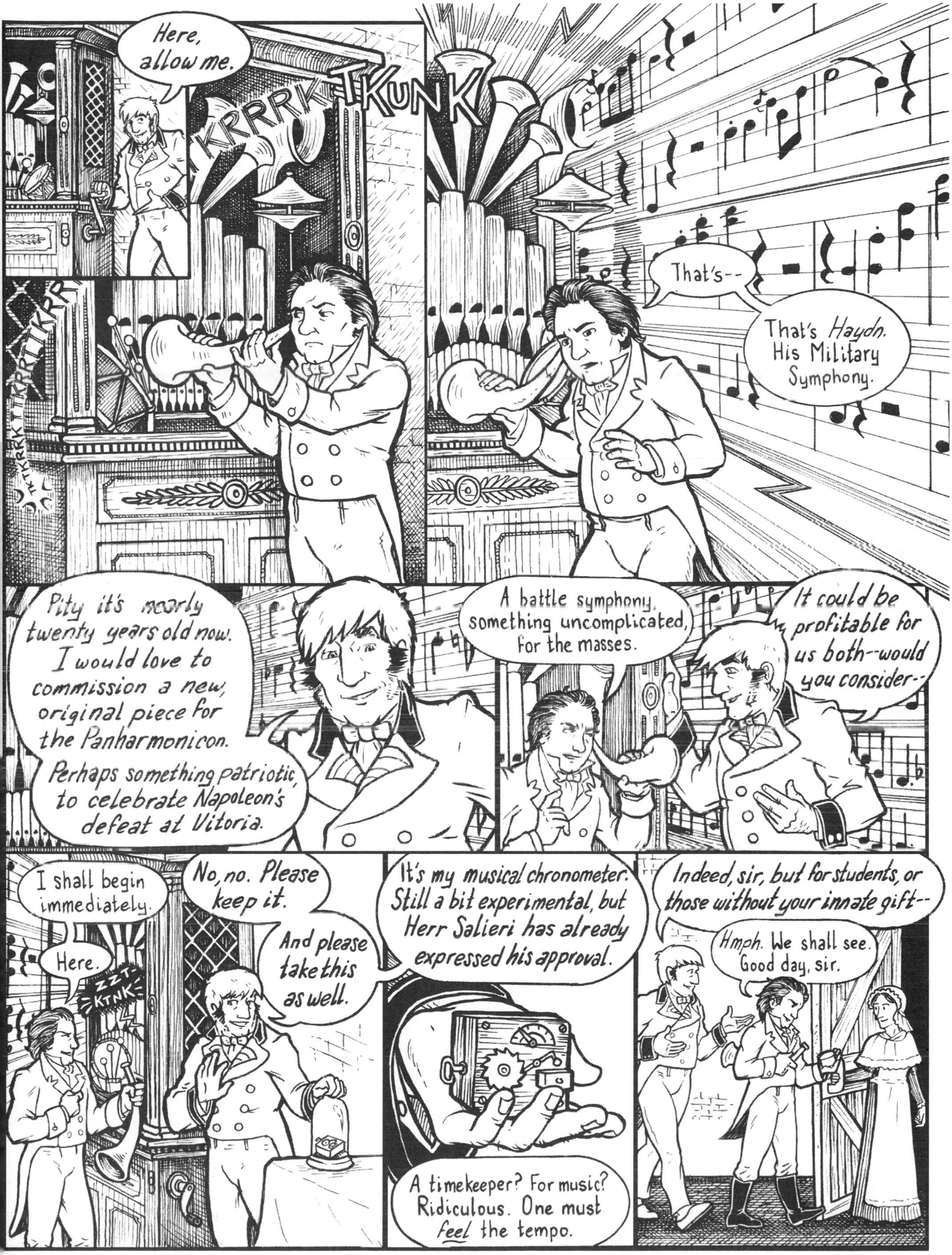

Here, allow me.
KRRRK
TKUNK
That's--
That's *Haydn.* His Military Symphony.
Pity it's nearly twenty years old now. I would love to commission a new, original piece for the Panharmonicon.
Perhaps something patriotic, to celebrate Napoleon's defeat at Vitoria.
A battle symphony, something uncomplicated, for the masses.
It could be profitable for us both--would you consider--
I shall begin immediately.
Here.
ZZT KTNK
No, no. Please keep it.
And please take this as well.
It's my musical chronometer. Still a bit experimental, but Herr Salieri has already expressed his approval.
A timekeeper? For music? Ridiculous. One must *feel* the tempo.
Indeed, sir, but for students, or those without your innate gift--
Hmph. We shall see. Good day, sir.

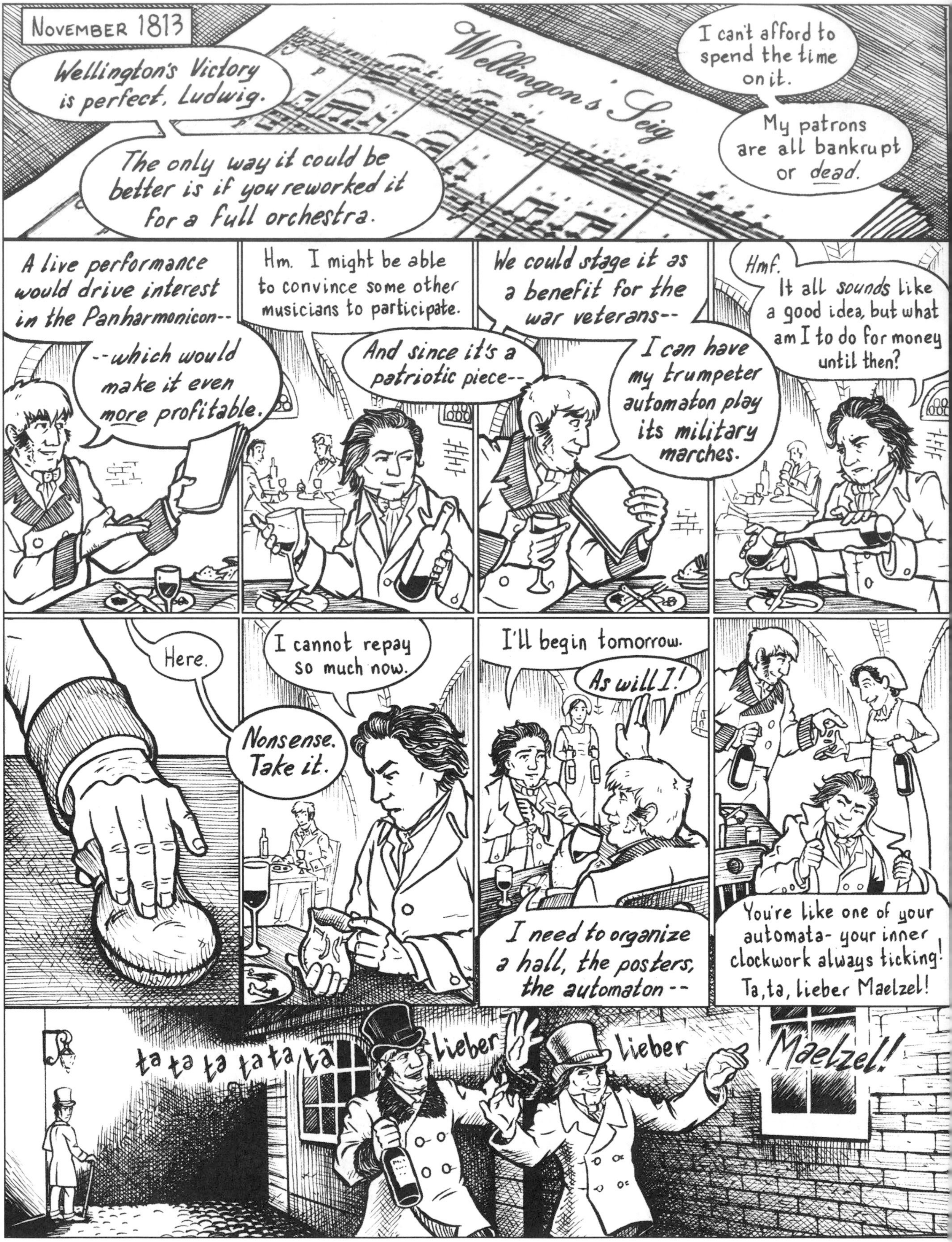

November 1813
Wellington's Victory is perfect, Ludwig.
The only way it could be better is if you reworked it for a full orchestra.
Wellingon's Seig
I can't afford to spend the time on it.
My patrons are all bankrupt or dead.
A live performance would drive interest in the Panharmonicon--
--which would make it even more profitable.
Hm. I might be able to convince some other musicians to participate.
And since it's a patriotic piece--
We could stage it as a benefit for the war veterans--
I can have my trumpeter automaton play its military marches.
Hmf.
It all sounds like a good idea, but what am I to do for money until then?
Here.
I cannot repay so much now.
Nonsense. Take it.
I'll begin tomorrow.
As will I!
I need to organize a hall, the posters, the automaton--
You're like one of your automata- your inner clockwork always ticking!
Ta, ta, lieber Maelzel!
ta ta ta tata ta lieber lieber Maelzel!

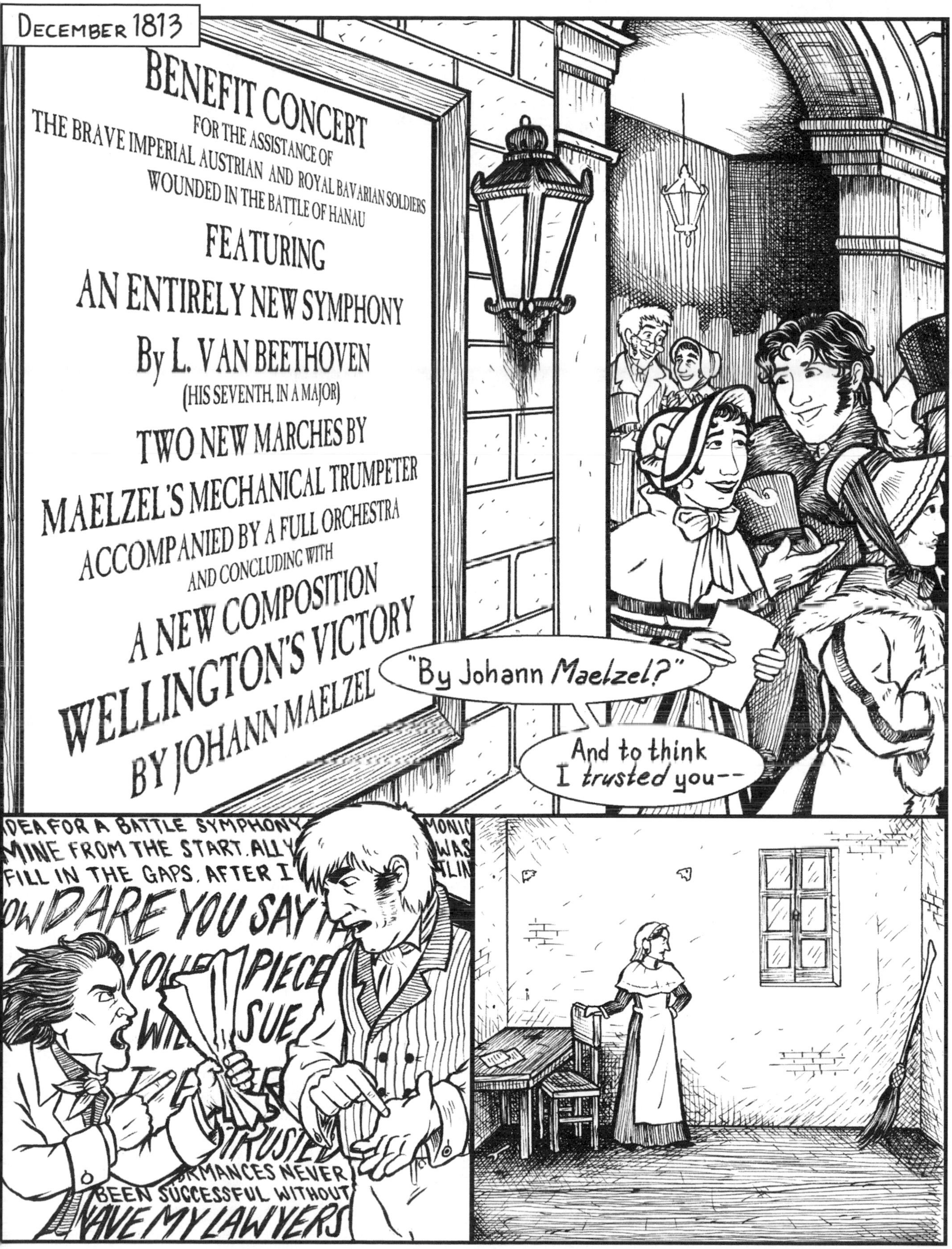
December 1813
BENEFIT CONCERT
FOR THE ASSISTANCE OF
THE BRAVE IMPERIAL AUSTRIAN AND ROYAL BAVARIAN SOLDIERS
WOUNDED IN THE BATTLE OF HANAU
FEATURING
AN ENTIRELY NEW SYMPHONY
By L. VAN BEETHOVEN
(HIS SEVENTH, IN A MAJOR)
TWO NEW MARCHES BY
MAELZEL'S MECHANICAL TRUMPETER
ACCOMPANIED BY A FULL ORCHESTRA
AND CONCLUDING WITH
A NEW COMPOSITION
WELLINGTON'S VICTORY
BY JOHANN MAELZEL
"By Johann Maelzel?"
And to think I trusted you--
DEA FOR A BATTLE SYMPHONY
MINE FROM THE START. ALL
FILL IN THE GAPS. AFTER I
DARE YOU SAY
PIECE
SUE
TRUSTED
RMANCES NEVER
BEEN SUCCESSFUL WITHOUT
AVE MY LAWYERS

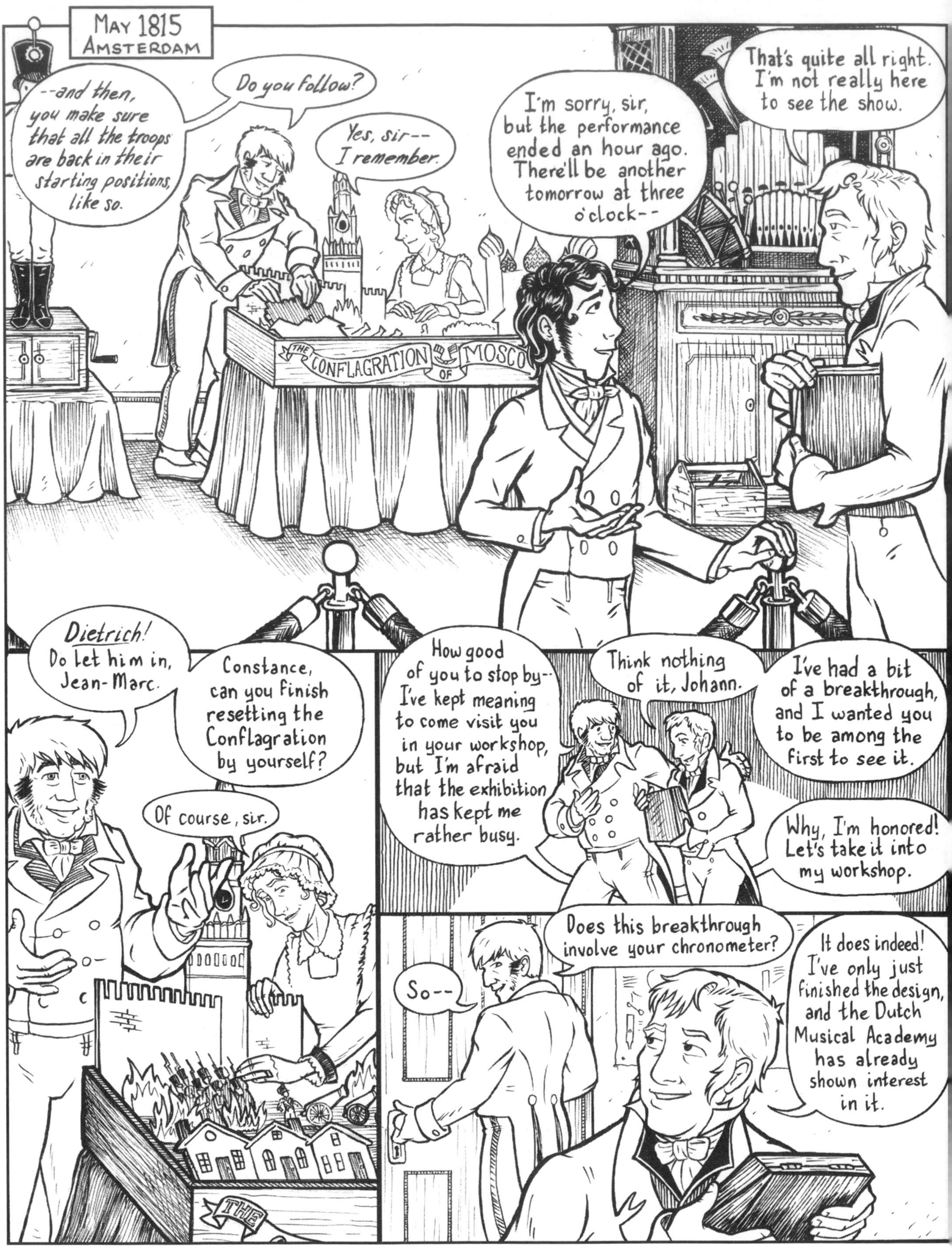
May 1815 Amsterdam
--and then, you make sure that all the troops are back in their starting positions, like so.
Do you follow?
Yes, sir-- I remember.
The Conflagration of Mosco
I'm sorry, sir, but the performance ended an hour ago. There'll be another tomorrow at three o'clock--
That's quite all right. I'm not really here to see the show.
Dietrich! Do let him in, Jean-Marc.
Constance, can you finish resetting the Conflagration by yourself?
Of course, sir.
The
How good of you to stop by-- I've kept meaning to come visit you in your workshop, but I'm afraid that the exhibition has kept me rather busy.
Think nothing of it, Johann.
I've had a bit of a breakthrough, and I wanted you to be among the first to see it.
Why, I'm honored! Let's take it into my workshop.
So--
Does this breakthrough involve your chronometer?
It does indeed! I've only just finished the design, and the Dutch Musical Academy has already shown interest in it.

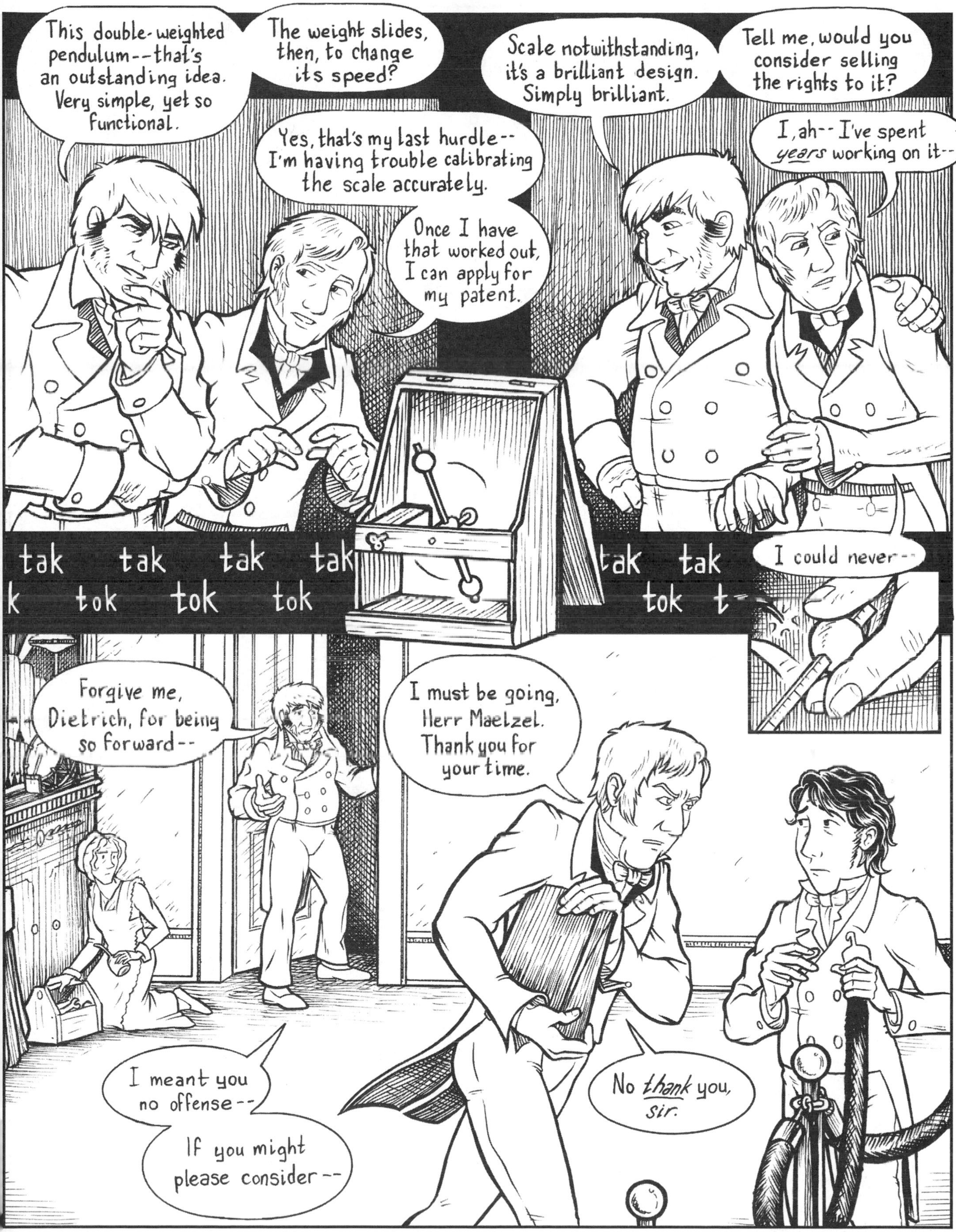

This double-weighted pendulum--that's an outstanding idea. Very simple, yet so functional.
The weight slides, then, to change its speed?
Yes, that's my last hurdle-- I'm having trouble calibrating the scale accurately.
Once I have that worked out, I can apply for my patent.
Scale notwithstanding, it's a brilliant design. Simply brilliant.
Tell me, would you consider selling the rights to it?
I, ah-- I've spent years working on it--
tak tak tak tak
k tok tok tok
tak tak
tok t-
I could never--
Forgive me, Dietrich, for being so forward--
I must be going, Herr Maelzel. Thank you for your time.
I meant you no offense--
If you might please consider--
No thank you, sir.

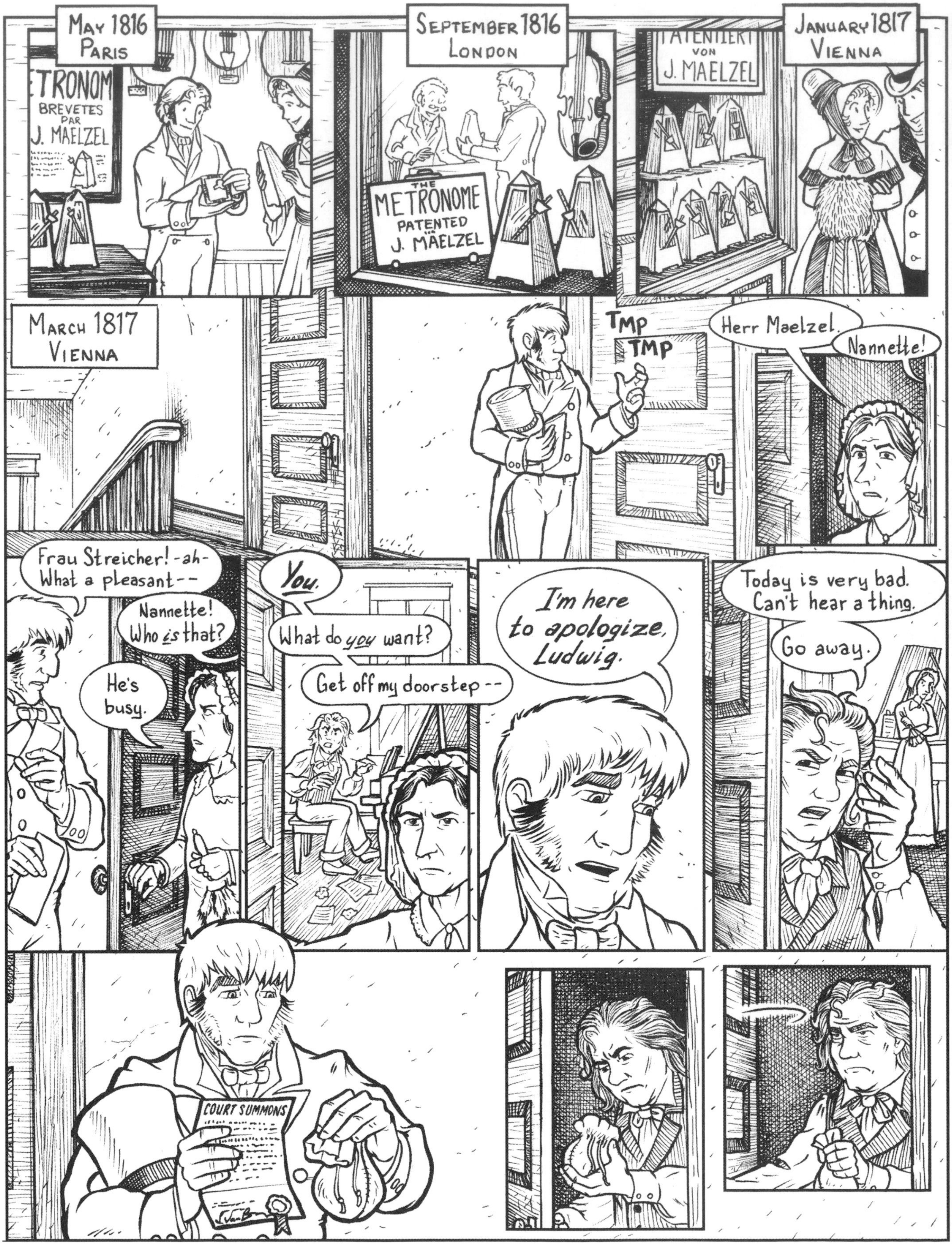
May 1816
Paris
ETRONOM
BREVETES PAR
J. MAELZEL
September 1816
London
THE METRONOME PATENTED J. MÄELZEL
January 1817
Vienna
J. MAELZEL
March 1817
Vienna
TMP
TMP
Herr Maelzel.
Nannette!
Frau Streicher! -ah- What a pleasant --
Nannette! Who is that?
He's busy.
You.
What do you want?
Get off my doorstep --
I'm here to apologize, Ludwig.
Today is very bad. Can't hear a thing.
Go away.
COURT SUMMONS

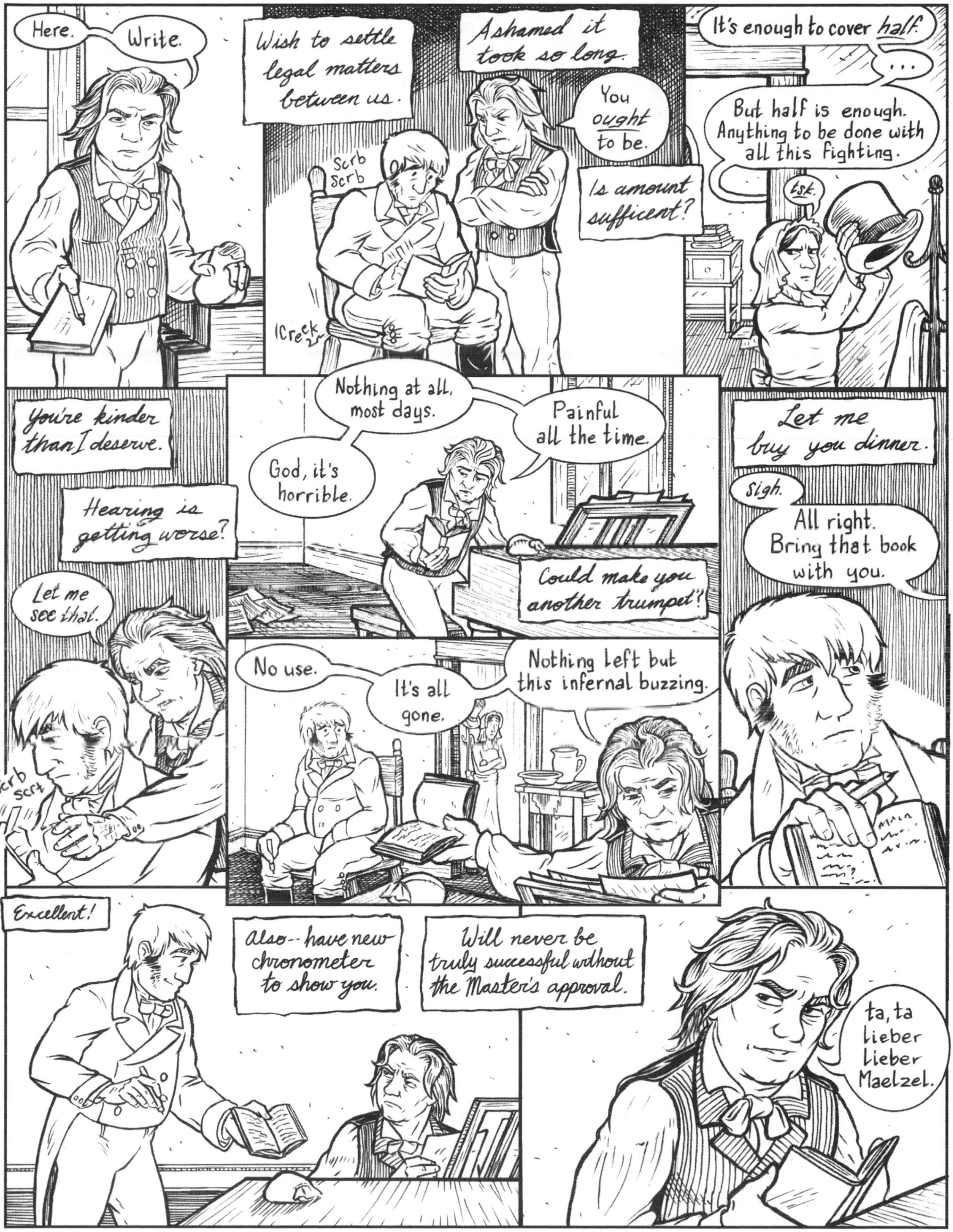
Here.
Write.
Wish to settle legal matters between us.
Ashamed it took so long.
Scrb Scrb
Creek
You ought to be.
Is amount sufficent?
It's enough to cover half.
...
But half is enough. Anything to be done with all this fighting.
tsk.
You're kinder than I deserve.
Hearing is getting worse?
Let me see that.
Scrb Scrb
Nothing at all, most days.
Painful all the time.
God, it's horrible.
Could make you another trumpet?
No use.
It's all gone.
Nothing left but this infernal buzzing.
Let me buy you dinner.
Sigh.
All right. Bring that book with you.
Excellent!
Also--have new chronometer to show you.
Will never be truly successful without the Master's approval.
ta, ta lieber lieber Maelzel.

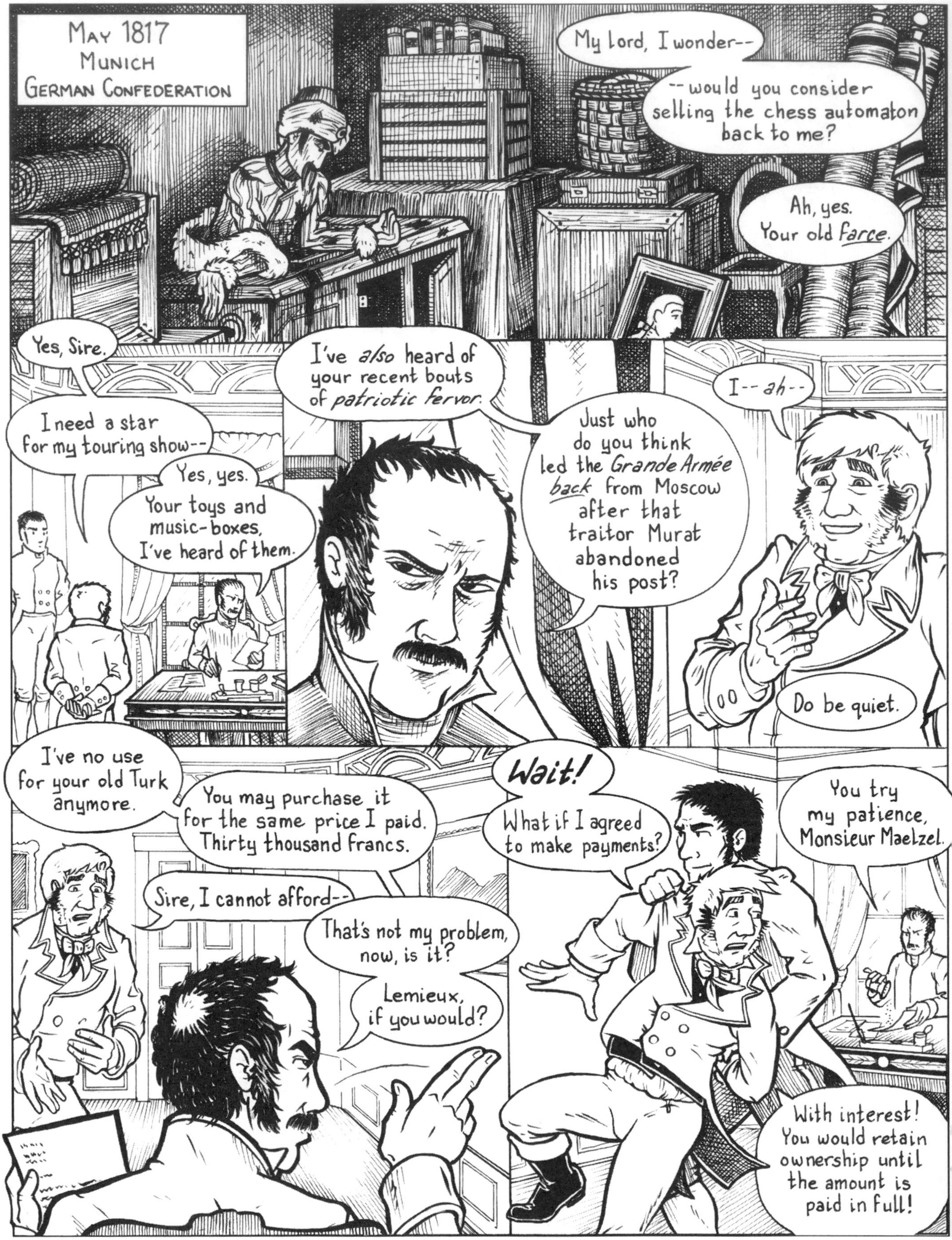
May 1817
Munich
German Confederation
My Lord, I wonder--
--would you consider selling the chess automaton back to me?
Ah, yes. Your old farce.
Yes, Sire.
I need a star for my touring show--
Yes, yes. Your toys and music-boxes, I've heard of them.
I've also heard of your recent bouts of patriotic fervor.
Just who do you think led the Grande Armée back from Moscow after that traitor Murat abandoned his post?
I--ah--
Do be quiet.
I've no use for your old Turk anymore.
You may purchase it for the same price I paid. Thirty thousand francs.
Sire, I cannot afford--
That's not my problem, now, is it?
Lemieux, if you would?
Wait!
What if I agreed to make payments?
You try my patience, Monsieur Maelzel.
With interest! You would retain ownership until the amount is paid in full!

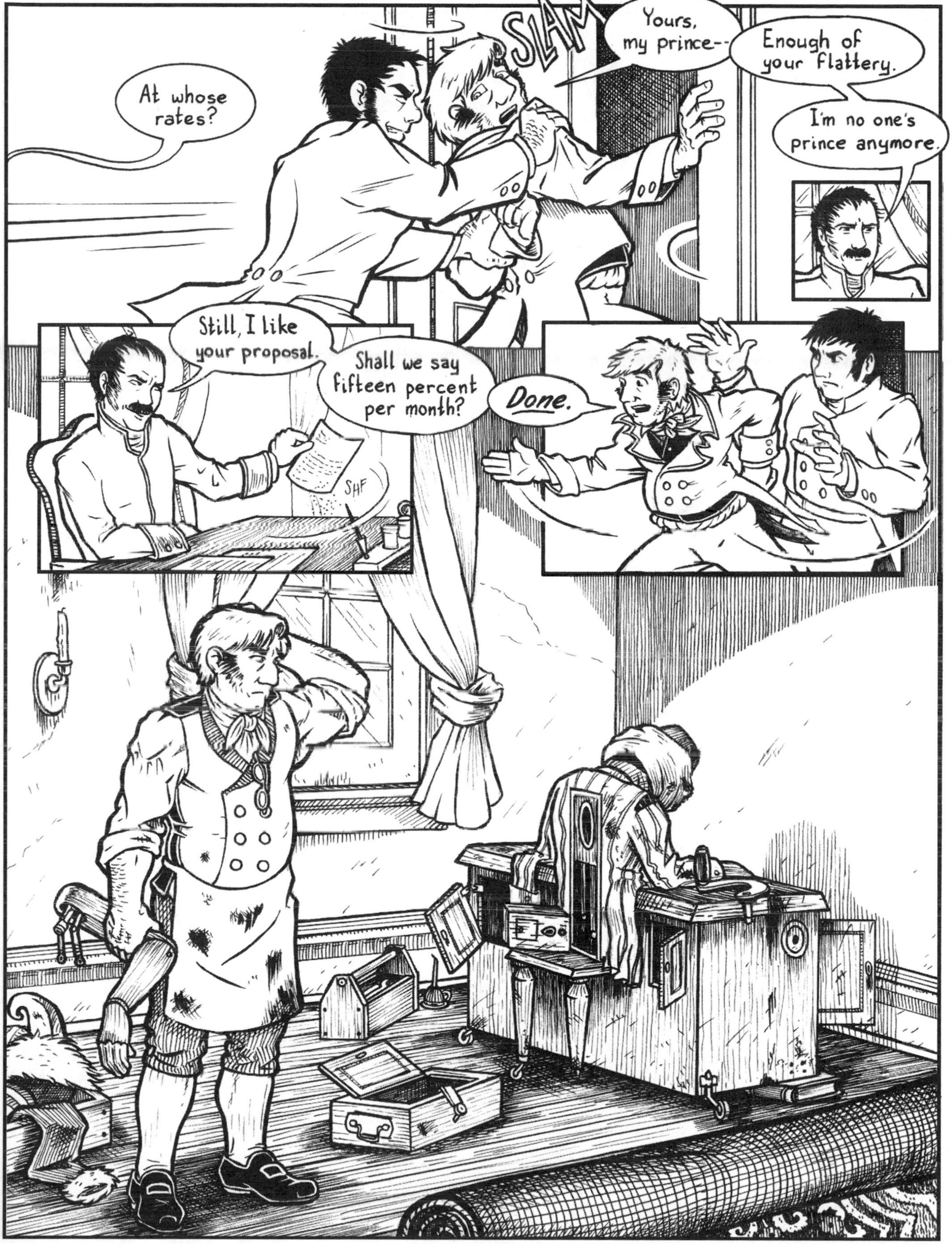
At whose rates?
SLAM
Yours, my prince--
Enough of your flattery.
I'm no one's prince anymore.
Still, I like your proposal.
Shall we say fifteen percent per month?
SHF
Done.

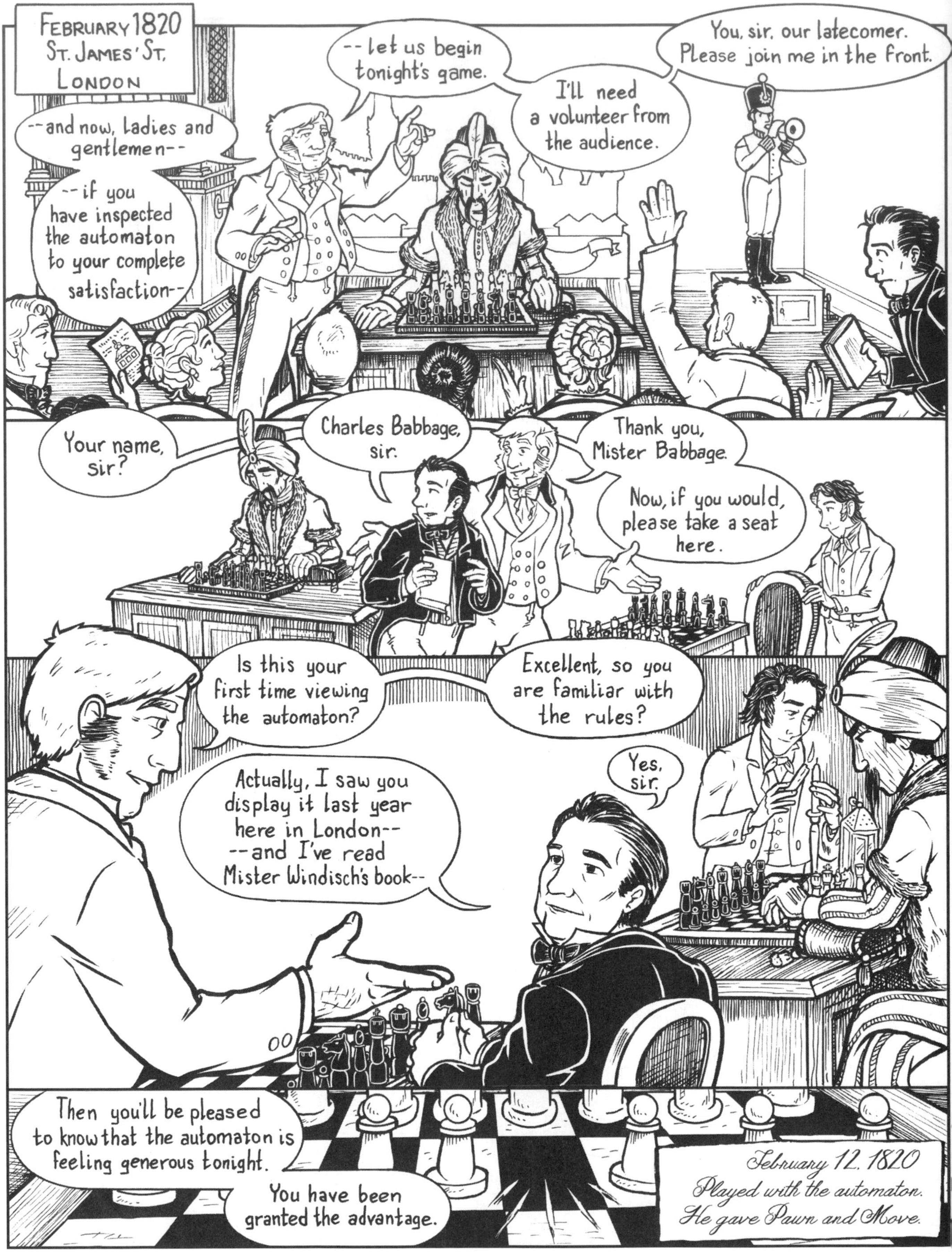
February 1820
St. James' St, London
--and now, ladies and gentlemen--
--if you have inspected the automaton to your complete satisfaction--
--let us begin tonight's game.
I'll need a volunteer from the audience.
You, sir, our latecomer. Please join me in the front.
Your name, sir?
Charles Babbage, sir.
Thank you, Mister Babbage.
Now, if you would, please take a seat here.
Is this your first time viewing the automaton?
Actually, I saw you display it last year here in London--
--and I've read Mister Windisch's book--
Excellent, so you are familiar with the rules?
Yes, sir.
Then you'll be pleased to know that the automaton is feeling generous tonight.
You have been granted the advantage.
February 12, 1820
Played with the automaton.
He gave Pawn and Move.

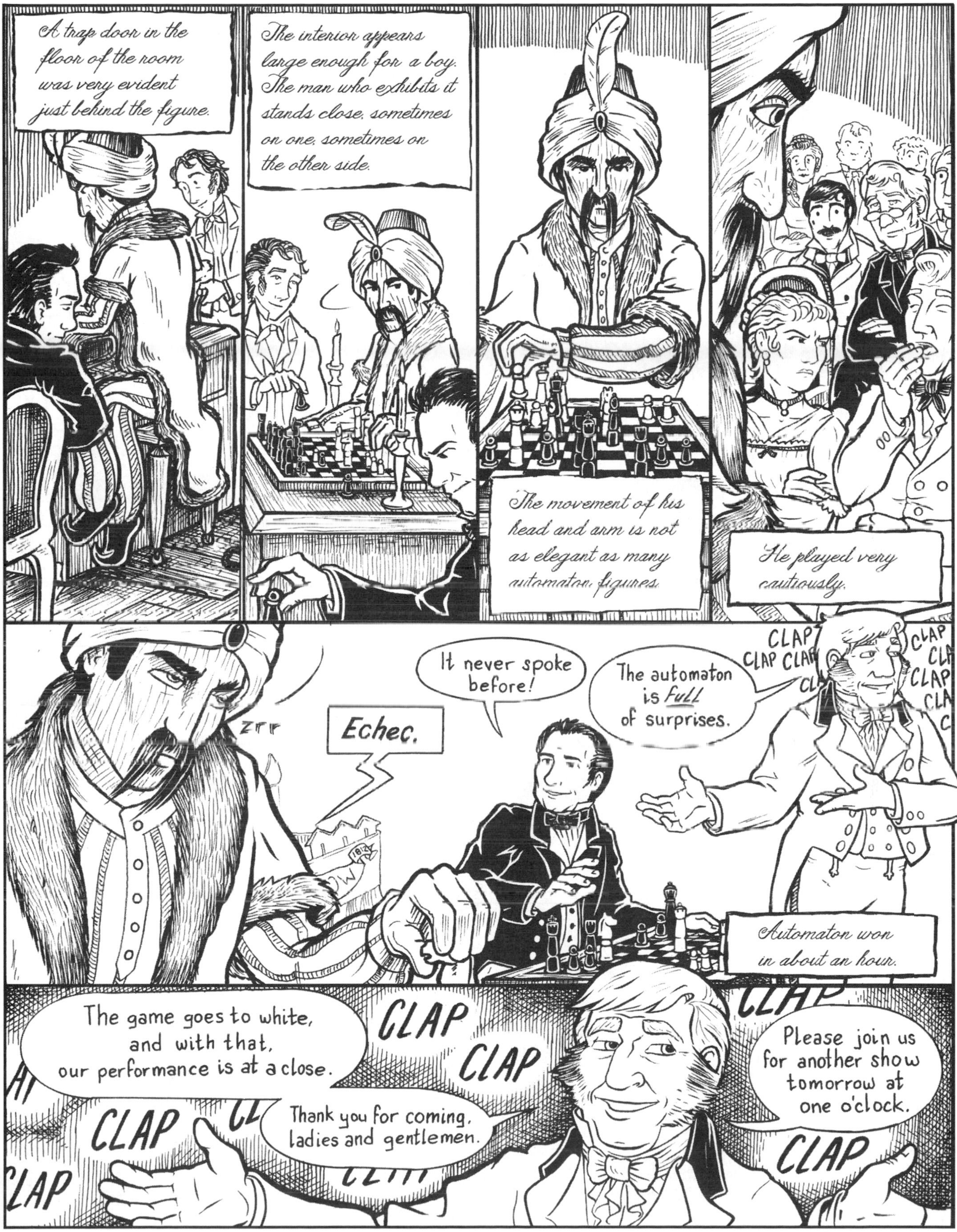
A trap door in the floor of the room was very evident just behind the figure.
The interior appears large enough for a boy. The man who exhibits it stands close, sometimes on one, sometimes on the other side.
The movement of his head and arm is not as elegant as many automaton figures.
He played very cautiously.
Zrr
Echec.
It never spoke before!
The automaton is full of surprises.
CLAP CLAP CLAP CLAP
Automaton won in about an hour.
The game goes to white, and with that, our performance is at a close.
CLAP
CLAP
Thank you for coming, ladies and gentlemen.
CLAP
CLAP
Please join us for another show tomorrow at one o'clock.
CLAP

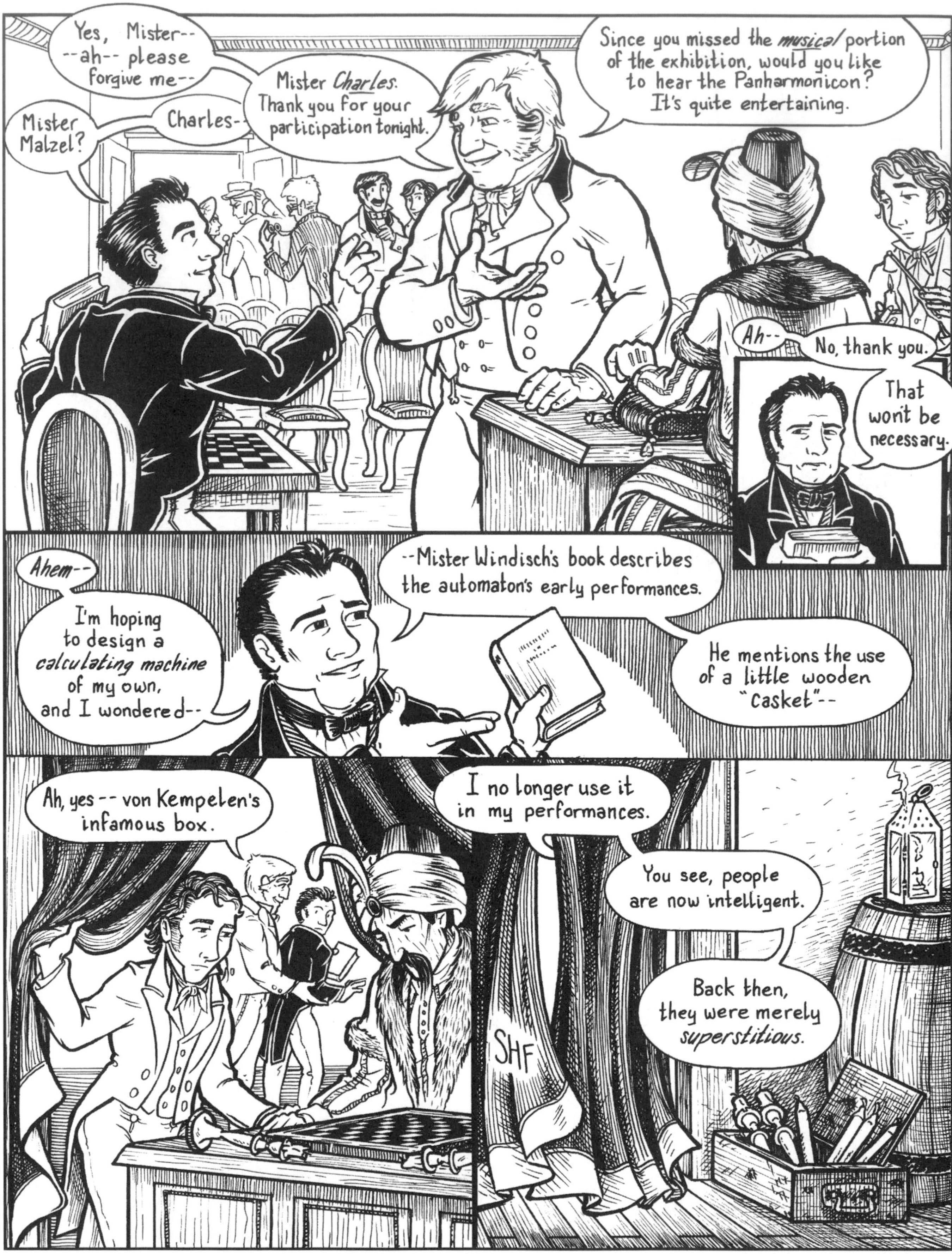
Mister Malzel?
Yes, Mister-- --ah-- please forgive me--
Charles-
Mister Charles. Thank you for your participation tonight.
Since you missed the musical portion of the exhibition, would you like to hear the Panharmonicon? It's quite entertaining.
Ah--
No, thank you.
That won't be necessary.
Ahem--
I'm hoping to design a calculating machine of my own, and I wondered--
--Mister Windisch's book describes the automaton's early performances.
He mentions the use of a little wooden "casket"--
Ah, yes -- von Kempelen's infamous box.
I no longer use it in my performances.
You see, people are now intelligent.
Back then, they were merely superstitious.
SHF

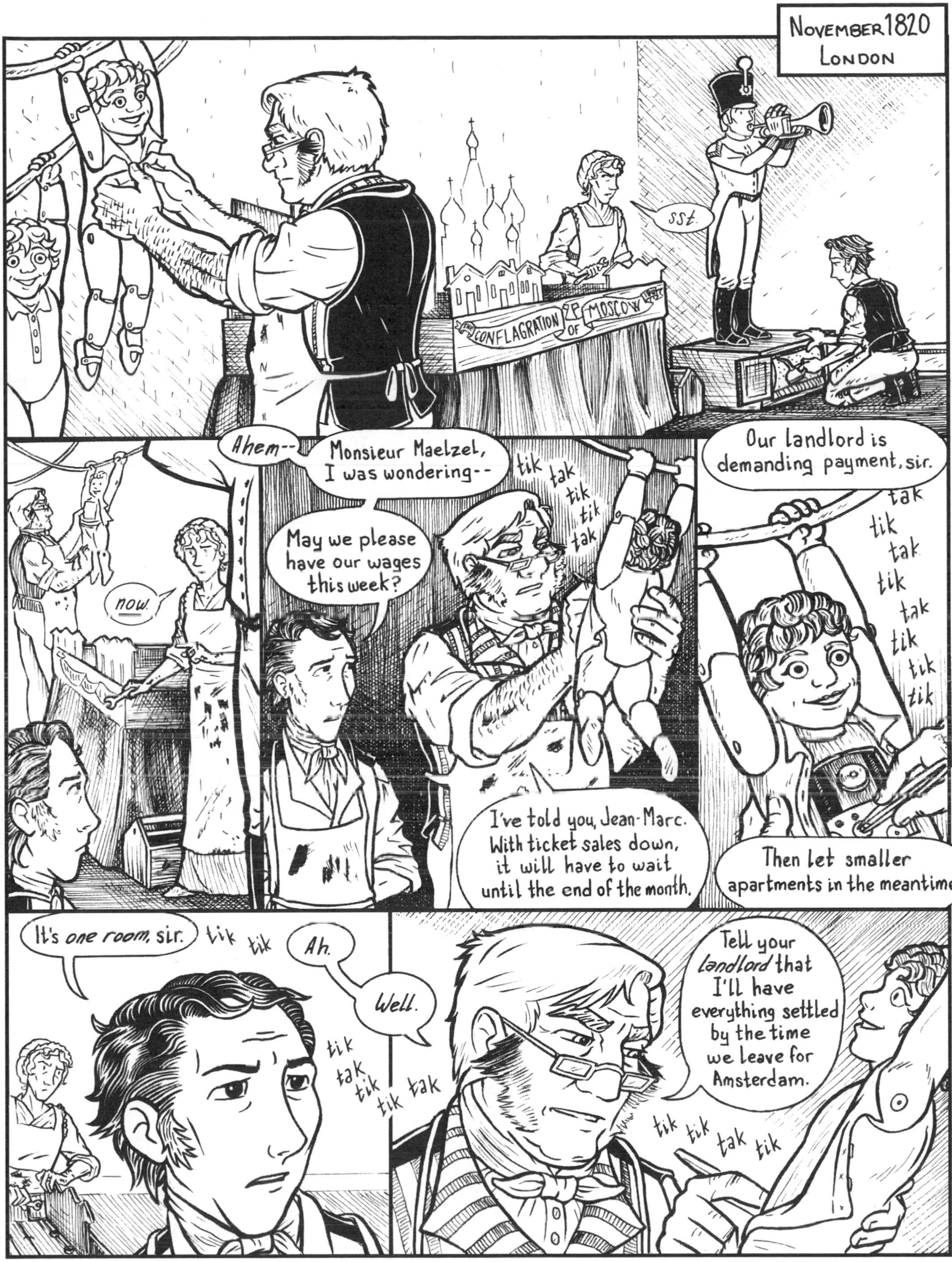
November 1820
London
THE CONFLAGRATION OF MOSCOW
sst.
Ahem--
now.
Monsieur Maelzel, I was wondering--
May we please have our wages this week?
tik tak tik tik tak
I've told you, Jean-Marc. With ticket sales down, it will have to wait until the end of the month.
Our landlord is demanding payment, sir.
tak tik tak tik tak tik tik tik
Then let smaller apartments in the meantime.
It's *one room*, sir.
tik tik
Ah.
Well.
tik tak tik tik tak
Tell your *landlord* that I'll have everything settled by the time we leave for Amsterdam.
tik tik tak tik

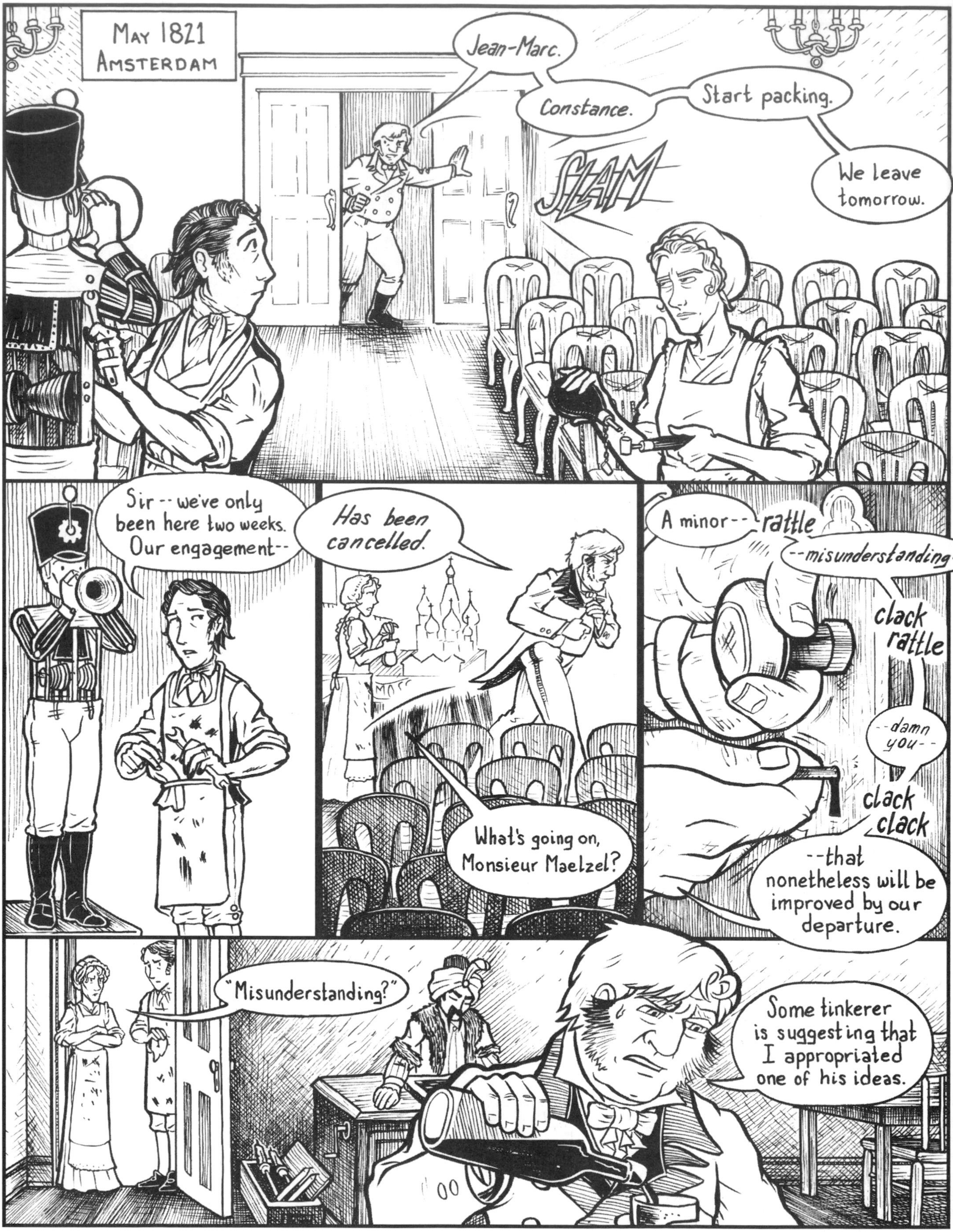
May 1821
Amsterdam
Jean-Marc.
Constance.
Start packing.
We leave tomorrow.
SLAM
Sir -- we've only been here two weeks. Our engagement--
Has been cancelled.
What's going on, Monsieur Maelzel?
A minor--
rattle
--misunderstanding-
clack
rattle
--damn you--
clack
clack
--that nonetheless will be improved by our departure.
"Misunderstanding?"
Some tinkerer is suggesting that I appropriated one of his ideas.

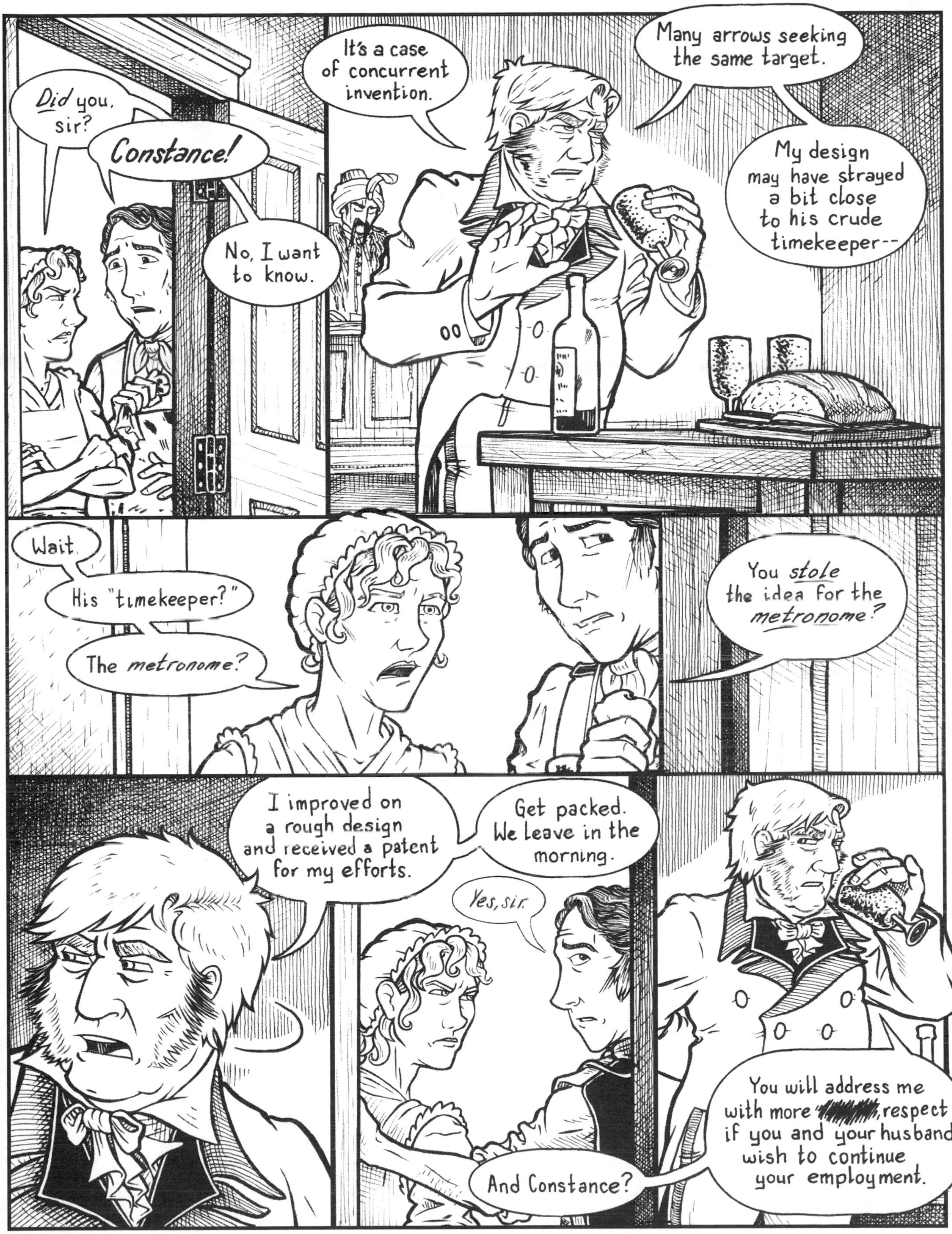
Did you, sir?
Constance!
No, I want to know.
It's a case of concurrent invention.
Many arrows seeking the same target.
My design may have strayed a bit close to his crude timekeeper--
Wait.
His "timekeeper?"
The metronome?
You stole the idea for the metronome?
I improved on a rough design and received a patent for my efforts.
Get packed. We leave in the morning.
Yes, sir.
And Constance?
You will address me with more [redacted], respect if you and your husband wish to continue your employment.

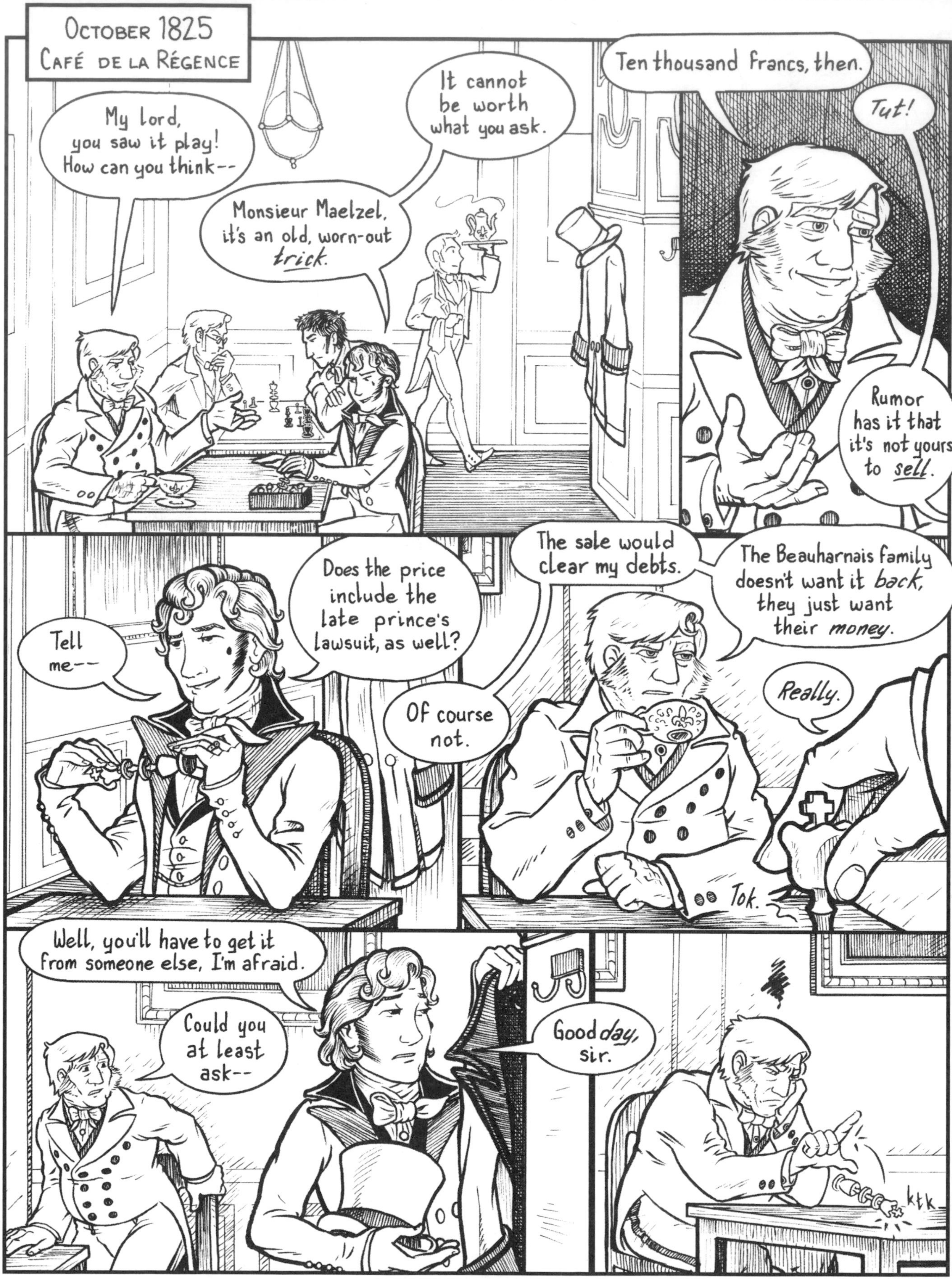
October 1825
Café de la Régence
My lord, you saw it play! How can you think--
It cannot be worth what you ask.
Monsieur Maelzel, it's an old, worn-out *trick*.
Ten thousand francs, then.
Tut!
Rumor has it that it's not yours to *sell*.
Tell me--
Does the price include the late prince's lawsuit, as well?
The sale would clear my debts.
The Beauharnais family doesn't want it *back*, they just want their *money*.
Of course not.
Really.
Tok.
Well, you'll have to get it from someone else, I'm afraid.
Could you at least ask--
Good *day*, sir.
ktk

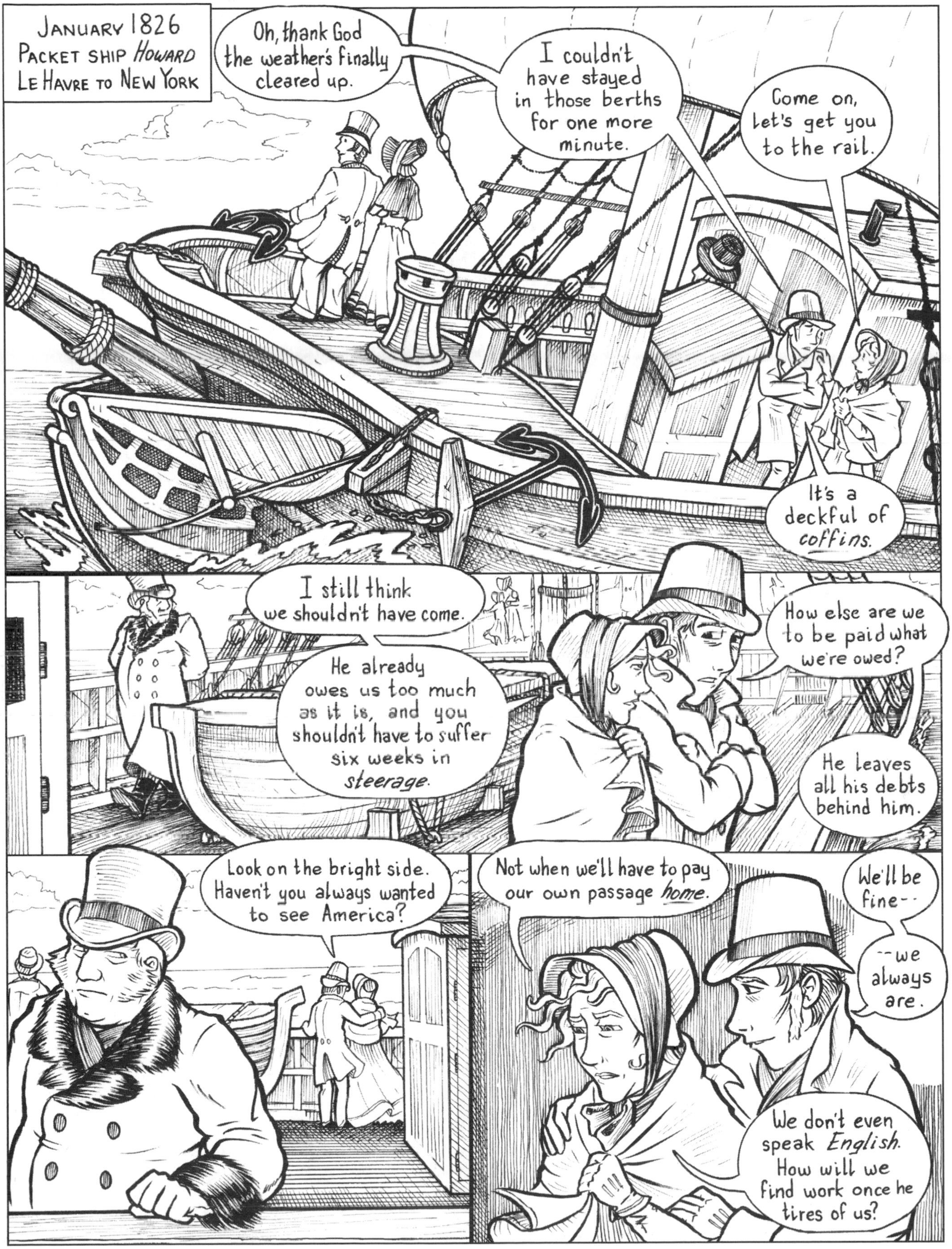
January 1826
Packet ship *Howard*
Le Havre to New York
Oh, thank God the weather's finally cleared up.
I couldn't have stayed in those berths for one more minute.
Come on, let's get you to the rail.
It's a deckful of *coffins*.
I still think we shouldn't have come.
He already owes us too much as it is, and you shouldn't have to suffer six weeks in *steerage*.
How else are we to be paid what we're owed?
He leaves all his debts behind him.
Look on the bright side. Haven't you always wanted to see America?
Not when we'll have to pay our own passage *home*.
We'll be fine--
--we always are.
We don't even speak *English*. How will we find work once he tires of us?

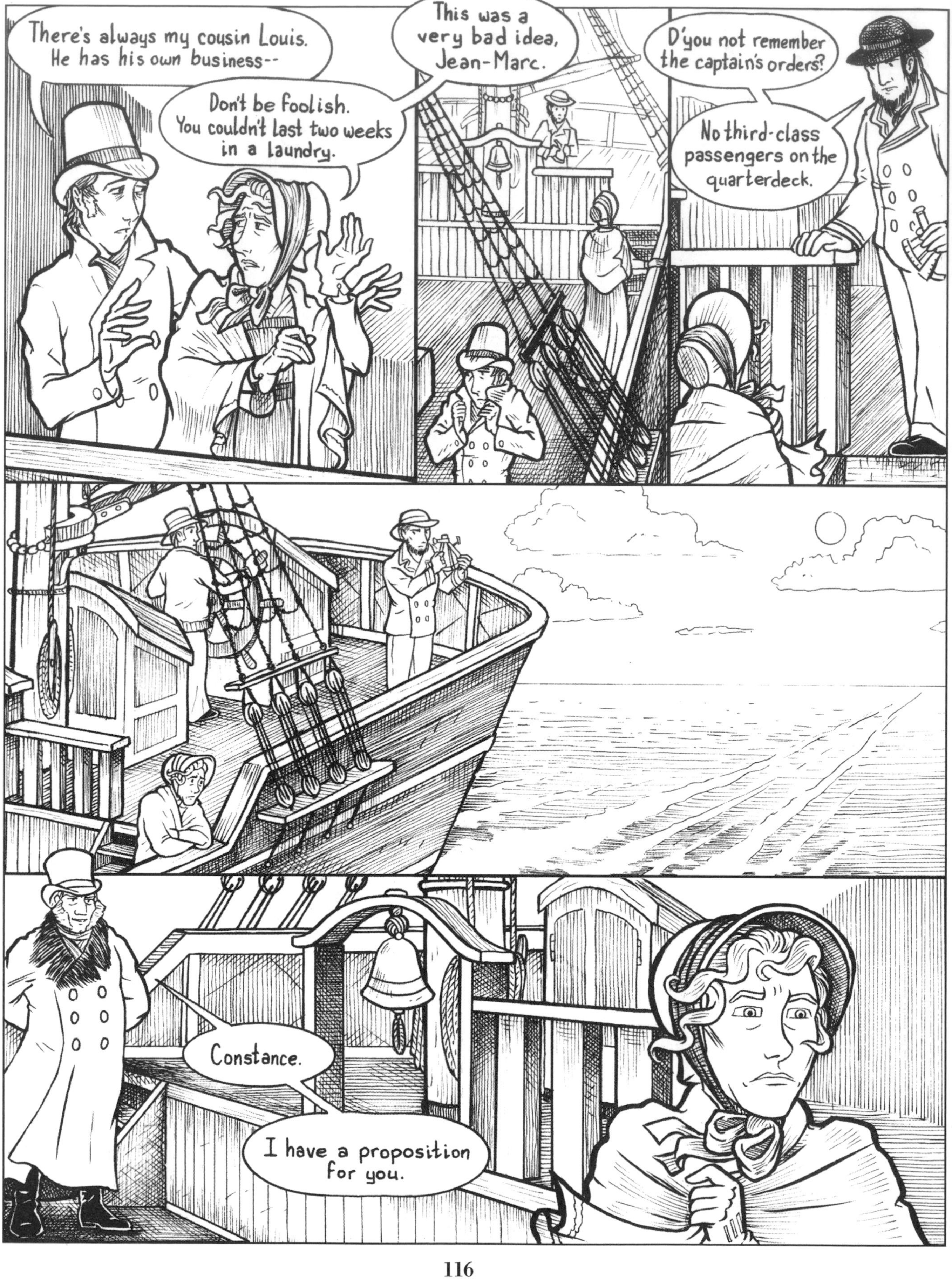
There's always my cousin Louis. He has his own business--
Don't be foolish. You couldn't last two weeks in a laundry.
This was a very bad idea, Jean-Marc.
D'you not remember the captain's orders?
No third-class passengers on the quarterdeck.
Constance.
I have a proposition for you.

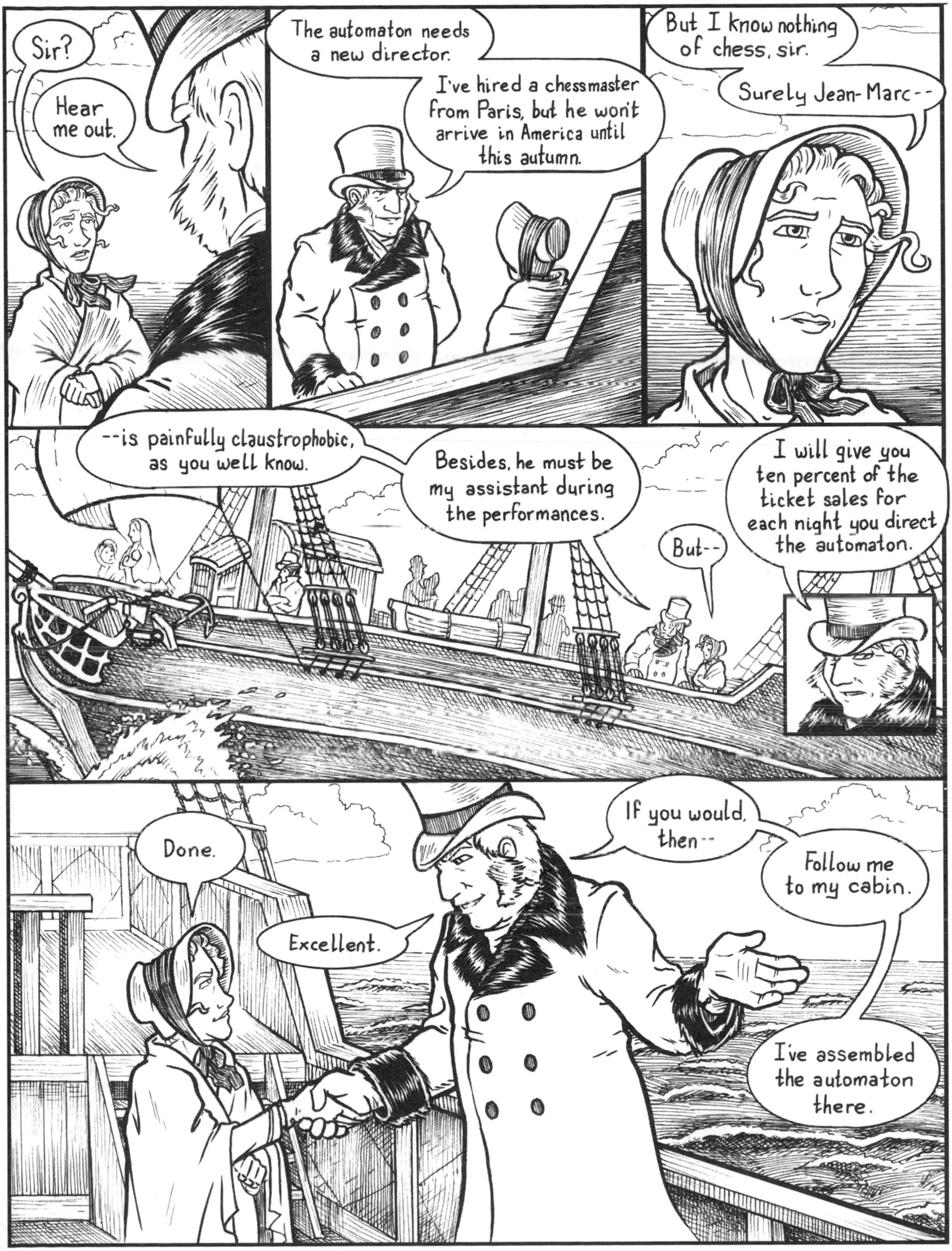
Sir?
Hear me out.
The automaton needs a new director.
I've hired a chessmaster from Paris, but he won't arrive in America until this autumn.
But I know nothing of chess, sir.
Surely Jean-Marc--
--is painfully claustrophobic, as you well know.
Besides, he must be my assistant during the performances.
But--
I will give you ten percent of the ticket sales for each night you direct the automaton.
Done.
Excellent.
If you would, then--
Follow me to my cabin.
I've assembled the automaton there.

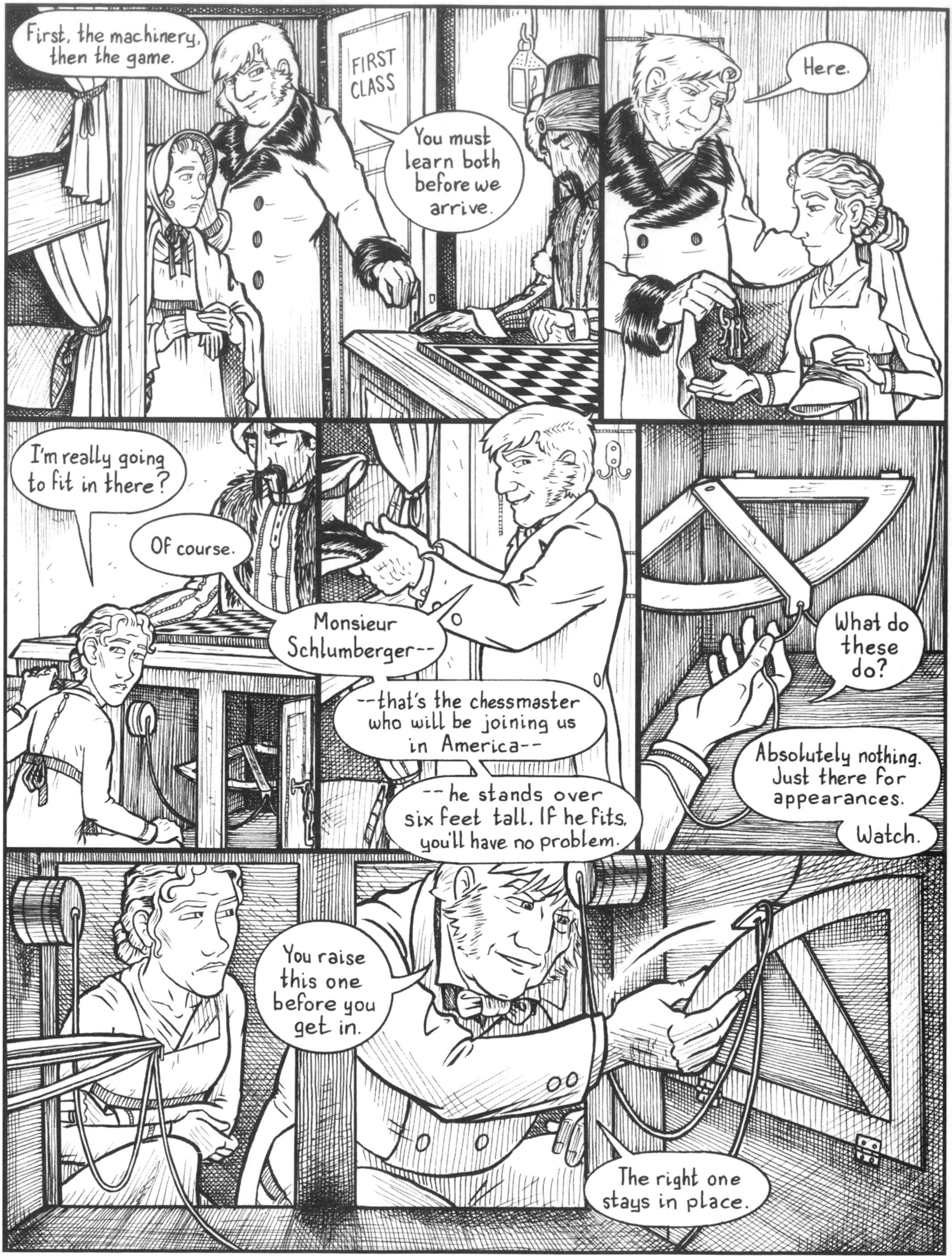
First, the machinery, then the game.
FIRST CLASS
You must learn both before we arrive.
Here.
I'm really going to fit in there?
Of course.
Monsieur Schlumberger--
--that's the chessmaster who will be joining us in America--
--he stands over six feet tall. If he fits, you'll have no problem.
What do these do?
Absolutely nothing. Just there for appearances.
Watch.
You raise this one before you get in.
The right one stays in place.

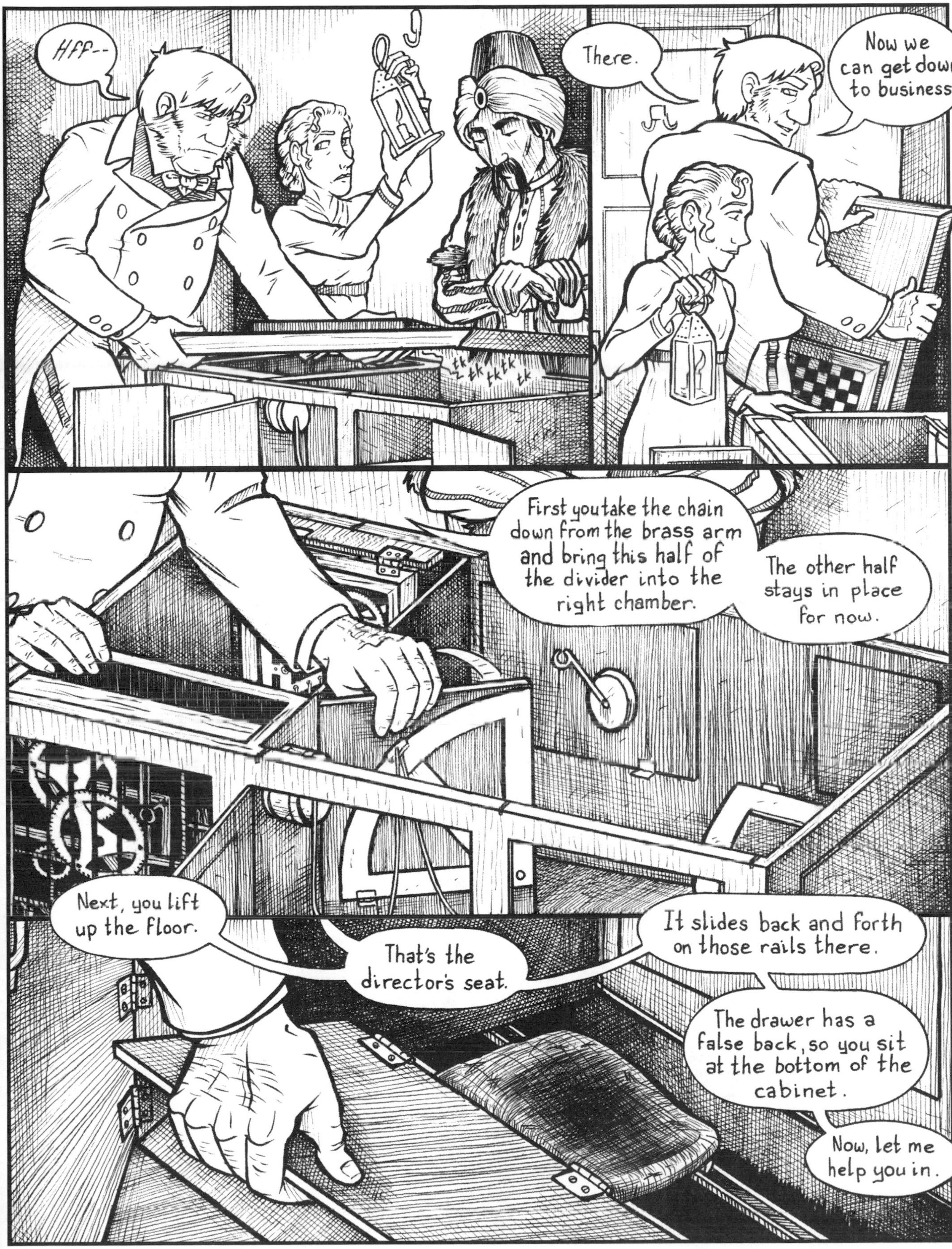
Hff--
There.
Now we can get down to business.
First you take the chain down from the brass arm and bring this half of the divider into the right chamber.
The other half stays in place for now.
Next, you lift up the floor.
That's the director's seat.
It slides back and forth on those rails there.
The drawer has a false back, so you sit at the bottom of the cabinet.
Now, let me help you in.

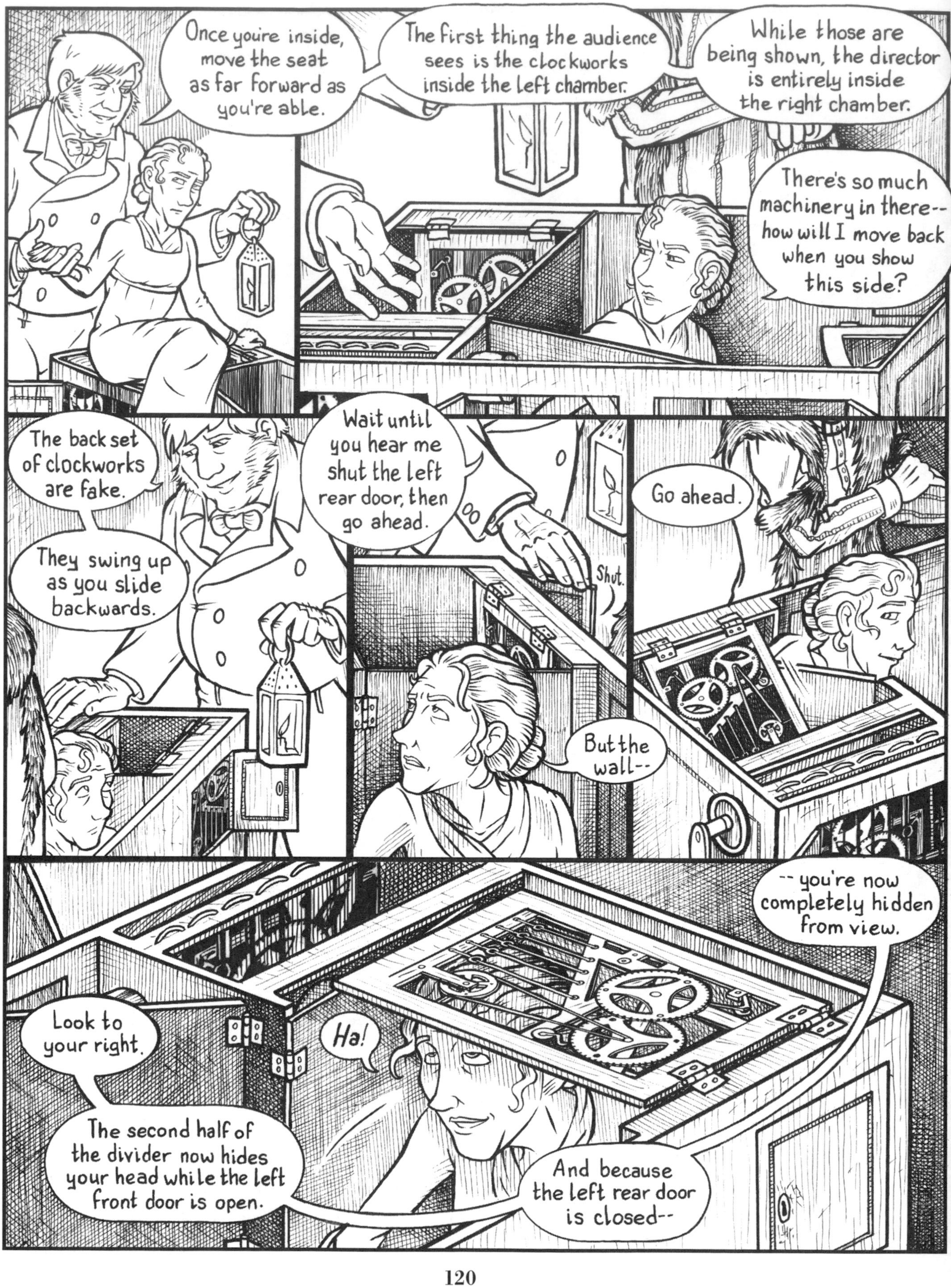
Once youre inside, move the seat as far forward as you're able.
The first thing the audience sees is the clockworks inside the left chamber.
While those are being shown, the director is entirely inside the right chamber.
There's so much machinery in there--how will I move back when you show this side?
The back set of clockworks are fake.
They swing up as you slide backwards.
Wait until you hear me shut the left rear door, then go ahead.
Shut.
But the wall--
Go ahead.
Look to your right.
Ha!
The second half of the divider now hides your head while the left front door is open.
And because the left rear door is closed--
-- you're now completely hidden from view.

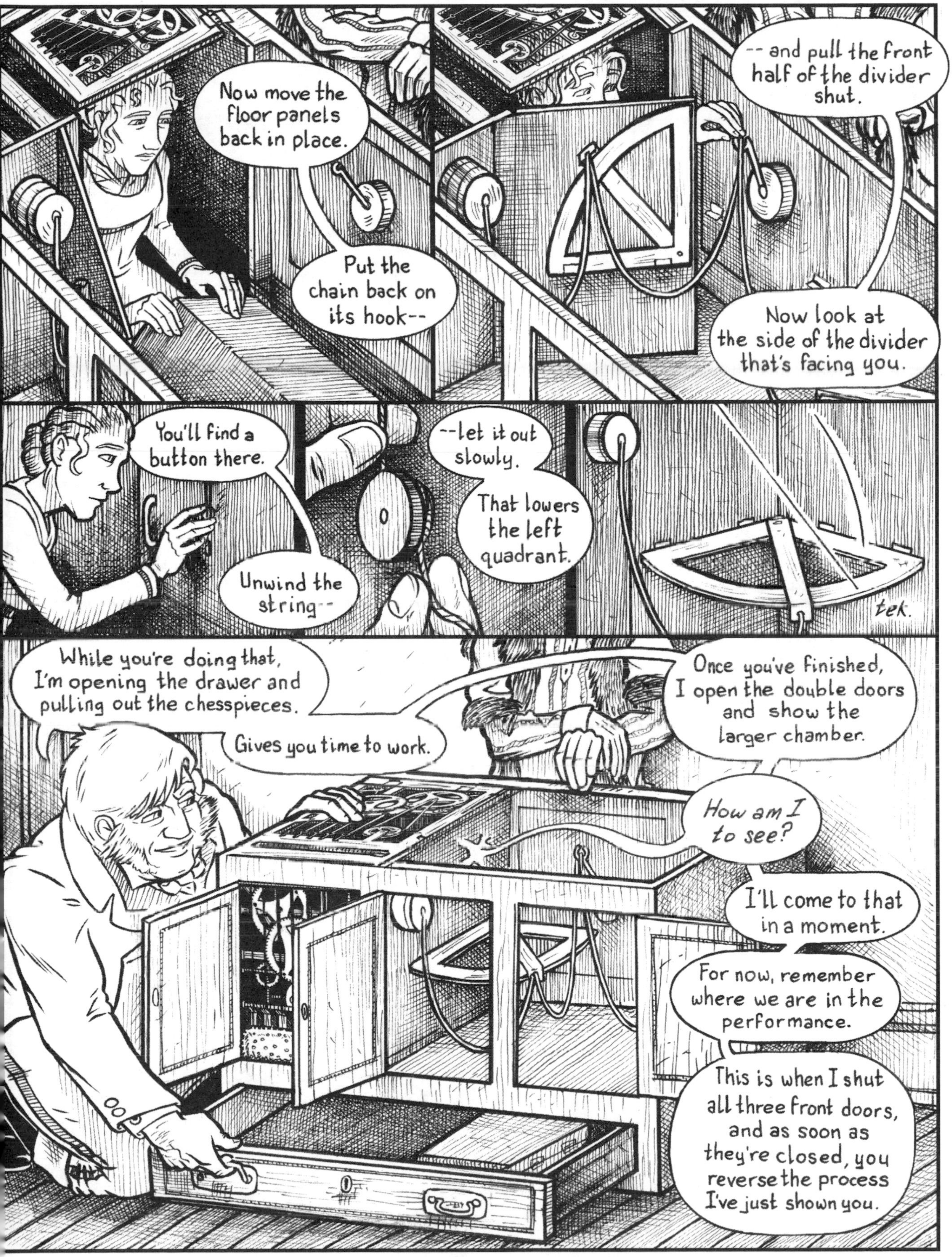
Now move the floor panels back in place.
Put the chain back on its hook--
-- and pull the front half of the divider shut.
Now look at the side of the divider that's facing you.
You'll find a button there.
Unwind the string--
--let it out slowly.
That lowers the left quadrant.
tek.
While you're doing that, I'm opening the drawer and pulling out the chesspieces.
Gives you time to work.
Once you've finished, I open the double doors and show the larger chamber.
How am I to see?
I'll come to that in a moment.
For now, remember where we are in the performance.
This is when I shut all three front doors, and as soon as they're closed, you reverse the process I've just shown you.

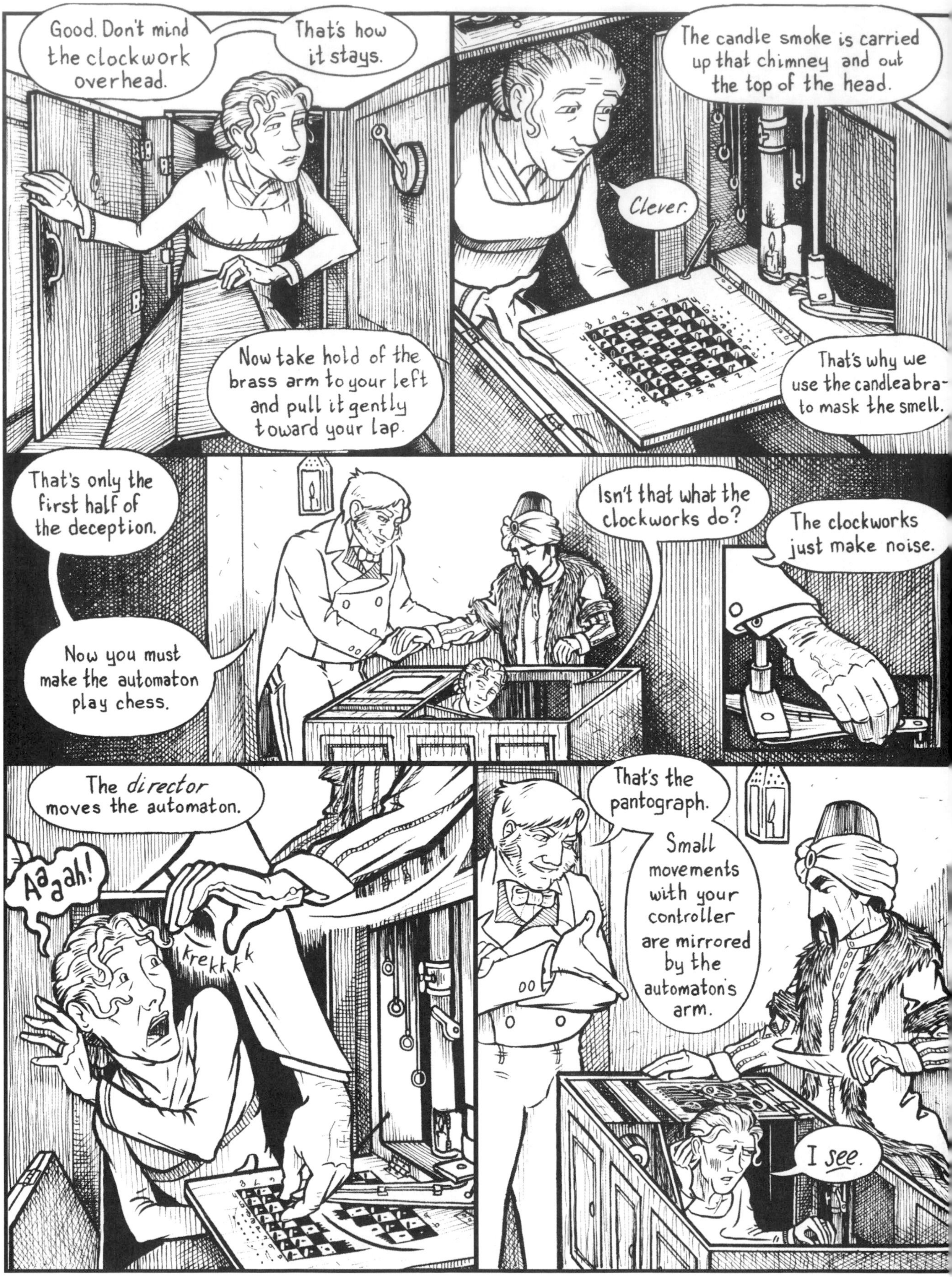
Good. Don't mind the clockwork overhead.
That's how it stays.
Now take hold of the brass arm to your left and pull it gently toward your lap.
The candle smoke is carried up that chimney and out the top of the head.
Clever.
That's why we use the candleabra to mask the smell.
That's only the first half of the deception.
Now you must make the automaton play chess.
Isn't that what the clockworks do?
The clockworks just make noise.
The *director* moves the automaton.
Aaaah!
krekkkk
That's the pantograph.
Small movements with your controller are mirrored by the automaton's arm.
I *see*.

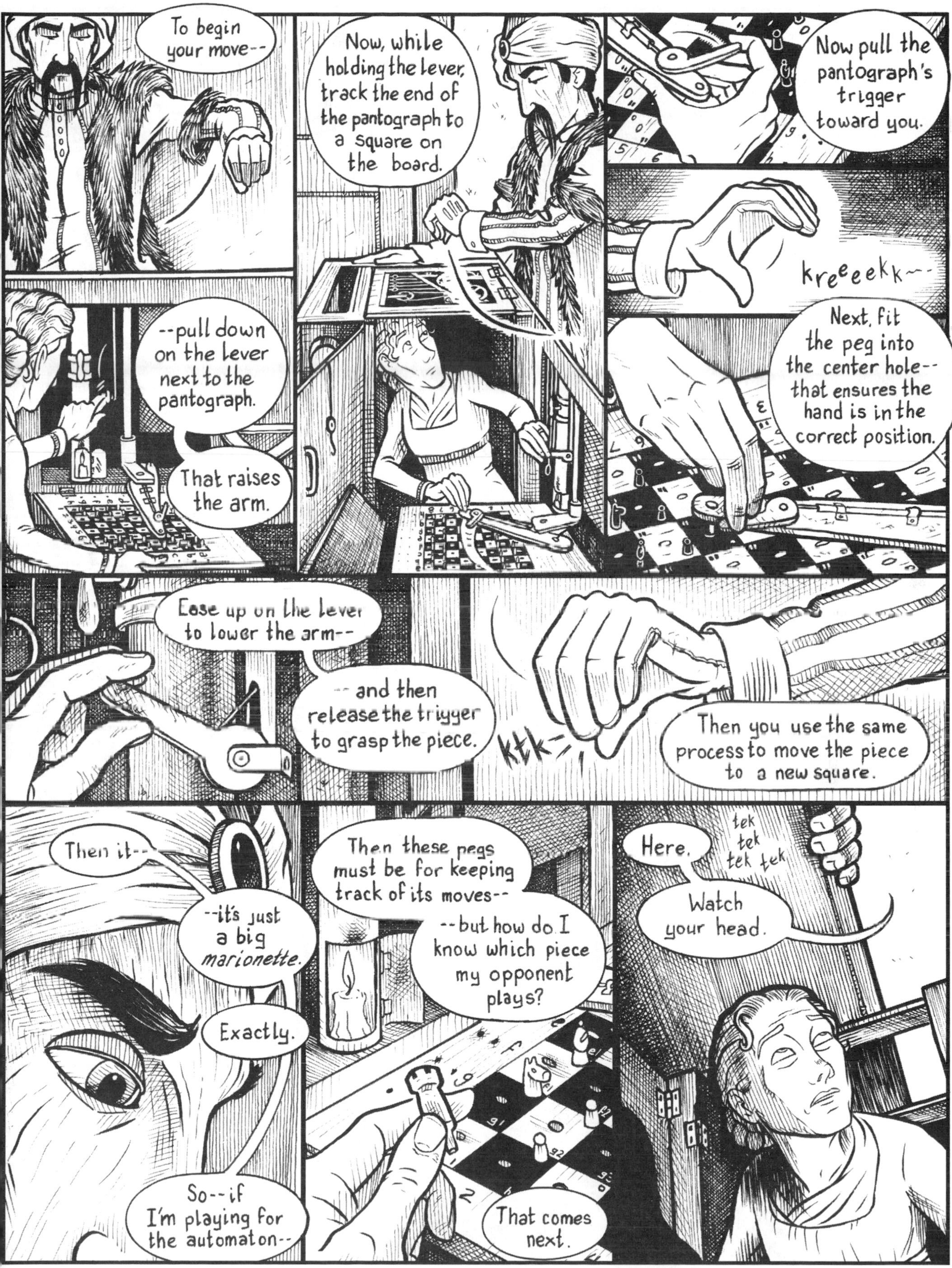

To begin your move--
Now, while holding the lever, track the end of the pantograph to a square on the board.
Now pull the pantograph's trigger toward you.
kreeeekk--
--pull down on the lever next to the pantograph.
That raises the arm.
Next, fit the peg into the center hole--that ensures the hand is in the correct position.
Ease up on the lever to lower the arm--
--and then release the trigger to grasp the piece.
ktk--
Then you use the same process to move the piece to a new square.
Then it--
--it's just a big *marionette*.
Exactly.
So--if I'm playing for the automaton--
Then these pegs must be for keeping track of its moves--
--but how do I know which piece my opponent plays?
That comes next.
Here.
tek tek tek tek
Watch your head.

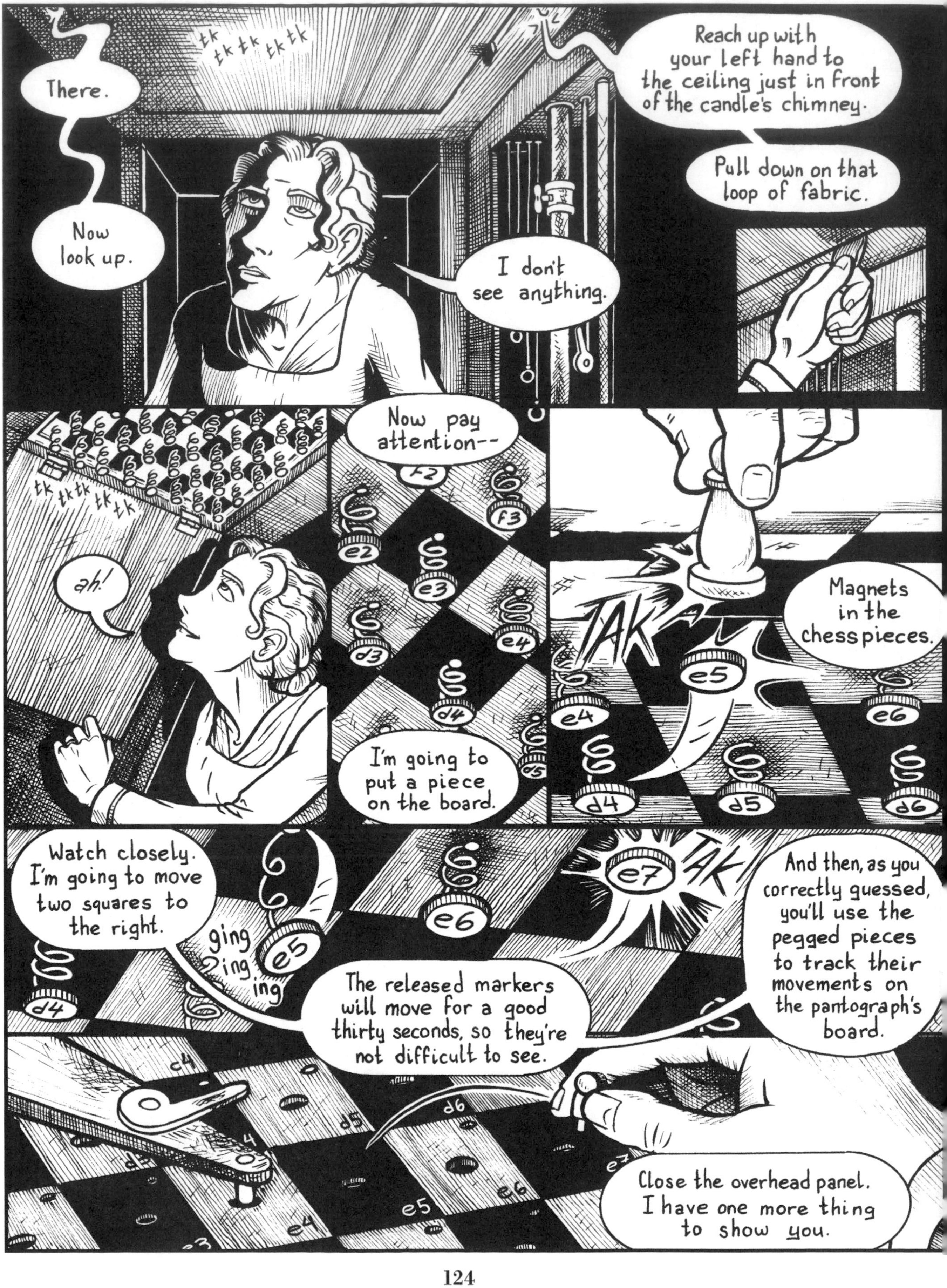

tk tk tk tk tk
There.
Now look up.
I don't see anything.
Reach up with your left hand to the ceiling just in front of the candle's chimney.
Pull down on that loop of fabric.
tk tk tk tk tk
ah!
Now pay attention--
f2
f3
e2
e3
e4
d3
d4
d5
I'm going to put a piece on the board.
TAK
Magnets in the chesspieces.
e5
e4
e6
d4
d5
d6
Watch closely. I'm going to move two squares to the right.
ging ing ing
e5
e6
e7
TAK
d4
And then, as you correctly guessed, you'll use the pegged pieces to track their movements on the pantograph's board.
The released markers will move for a good thirty seconds, so they're not difficult to see.
c4
d5
d6
e4
e5
e6
e7
Close the overhead panel. I have one more thing to show you.

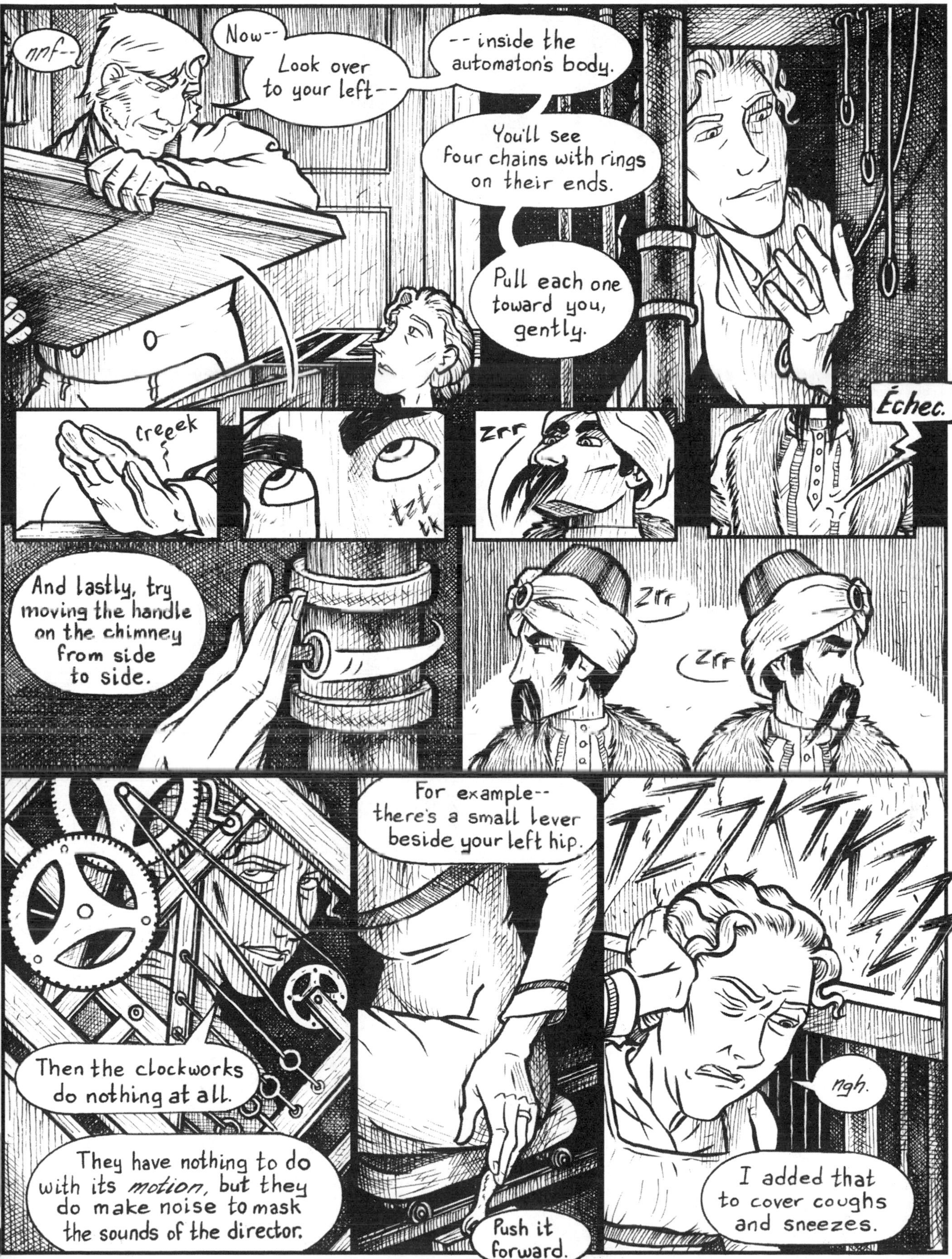
nnf--
Now-- Look over to your left--
--inside the automaton's body.
You'll see four chains with rings on their ends.
Pull each one toward you, gently.
creeek
tzt tk
Zrr
Échec.
And lastly, try moving the handle on the chimney from side to side.
Zrr
Zrr
Then the clockworks do nothing at all.
They have nothing to do with its *motion*, but they do make noise to mask the sounds of the director.
For example-- there's a small lever beside your left hip.
Push it forward.
TZZKTKZZ
ngh.
I added that to cover coughs and sneezes.

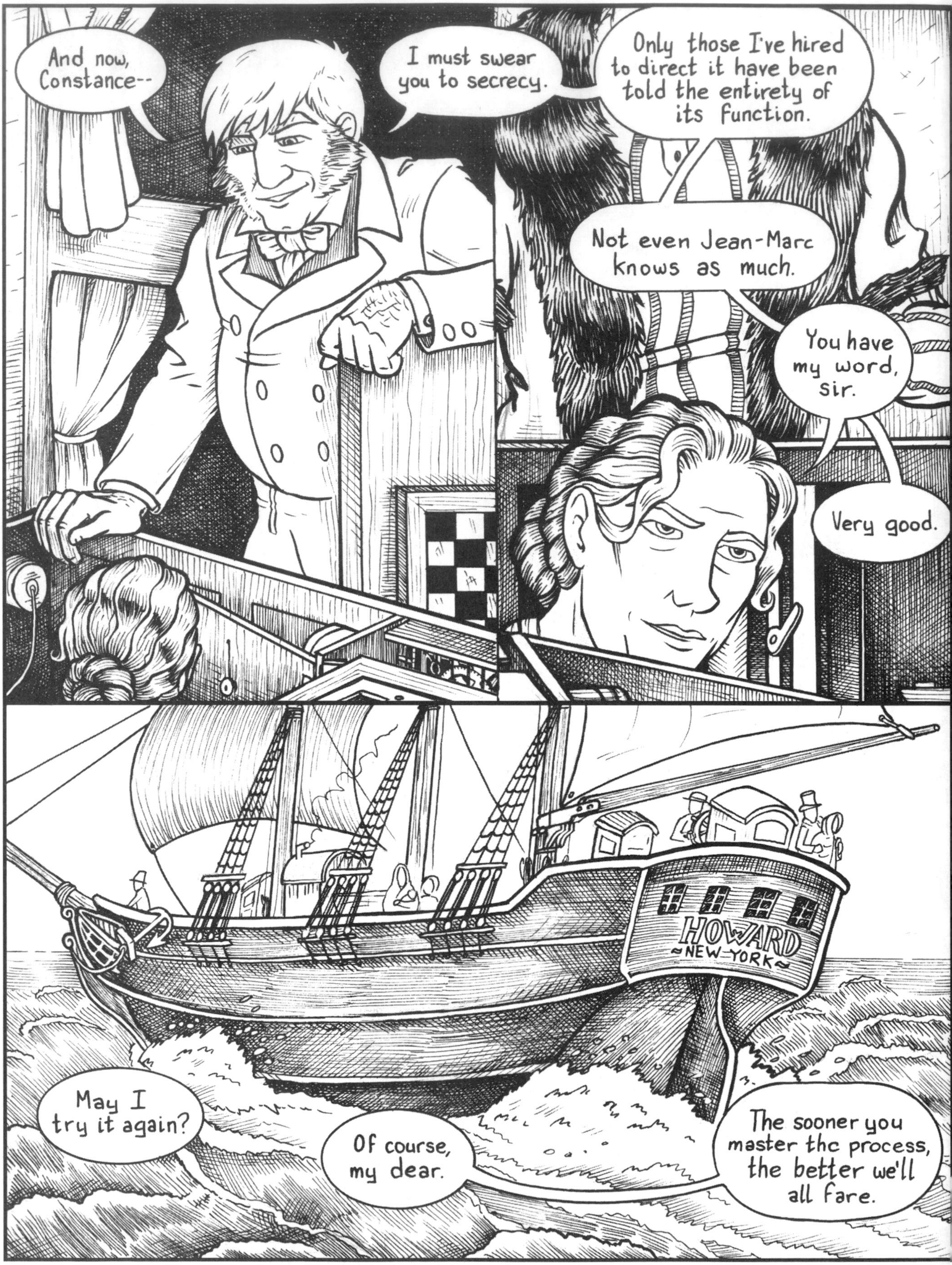
And now, Constance--
I must swear you to secrecy.
Only those I've hired to direct it have been told the entirety of its function.
Not even Jean-Marc knows as much.
You have my word, sir.
Very good.
HOWARD
NEW-YORK
May I try it again?
Of course, my dear.
The sooner you master thc process, the better we'll all fare.

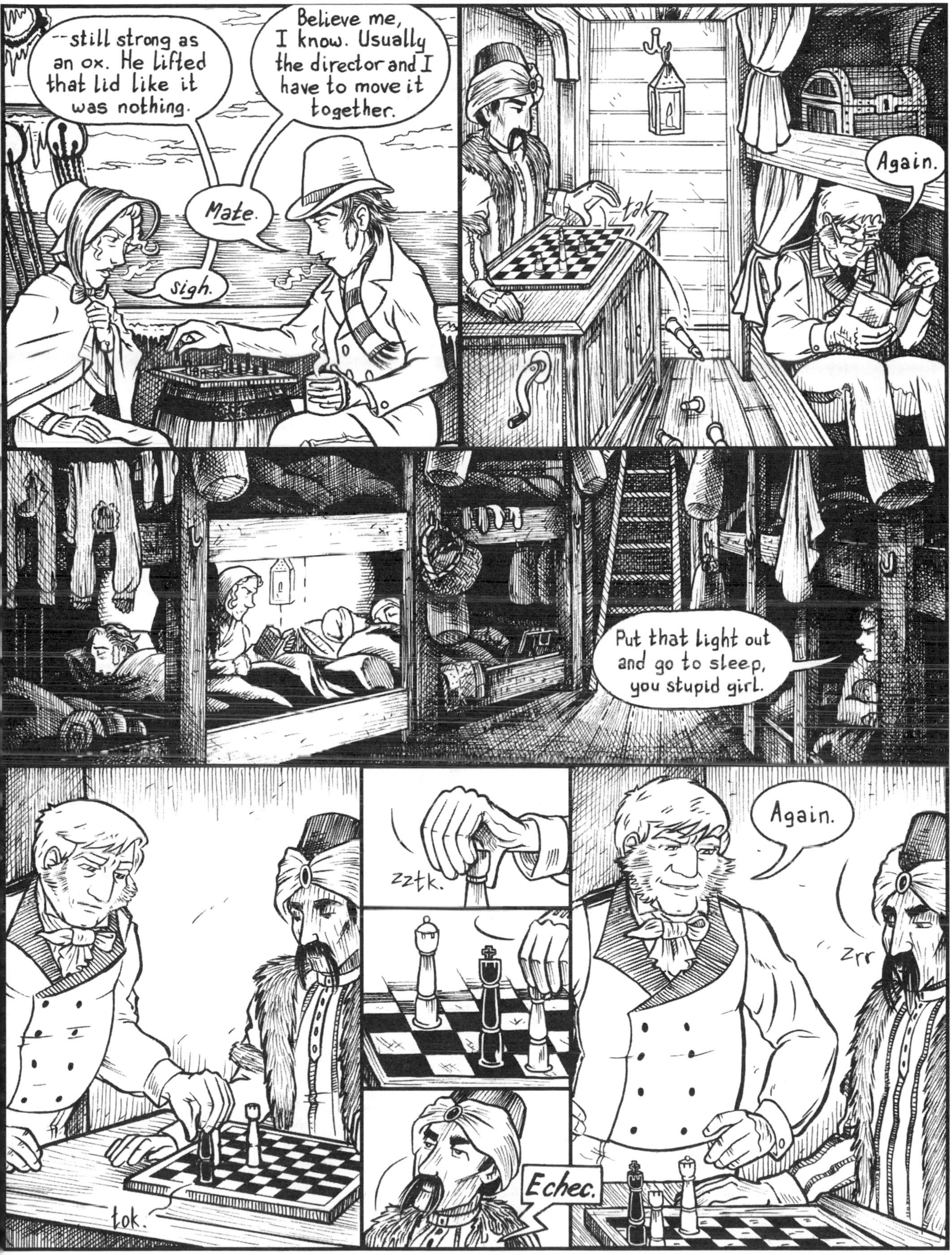
--still strong as an ox. He lifted that lid like it was nothing.
Believe me, I know. Usually the director and I have to move it together.
Mate.
sigh.
tak
Again.
Put that light out and go to sleep, you stupid girl.
tok.
zztk.
Echec.
Again.
zrr

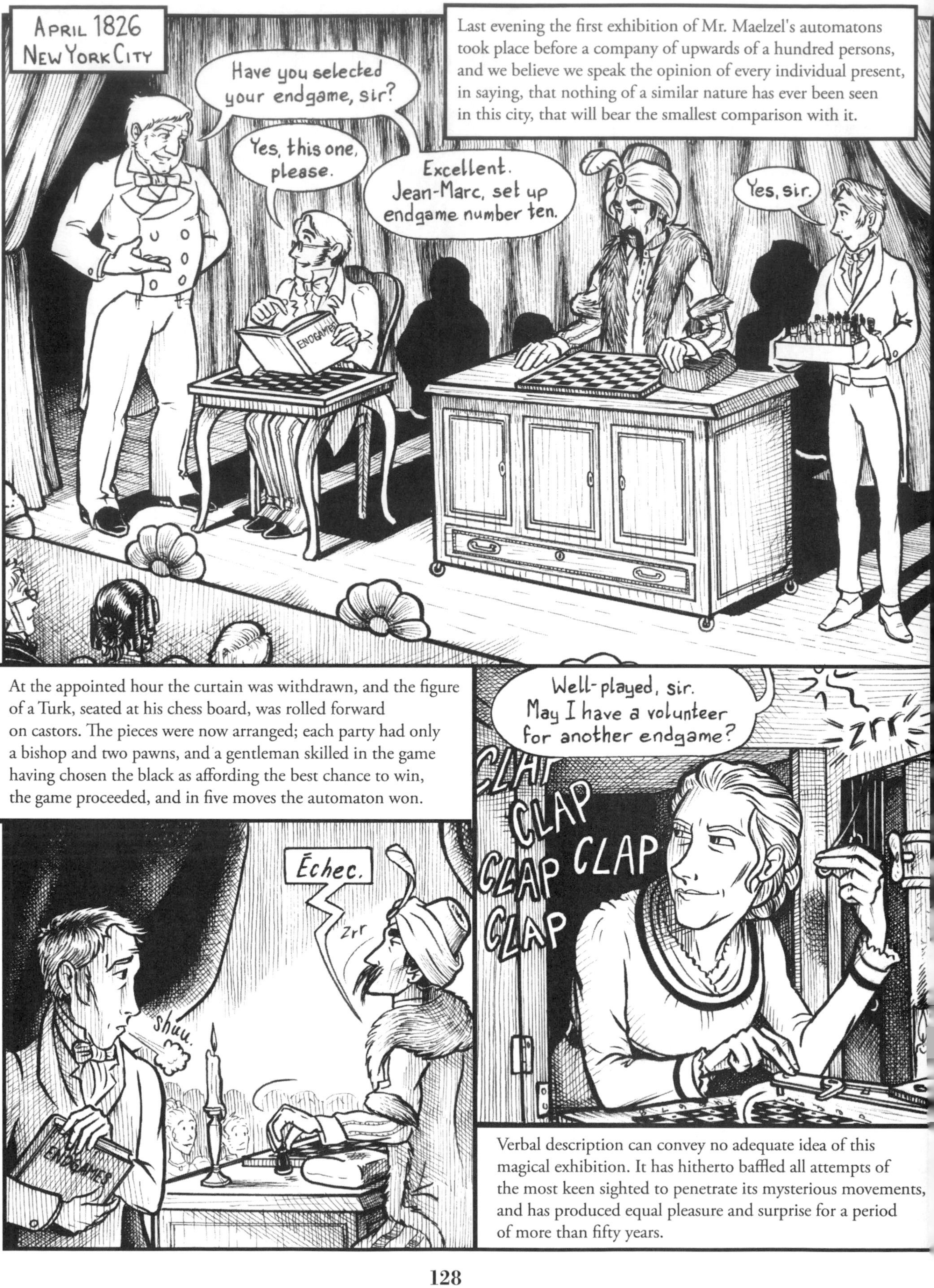
April 1826
New York City
Last evening the first exhibition of Mr. Maelzel's automatons took place before a company of upwards of a hundred persons, and we believe we speak the opinion of every individual present, in saying, that nothing of a similar nature has ever been seen in this city, that will bear the smallest comparison with it.
Have you selected your endgame, sir?
Yes, this one, please.
Excellent. Jean-Marc, set up endgame number ten.
Yes, sir.
ENDGAMES
At the appointed hour the curtain was withdrawn, and the figure of a Turk, seated at his chess board, was rolled forward on castors. The pieces were now arranged; each party had only a bishop and two pawns, and a gentleman skilled in the game having chosen the black as affording the best chance to win, the game proceeded, and in five moves the automaton won.
Échec.
zrr
shuu.
ENDGAMES
Well-played, sir. May I have a volunteer for another endgame?
zrr
CLAP
CLAP
CLAP
CLAP
CLAP
Verbal description can convey no adequate idea of this magical exhibition. It has hitherto baffled all attempts of the most keen sighted to penetrate its mysterious movements, and has produced equal pleasure and surprise for a period of more than fifty years.

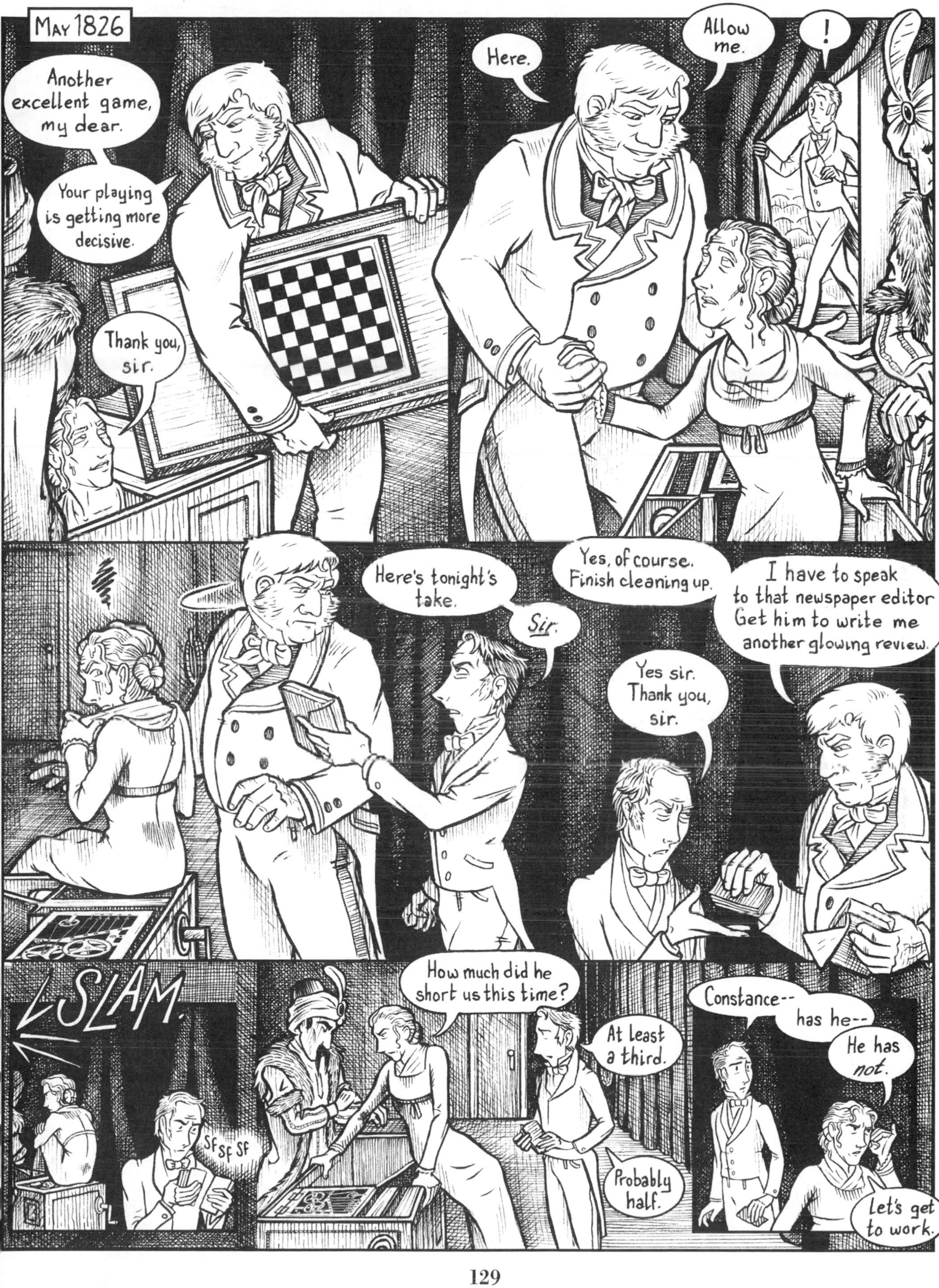
May 1826
Another excellent game, my dear.
Your playing is getting more decisive.
Thank you, sir.
Here.
Allow me.
!
Here's tonight's take.
Sir.
Yes, of course. Finish cleaning up.
I have to speak to that newspaper editor Get him to write me another glowing review.
Yes sir. Thank you, sir.
SLAM.
Sf sf sf
How much did he short us this time?
At least a third.
Probably half.
Constance--
has he--
He has not.
Let's get to work.

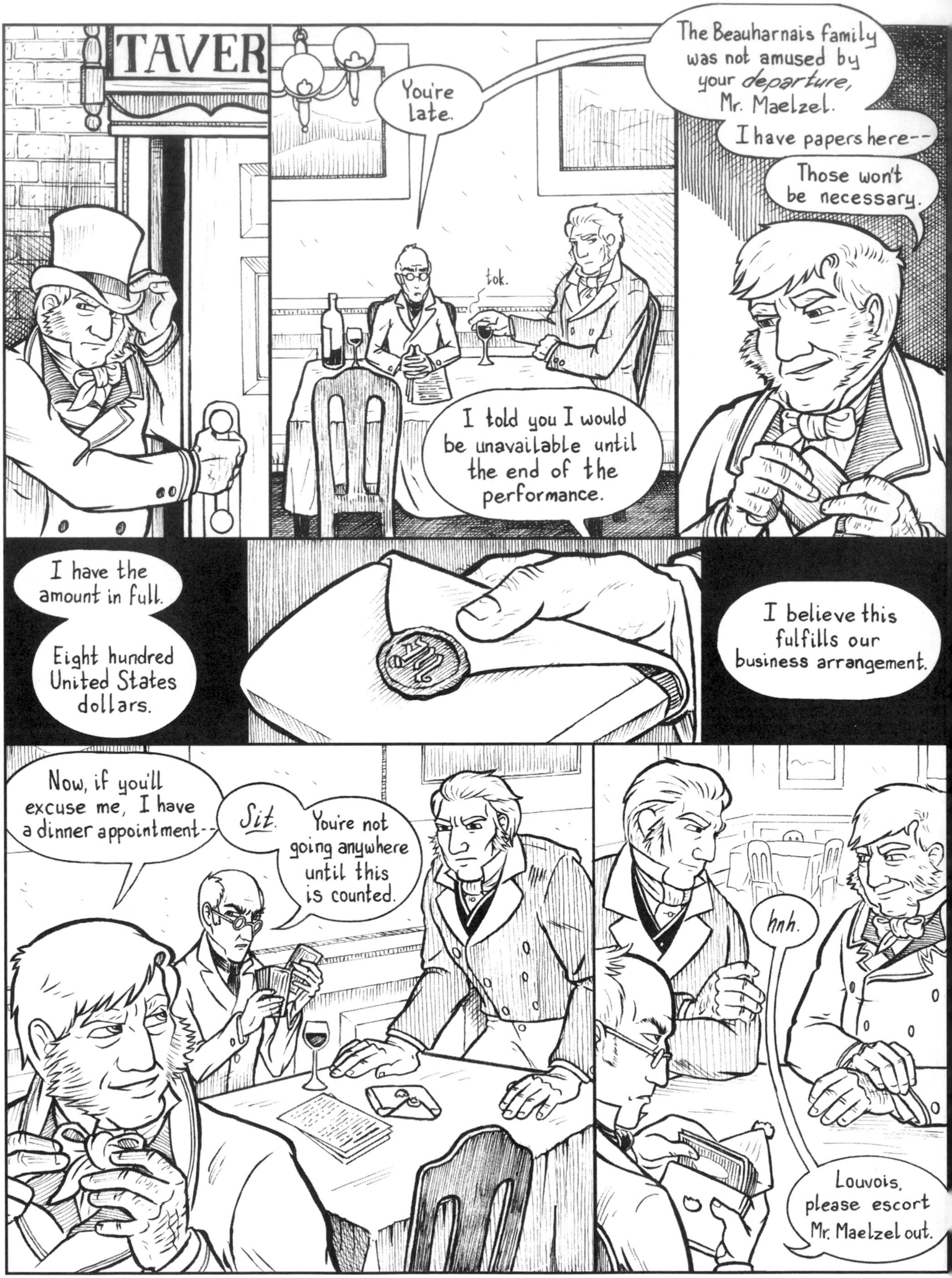
TAVER
You're late.
The Beauharnais family was not amused by your *departure,* Mr. Maelzel.
I have papers here--
Those won't be necessary.
tok.
I told you I would be unavailable until the end of the performance.
I have the amount in full.
Eight hundred United States dollars.
I believe this fulfills our business arrangement.
Now, if you'll excuse me, I have a dinner appointment--
Sit.
You're not going anywhere until this is counted.
hnh.
Louvois, please escort Mr. Maelzel out.

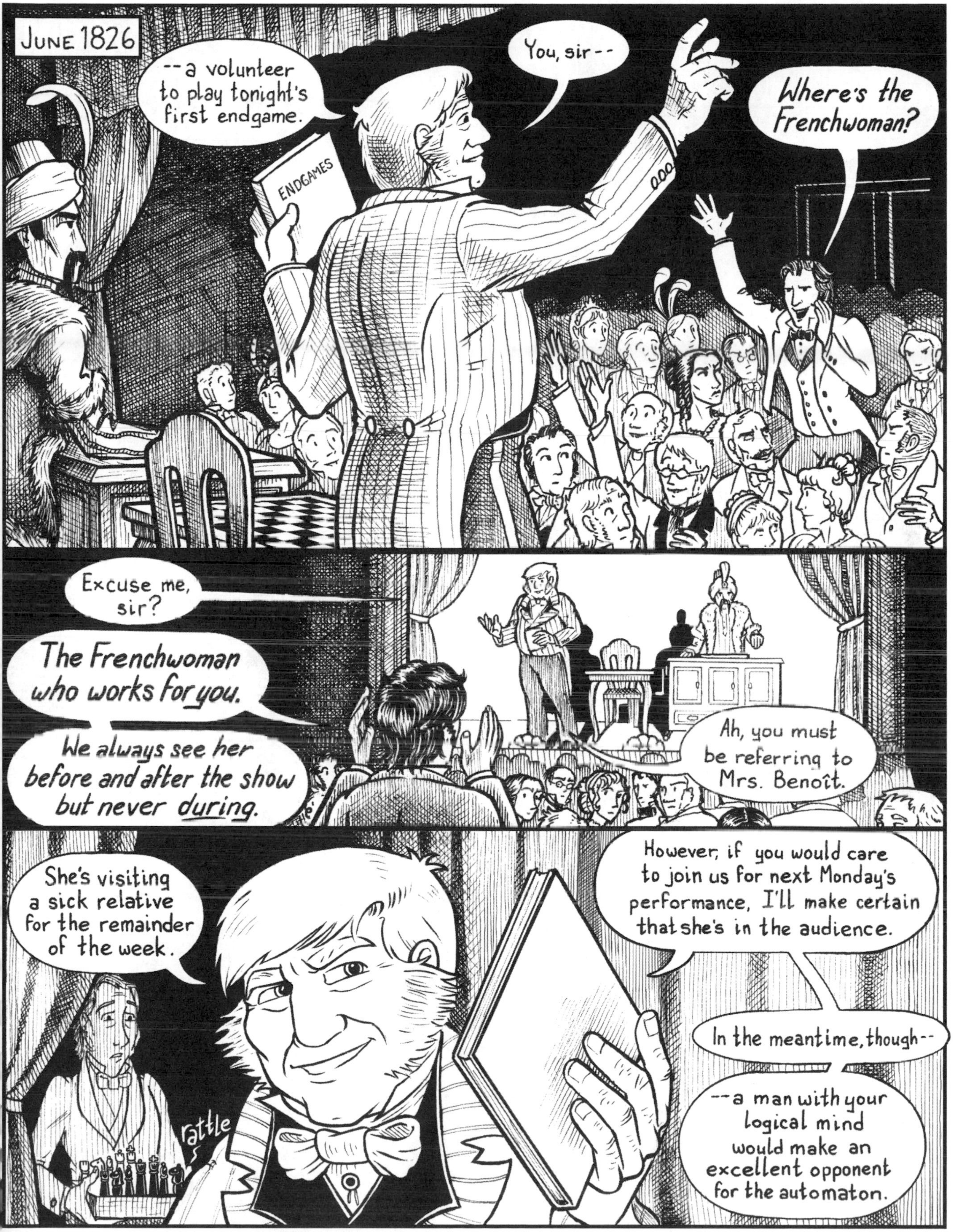
June 1826
--a volunteer to play tonight's first endgame.
You, sir--
Where's the Frenchwoman?
ENDGAMES
Excuse me, sir?
The Frenchwoman who works for you.
We always see her before and after the show but never during.
Ah, you must be referring to Mrs. Benoît.
She's visiting a sick relative for the remainder of the week.
However, if you would care to join us for next Monday's performance, I'll make certain that she's in the audience.
In the meantime, though--
--a man with your logical mind would make an excellent opponent for the automaton.
rattle

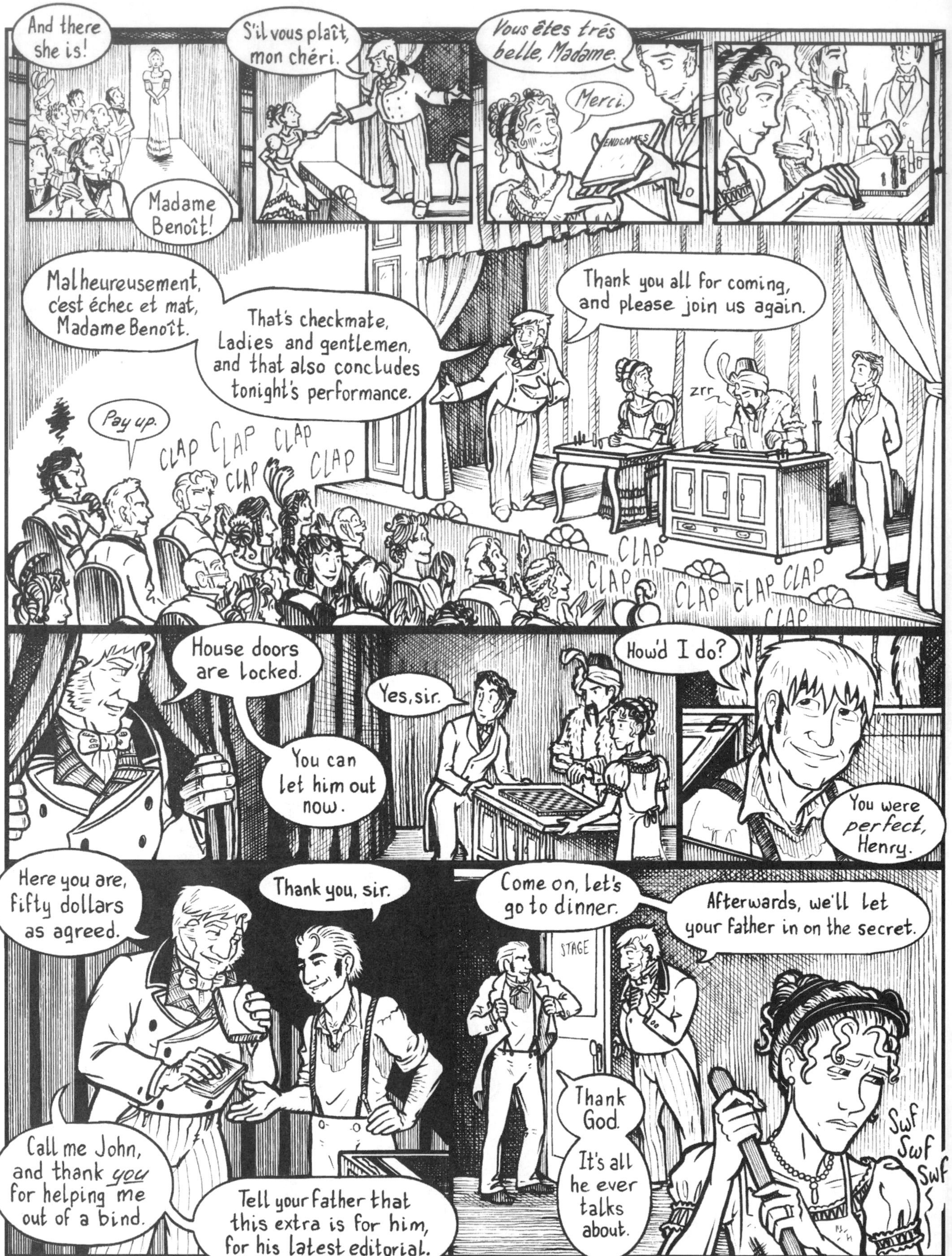

And there she is!
Madame Benoît!
S'il vous plaît, mon chéri.
Vous êtes trés belle, Madame.
Merci.
ENDGAMES
Malheureusement, c'est échec et mat, Madame Benoît.
That's checkmate, ladies and gentlemen, and that also concludes tonight's performance.
Thank you all for coming, and please join us again.
Pay up.
zrr
CLAP CLAP CLAP CLAP CLAP
CLAP CLAP CLAP CLAP CLAP
House doors are locked.
You can let him out now.
Yes, sir.
How'd I do?
You were *perfect*, Henry.
Here you are, fifty dollars as agreed.
Thank you, sir.
Call me John, and thank _you_ for helping me out of a bind.
Tell your father that this extra is for him, for his latest editorial.
Come on, let's go to dinner.
Afterwards, we'll let your father in on the secret.
STAGE
Thank God.
It's all he ever talks about.
Swf Swf Swf

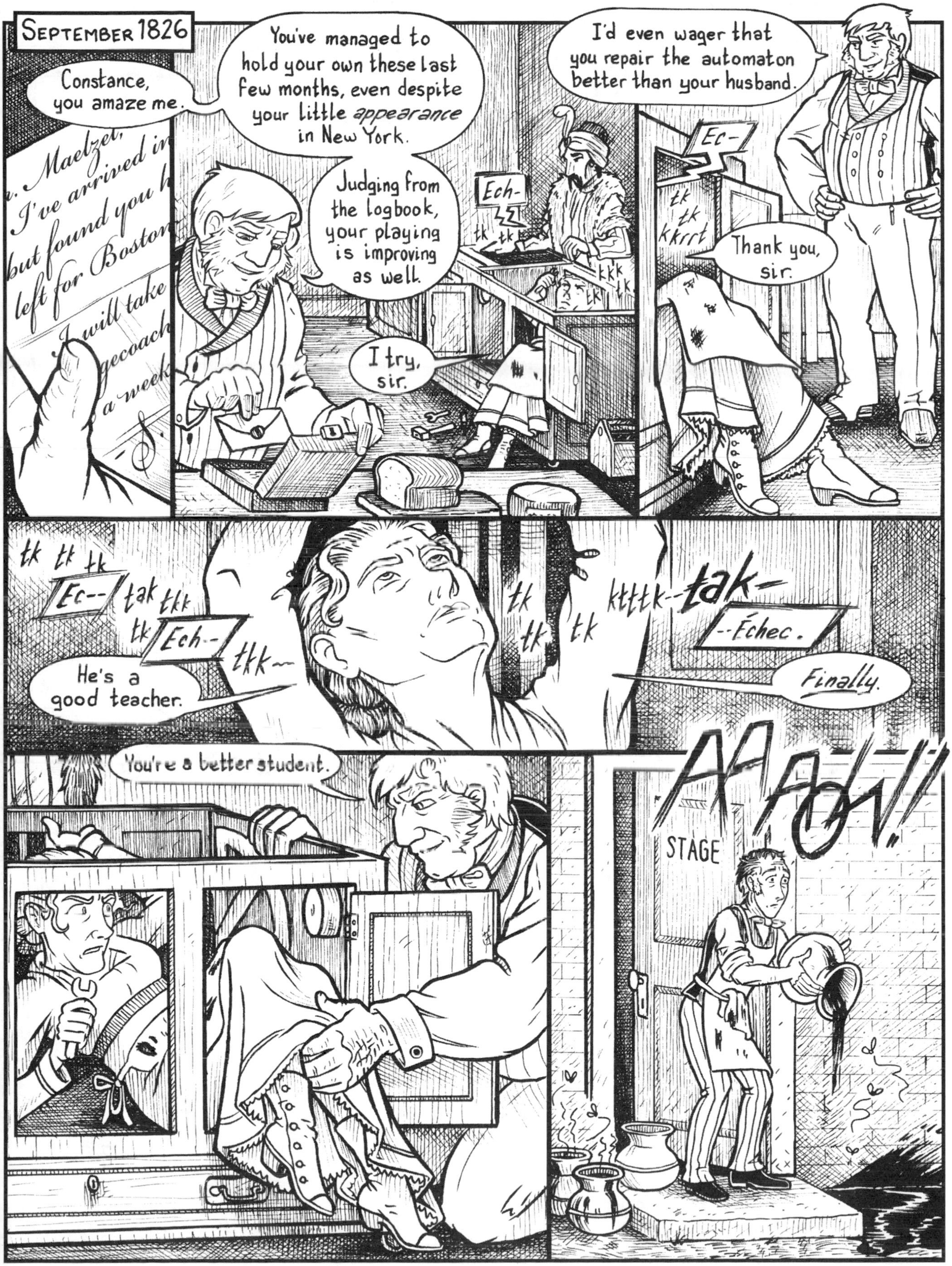
September 1826
Constance, you amaze me.
You've managed to hold your own these last few months, even despite your little *appearance* in New York.
Judging from the logbook, your playing is improving as well.
Ech-
tk tk
I try, sir.
I'd even wager that you repair the automaton better than your husband.
Ec-
tk tk kkrrt
Thank you, sir.
tk tk tk
Ec--
tak tkk tk
Ech--
tkk--
He's a good teacher.
tk tk tk kkttk--tak--
--Échec.
Finally.
You're a better student.
AAAOW!!
STAGE

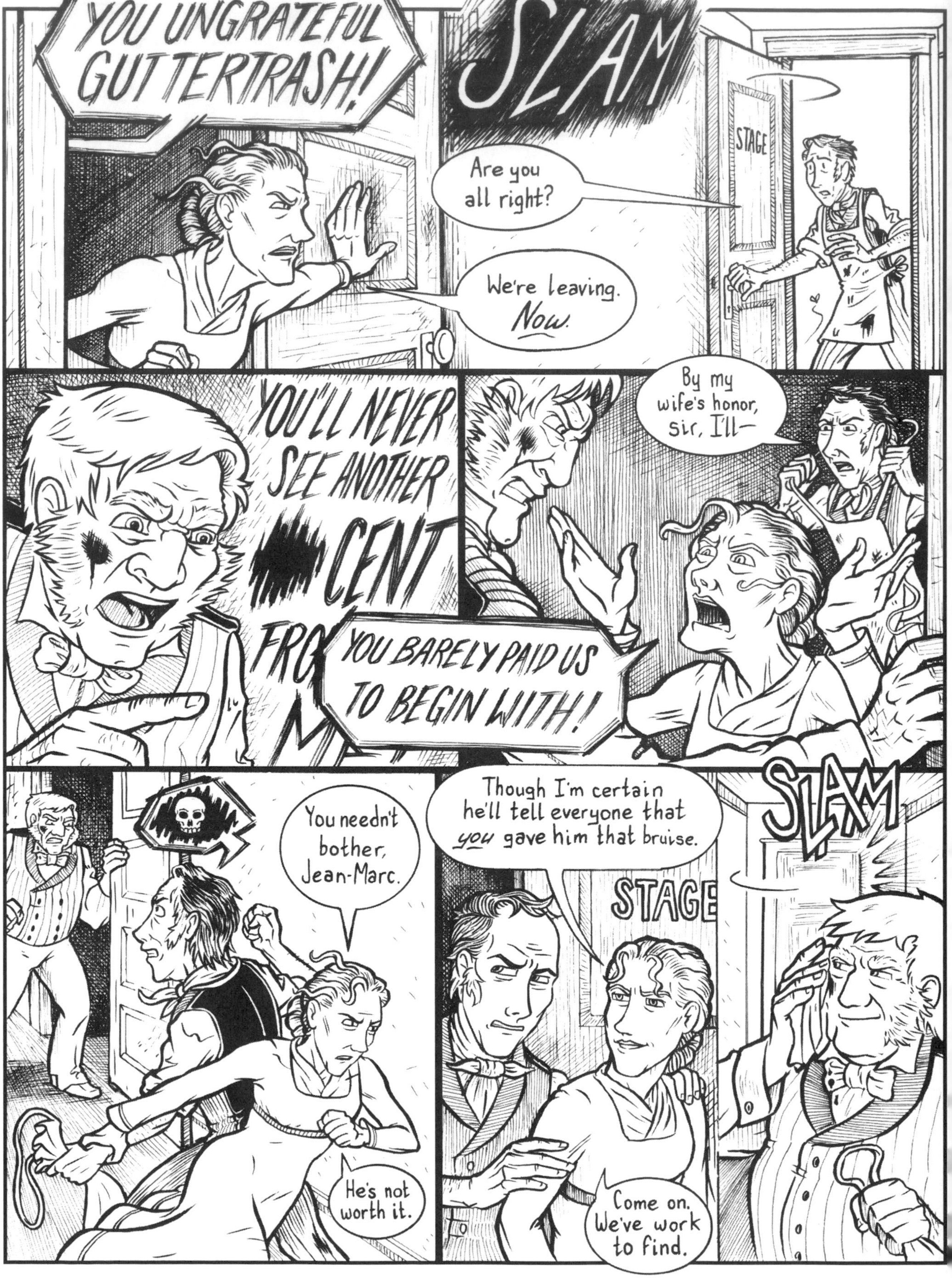
YOU UNGRATEFUL GUTTERTRASH!
SLAM
STAGE
Are you all right?
We're leaving. Now.
YOU'LL NEVER SEE ANOTHER CENT FRO M
By my wife's honor, sir, I'll—
YOU BARELY PAID US TO BEGIN WITH!
You needn't bother, Jean-Marc.
He's not worth it.
Though I'm certain he'll tell everyone that you gave him that bruise.
STAGE
SLAM
Come on. We've work to find.

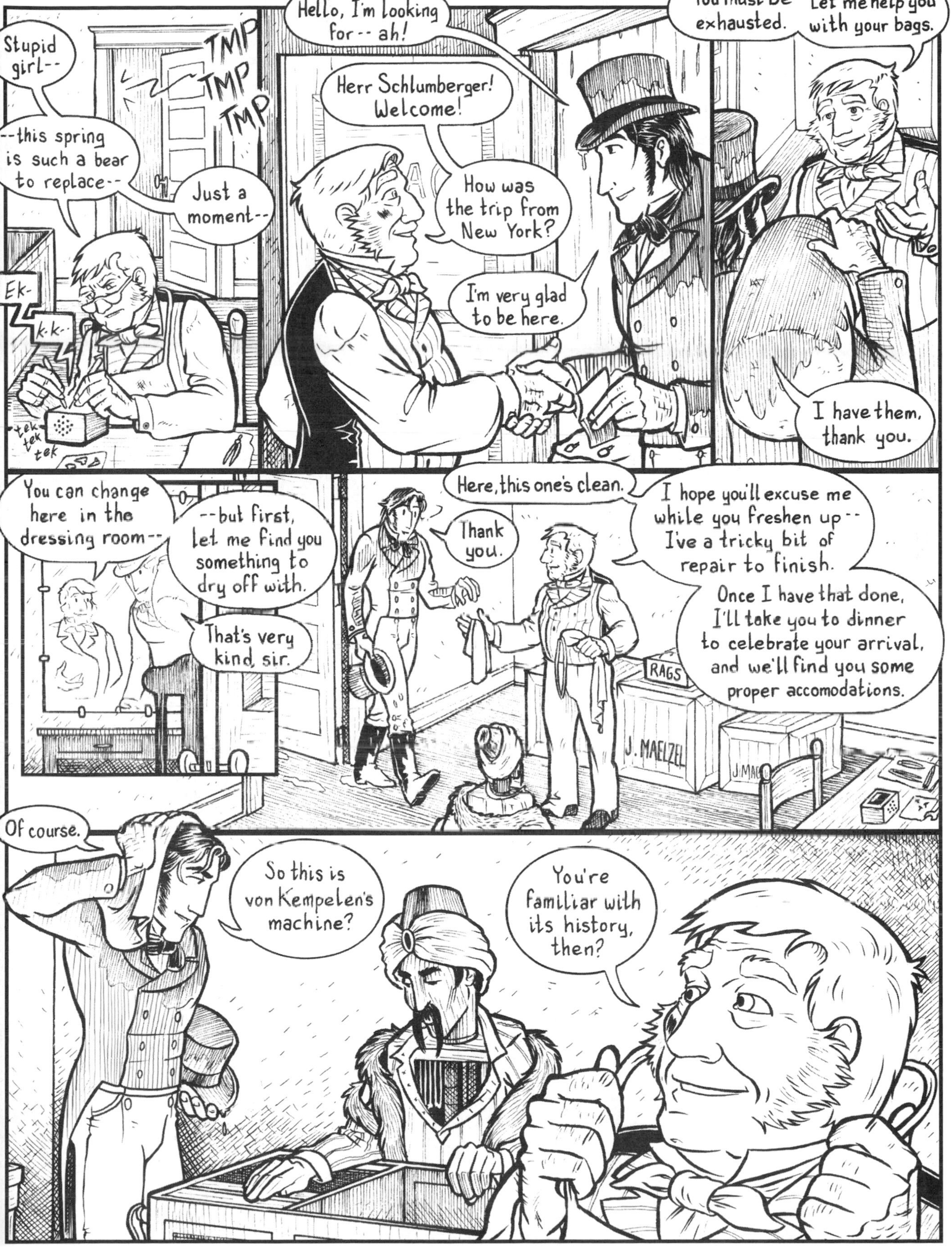
Stupid girl--
--this spring is such a bear to replace--
Just a moment--
TMP TMP TMP
Ek-
k-k-
tek tek tek
Hello, I'm looking for -- ah!
Herr Schlumberger! Welcome!
How was the trip from New York?
I'm very glad to be here.
You must be exhausted.
Let me help you with your bags.
I have them, thank you.
You can change here in the dressing room--
--but first, let me find you something to dry off with.
That's very kind, sir.
Here, this one's clean.
Thank you.
I hope you'll excuse me while you freshen up-- I've a tricky bit of repair to finish.
Once I have that done, I'll take you to dinner to celebrate your arrival, and we'll find you some proper accomodations.
RAGS
J. MAELZEL
Of course.
So this is von Kempelen's machine?
You're familiar with its history, then?

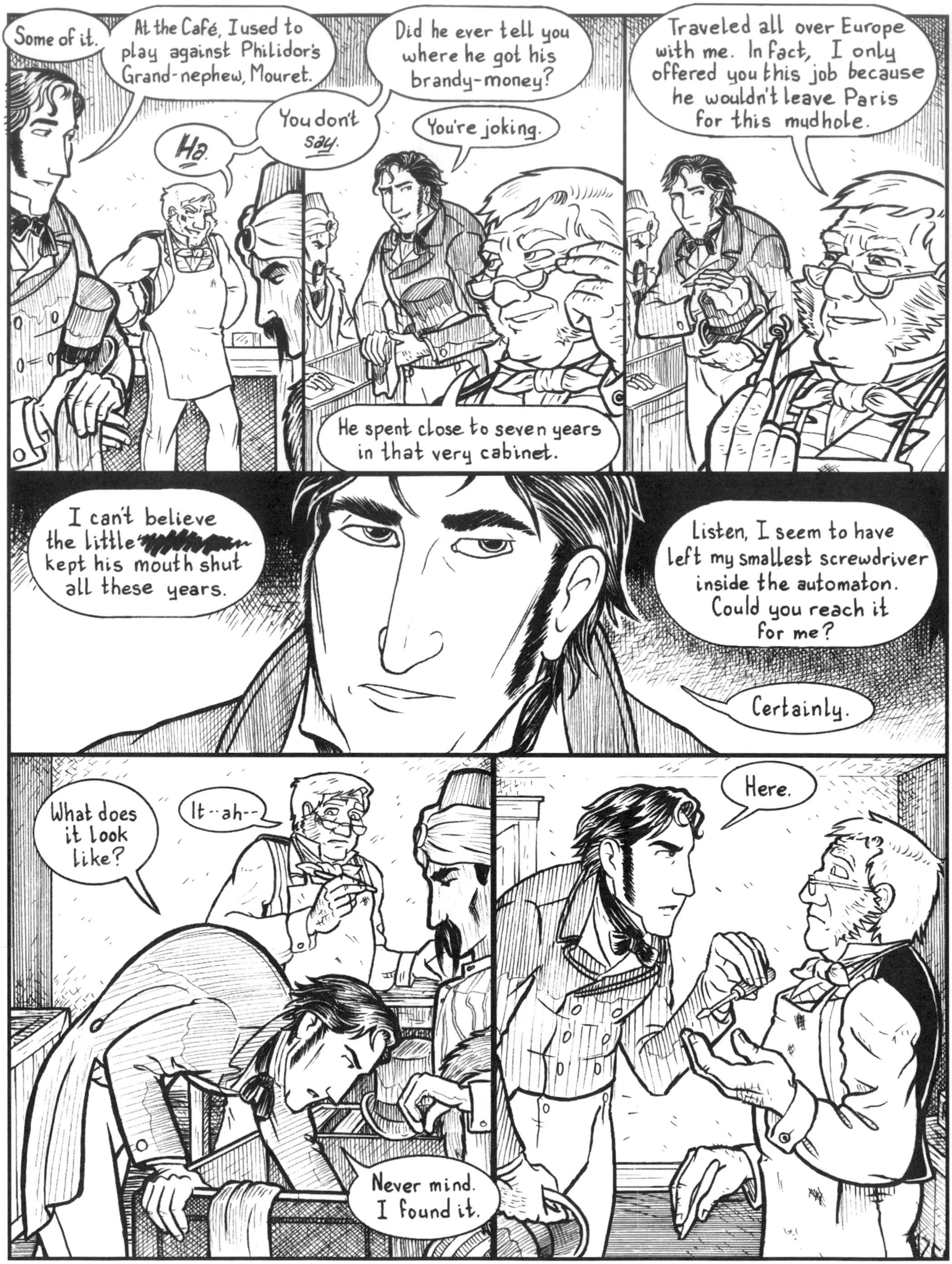
Some of it.
At the Café, I used to play against Philidor's Grand-nephew, Mouret.
Ha.
You don't say.
Did he ever tell you where he got his brandy-money?
You're joking.
He spent close to seven years in that very cabinet.
Traveled all over Europe with me. In fact, I only offered you this job because he wouldn't leave Paris for this mudhole.
I can't believe the little [redacted] kept his mouth shut all these years.
Listen, I seem to have left my smallest screwdriver inside the automaton. Could you reach it for me?
Certainly.
What does it look like?
It--ah--
Never mind. I found it.
Here.

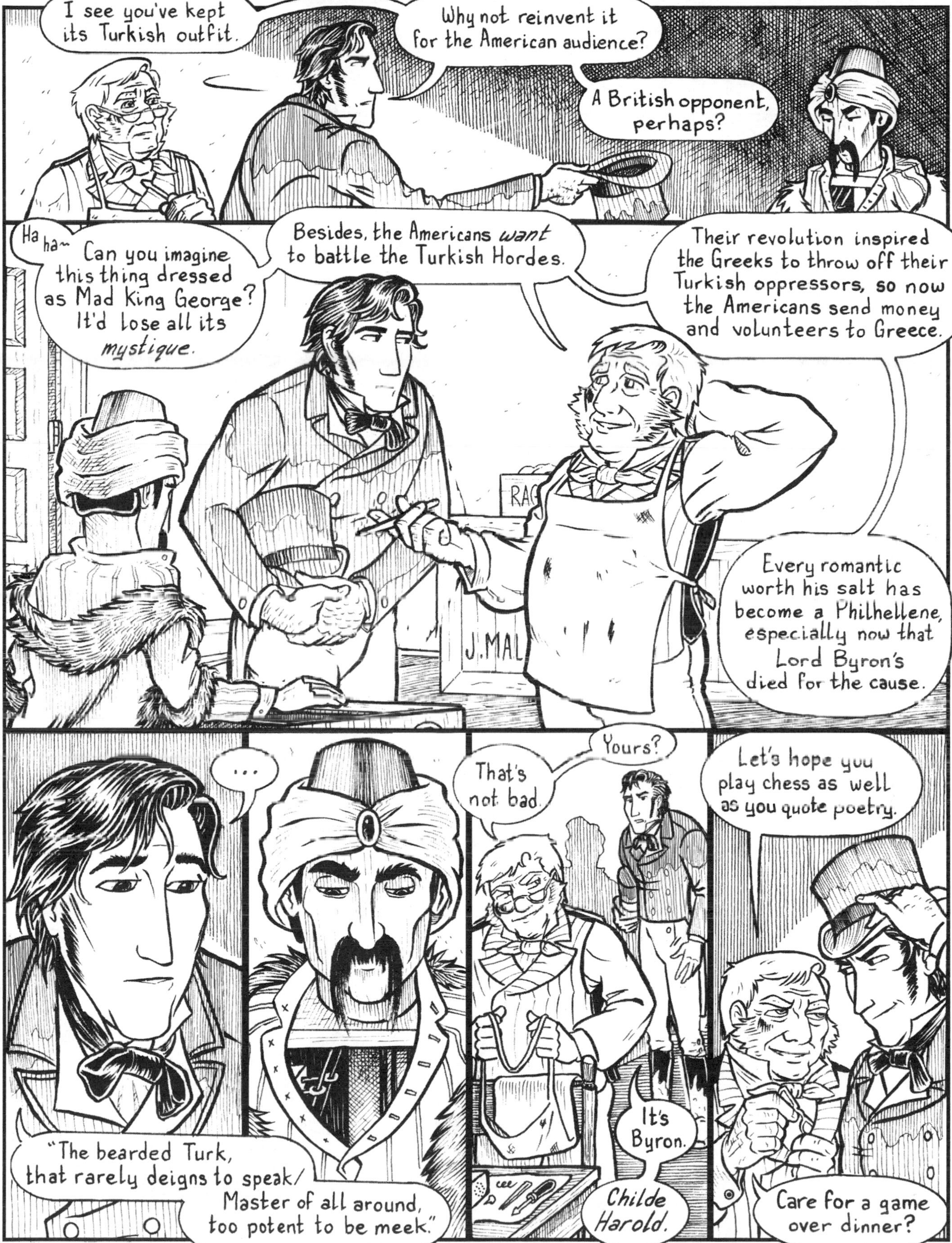
I see you've kept its Turkish outfit.
Why not reinvent it for the American audience?
A British opponent, perhaps?
Ha ha~ Can you imagine this thing dressed as Mad King George? It'd lose all its *mystique*.
Besides, the Americans *want* to battle the Turkish Hordes.
Their revolution inspired the Greeks to throw off their Turkish oppressors, so now the Americans send money and volunteers to Greece.
Every romantic worth his salt has become a Philhellene, especially now that Lord Byron's died for the cause.
RAG
J. MAL
...
"The bearded Turk, that rarely deigns to speak/ Master of all around, too potent to be meek."
That's not bad.
Yours?
It's Byron.
Childe Harold.
Let's hope you play chess as well as you quote poetry.
Care for a game over dinner?

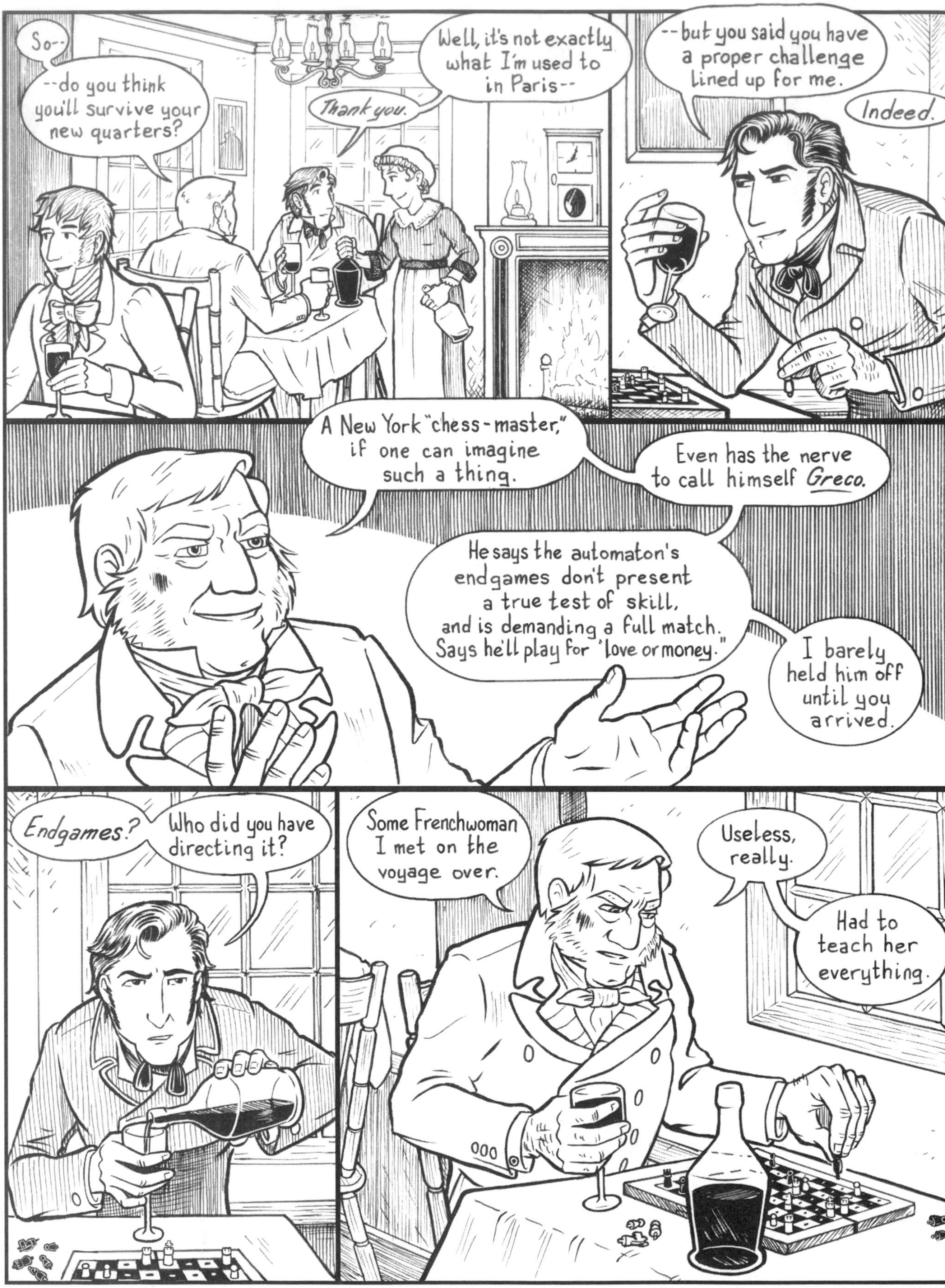
So--
--do you think you'll survive your new quarters?
Thank you.
Well, it's not exactly what I'm used to in Paris--
--but you said you have a proper challenge lined up for me.
Indeed.
A New York "chess-master," if one can imagine such a thing.
Even has the nerve to call himself Greco.
He says the automaton's endgames don't present a true test of skill, and is demanding a full match. Says he'll play for "love or money."
I barely held him off until you arrived.
Endgames?
Who did you have directing it?
Some Frenchwoman I met on the voyage over.
Useless, really.
Had to teach her everything.

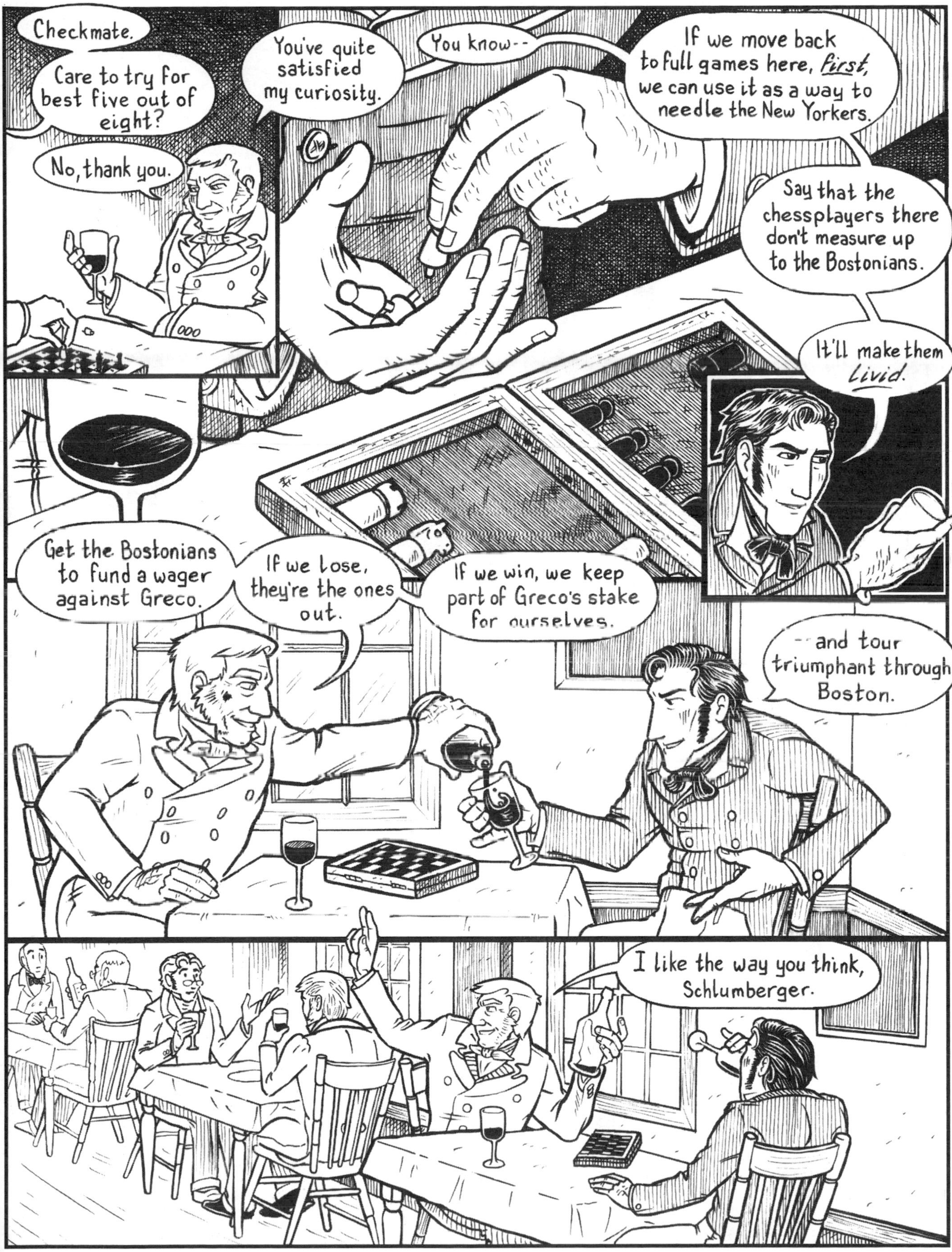
Checkmate.
Care to try for best five out of eight?
No, thank you.
You've quite satisfied my curiosity.
You know--
If we move back to full games here, *first*, we can use it as a way to needle the New Yorkers.
Say that the chessplayers there don't measure up to the Bostonians.
It'll make them *livid*.
Get the Bostonians to fund a wager against Greco.
If we lose, they're the ones out.
If we win, we keep part of Greco's stake for ourselves.
--and tour triumphant through Boston.
I like the way you think, Schlumberger.

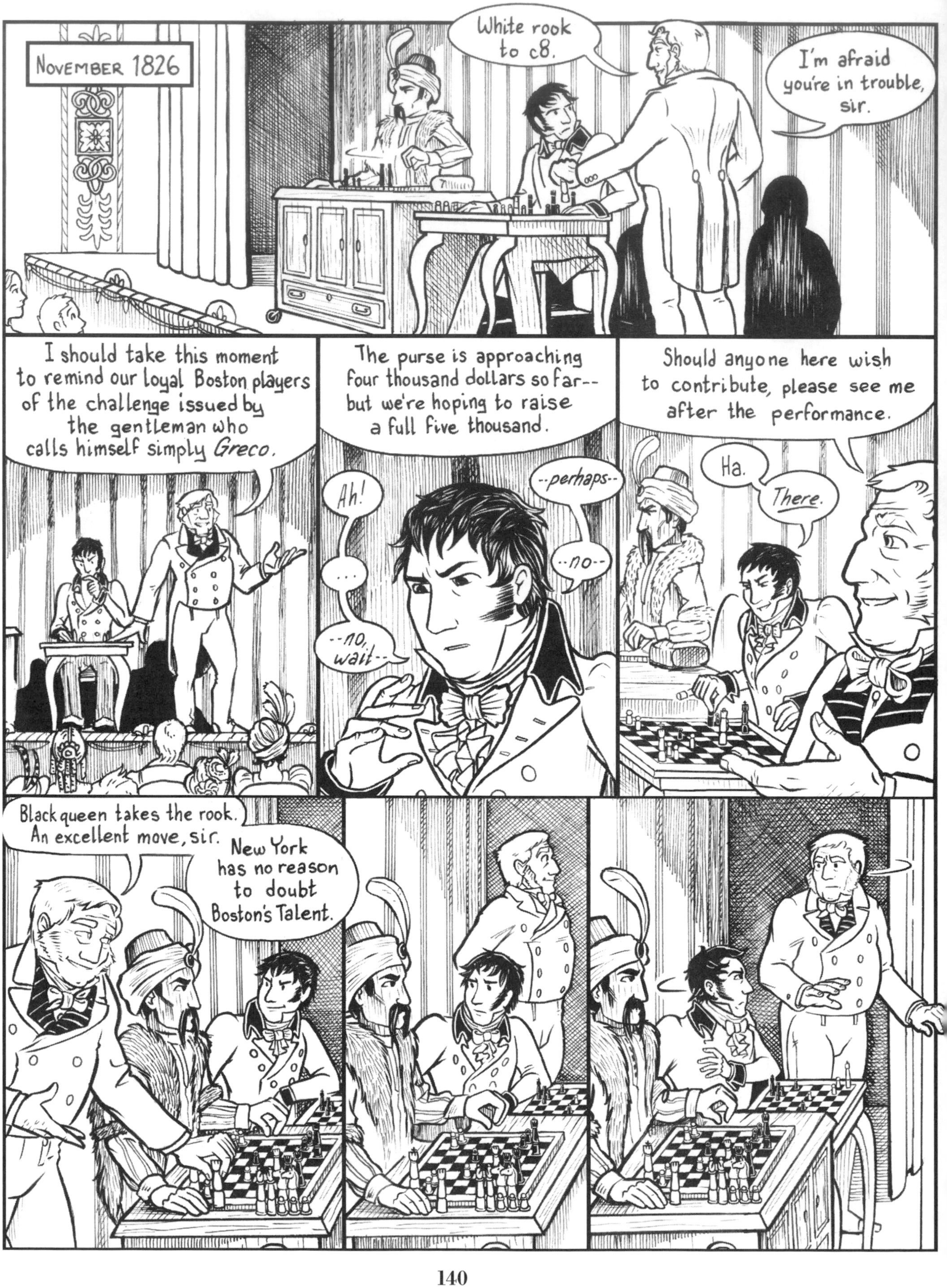
November 1826
White rook to c8.
I'm afraid you're in trouble, sir.
I should take this moment to remind our loyal Boston players of the challenge issued by the gentleman who calls himself simply *Greco*.
The purse is approaching four thousand dollars so far-- but we're hoping to raise a full five thousand.
Ah!
...
--no, wait--
--perhaps--
--no--
Should anyone here wish to contribute, please see me after the performance.
Ha.
There.
Black queen takes the rook. An excellent move, sir.
New York has no reason to doubt Boston's Talent.

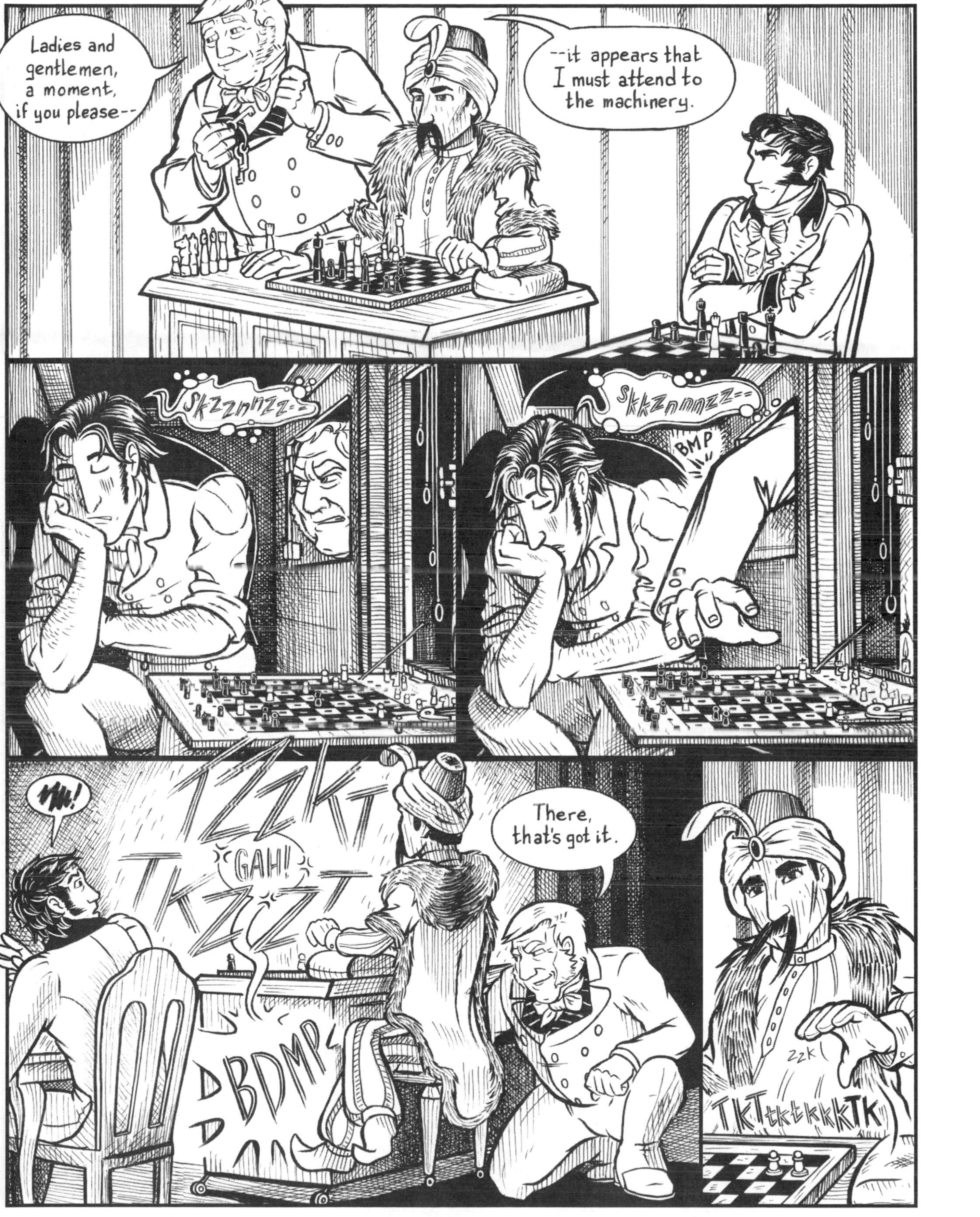
Ladies and gentlemen, a moment, if you please--
--it appears that I must attend to the machinery.
Skzznnnzz--
Skkznnnnzz--
BMP
GAH!
There, that's got it.
DBDMP
TKTtktkkkkTK

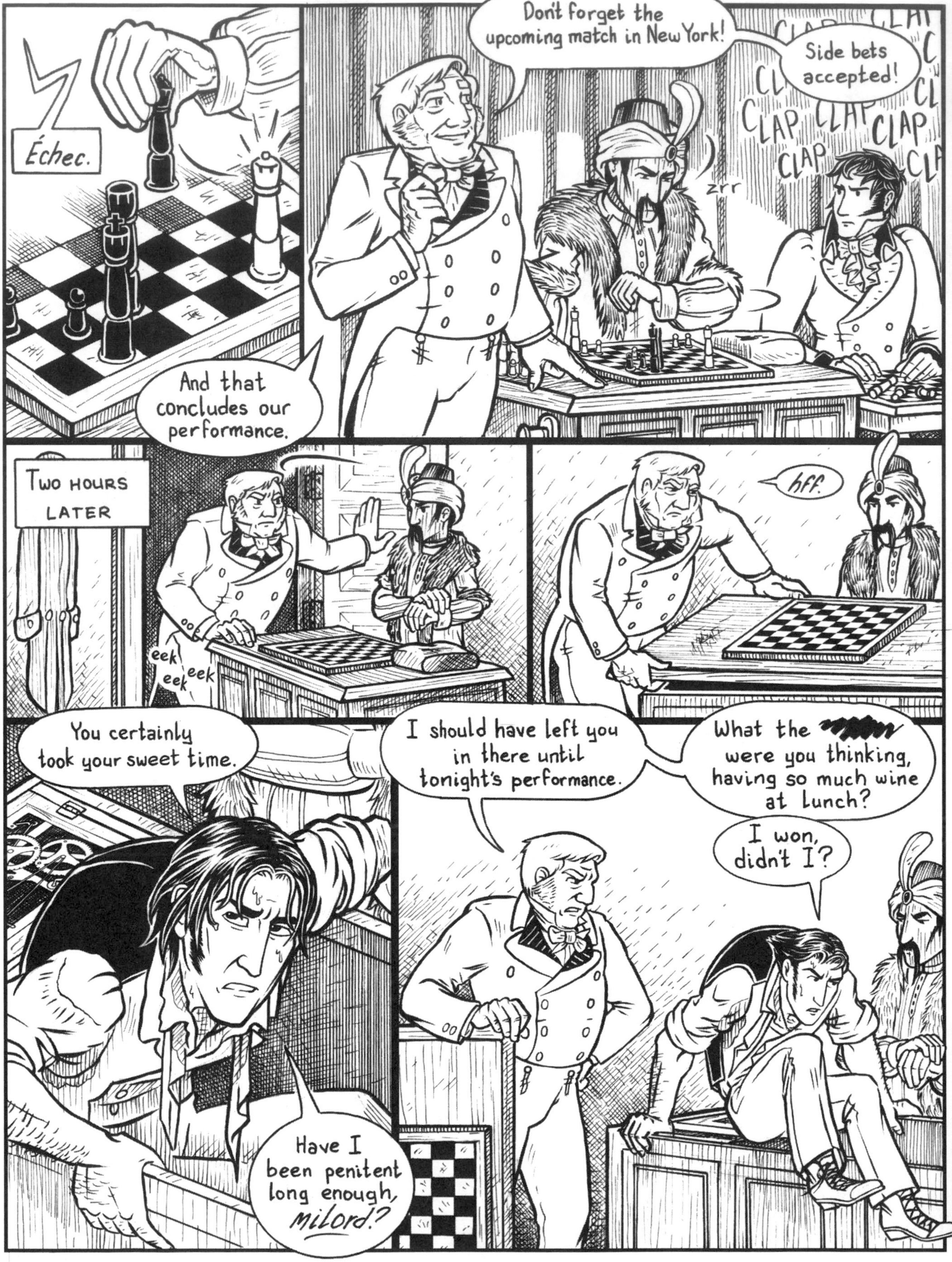
Échec.
And that concludes our performance.
Don't forget the upcoming match in New York!
Side bets accepted!
CLAP CLAP CLAP CLAP CLAP
zrr
Two hours later
eek eek eek
hff.
You certainly took your sweet time.
Have I been penitent long enough, milord?
I should have left you in there until tonight's performance.
What the [redacted] were you thinking, having so much wine at lunch?
I won, didn't I?

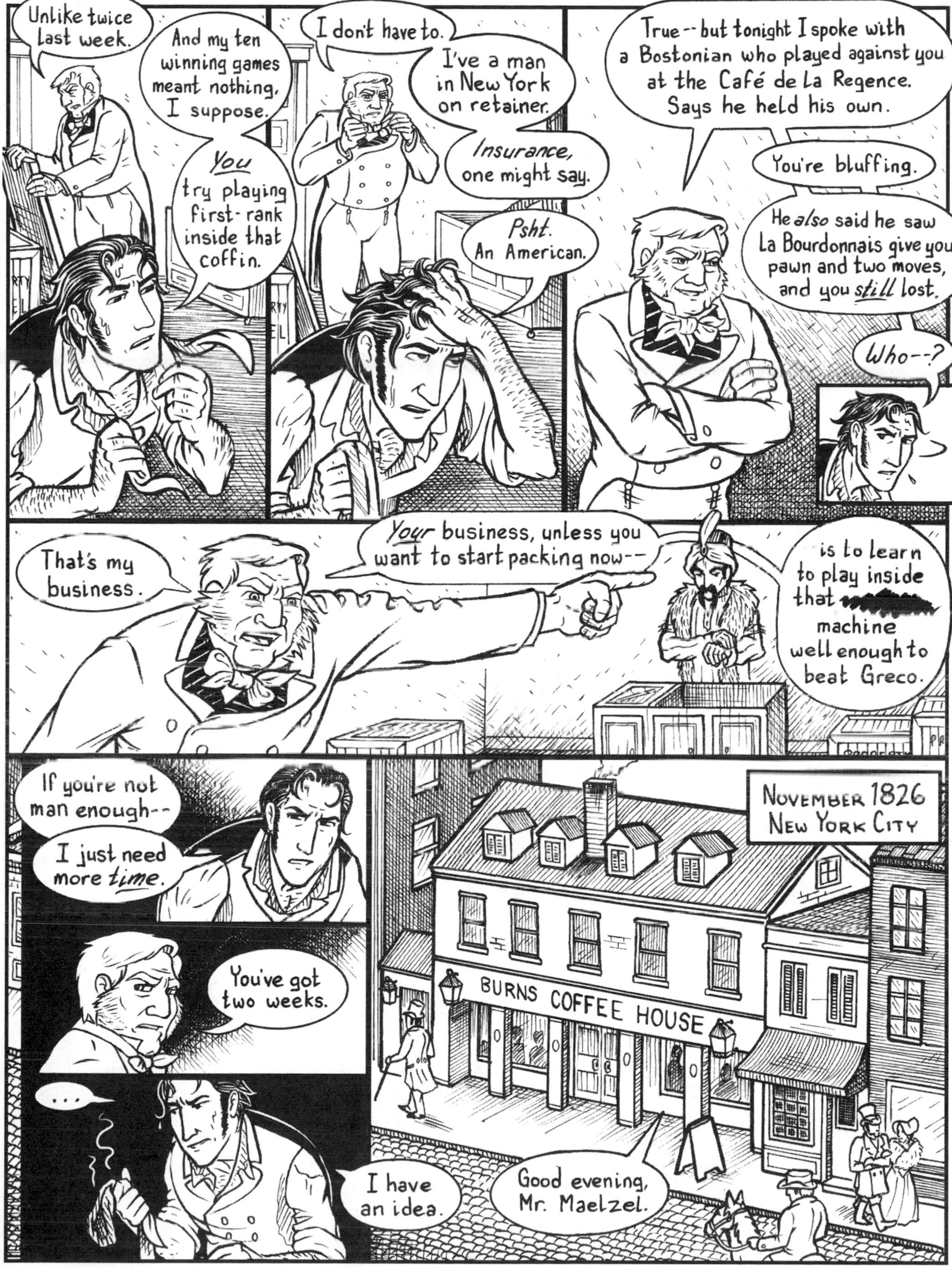
Unlike twice last week.
And my ten winning games meant nothing, I suppose.
You try playing first-rank inside that coffin.
I don't have to.
I've a man in New York on retainer.
Insurance, one might say.
Psht. An American.
True -- but tonight I spoke with a Bostonian who played against you at the Café de La Regence. Says he held his own.
You're bluffing.
He also said he saw La Bourdonnais give you pawn and two moves, and you still lost.
Who--?
That's my business.
Your business, unless you want to start packing now--
is to learn to play inside that [redacted] machine well enough to beat Greco.
If you're not man enough--
I just need more time.
You've got two weeks.
. . .
I have an idea.
November 1826 New York City
BURNS COFFEE HOUSE
Good evening, Mr. Maelzel.

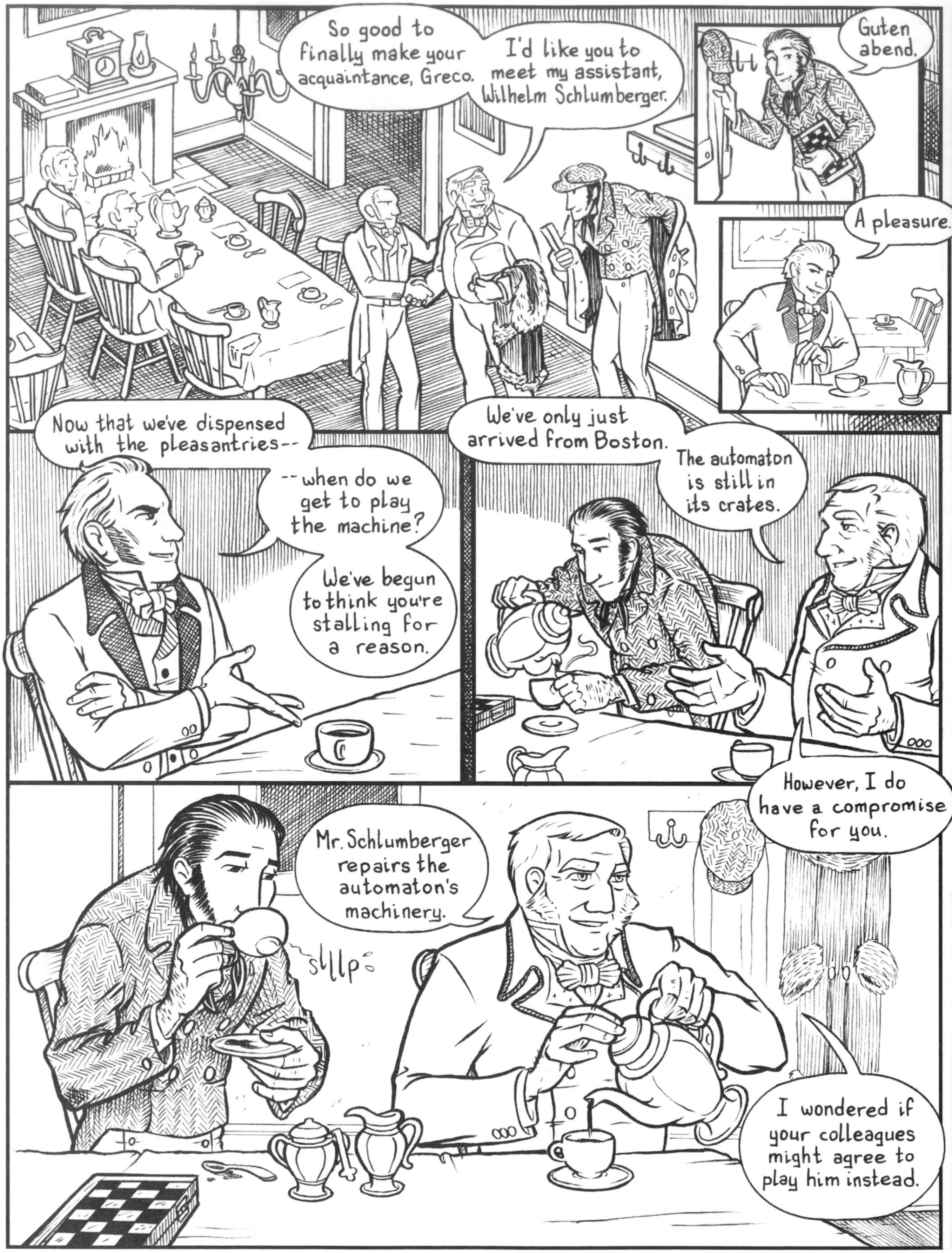
So good to finally make your acquaintance, Greco.
I'd like you to meet my assistant, Wilhelm Schlumberger.
Guten abend.
A pleasure.
Now that we've dispensed with the pleasantries--
--when do we get to play the machine?
We've begun to think you're stalling for a reason.
We've only just arrived from Boston.
The automaton is still in its crates.
However, I do have a compromise for you.
Mr. Schlumberger repairs the automaton's machinery.
sllp
I wondered if your colleagues might agree to play him instead.

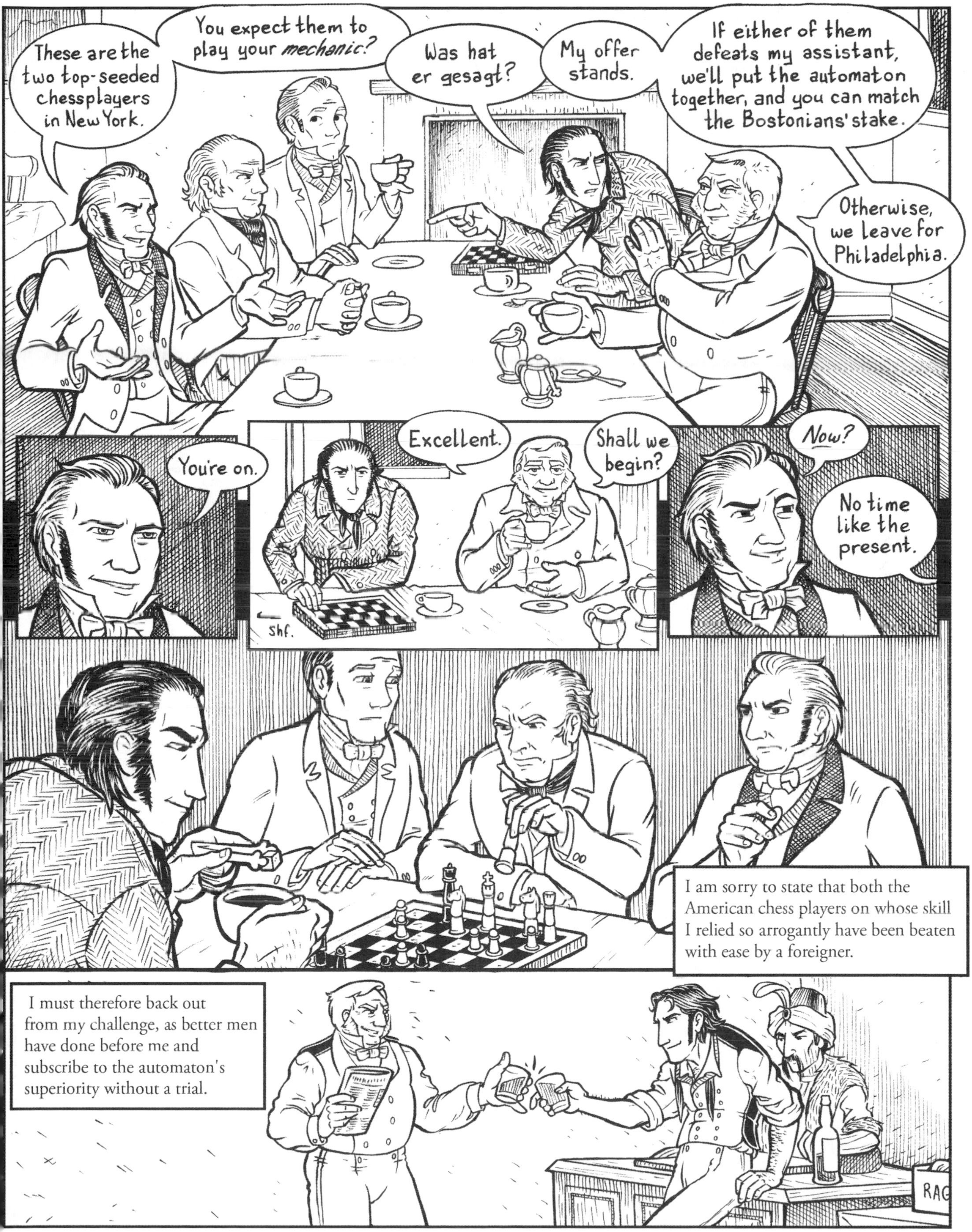
These are the two top-seeded chessplayers in New York.
You expect them to play your *mechanic*?
Was hat er gesagt?
My offer stands.
If either of them defeats my assistant, we'll put the automaton together, and you can match the Bostonians' stake.
Otherwise, we leave for Philadelphia.
You're on.
Excellent.
Shall we begin?
shf.
Now?
No time like the present.
I am sorry to state that both the American chess players on whose skill I relied so arrogantly have been beaten with ease by a foreigner.
I must therefore back out from my challenge, as better men have done before me and subscribe to the automaton's superiority without a trial.
RAG

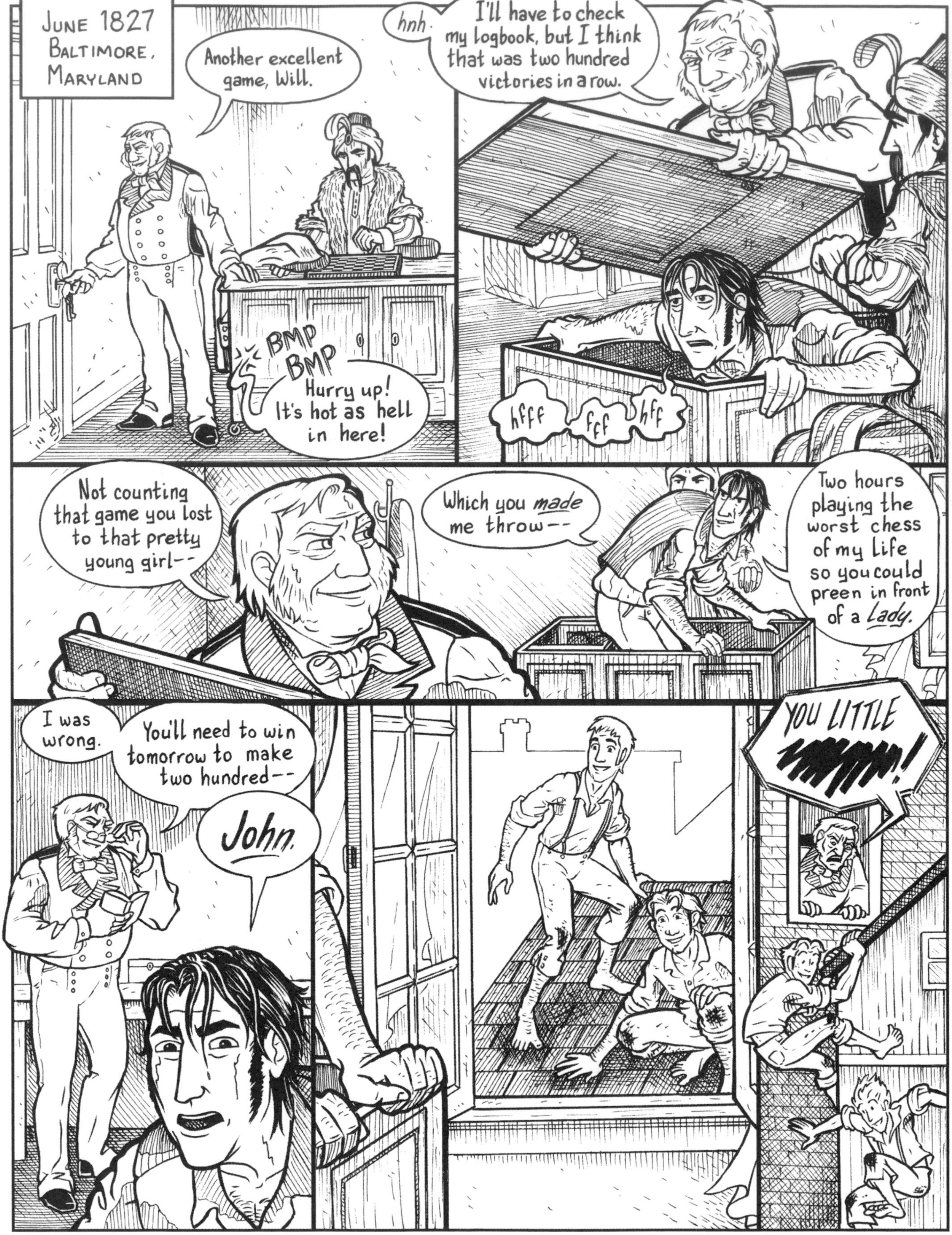

June 1827
Baltimore, Maryland
Another excellent game, Will.
BMP BMP
Hurry up! It's hot as hell in here!
hnh.
I'll have to check my logbook, but I think that was two hundred victories in a row.
hfff fff hff
Not counting that game you lost to that pretty young girl--
Which you *made* me throw--
Two hours playing the worst chess of my life so you could preen in front of a *Lady*.
I was wrong.
You'll need to win tomorrow to make two hundred--
John.
YOU LITTLE [redacted]!

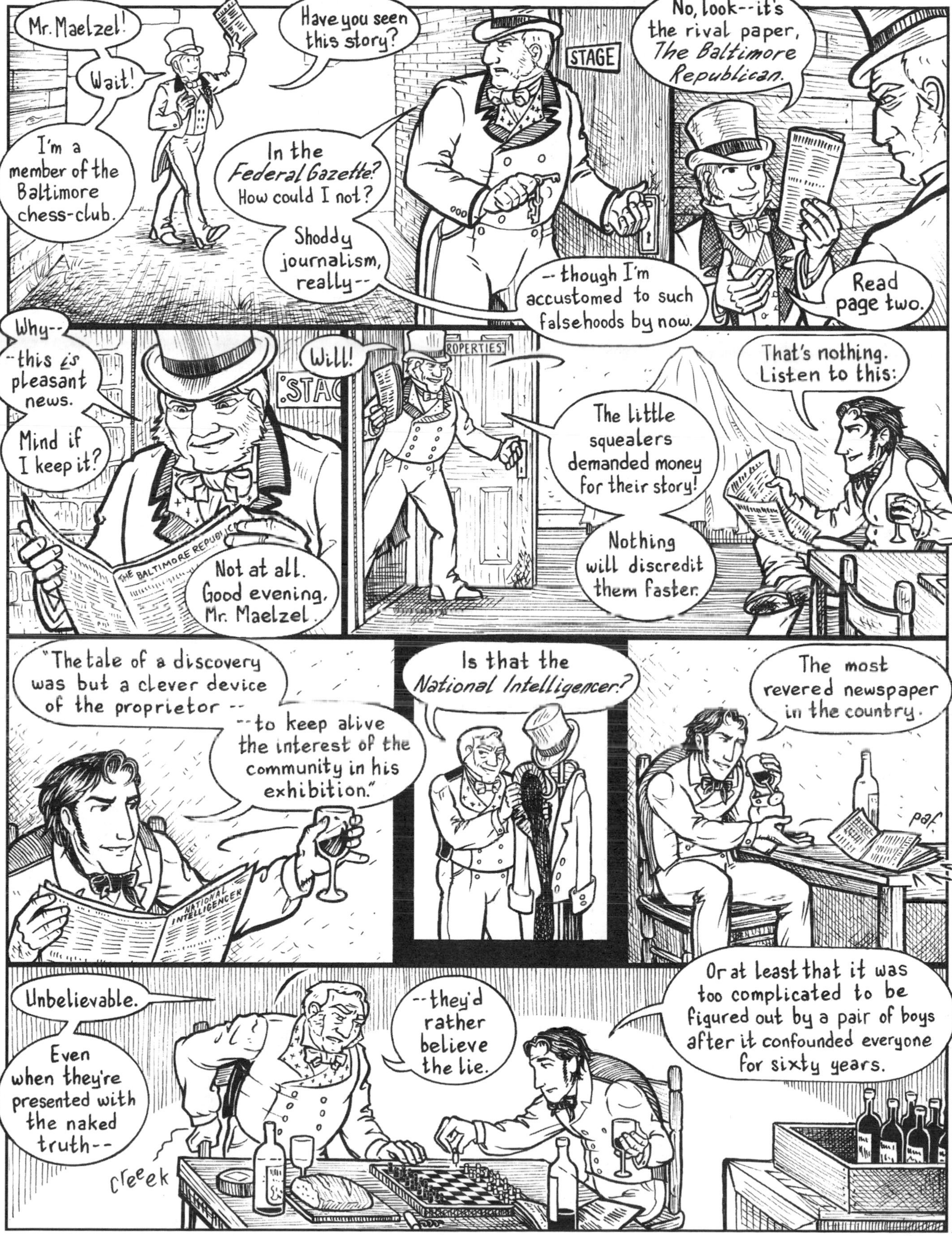
Mr. Maelzel!
Wait!
I'm a member of the Baltimore chess-club.
Have you seen this story?
In the *Federal Gazette*? How could I not?
Shoddy journalism, really--
--though I'm accustomed to such falsehoods by now.
STAGE
No, look--it's the rival paper, *The Baltimore Republican*.
Read page two.
Why--
--this *is* pleasant news.
Mind if I keep it?
THE BALTIMORE REPUBLICAN
Not at all. Good evening, Mr. Maelzel.
Will!
PROPERTIES
The little squealers demanded money for their story!
Nothing will discredit them faster.
That's nothing. Listen to this:
"The tale of a discovery was but a clever device of the proprietor --
--to keep alive the interest of the community in his exhibition."
NATIONAL INTELLIGENCER
Is that the *National Intelligencer*?
The most revered newspaper in the country.
paf
Unbelievable.
Even when they're presented with the naked truth--
--they'd rather believe the lie.
creeek
Or at least that it was too complicated to be figured out by a pair of boys after it confounded everyone for sixty years.

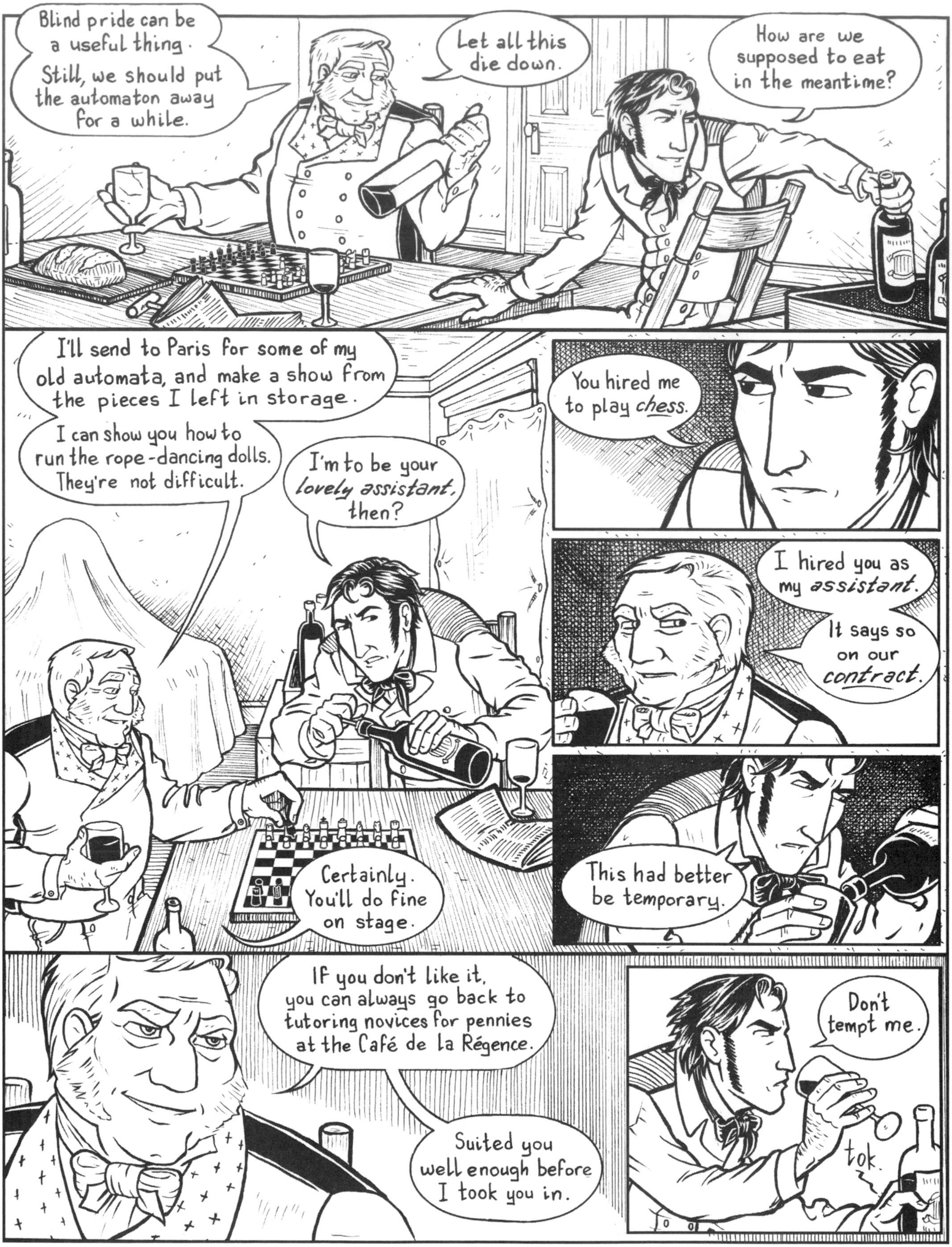
Blind pride can be a useful thing. Still, we should put the automaton away for a while.
Let all this die down.
How are we supposed to eat in the meantime?
I'll send to Paris for some of my old automata, and make a show from the pieces I left in storage.
I can show you how to run the rope-dancing dolls. They're not difficult.
I'm to be your *lovely assistant*, then?
Certainly. You'll do fine on stage.
You hired me to play *chess*.
I hired you as my *assistant*.
It says so on our *contract*.
This had better be temporary.
If you don't like it, you can always go back to tutoring novices for pennies at the Café de la Régence.
Suited you well enough before I took you in.
Don't tempt me.
tok.

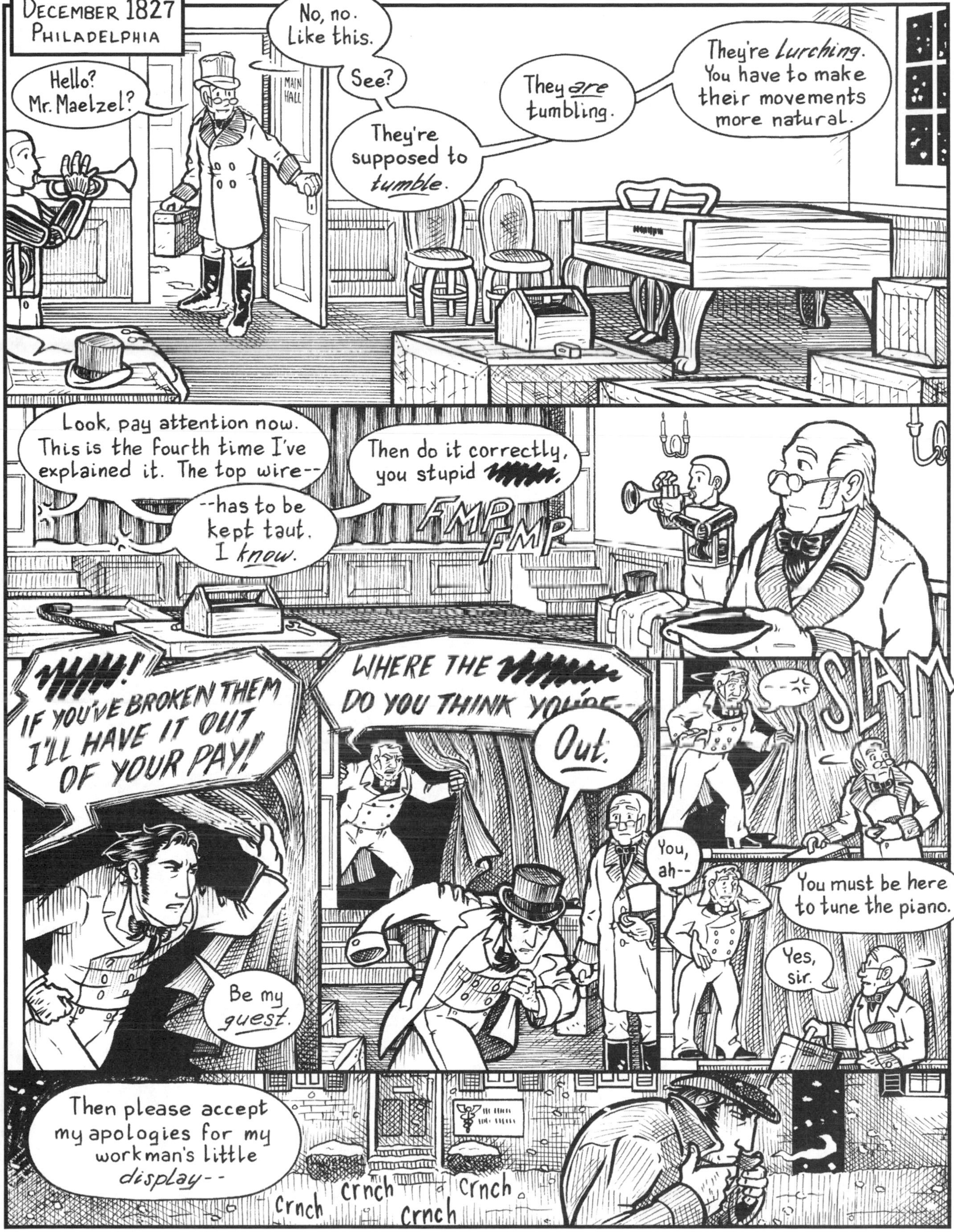
December 1827
Philadelphia
Hello? Mr. Maelzel?
No, no. Like this.
See?
They're supposed to tumble.
They are tumbling.
They're lurching. You have to make their movements more natural.
Look, pay attention now. This is the fourth time I've explained it. The top wire--
--has to be kept taut. I know.
Then do it correctly, you stupid [redacted].
FMP FMP
[redacted]! IF YOU'VE BROKEN THEM I'LL HAVE IT OUT OF YOUR PAY!
Be my guest.
WHERE THE [redacted] DO YOU THINK
Out.
SLAM
You, ah--
You must be here to tune the piano.
Yes, sir.
Then please accept my apologies for my workman's little display--
crnch crnch crnch crnch

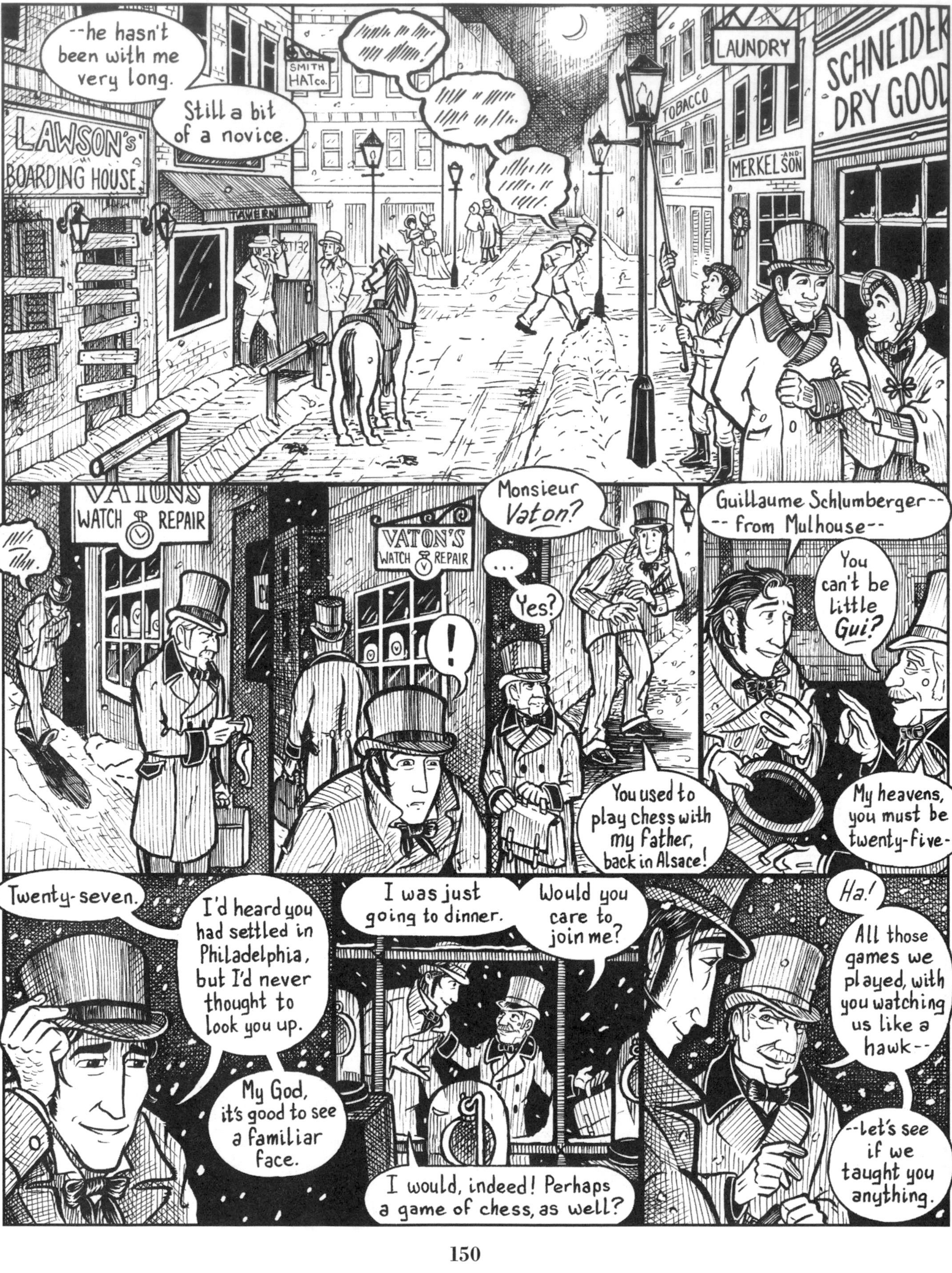
--he hasn't been with me very long.
Still a bit of a novice.
SMITH HAT Co.
LAWSON's BOARDING HOUSE
TAVERN
LAUNDRY
TOBACCO
SCHNEIDER DRY GOOD
MERKEL AND SON
VATON'S WATCH REPAIR
VATON'S WATCH REPAIR
!
Monsieur Vaton?
...
Yes?
You used to play chess with my father, back in Alsace!
Guillaume Schlumberger-- --from Mulhouse--
You can't be little Gui?
My heavens, you must be twenty-five--
Twenty-seven.
I'd heard you had settled in Philadelphia, but I'd never thought to look you up.
My God, it's good to see a familiar face.
I was just going to dinner.
Would you care to join me?
I would, indeed! Perhaps a game of chess, as well?
Ha!
All those games we played, with you watching us like a hawk--
--let's see if we taught you anything.

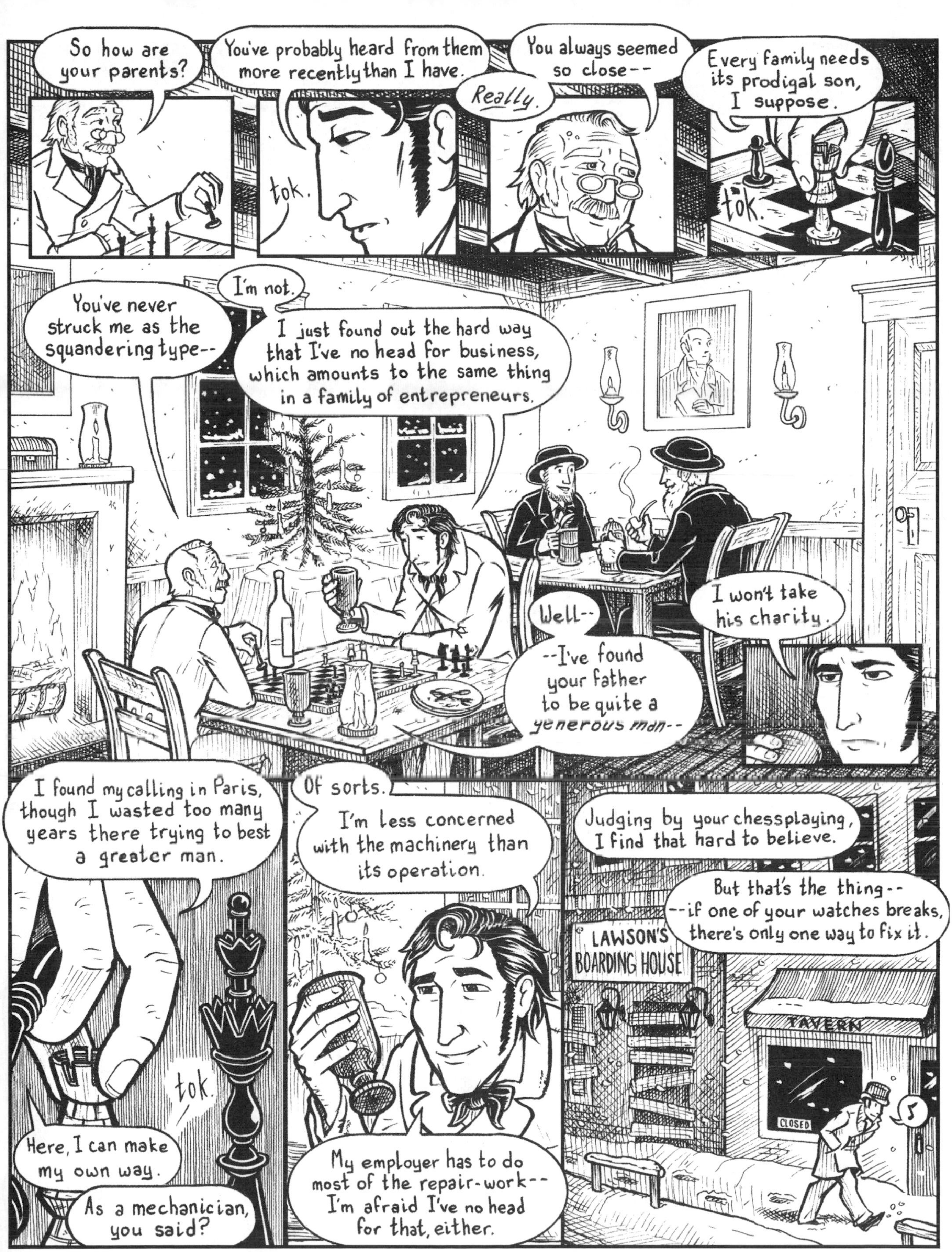
So how are your parents?
You've probably heard from them more recently than I have.
tok.
Really.
You always seemed so close--
Every family needs its prodigal son, I suppose.
tok.
You've never struck me as the squandering type--
I'm not.
I just found out the hard way that I've no head for business, which amounts to the same thing in a family of entrepreneurs.
Well--
--I've found your father to be quite a generous man--
I won't take his charity.
I found my calling in Paris, though I wasted too many years there trying to best a greater man.
tok.
Here, I can make my own way.
As a mechanician, you said?
Of sorts.
I'm less concerned with the machinery than its operation.
My employer has to do most of the repair-work--I'm afraid I've no head for that, either.
Judging by your chessplaying, I find that hard to believe.
But that's the thing--
--if one of your watches breaks, there's only one way to fix it.
LAWSON'S BOARDING HOUSE
TAVERN
CLOSED

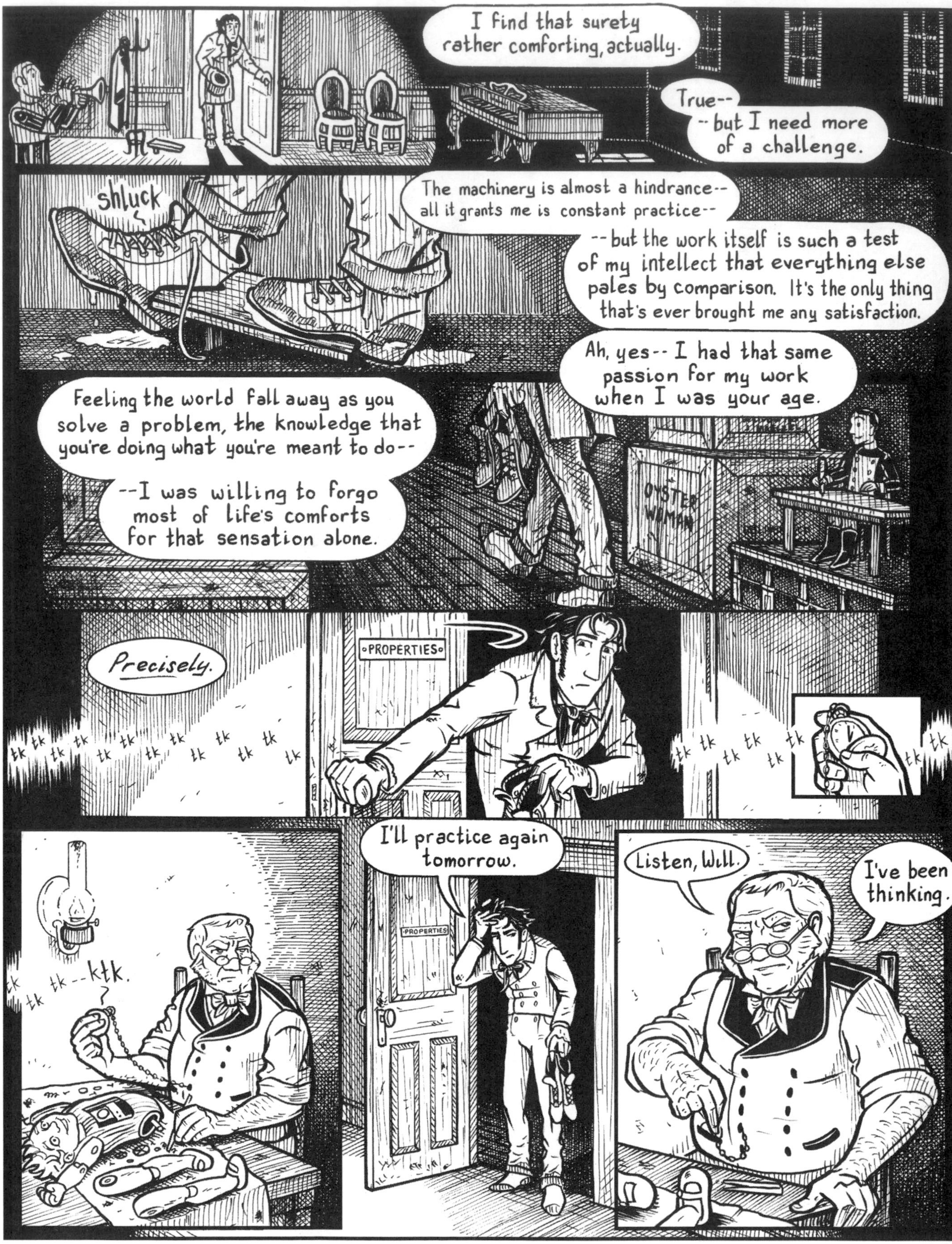
I find that surety rather comforting, actually.
True--
--but I need more of a challenge.
shluck
The machinery is almost a hindrance--all it grants me is constant practice--
--but the work itself is such a test of my intellect that everything else pales by comparison. It's the only thing that's ever brought me any satisfaction.
Ah, yes--I had that same passion for my work when I was your age.
Feeling the world fall away as you solve a problem, the knowledge that you're doing what you're meant to do--
--I was willing to forgo most of life's comforts for that sensation alone.
OYSTER WOMAN
Precisely.
PROPERTIES
tk tk tk tk tk tk tk tk tk tk tk tk
tk tk tk tk tk tk tk tk
tk tk tk--ktk.
I'll practice again tomorrow.
PROPERTIES
Listen, Will.
I've been thinking.

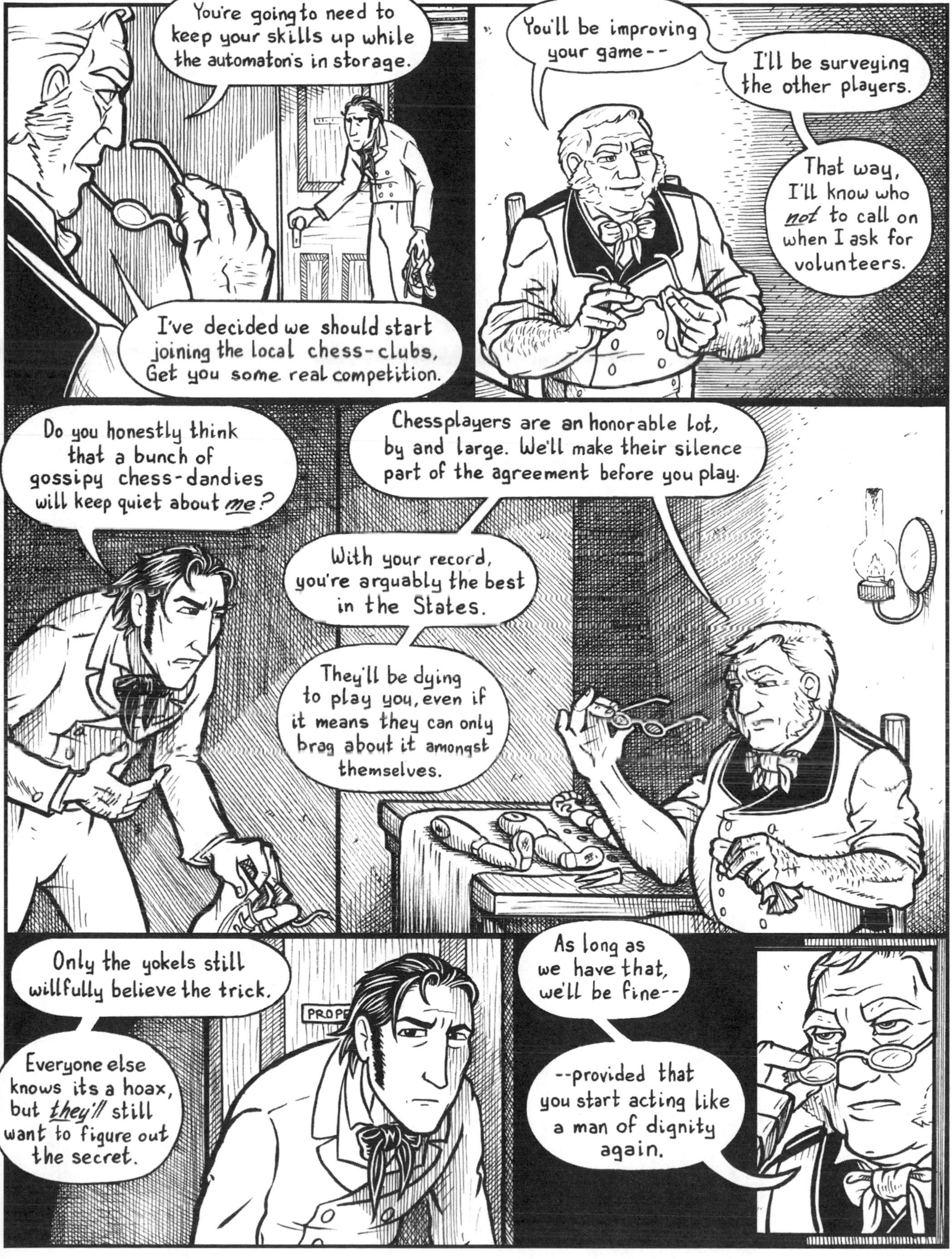
You're going to need to keep your skills up while the automaton's in storage.
I've decided we should start joining the local chess-clubs, Get you some real competition.
You'll be improving your game--
I'll be surveying the other players.
That way, I'll know who not to call on when I ask for volunteers.
Do you honestly think that a bunch of gossipy chess-dandies will keep quiet about me?
Chessplayers are an honorable lot, by and large. We'll make their silence part of the agreement before you play.
With your record, you're arguably the best in the States.
They'll be dying to play you, even if it means they can only brag about it amongst themselves.
Only the yokels still willfully believe the trick.
Everyone else knows its a hoax, but they'll still want to figure out the secret.
PROP
As long as we have that, we'll be fine--
--provided that you start acting like a man of dignity again.

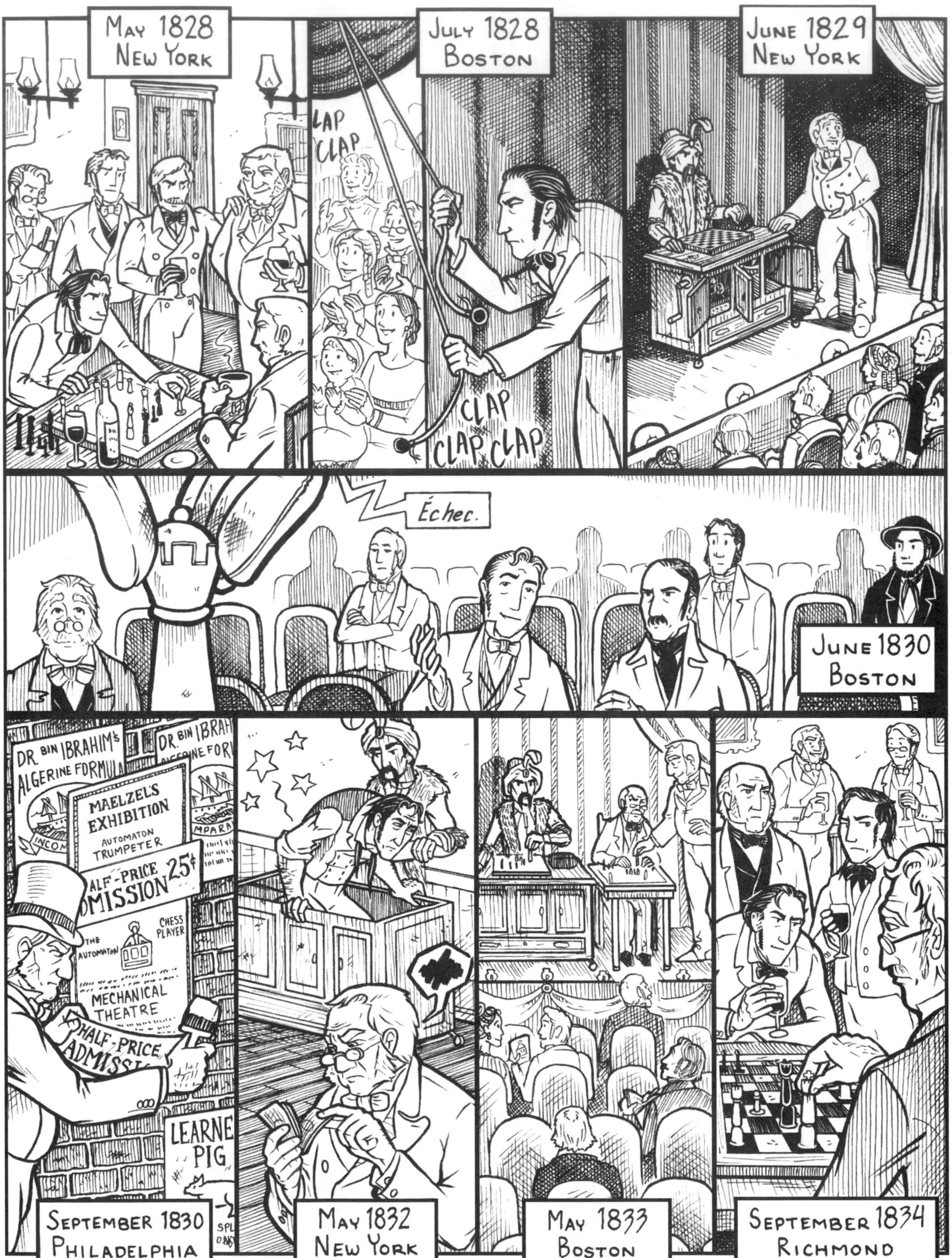
May 1828
New York
July 1828
Boston
CLAP
CLAP
CLAP
CLAP CLAP
June 1829
New York
Échec.
June 1830
Boston
DR. BIN IBRAHIM'S
ALGERINE FORMU
INCOM
DR. BIN IBRAHI
ALGERINE FORM
MPARA
MAELZEL'S
EXHIBITION
AUTOMATON
TRUMPETER
ALF-PRICE
MISSION 25¢
THE AUTOMATON
CHESS PLAYER
MECHANICAL
THEATRE
HALF-PRICE
ADMISS
LEARNE
PIG
September 1830
Philadelphia
May 1832
New York
May 1833
Boston
September 1834
Richmond

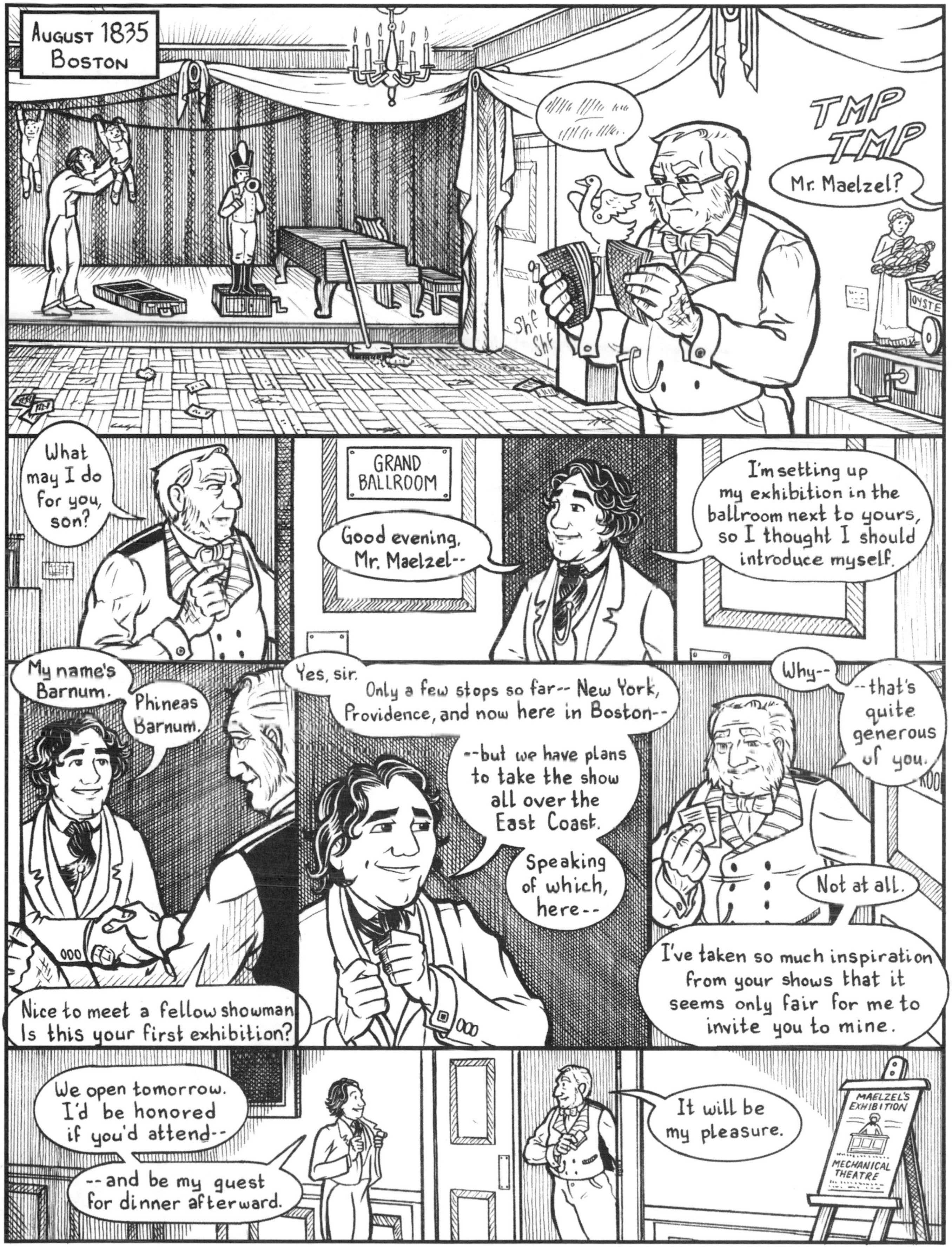
August 1835
Boston
TMP TMP
Mr. Maelzel?
What may I do for you, son?
GRAND BALLROOM
Good evening, Mr. Maelzel--
I'm setting up my exhibition in the ballroom next to yours, so I thought I should introduce myself.
My name's Barnum.
Phineas Barnum.
Nice to meet a fellow showman. Is this your first exhibition?
Yes, sir.
Only a few stops so far-- New York, Providence, and now here in Boston--
--but we have plans to take the show all over the East Coast.
Speaking of which, here--
Why--
--that's quite generous of you.
Not at all.
I've taken so much inspiration from your shows that it seems only fair for me to invite you to mine.
We open tomorrow. I'd be honored if you'd attend--
--and be my quest for dinner afterward.
It will be my pleasure.
MAELZEL'S EXHIBITION
MECHANICAL THEATRE

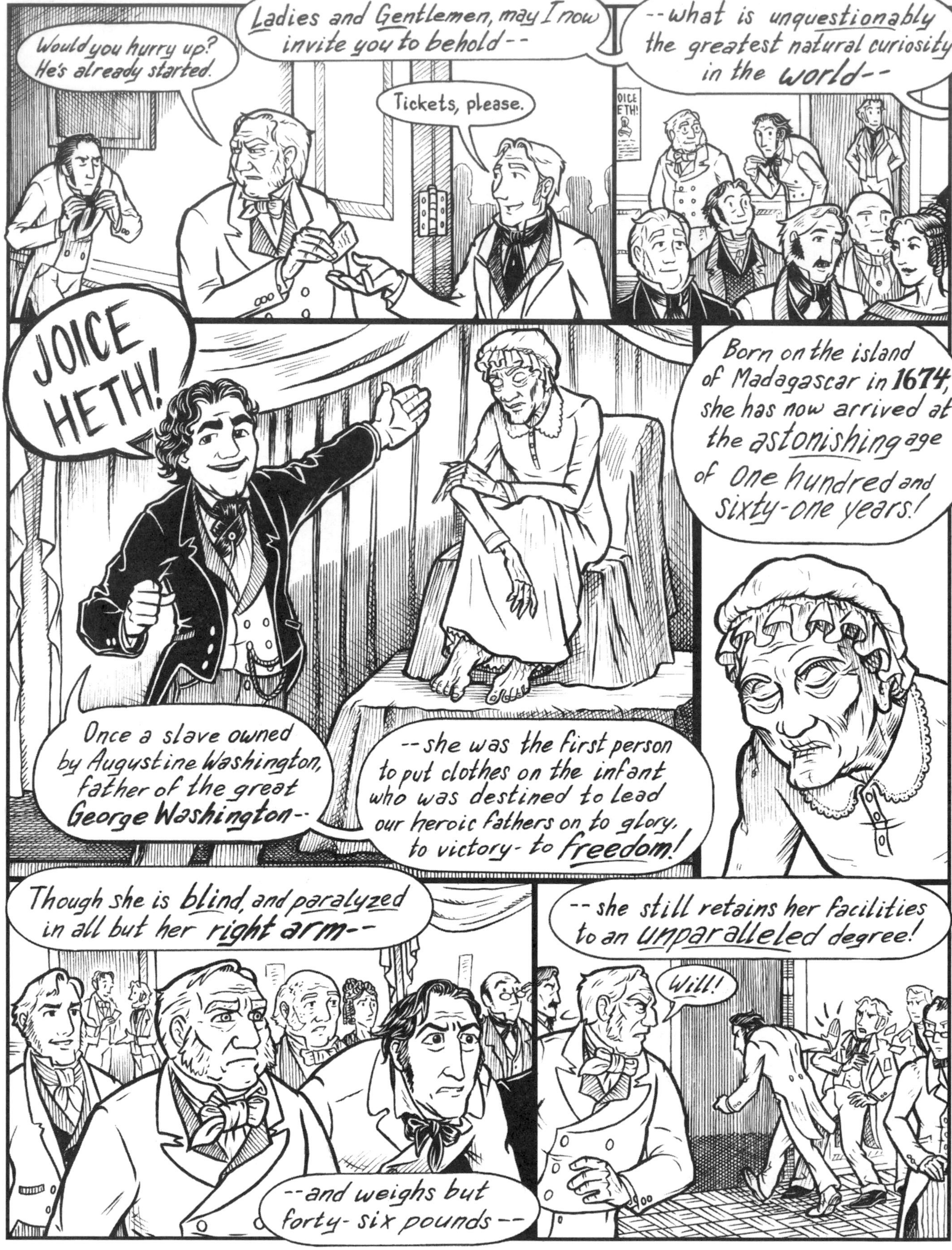
Would you hurry up? He's already started.
Ladies and Gentlemen, may I now invite you to behold--
Tickets, please.
--what is unquestionably the greatest natural curiosity in the world--
JOICE HETH!
Born on the island of Madagascar in 1674, she has now arrived at the astonishing age of one hundred and sixty-one years!
Once a slave owned by Augustine Washington, father of the great George Washington--
--she was the first person to put clothes on the infant who was destined to lead our heroic fathers on to glory, to victory- to freedom!
Though she is blind, and paralyzed in all but her right arm--
--and weighs but forty- six pounds--
--she still retains her facilities to an unparalleled degree!
Will!

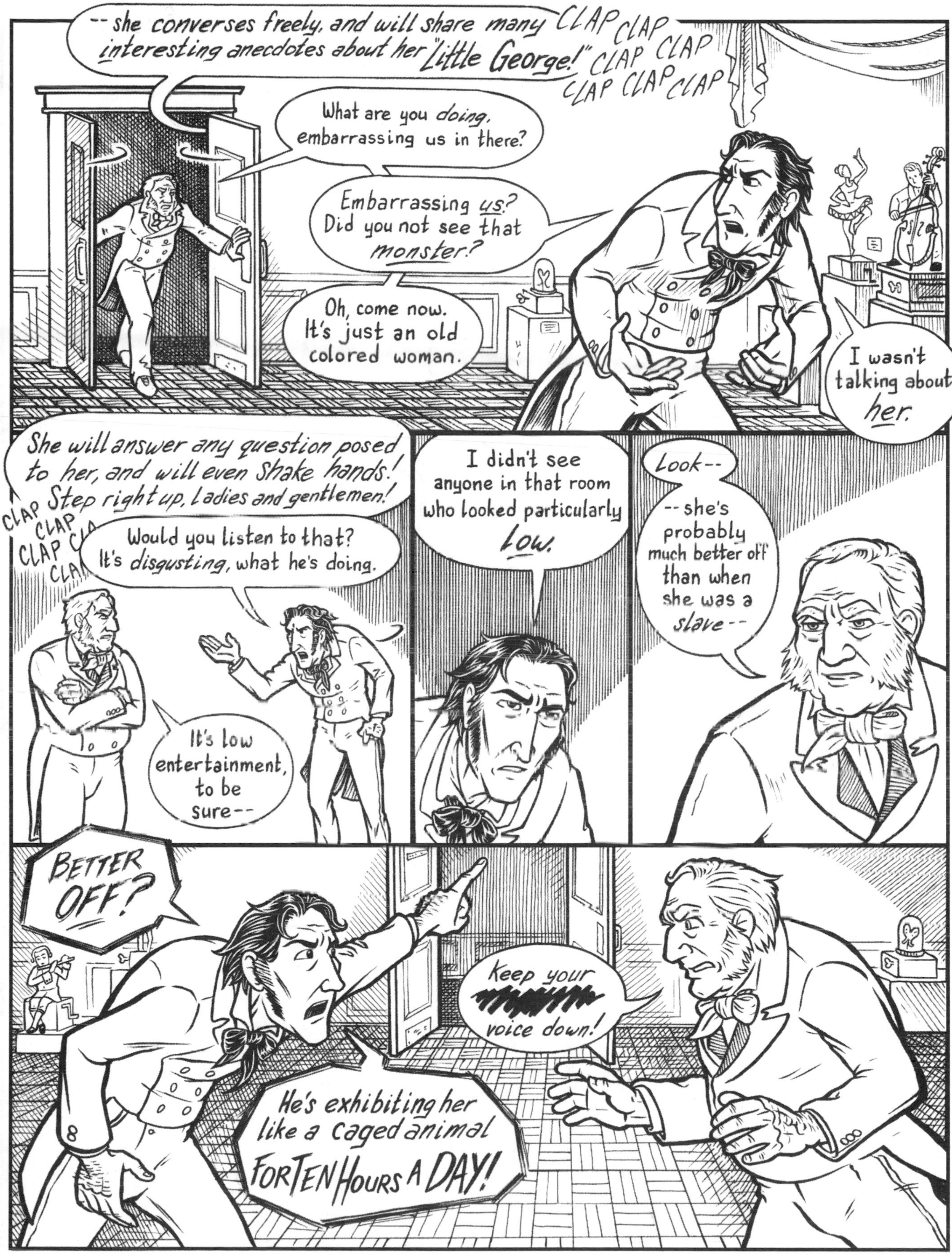
-- she converses freely, and will share many interesting anecdotes about her "Little George!"
CLAP CLAP CLAP CLAP CLAP CLAP CLAP
What are you doing, embarrassing us in there?
Embarrassing us? Did you not see that monster?
Oh, come now. It's just an old colored woman.
I wasn't talking about her.
She will answer any question posed to her, and will even shake hands! Step right up, Ladies and gentlemen!
CLAP CLAP CLAP
Would you listen to that? It's disgusting, what he's doing.
It's low entertainment, to be sure--
I didn't see anyone in that room who looked particularly low.
Look--
-- she's probably much better off than when she was a slave--
BETTER OFF?
He's exhibiting her like a caged animal FOR TEN HOURS A DAY!
Keep your [redacted] voice down!

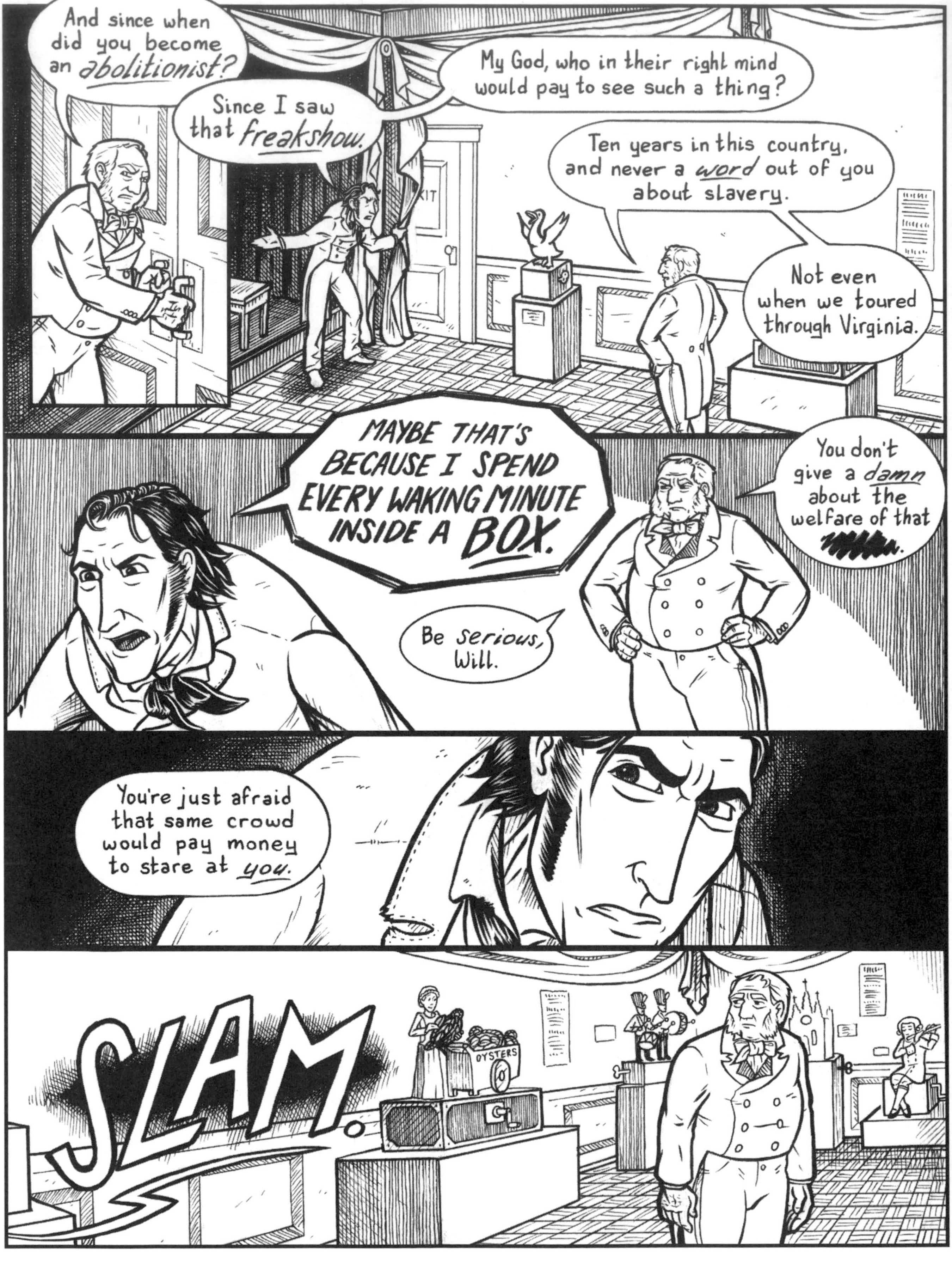
And since when did you become an *abolitionist?*
Since I saw that *freakshow.*
My God, who in their right mind would pay to see such a thing?
Ten years in this country, and never a *word* out of you about slavery.
Not even when we toured through Virginia.
MAYBE THAT'S BECAUSE I SPEND EVERY WAKING MINUTE INSIDE A *BOX.*
You don't give a *damn* about the welfare of that [redacted].
Be *serious,* Will.
You're just afraid that same crowd would pay money to stare at *you.*
OYSTERS
SLAM.

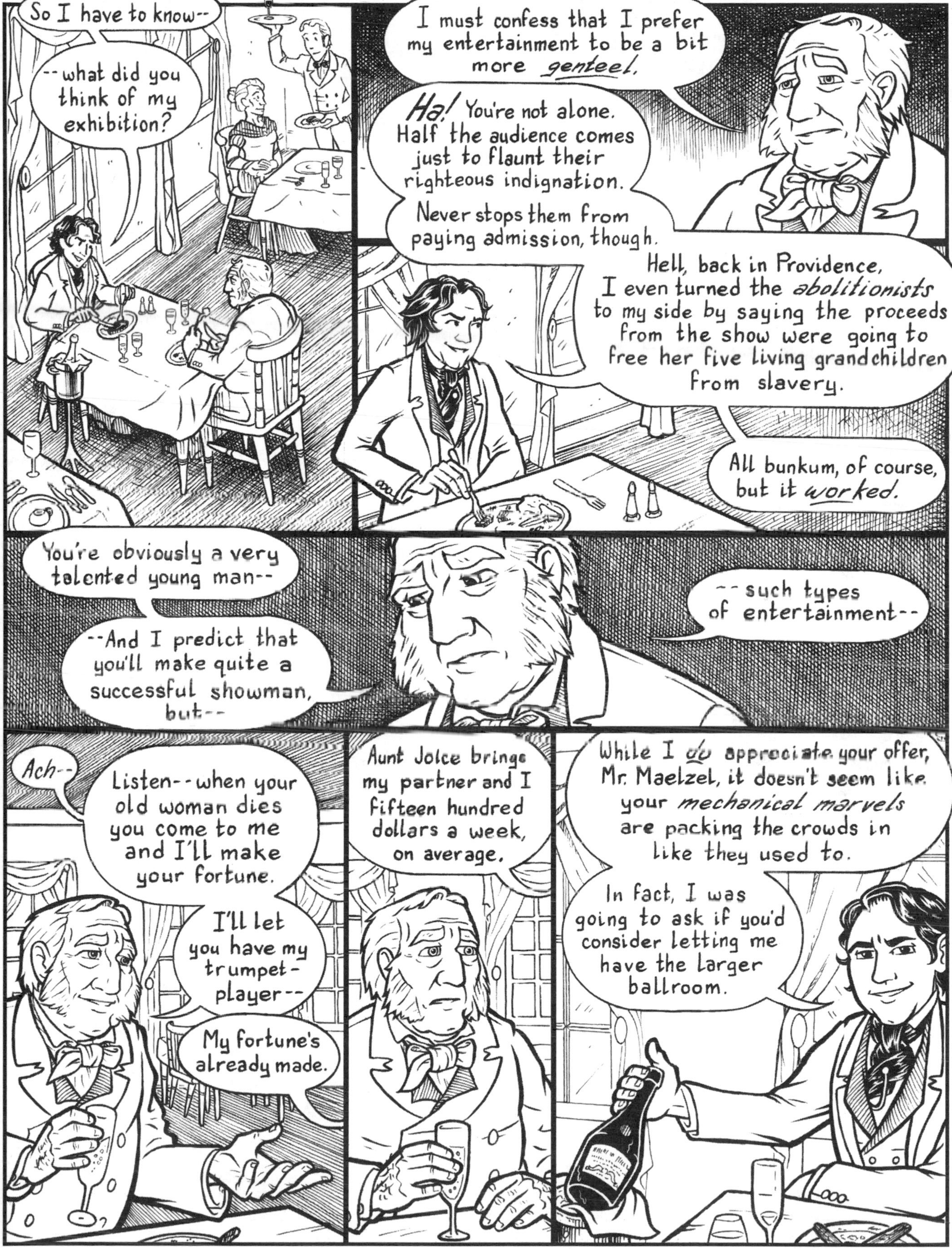
So I have to know--
--what did you think of my exhibition?
I must confess that I prefer my entertainment to be a bit more genteel.
Ha! You're not alone. Half the audience comes just to flaunt their righteous indignation.
Never stops them from paying admission, though.
Hell, back in Providence, I even turned the abolitionists to my side by saying the proceeds from the show were going to free her five living grandchildren from slavery.
All bunkum, of course, but it worked.
You're obviously a very talented young man--
--And I predict that you'll make quite a successful showman, but--
--such types of entertainment--
Ach--
Listen--when your old woman dies you come to me and I'll make your fortune.
I'll let you have my trumpet-player--
My fortune's already made.
Aunt Joice brings my partner and I fifteen hundred dollars a week, on average.
While I do appreciate your offer, Mr. Maelzel, it doesn't seem like your mechanical marvels are packing the crowds in like they used to.
In fact, I was going to ask if you'd consider letting me have the larger ballroom.

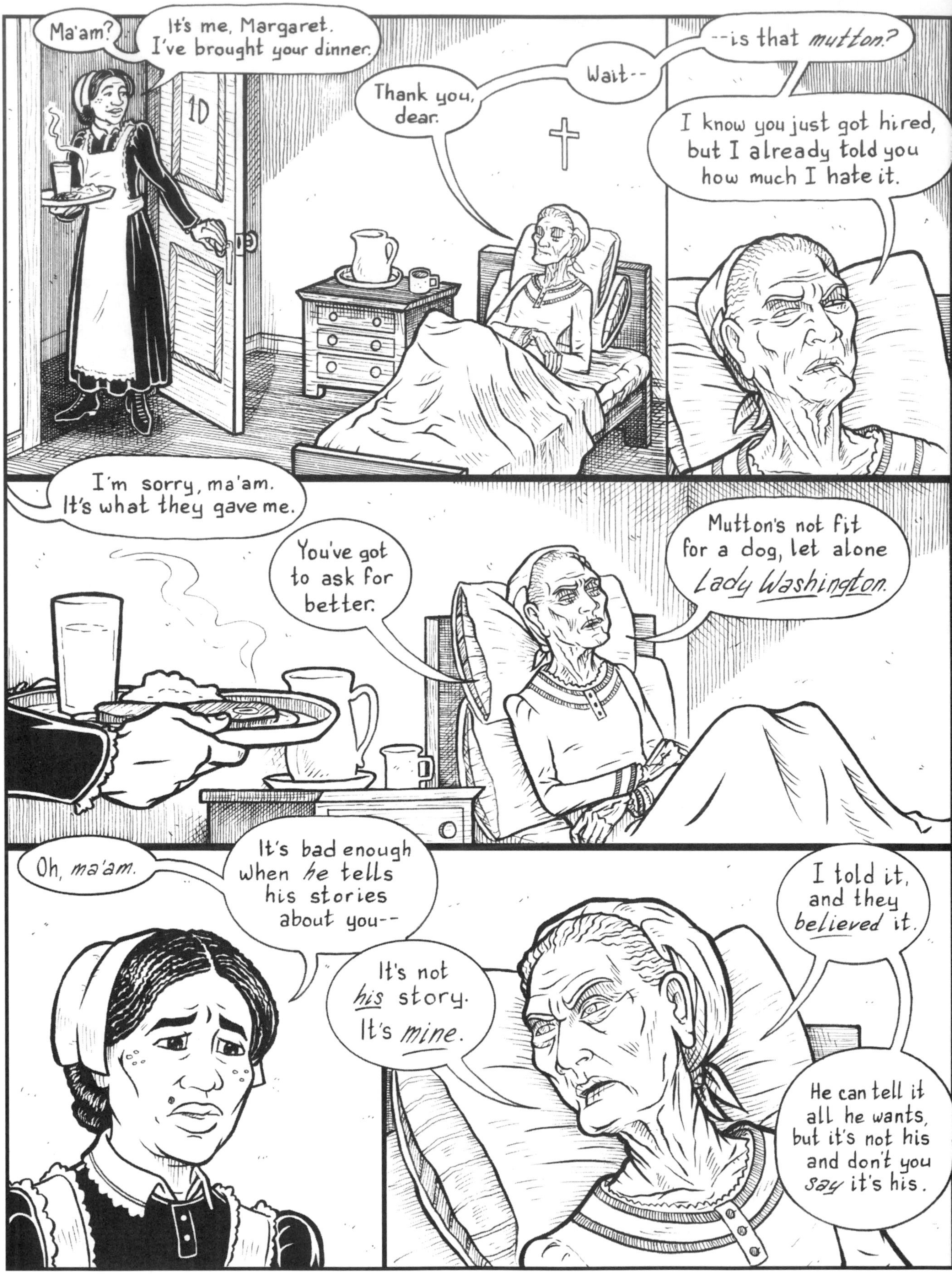
Ma'am?
It's me, Margaret. I've brought your dinner.
Thank you, dear.
Wait--
--is that *mutton?*
I know you just got hired, but I already told you how much I hate it.
I'm sorry, ma'am. It's what they gave me.
You've got to ask for better.
Mutton's not fit for a dog, let alone *Lady Washington.*
Oh, *ma'am.*
It's bad enough when *he* tells his stories about you--
It's not *his* story. It's *mine.*
I told it, and they *believed* it.
He can tell it all he wants, but it's not his and don't you *say* it's his.

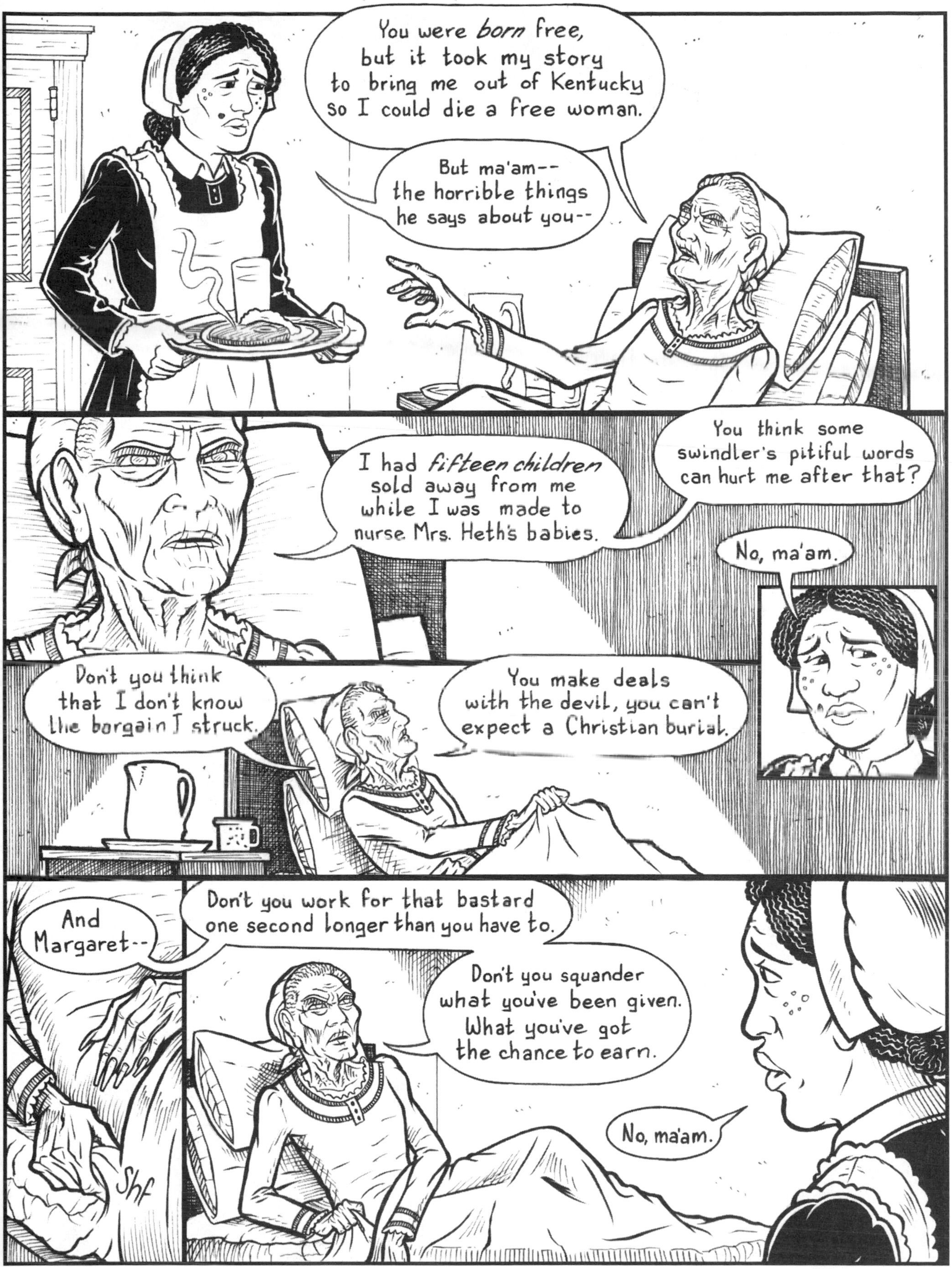
You were *born* free, but it took my story to bring me out of Kentucky so I could die a free woman.
But ma'am-- the horrible things he says about you--
I had *fifteen children* sold away from me while I was made to nurse Mrs. Heth's babies.
You think some swindler's pitiful words can hurt me after that?
No, ma'am.
Don't you think that I don't know the bargain I struck.
You make deals with the devil, you can't expect a Christian burial.
And Margaret--
Don't you work for that bastard one second longer than you have to.
Don't you squander what you've been given. What you've got the chance to earn.
No, ma'am.
Shf

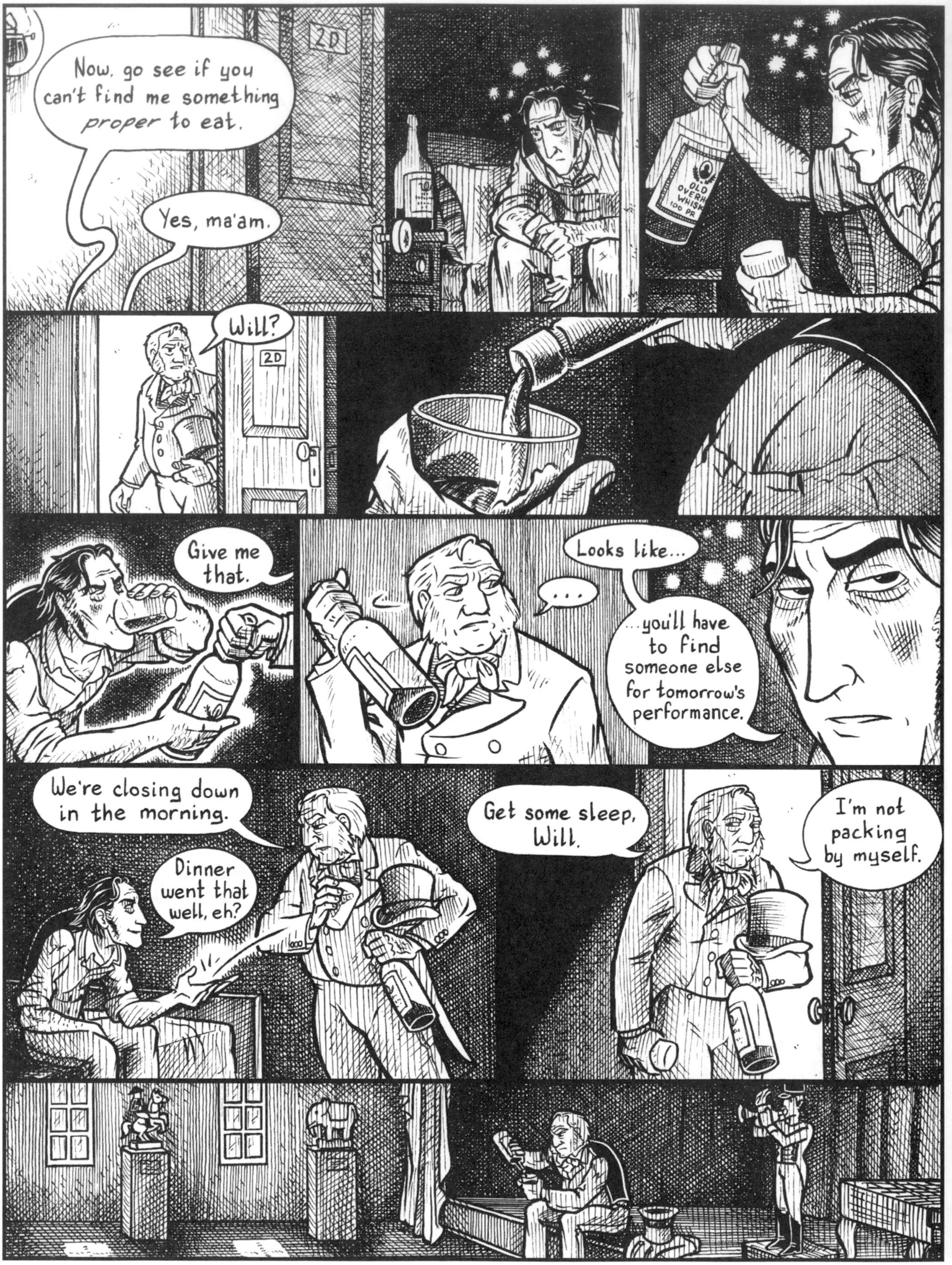

Now, go see if you can't find me something *proper* to eat.
Yes, ma'am.
Will?
Give me that.
. . .
Looks like...
...you'll have to find someone else for tomorrow's performance.
We're closing down in the morning.
Dinner went that well, eh?
Get some sleep, Will.
I'm not packing by myself.

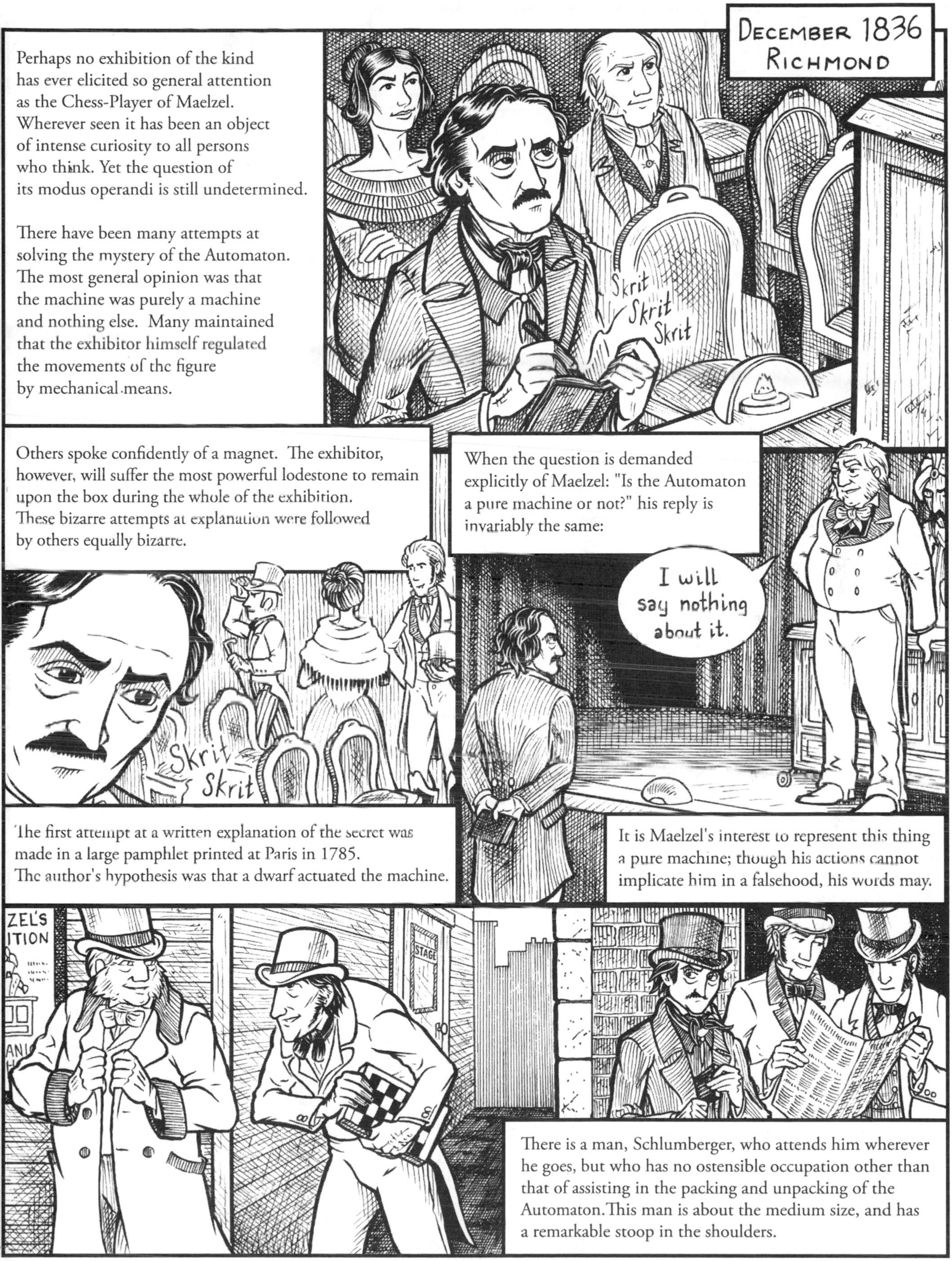
December 1836
Richmond
Perhaps no exhibition of the kind has ever elicited so general attention as the Chess-Player of Maelzel. Wherever seen it has been an object of intense curiosity to all persons who think. Yet the question of its modus operandi is still undetermined.
There have been many attempts at solving the mystery of the Automaton. The most general opinion was that the machine was purely a machine and nothing else. Many maintained that the exhibitor himself regulated the movements of the figure by mechanical means.
Skrit Skrit Skrit
Others spoke confidently of a magnet. The exhibitor, however, will suffer the most powerful lodestone to remain upon the box during the whole of the exhibition. These bizarre attempts at explanation were followed by others equally bizarre.
Skrit Skrit
The first attempt at a written explanation of the secret was made in a large pamphlet printed at Paris in 1785. The author's hypothesis was that a dwarf actuated the machine.
When the question is demanded explicitly of Maelzel: "Is the Automaton a pure machine or not?" his reply is invariably the same:
I will say nothing about it.
It is Maelzel's interest to represent this thing a pure machine; though his actions cannot implicate him in a falsehood, his words may.
ZEL'S
ITION
STAGE
There is a man, Schlumberger, who attends him wherever he goes, but who has no ostensible occupation other than that of assisting in the packing and unpacking of the Automaton. This man is about the medium size, and has a remarkable stoop in the shoulders.

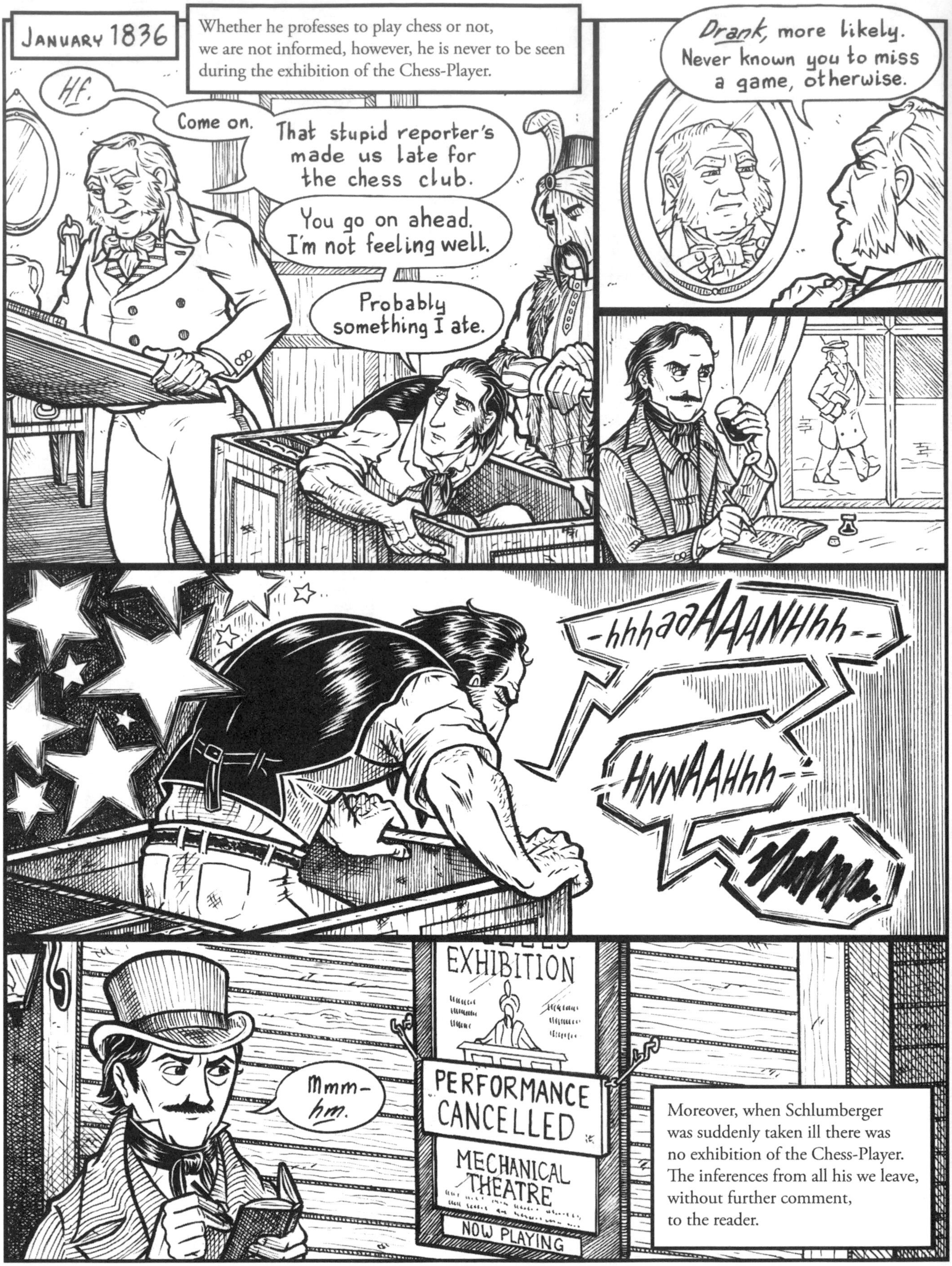
January 1836
Whether he professes to play chess or not, we are not informed, however, he is never to be seen during the exhibition of the Chess-Player.
Hf.
Come on.
That stupid reporter's made us late for the chess club.
You go on ahead. I'm not feeling well.
Probably something I ate.
Drank, more likely. Never known you to miss a game, otherwise.
-hhhaaAAANHhh--
HNNAAhhh-
EXHIBITION
PERFORMANCE CANCELLED
MECHANICAL THEATRE
NOW PLAYING
Mmm-hm.
Moreover, when Schlumberger was suddenly taken ill there was no exhibition of the Chess-Player. The inferences from all his we leave, without further comment, to the reader.

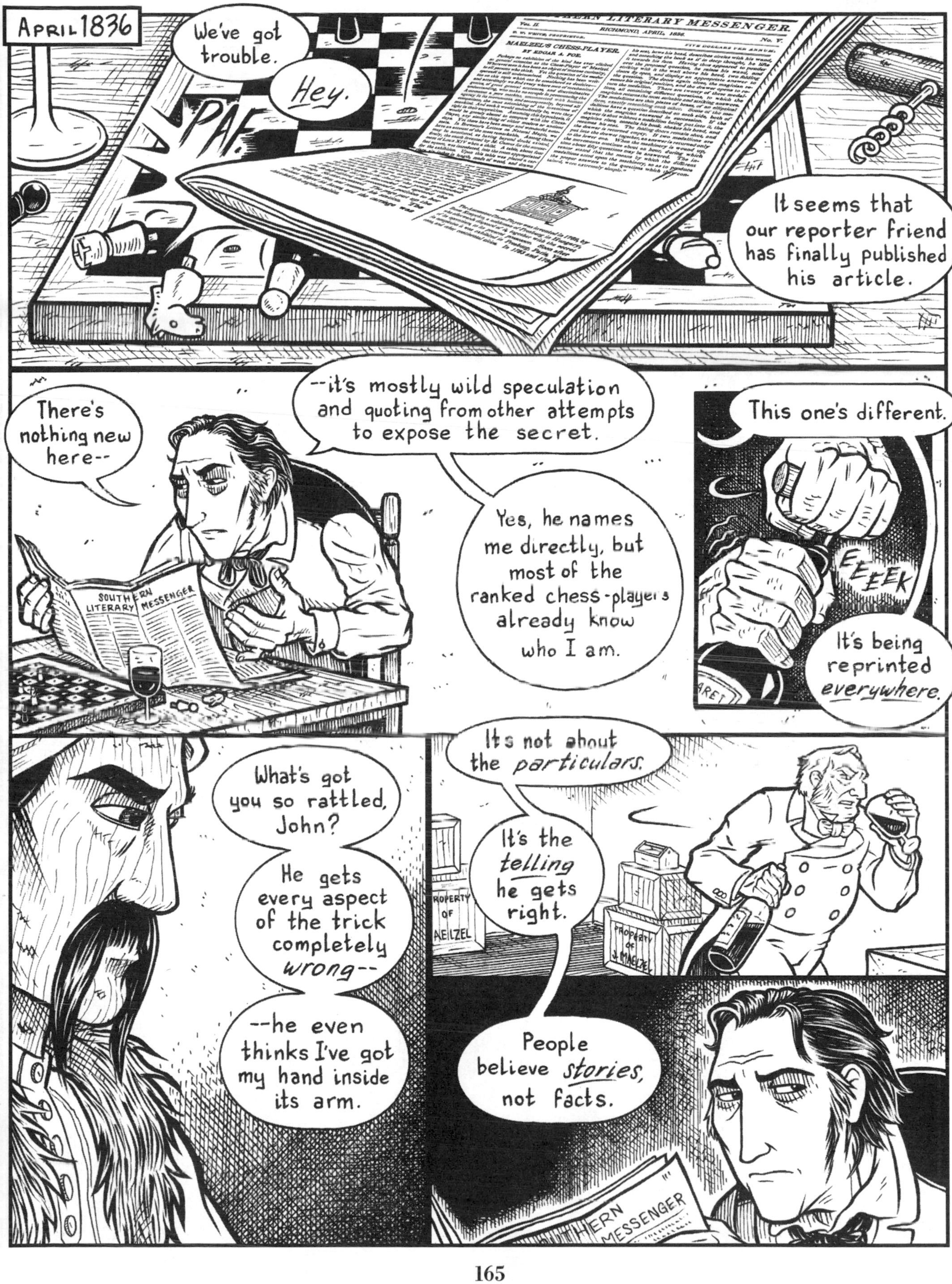
April 1836
We've got trouble.
Hey.
PAF.
MAELZEL'S CHESS-PLAYER.
BY EDGAR A. POE.
It seems that our reporter friend has finally published his article.
There's nothing new here--
--it's mostly wild speculation and quoting from other attempts to expose the secret.
Yes, he names me directly, but most of the ranked chess-players already know who I am.
SOUTHERN LITERARY MESSENGER
This one's different.
EEEEK
It's being reprinted *everywhere*.
What's got you so rattled, John?
He gets every aspect of the trick completely *wrong*--
--he even thinks I've got my hand inside its arm.
It's not about the *particulars*.
It's the *telling* he gets right.
People believe *stories*, not facts.

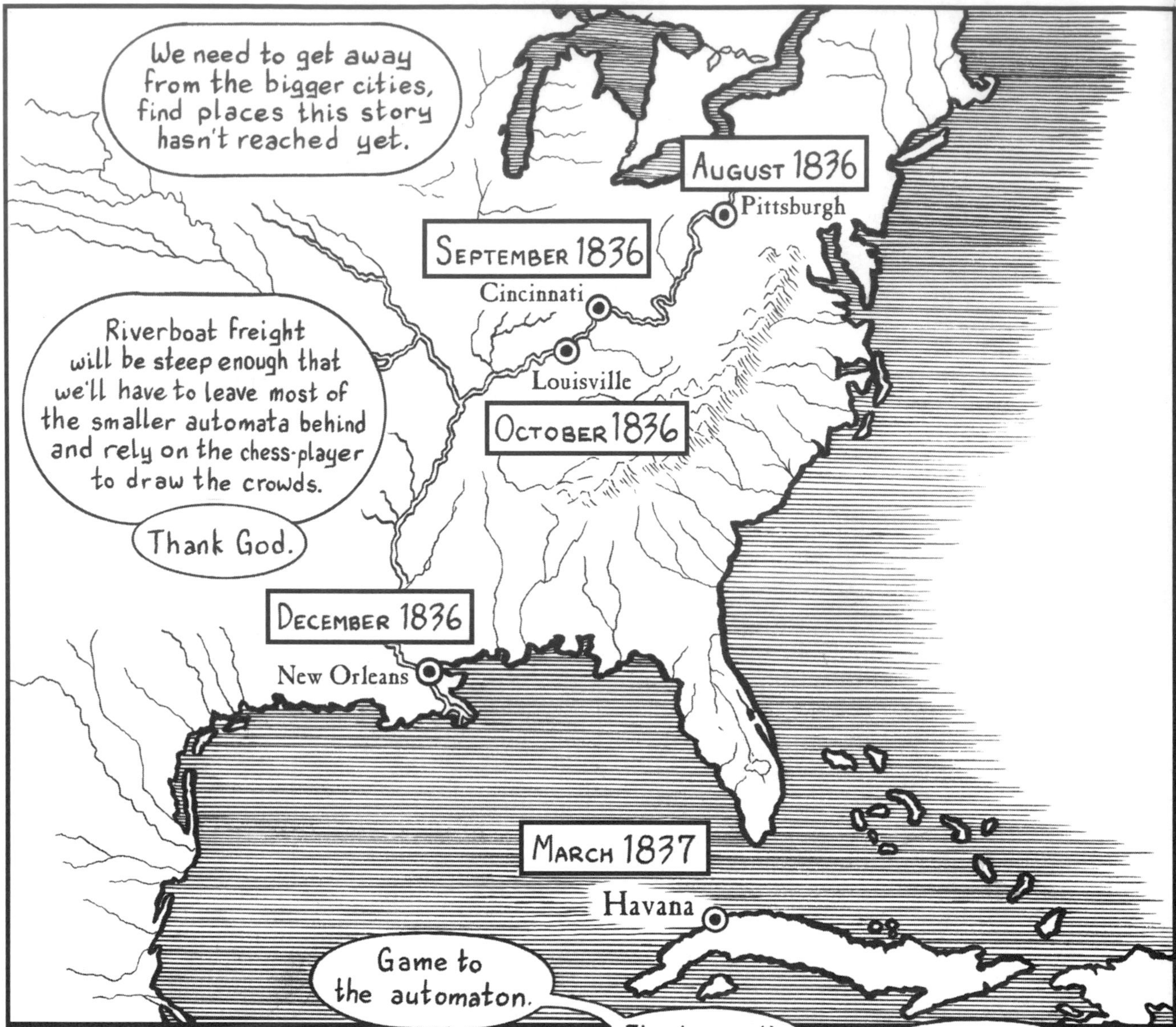
We need to get away from the bigger cities, find places this story hasn't reached yet.
August 1836
Pittsburgh
September 1836
Cincinnati
Louisville
Riverboat freight will be steep enough that we'll have to leave most of the smaller automata behind and rely on the chess-player to draw the crowds.
October 1836
Thank God.
December 1836
New Orleans
March 1837
Havana

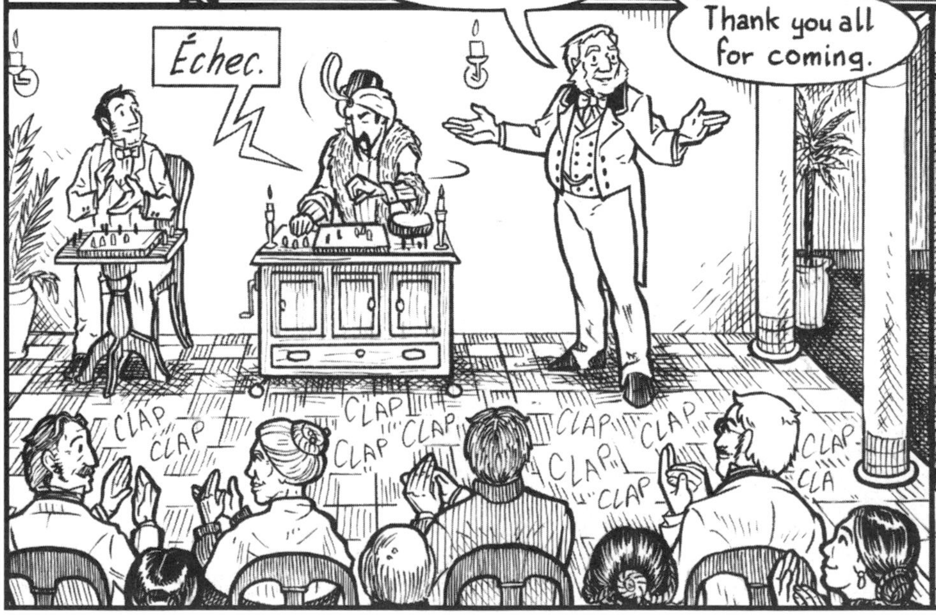
Game to the automaton.
Thank you all for coming.
Échec.
CLAP CLAP
CLAP CLAP CLAP
CLAP CLAP CLAP
CLAP CLAP
CLAP CLA

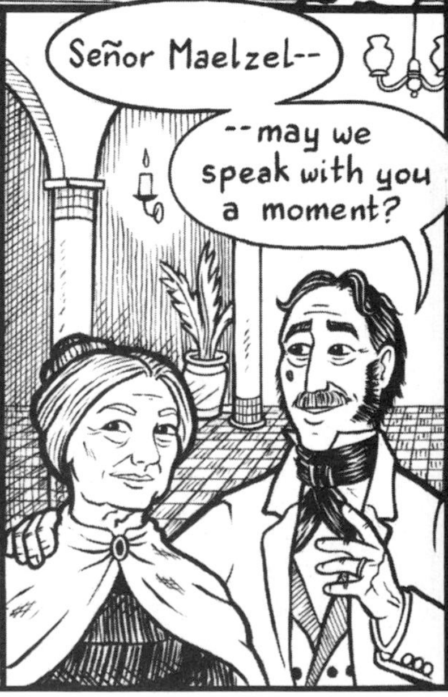
Señor Maelzel--
--may we speak with you a moment?

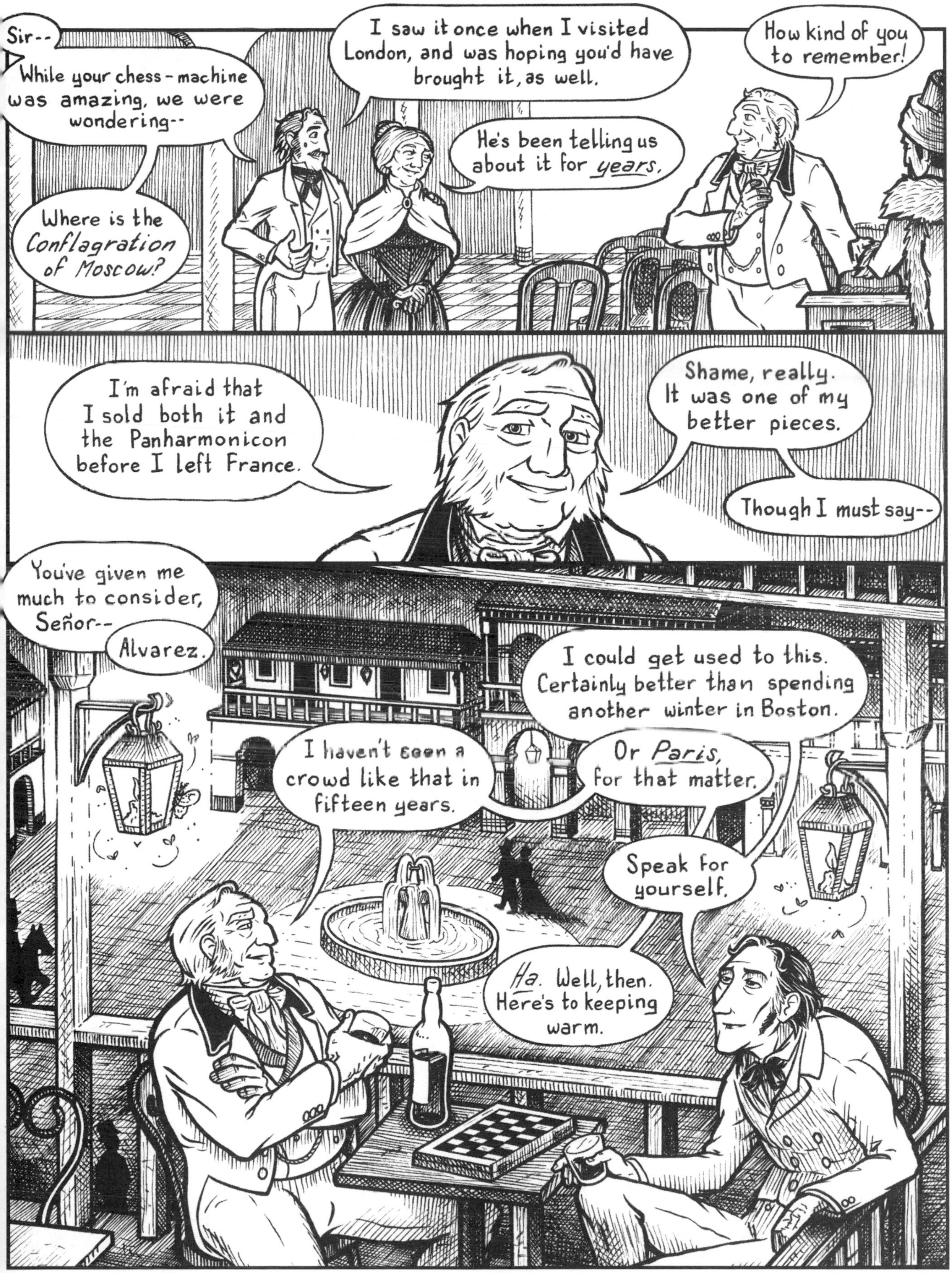

Sir--
While your chess-machine was amazing, we were wondering--
Where is the *Conflagration of Moscow?*
I saw it once when I visited London, and was hoping you'd have brought it, as well.
He's been telling us about it for years.
How kind of you to remember!
I'm afraid that I sold both it and the Panharmonicon before I left France.
Shame, really. It was one of my better pieces.
Though I must say--
You've given me much to consider, Señor--
Alvarez.
I could get used to this. Certainly better than spending another winter in Boston.
I haven't seen a crowd like that in fifteen years.
Or Paris, for that matter.
Speak for yourself.
Ha. Well, then. Here's to keeping warm.

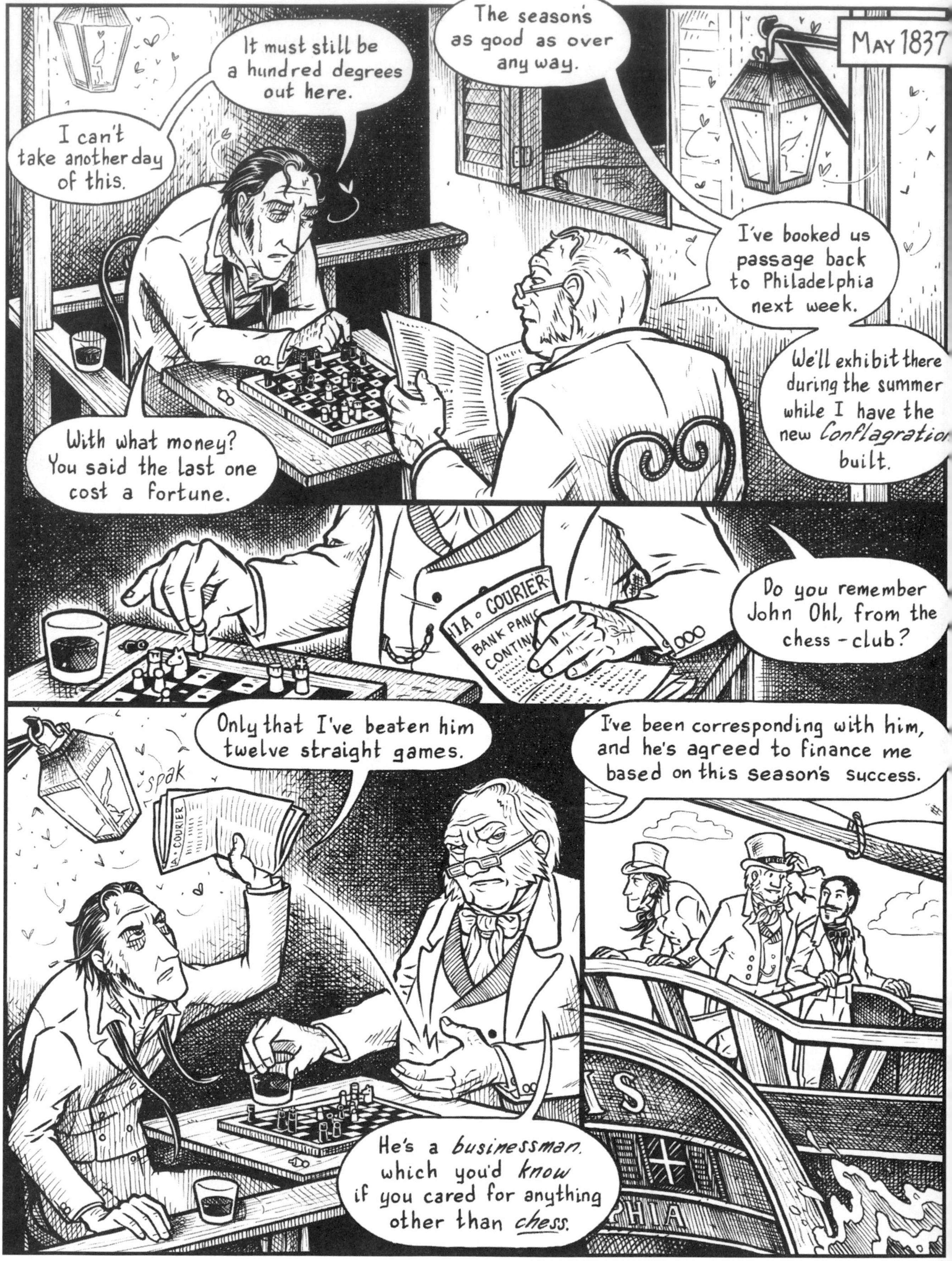
MAY 1837
I can't take another day of this.
It must still be a hundred degrees out here.
The season's as good as over any way.
I've booked us passage back to Philadelphia next week.
We'll exhibit there during the summer while I have the new *Conflagration* built.
With what money? You said the last one cost a fortune.
Do you remember John Ohl, from the chess-club?
COURIER
BANK PANIC CONTIN
Only that I've beaten him twelve straight games.
spak
I've been corresponding with him, and he's agreed to finance me based on this season's success.
He's a *businessman,* which you'd *know* if you cared for anything other than *chess.*

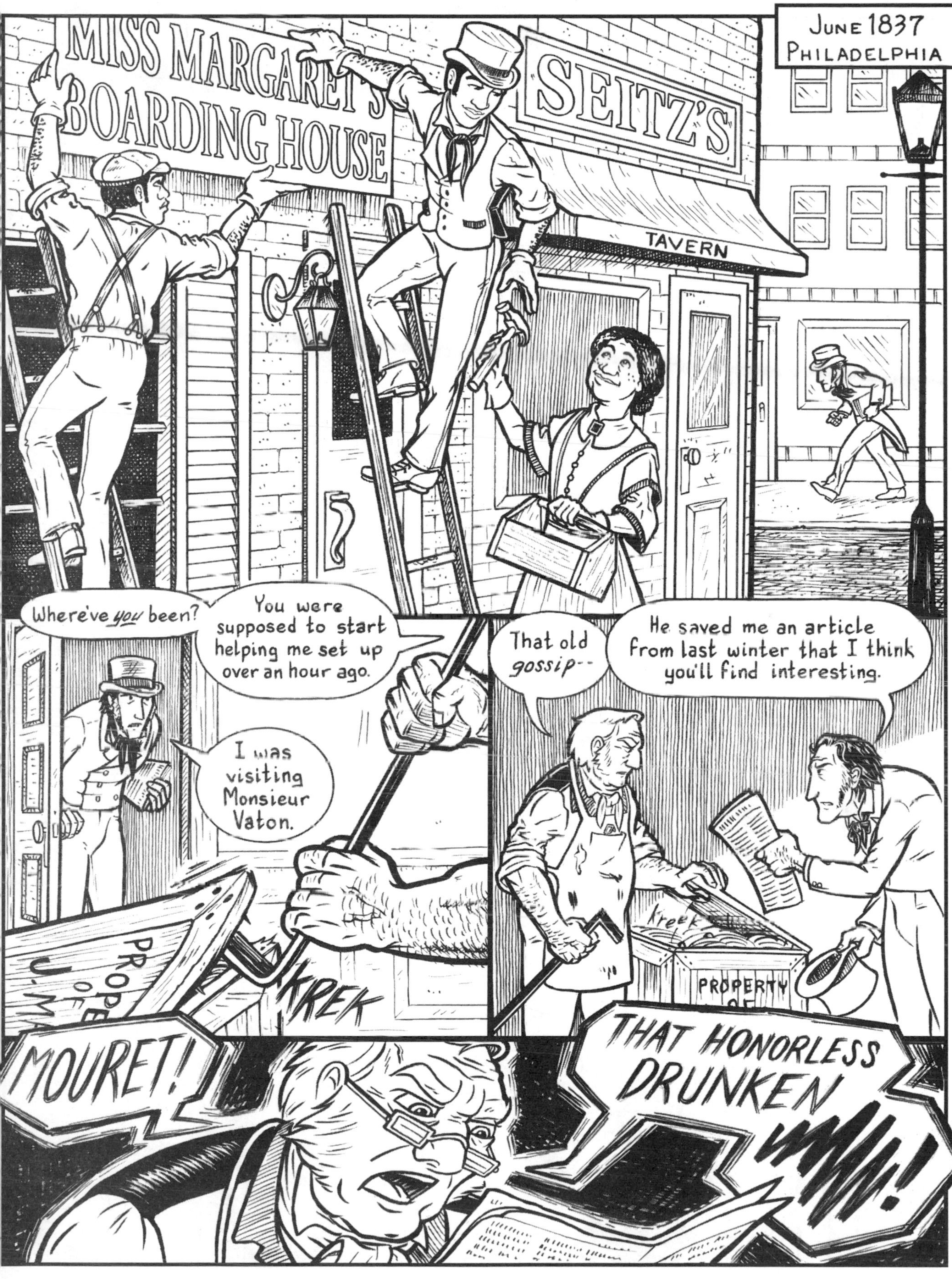
June 1837
Philadelphia
MISS MARGARET'S BOARDING HOUSE
SEITZ'S
TAVERN
Where've you been?
You were supposed to start helping me set up over an hour ago.
I was visiting Monsieur Vaton.
PROP OF J.M.
KREK
That old gossip--
He saved me an article from last winter that I think you'll find interesting.
kreek
PROPERTY OF
MOURET!
THAT HONORLESS DRUNKEN
VAMN!

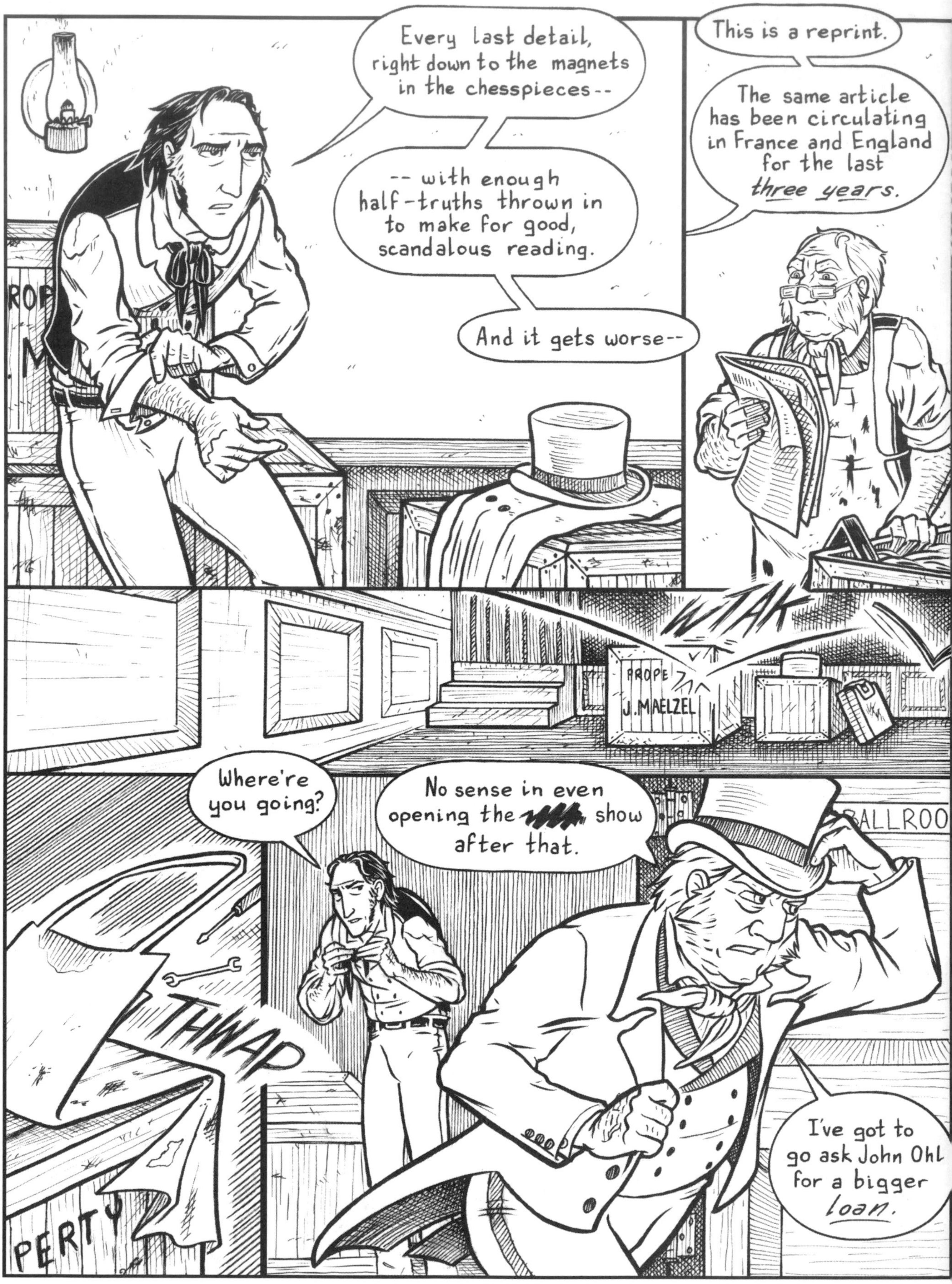
Every last detail, right down to the magnets in the chesspieces--
-- with enough half-truths thrown in to make for good, scandalous reading.
And it gets worse--
This is a reprint.
The same article has been circulating in France and England for the last *three years.*
ROP
WTAK
PROPE
J.MAELZEL
Where're you going?
No sense in even opening the [redacted] show after that.
BALLROO
THWAP
PERTY
I've got to go ask John Ohl for a bigger *loan.*

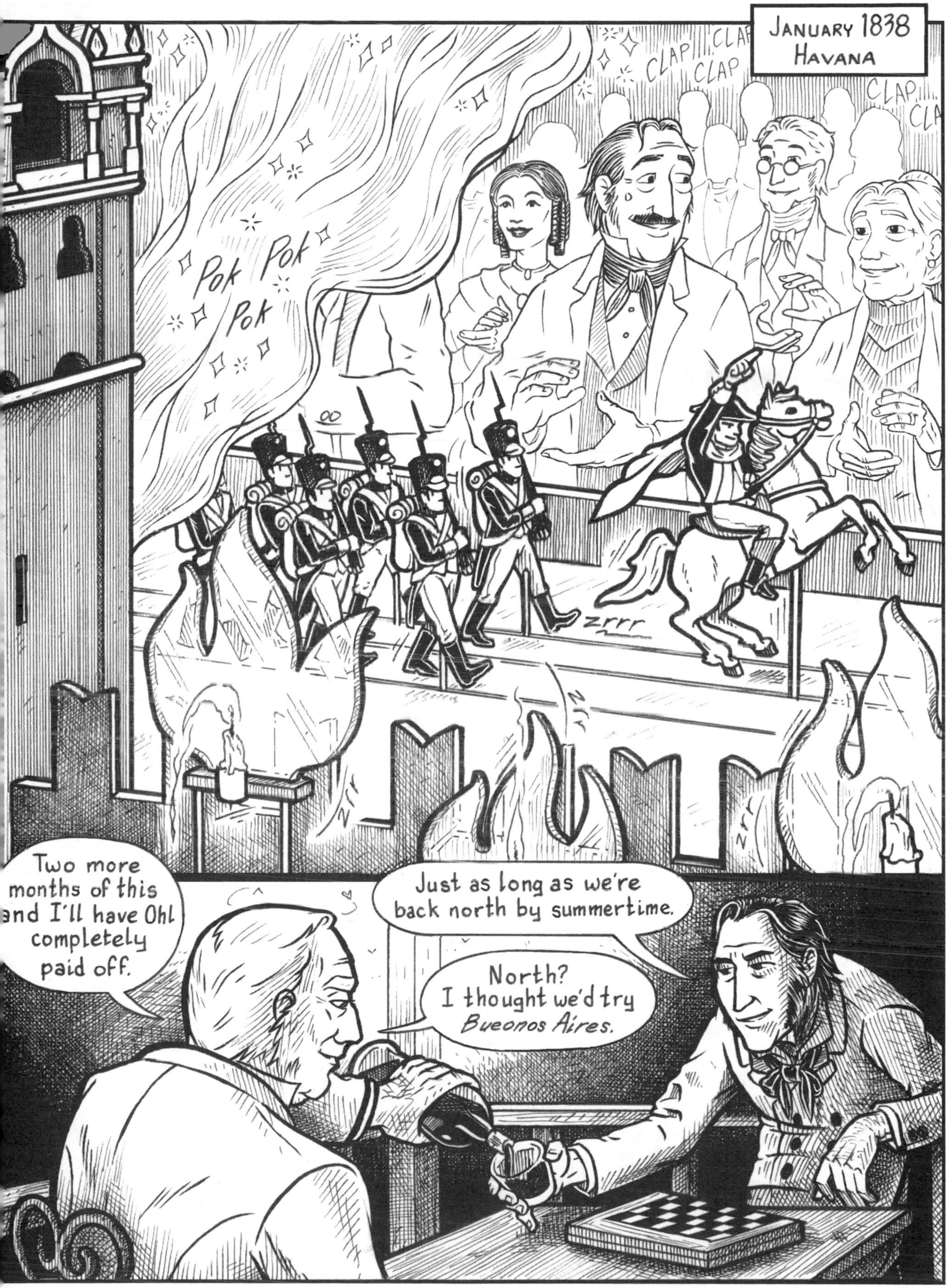

JANUARY 1838
HAVANA
CLAP CLAP CLAP
CLAP CLAP
Pok Pok Pok
zrrr
Two more months of this and I'll have Ohl completely paid off.
Just as long as we're back north by summertime.
North? I thought we'd try *Bueonos Aires*.

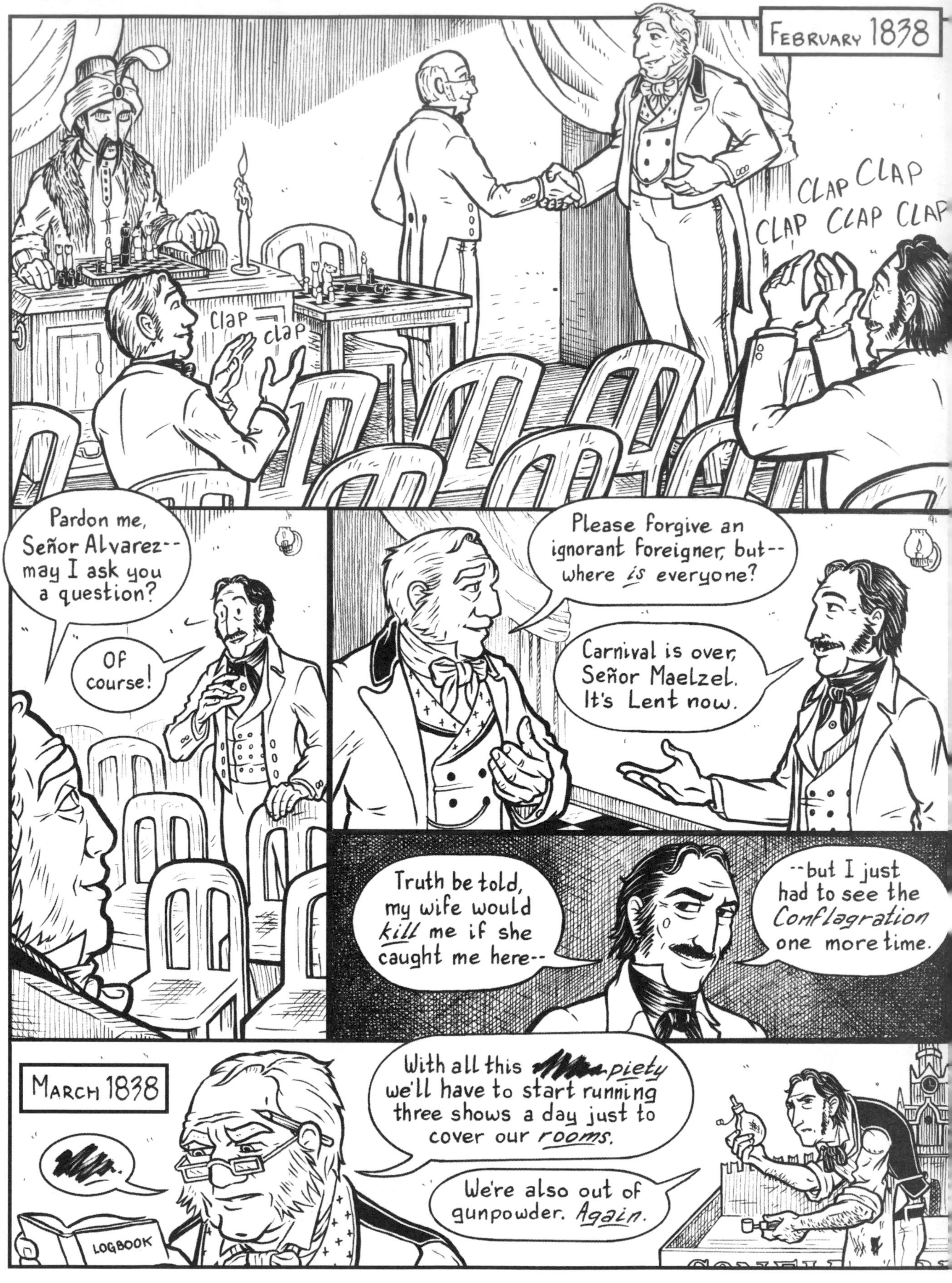
February 1838
clap clap
CLAP CLAP
CLAP CLAP CLAP
Pardon me, Señor Alvarez--may I ask you a question?
Of course!
Please forgive an ignorant foreigner, but--where *is* everyone?
Carnival is over, Señor Maelzel. It's Lent now.
Truth be told, my wife would *kill* me if she caught me here--
--but I just had to see the *Conflagration* one more time.
March 1838
[redacted].
With all this [redacted] *piety* we'll have to start running three shows a day just to cover our *rooms*.
We're also out of gunpowder. *Again*.
LOGBOOK

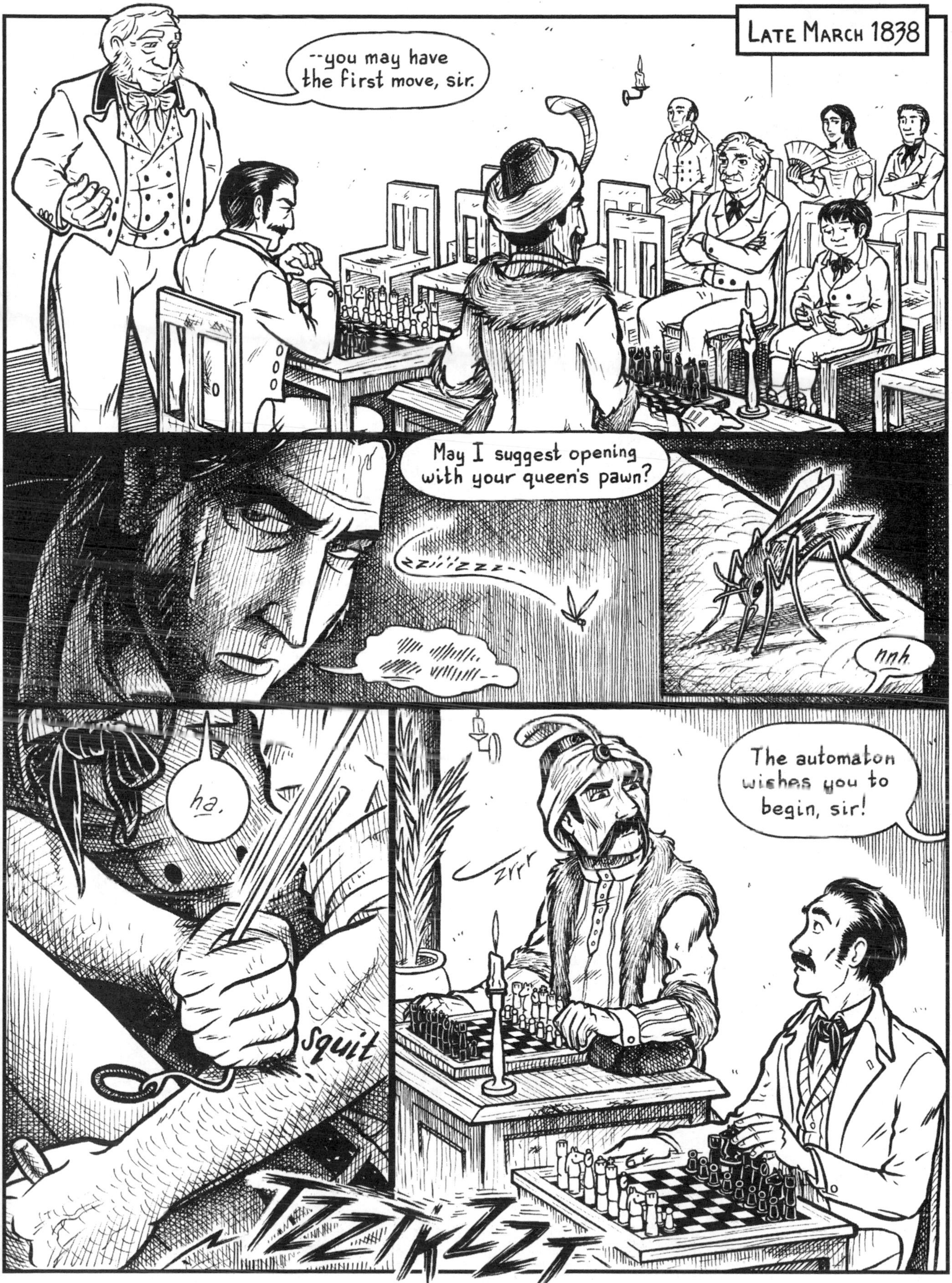

Late March 1838
--you may have the first move, sir.
May I suggest opening with your queen's pawn?
zzii'izzz--
nnh
ha.
squit
TZZTKZZT
zrrr
The automaton wishes you to begin, sir!

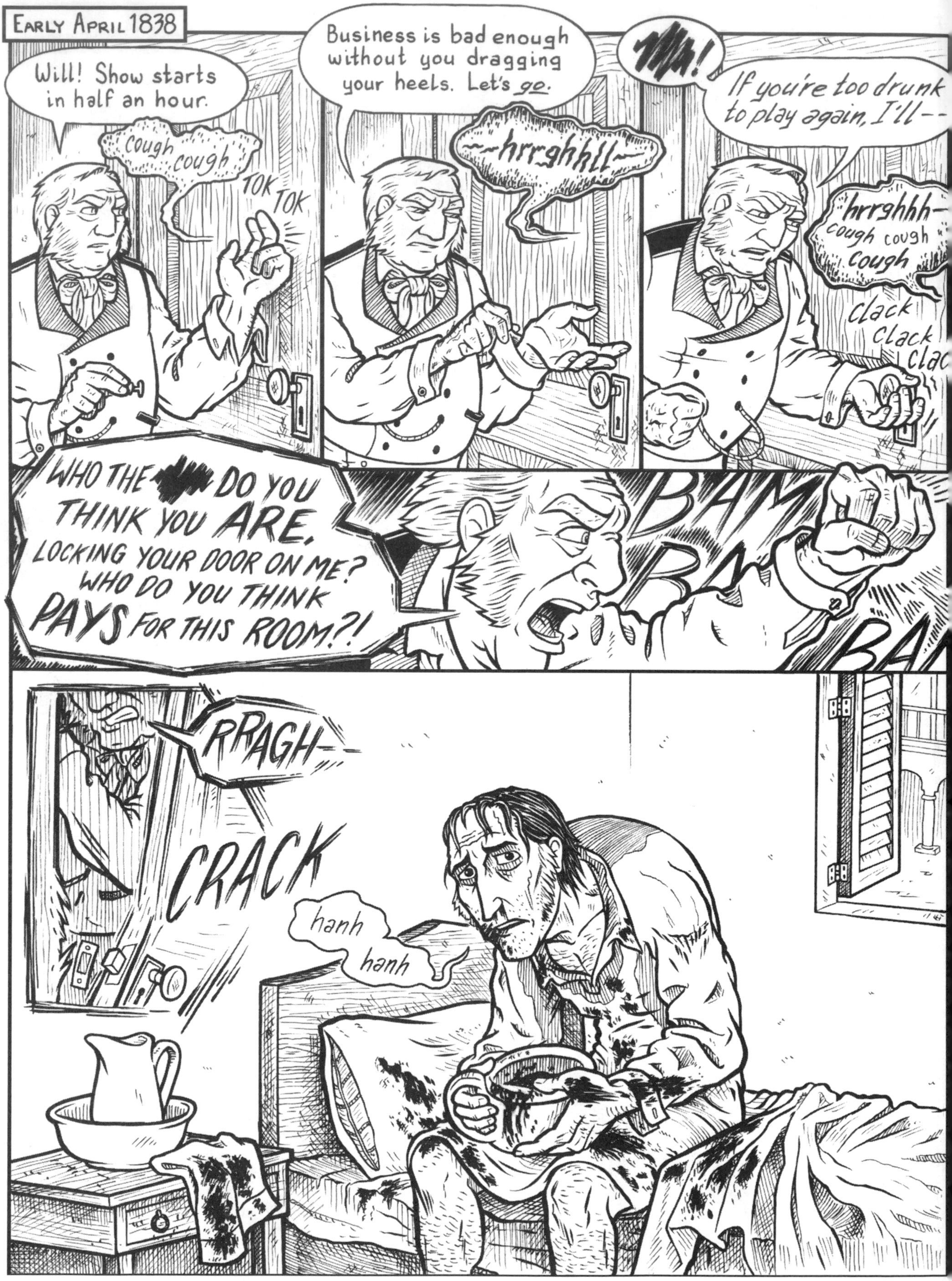

Early April 1838
Will! Show starts in half an hour.
cough cough
TOK TOK
Business is bad enough without you dragging your heels. Let's *go*.
~~hrrghhll~
[redacted]!
If you're too drunk to play again, I'll--
hrrghhh-- cough cough Cough
Clack Clack Clac
WHO THE [redacted] DO YOU THINK YOU ARE, LOCKING YOUR DOOR ON ME? WHO DO YOU THINK PAYS FOR THIS ROOM?!
BAM BAM BAM
RRAGH--
CRACK
hanh hanh

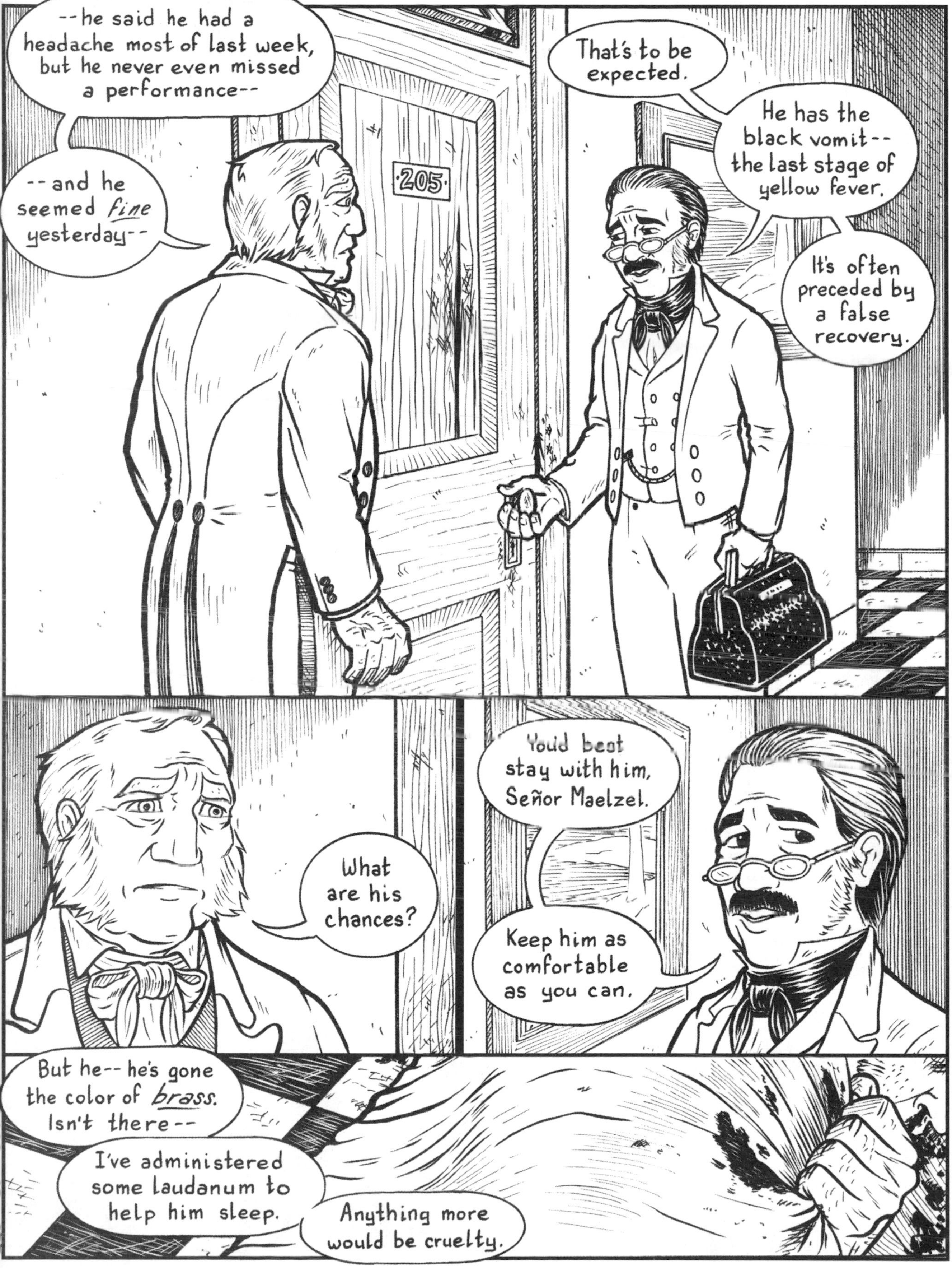
--he said he had a headache most of last week, but he never even missed a performance--
--and he seemed *fine* yesterday--
That's to be expected.
He has the black vomit--the last stage of yellow fever.
It's often preceded by a false recovery.
205
What are his chances?
You'd best stay with him, Señor Maelzel.
Keep him as comfortable as you can.
But he--he's gone the color of *brass*. Isn't there--
I've administered some laudanum to help him sleep.
Anything more would be cruelty.

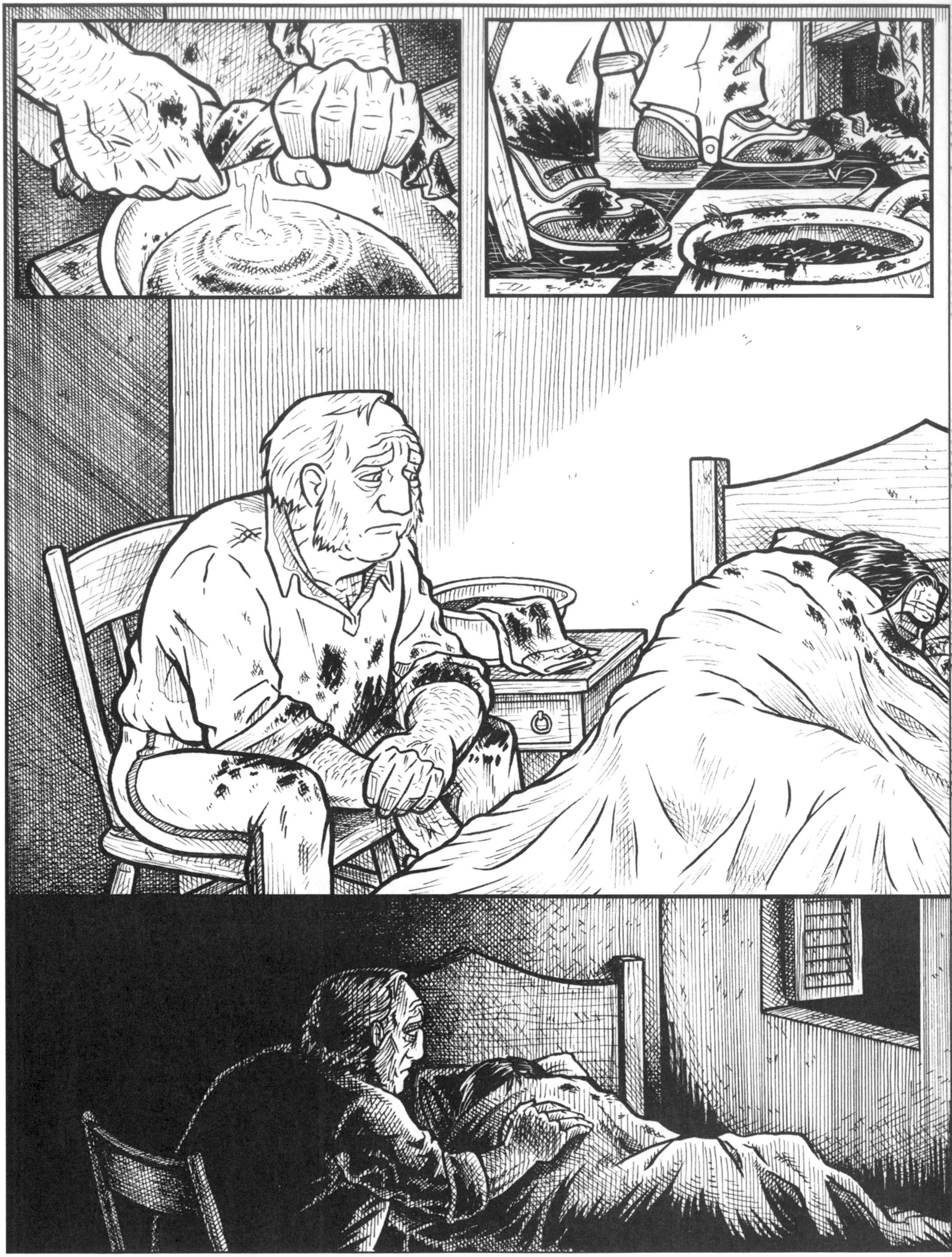

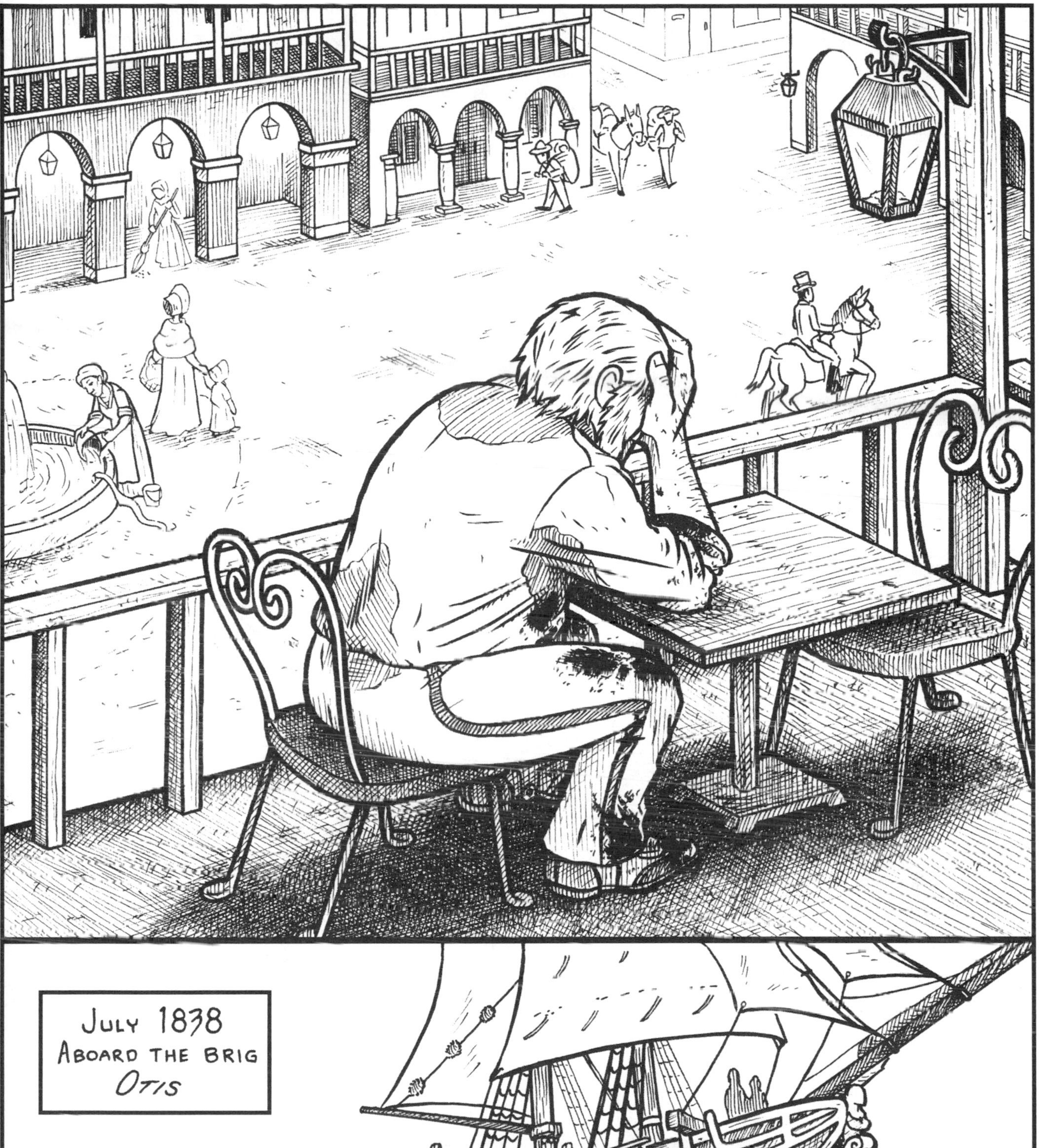

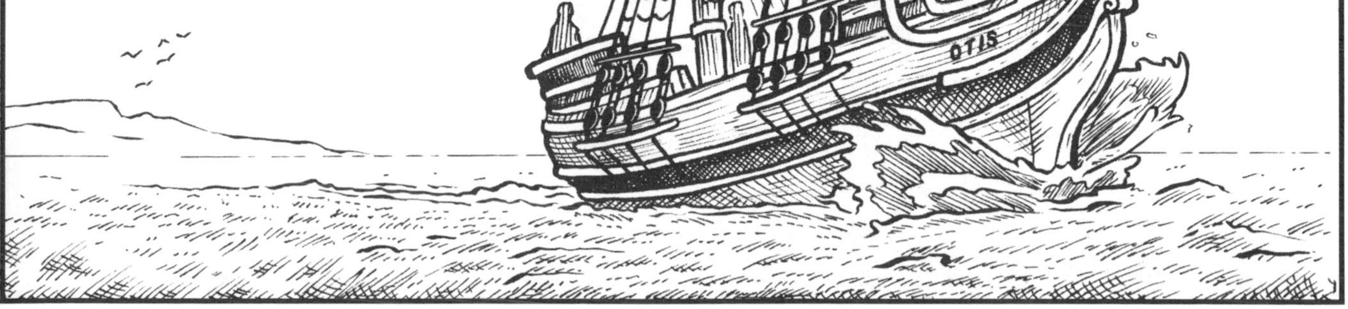
July 1838
Aboard the Brig
Otis
OTIS

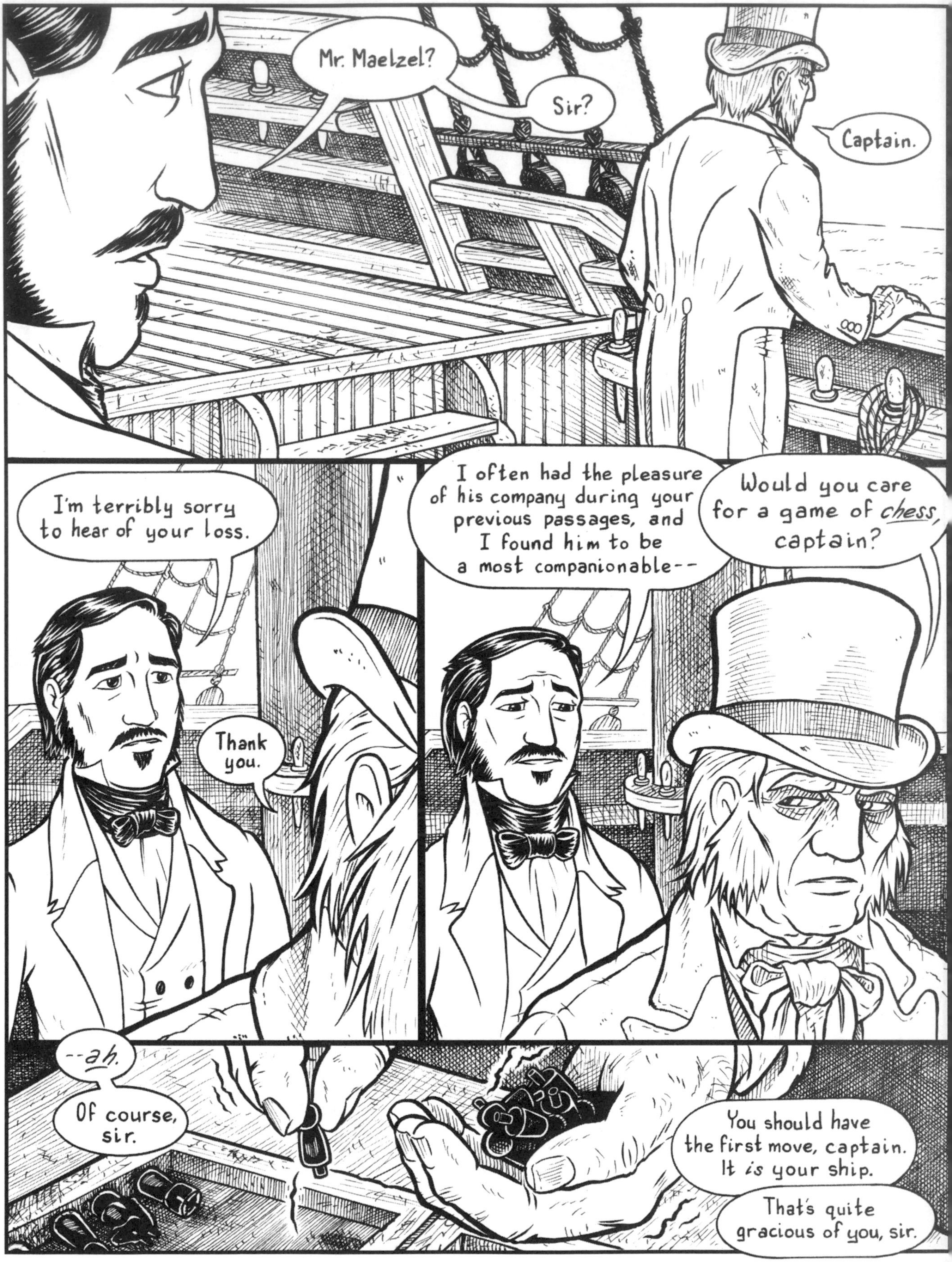
Mr. Maelzel?
Sir?
Captain.
I'm terribly sorry to hear of your loss.
Thank you.
I often had the pleasure of his company during your previous passages, and I found him to be a most companionable--
Would you care for a game of *chess*, captain?
--*ah.*
Of course, sir.
You should have the first move, captain. It *is* your ship.
That's quite gracious of you, sir.

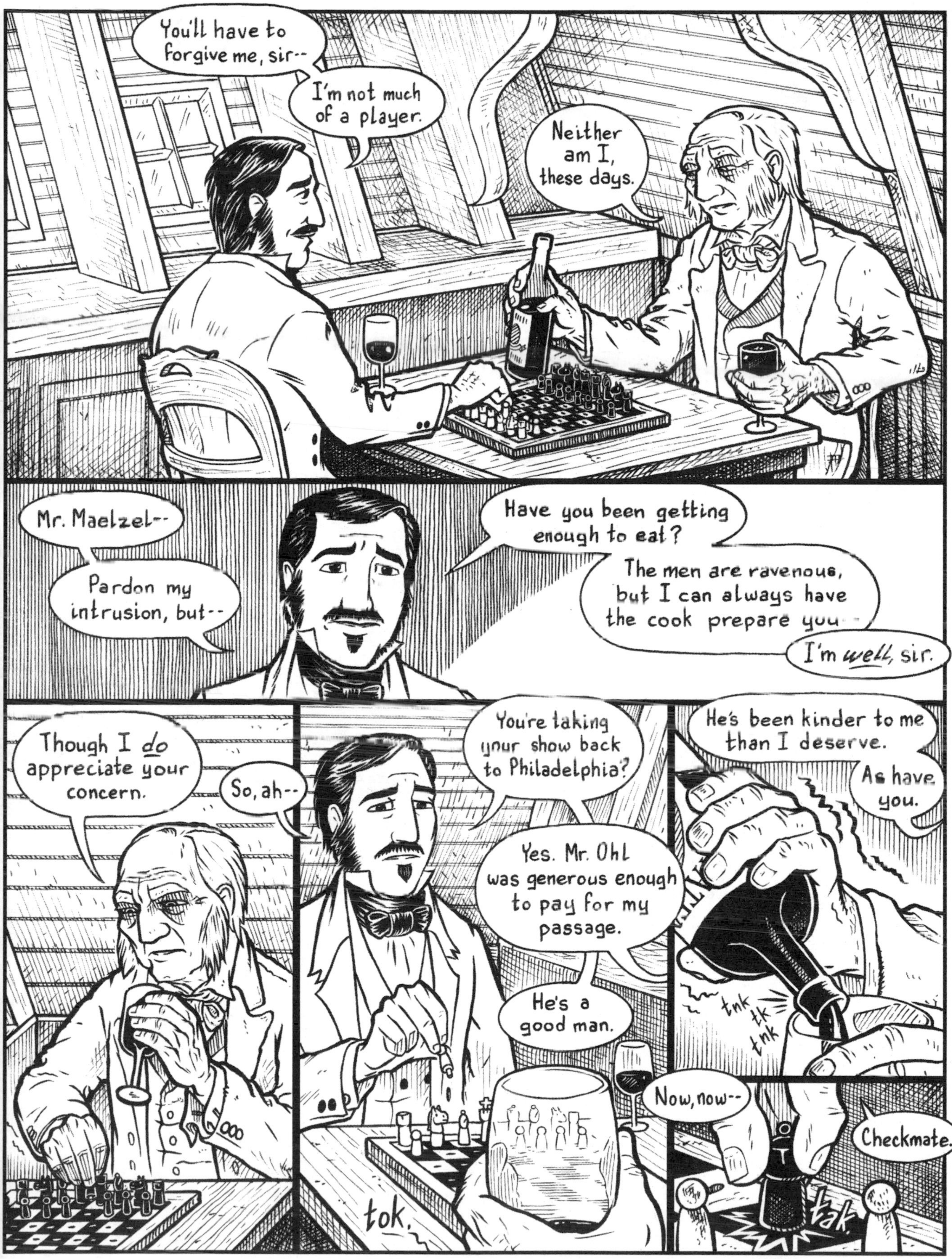

You'll have to forgive me, sir--
I'm not much of a player.
Neither am I, these days.
Mr. Maelzel--
Pardon my intrusion, but--
Have you been getting enough to eat?
The men are ravenous, but I can always have the cook prepare you--
I'm *well*, sir.
Though I *do* appreciate your concern.
So, ah--
You're taking your show back to Philadelphia?
Yes. Mr. Ohl was generous enough to pay for my passage.
He's a good man.
tok.
He's been kinder to me than I deserve.
As have you.
tnk tk tnk
Now, now--
Checkmate.
tak.

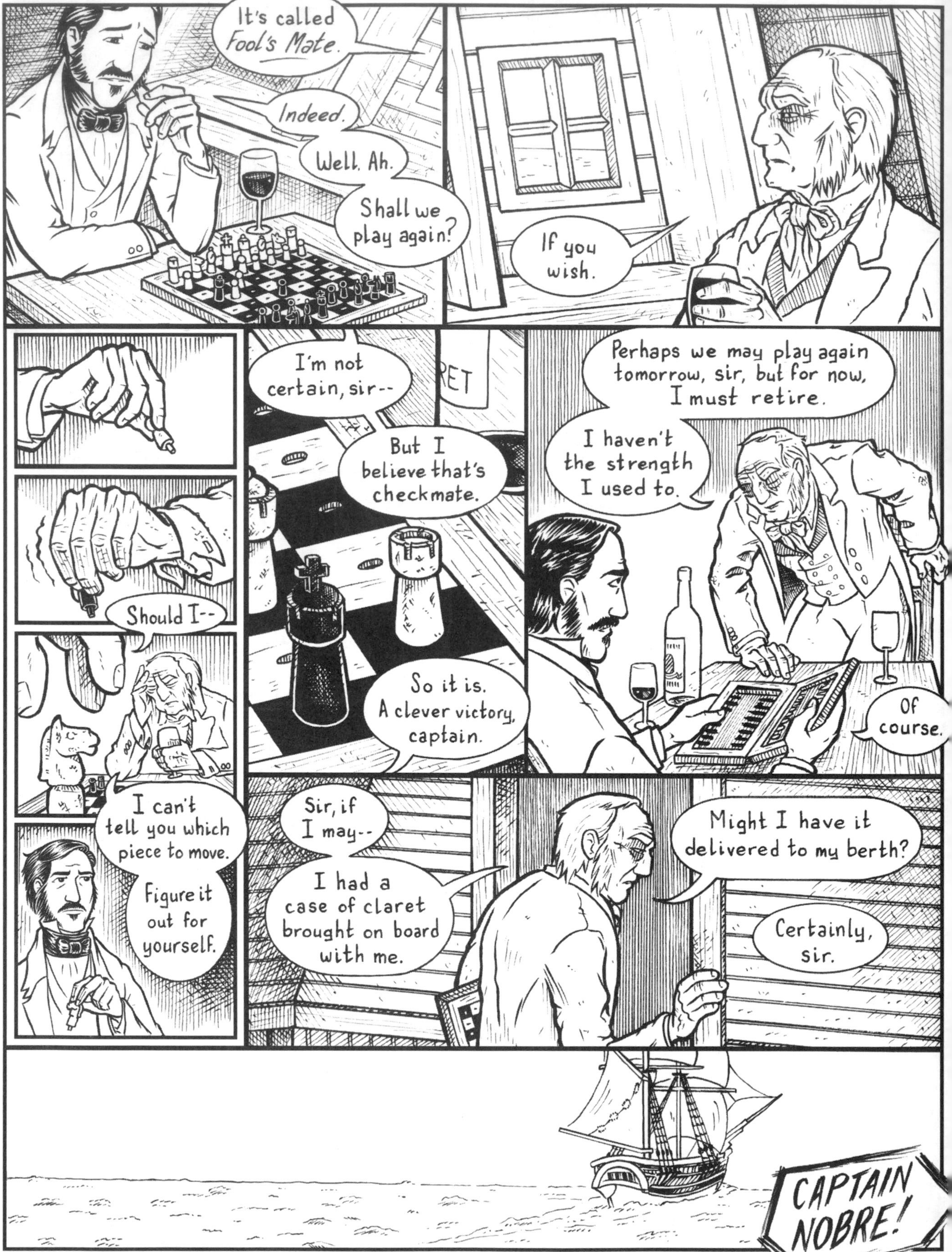
It's called Fool's Mate.
Indeed.
Well. Ah.
Shall we play again?
If you wish.
Should I--
I can't tell you which piece to move.
Figure it out for yourself.
I'm not certain, sir--
But I believe that's checkmate.
So it is. A clever victory, captain.
Perhaps we may play again tomorrow, sir, but for now, I must retire.
I haven't the strength I used to.
Of course.
Sir, if I may--
I had a case of claret brought on board with me.
Might I have it delivered to my berth?
Certainly, sir.
CAPTAIN NOBRE!

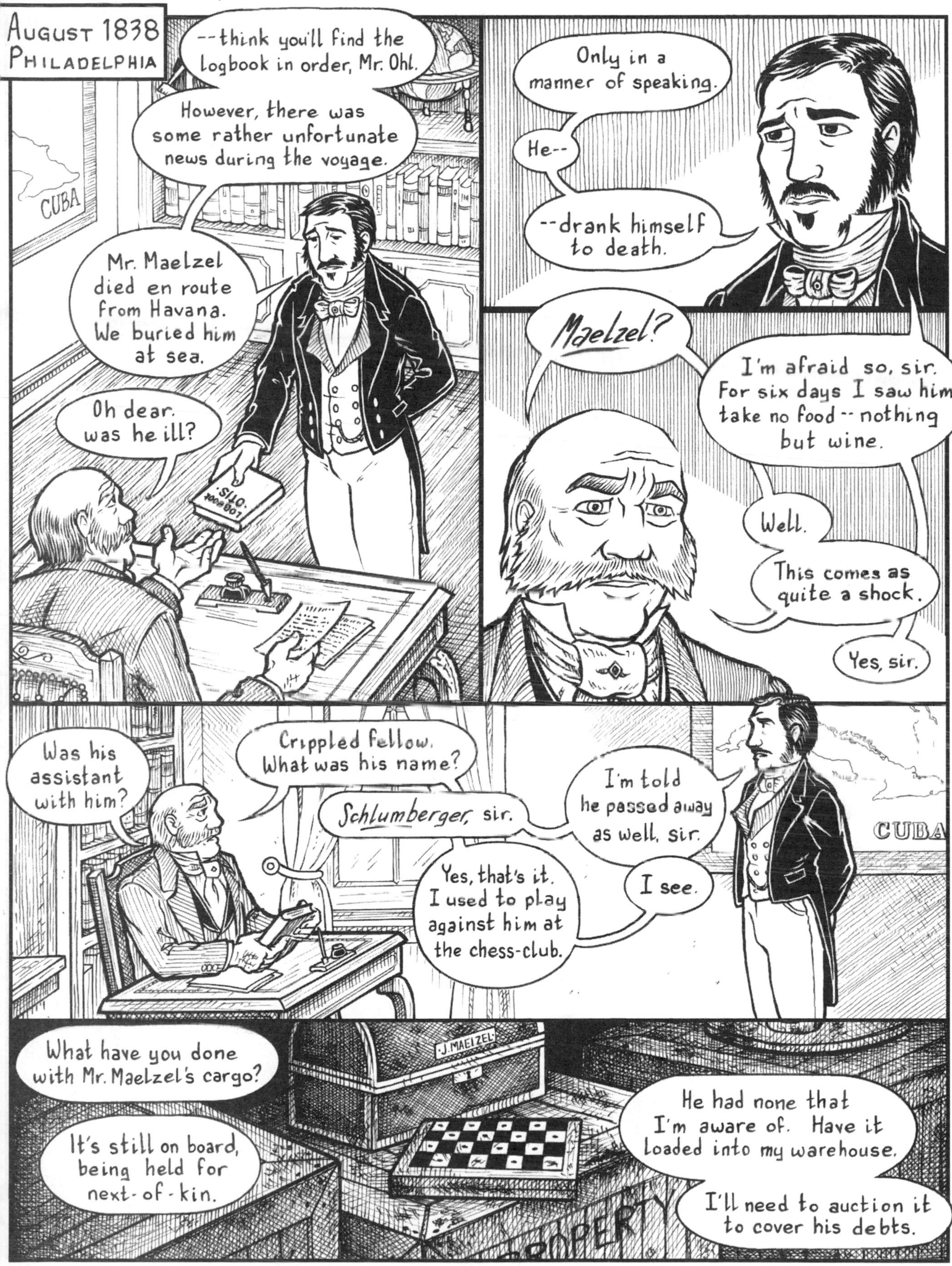
August 1838 Philadelphia
--think you'll find the logbook in order, Mr. Ohl.
However, there was some rather unfortunate news during the voyage.
Mr. Maelzel died en route from Havana. We buried him at sea.
Oh dear. was he ill?
Only in a manner of speaking.
He--
--drank himself to death.
Maelzel?
I'm afraid so, sir. For six days I saw him take no food -- nothing but wine.
Well.
This comes as quite a shock.
Yes, sir.
Was his assistant with him?
Crippled fellow. What was his name?
Schlumberger, sir.
Yes, that's it. I used to play against him at the chess-club.
I'm told he passed away as well, sir.
I see.
What have you done with Mr. Maelzel's cargo?
It's still on board, being held for next-of-kin.
He had none that I'm aware of. Have it loaded into my warehouse.
I'll need to auction it to cover his debts.

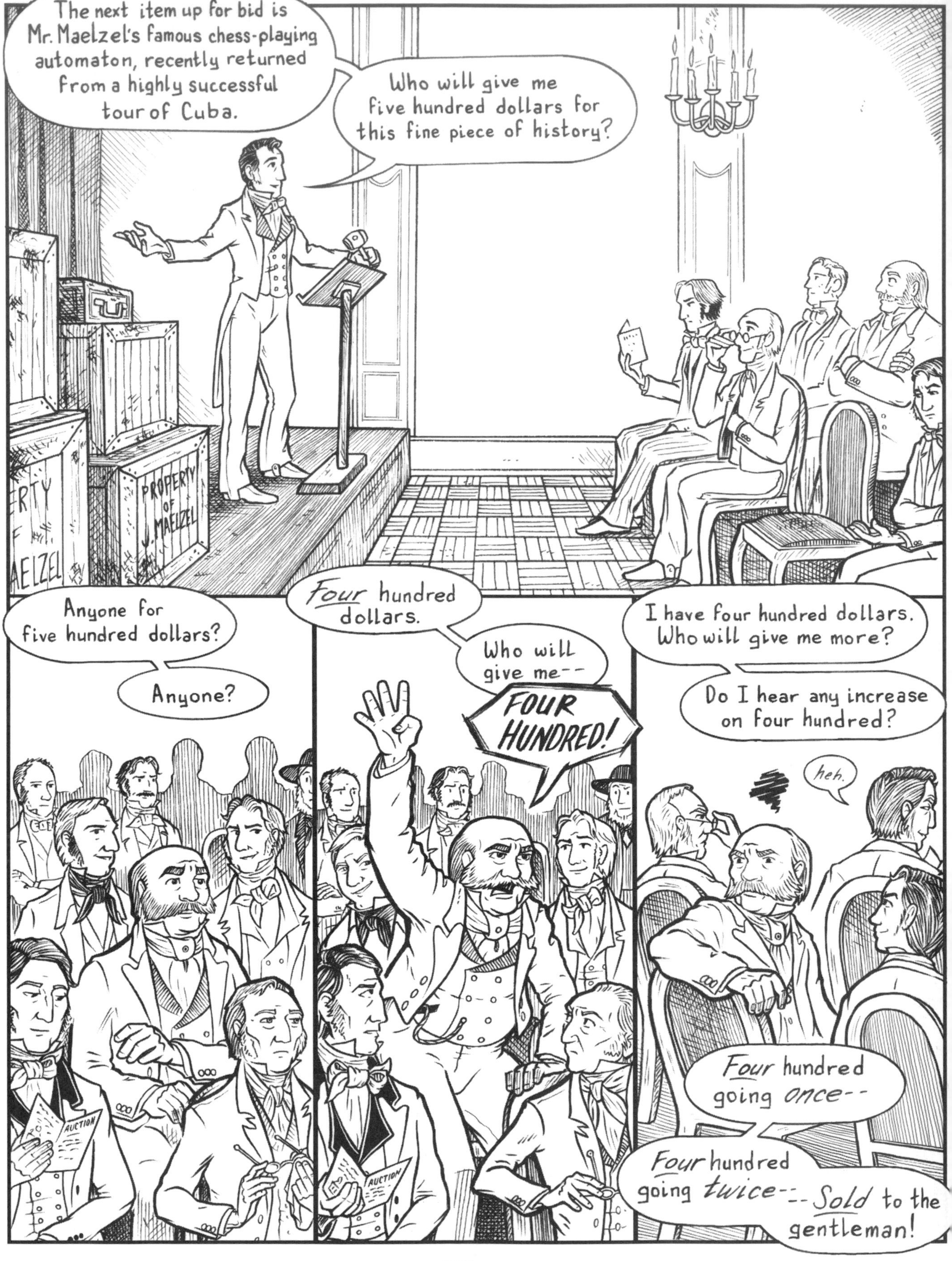
The next item up for bid is Mr. Maelzel's famous chess-playing automaton, recently returned from a highly successful tour of Cuba.
Who will give me five hundred dollars for this fine piece of history?
PROPERTY OF J. MAELZEL
Anyone for five hundred dollars?
Anyone?
Four hundred dollars.
Who will give me--
FOUR HUNDRED!
I have four hundred dollars. Who will give me more?
Do I hear any increase on four hundred?
heh.
Four hundred going once--
Four hundred going twice-- --Sold to the gentleman!

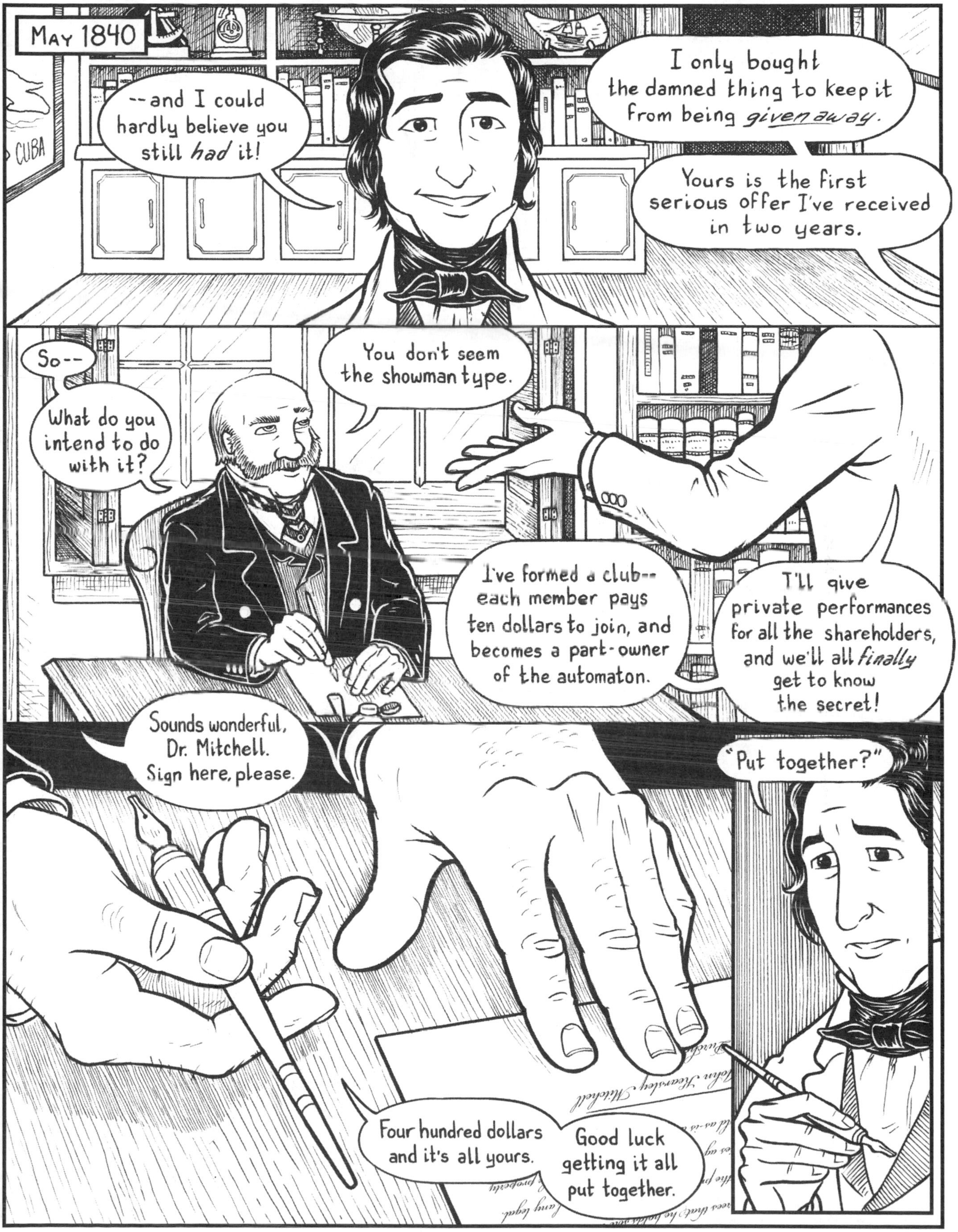
May 1840
--and I could hardly believe you still *had* it!
I only bought the damned thing to keep it from being given away.
Yours is the first serious offer I've received in two years.
So--
What do you intend to do with it?
You don't seem the showman type.
I've formed a club-- each member pays ten dollars to join, and becomes a part-owner of the automaton.
I'll give private performances for all the shareholders, and we'll all *finally* get to know the secret!
Sounds wonderful, Dr. Mitchell. Sign here, please.
"Put together?"
Four hundred dollars and it's all yours.
Good luck getting it all put together.

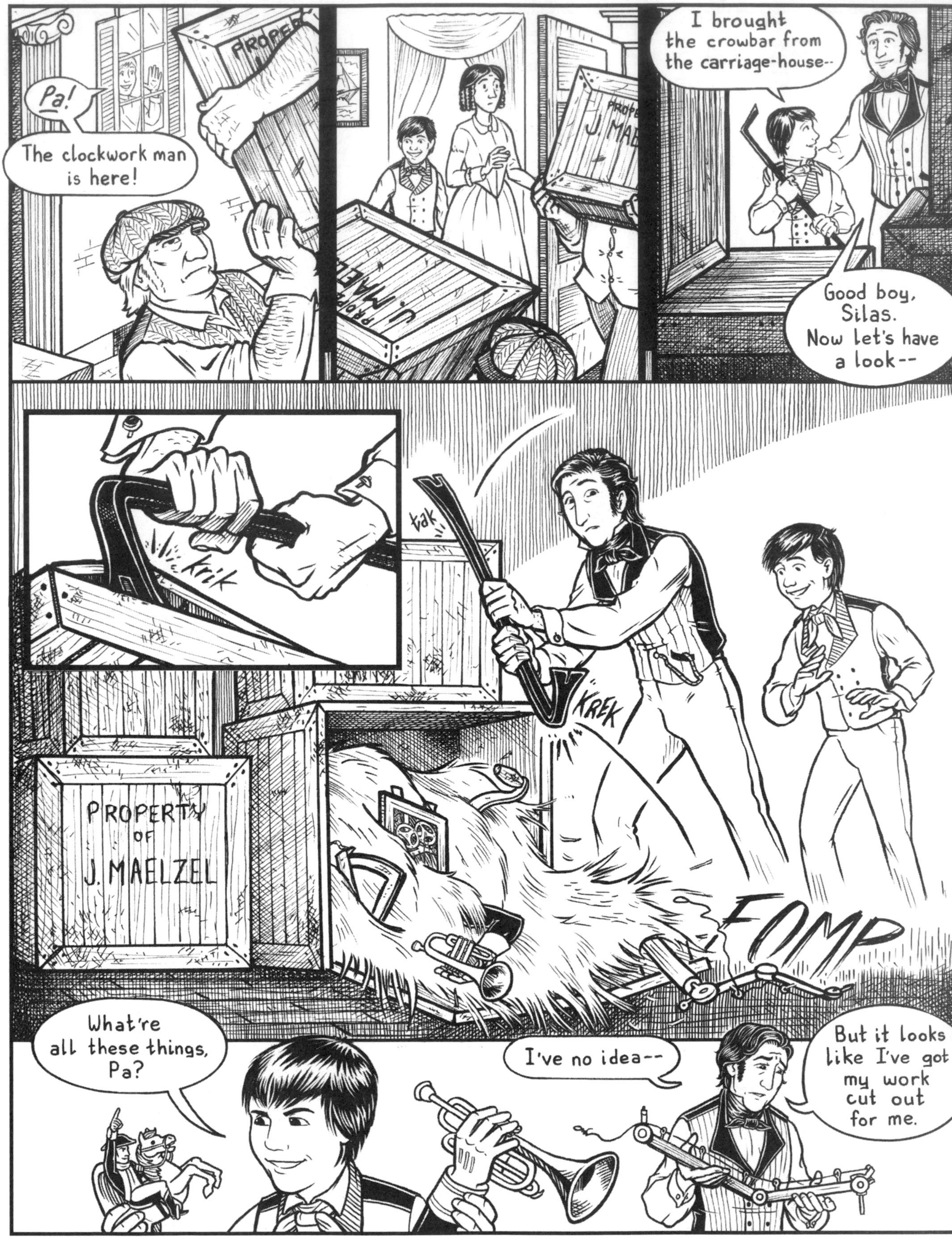
PROPER
Pa!
The clockwork man is here!
PROPE
J. MAE
J. MAELZ
PROP
I brought the crowbar from the carriage-house--
Good boy, Silas. Now let's have a look--
krik
tak
KREK
PROPERTY OF J. MAELZEL
FOMP
What're all these things, Pa?
I've no idea--
But it looks like I've got my work cut out for me.

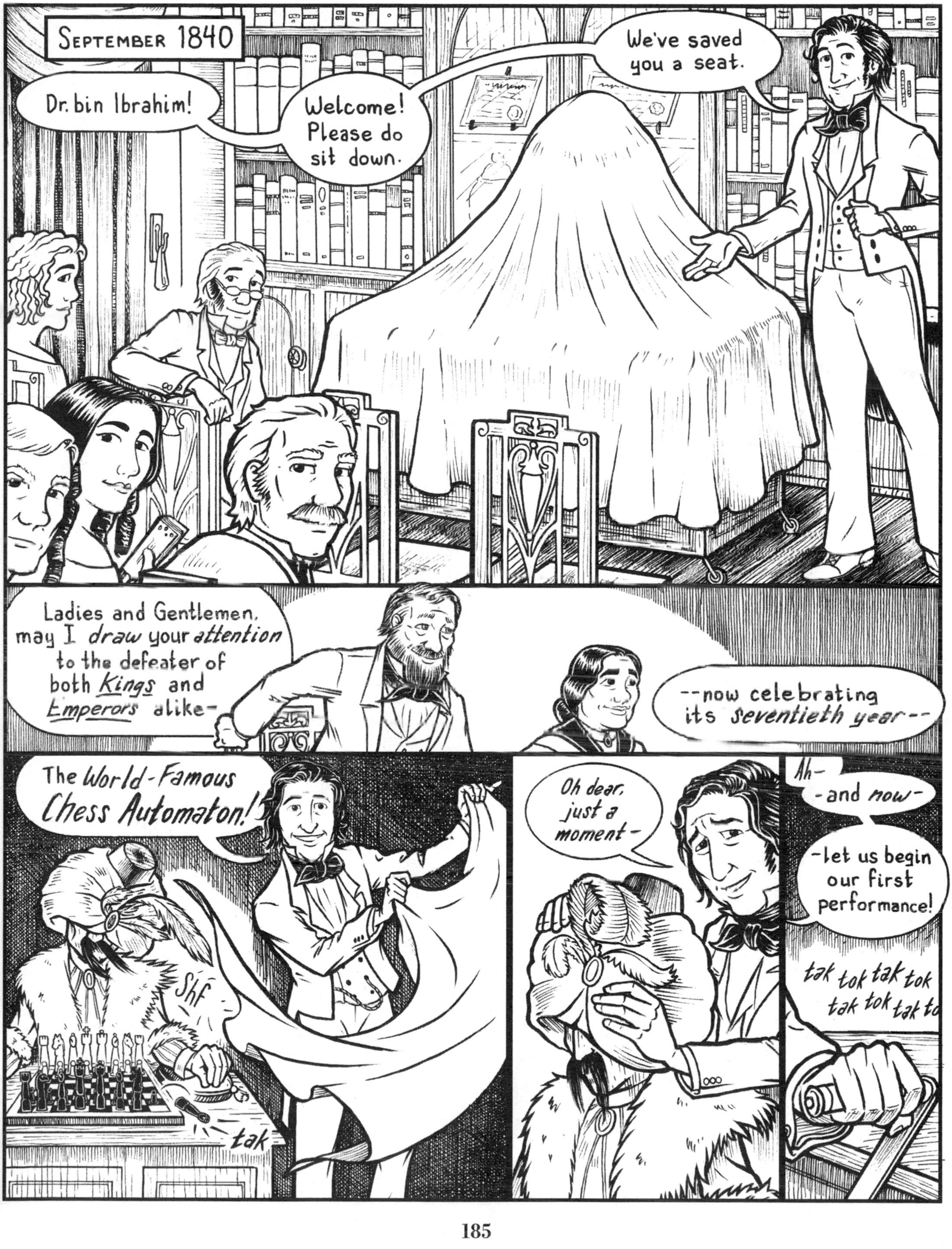
September 1840
Dr. bin Ibrahim!
Welcome! Please do sit down.
We've saved you a seat.
Ladies and Gentlemen, may I *draw* your *attention* to the defeater of both Kings and Emperors alike-
--now celebrating its *seventieth year*--
The *World-Famous Chess Automaton!*
Shf
tak
Oh dear, just a moment-
Ah-
-and *now*-
-let us begin our first performance!
tak tok tak tok
tak tok tak to

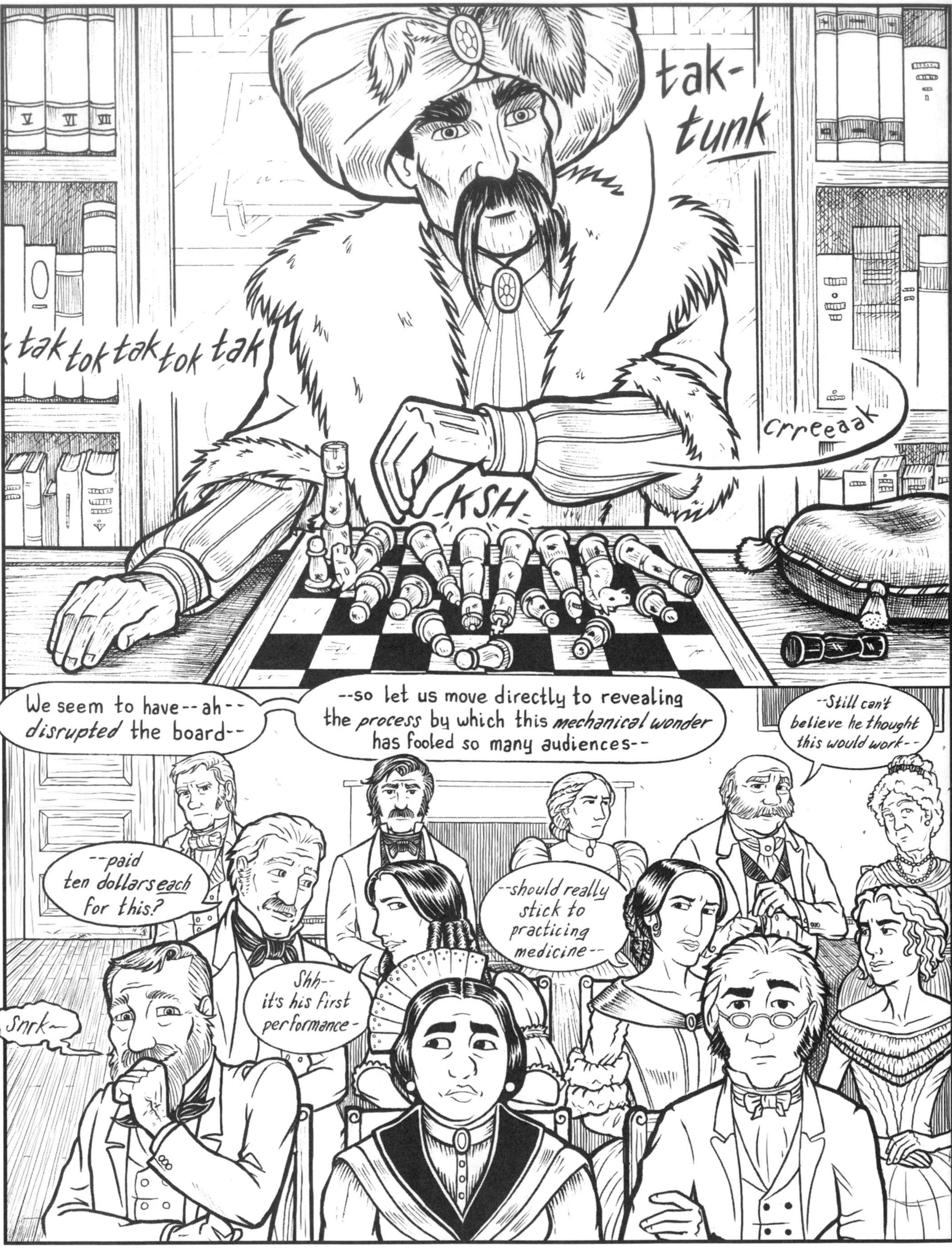
tak-
tunk
tak tok tak tok tak
crreeaak
KSH
We seem to have--ah-- disrupted the board--
--so let us move directly to revealing the process by which this mechanical wonder has fooled so many audiences--
--Still can't believe he thought this would work--
--paid ten dollars each for this?
--should really stick to practicing medicine--
Shh-- it's his first performance-
Snrk-

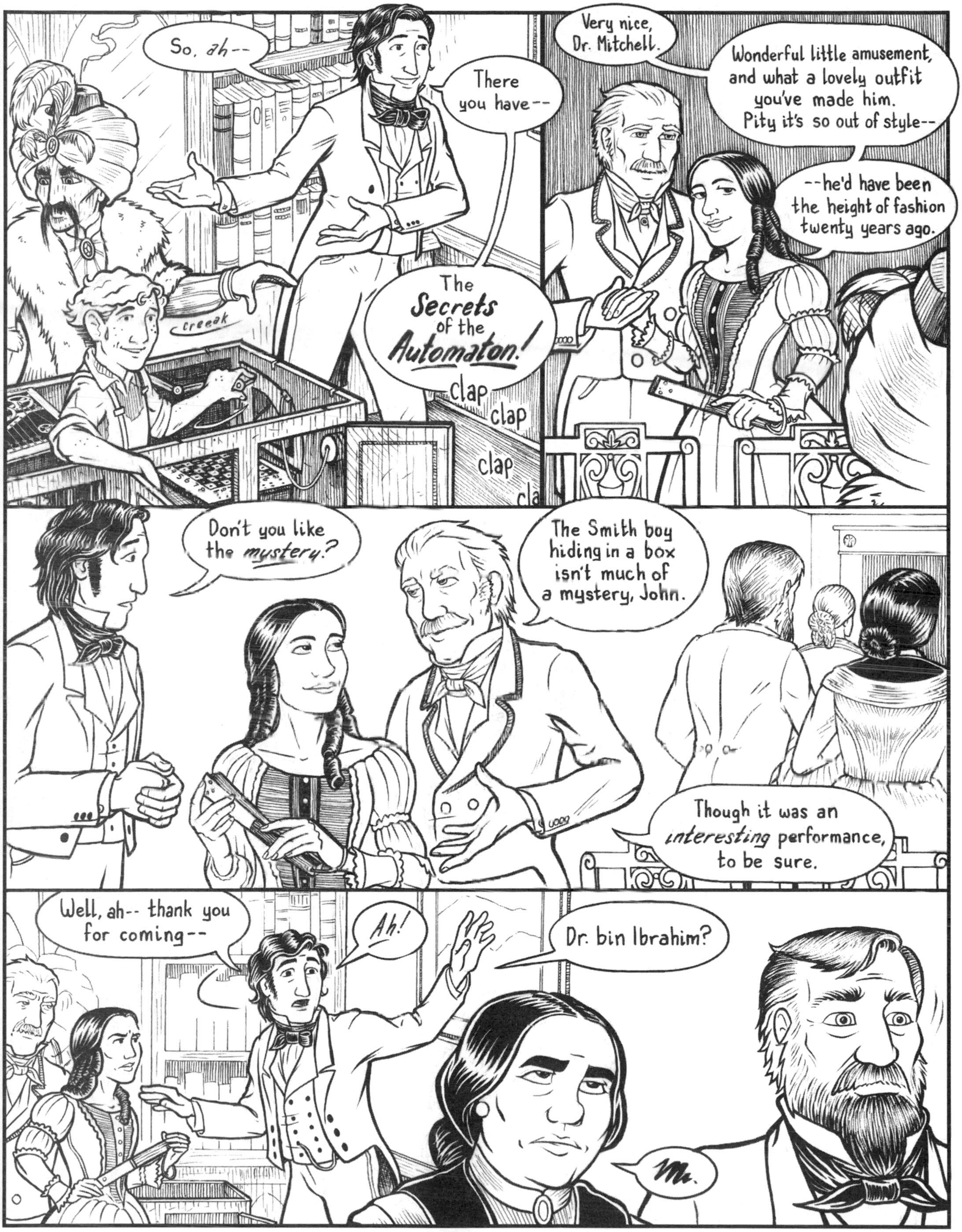
So, ah--
There you have--
The Secrets of the Automaton!
creeak
clap
clap
clap
cla
Very nice, Dr. Mitchell.
Wonderful little amusement, and what a lovely outfit you've made him. Pity it's so out of style--
--he'd have been the height of fashion twenty years ago.
Don't you like the mystery?
The Smith boy hiding in a box isn't much of a mystery, John.
Though it was an interesting performance, to be sure.
Well, ah-- thank you for coming--
Ah!
Dr. bin Ibrahim?
Mr.

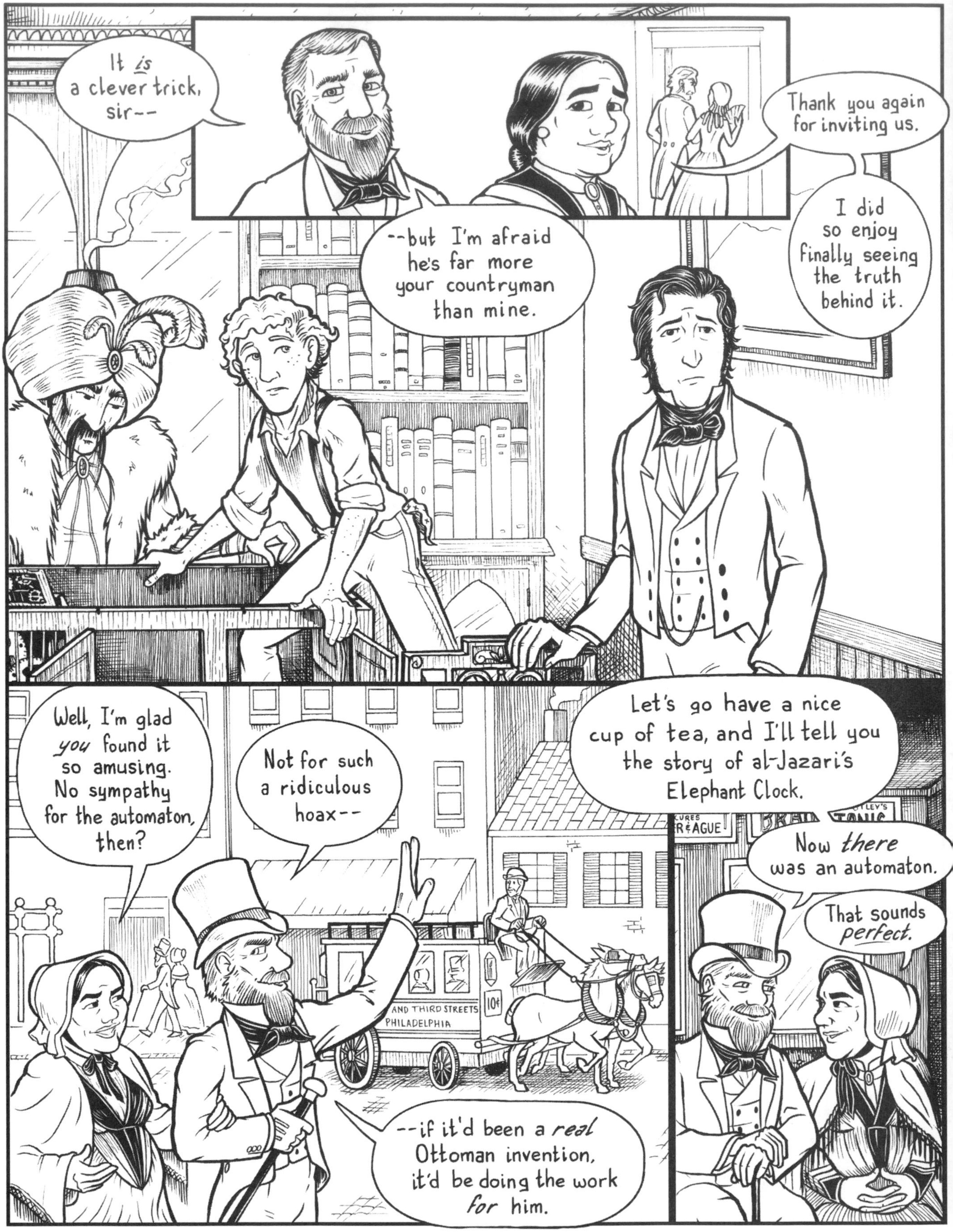
It *is* a clever trick, sir--
Thank you again for inviting us.
I did so enjoy finally seeing the truth behind it.
--but I'm afraid he's far more your countryman than mine.
Well, I'm glad *you* found it so amusing. No sympathy for the automaton, then?
Not for such a ridiculous hoax--
--if it'd been a *real* Ottoman invention, it'd be doing the work *for* him.
AND THIRD STREETS PHILADELPHIA
10¢
Let's go have a nice cup of tea, and I'll tell you the story of al-Jazari's Elephant Clock.
TONIC
Now *there* was an automaton.
That sounds *perfect*.

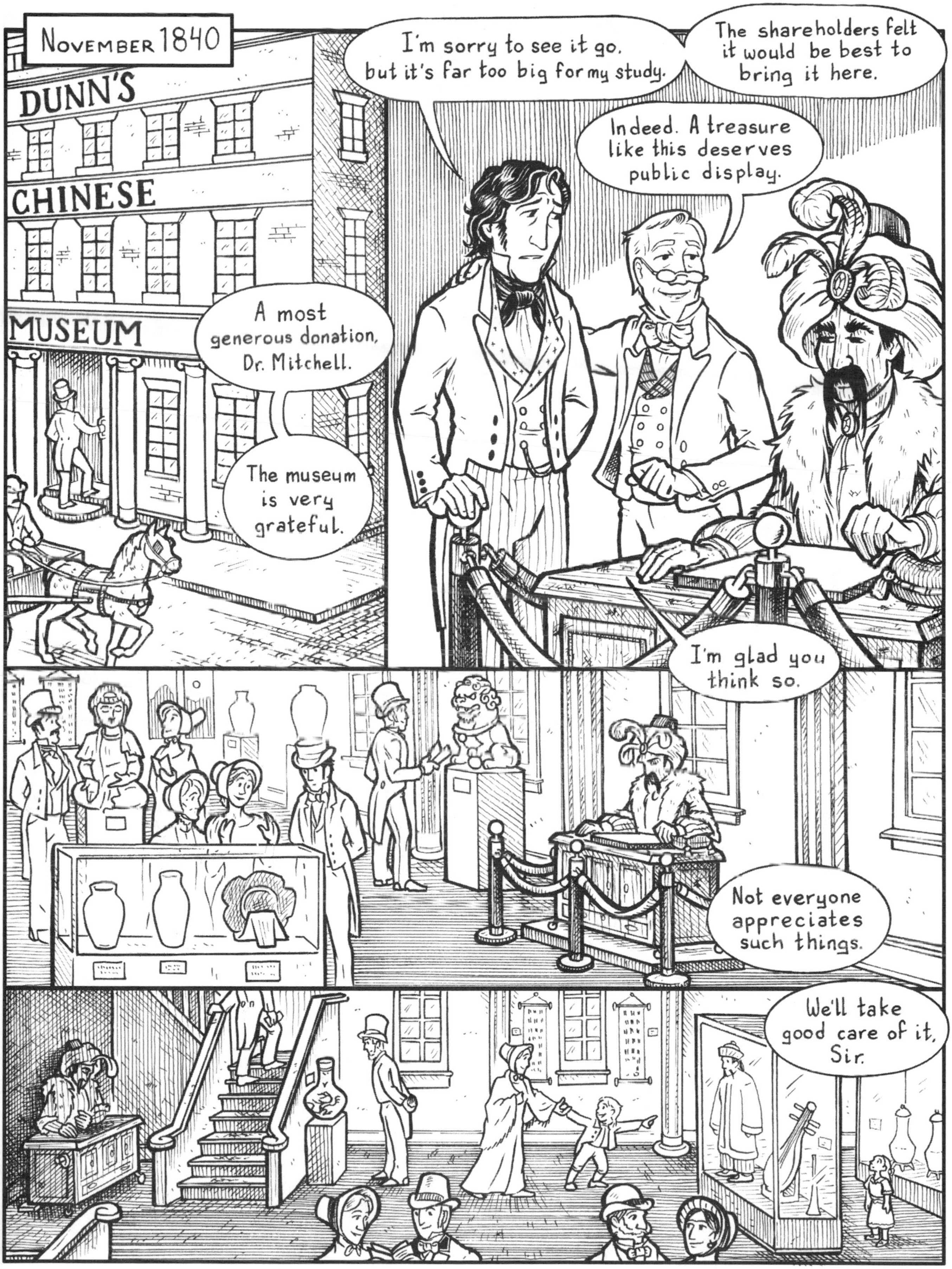
November 1840
DUNN'S
CHINESE
MUSEUM
I'm sorry to see it go, but it's far too big for my study.
The shareholders felt it would be best to bring it here.
Indeed. A treasure like this deserves public display.
A most generous donation, Dr. Mitchell.
The museum is very grateful.
I'm glad you think so.
Not everyone appreciates such things.
We'll take good care of it, Sir.

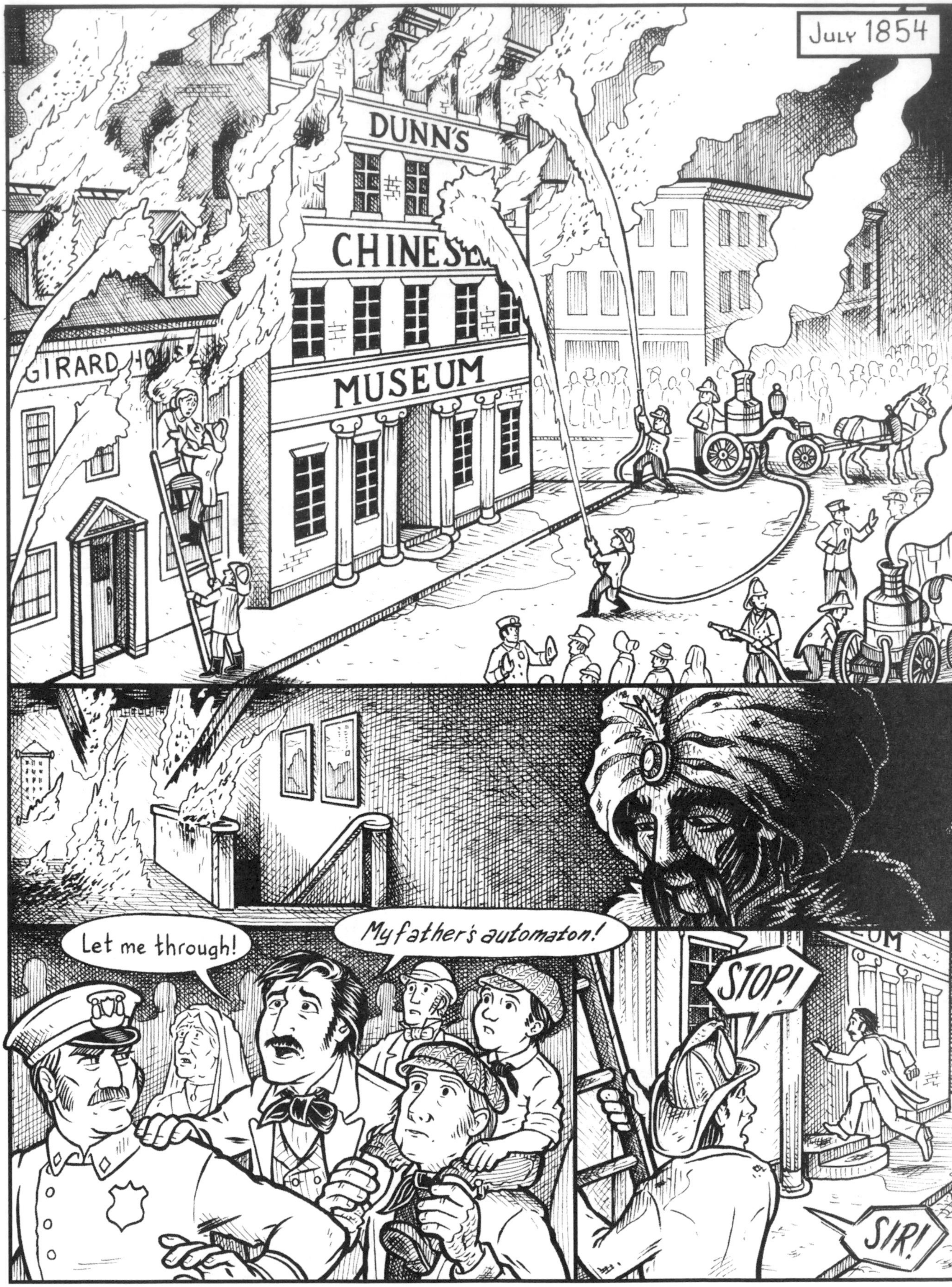
July 1854
DUNN'S
CHINESE
MUSEUM
GIRARD HOUSE
Let me through!
My father's automaton!
STOP!
SIR!

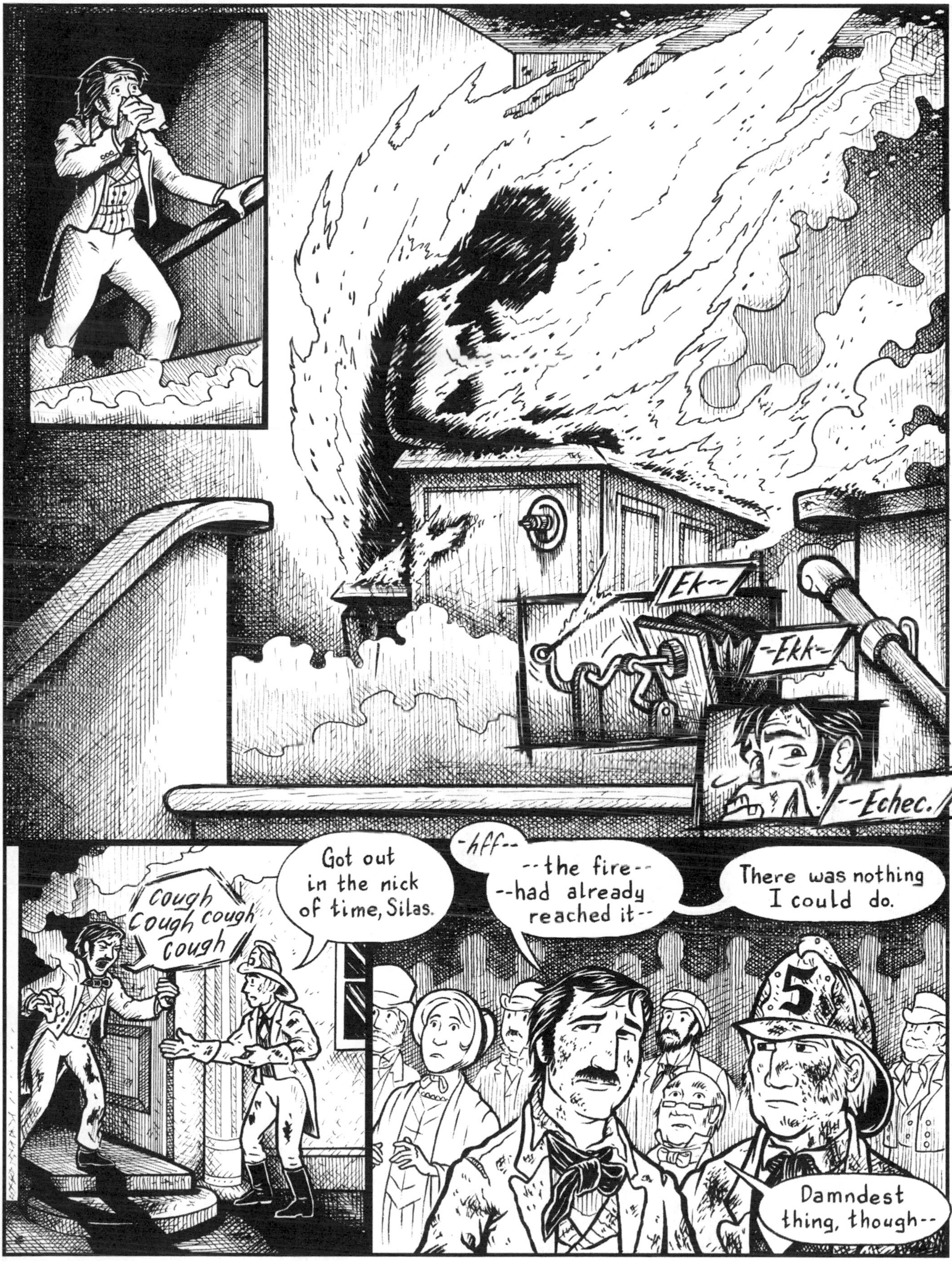
Ek--
-Ekk-
--Echec.
cough cough cough cough
Got out in the nick of time, Silas.
-hff--
--the fire-- --had already reached it--
There was nothing I could do.
Damndest thing, though--

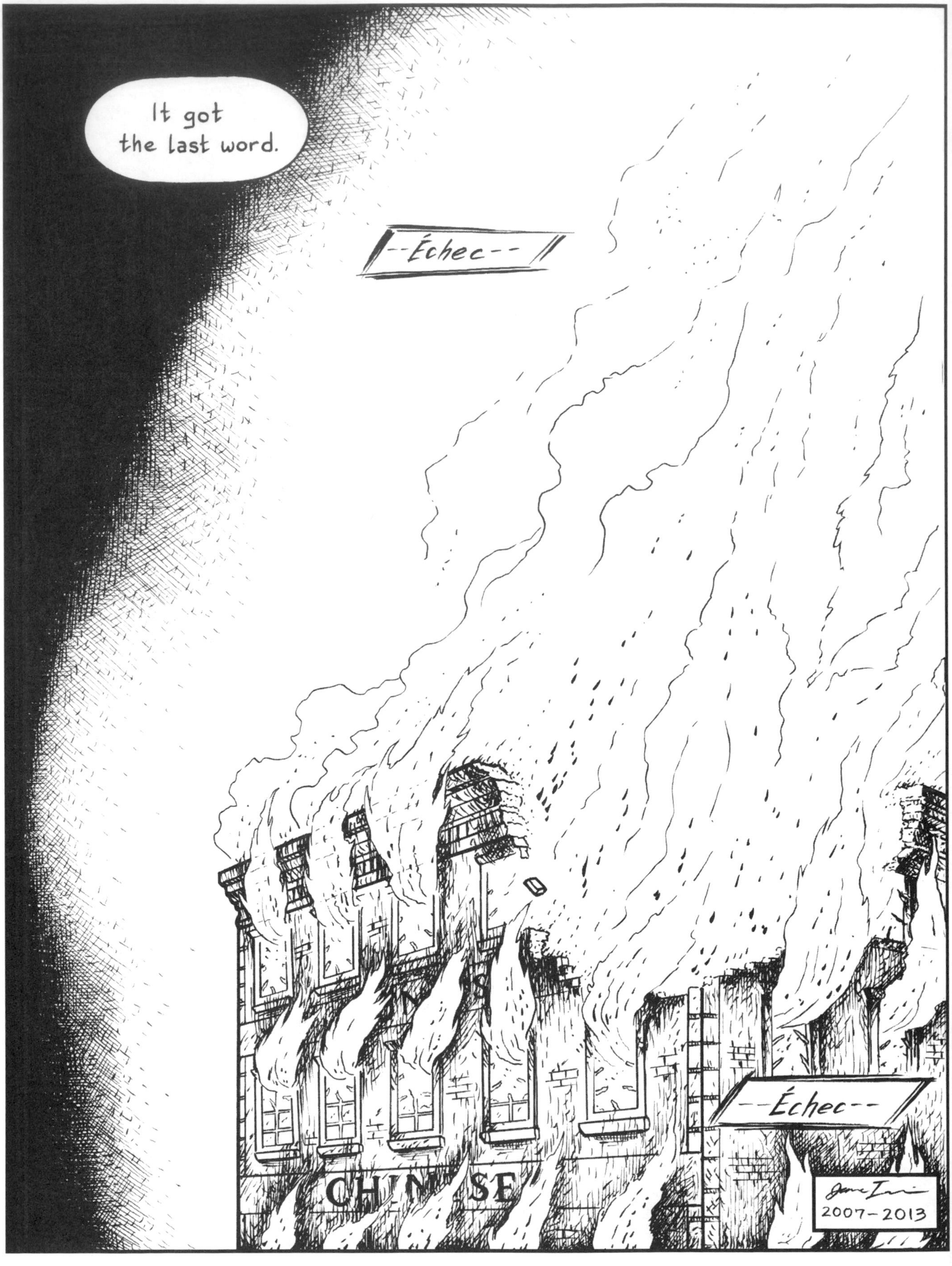
It got the last word.
--Échec--
--Échec--
CHI SE
2007–2013

NOTES

While *Clockwork Game* is ultimately historical fiction—I've taken too many liberties with history for me to pretend otherwise—I based my storytelling decisions as much in fact as I could, noting here when I used artistic license to better serve the narrative.

PAGE 11

Diyarbakır is a city in eastern Turkey, situated on the banks of the Tigris. Its city walls, made of black basalt, were ancient even in the thirteenth century, and are about three miles long. At the time the scene took place, the Artuqids called the city "Kara Amid" ("Kara" is Turkish for "black") due to the walls' dark color ("Diyarbakır").

PAGE 12

The mechanical elephant is based on designs for a water-clock by scientist and inventor al-Jazari, who served as the court engineer for the Artuqid kings. Al-Jazari is credited with an amazing spectrum of inventions, including several different clocks and water-raising devices (Al-Hassani).

The clock probably didn't stand in the courtyard, but rather in the palace itself, and it probably wasn't this big, but I couldn't resist giving it such a dramatic presentation.

PAGE 13

If you visit the 1001Inventions user channel on Youtube.com, you can watch an animation that shows more about how the elephant clock worked.

PAGE 16

Though his character is fictitious, Dr. bin Ibrahim is based on a real person, Dr. Ibrahim Ben Ali, for whose grandson the Ben Ali Stakes—a thoroughbred horse race held annually in Kentucky—is named ("Ben Ali Stakes").

PAGE 18

This scene takes place in the Great Gallery at Schönbrunn Palace. If you want a better look, the palace's website features an interactive video that even lets you see the frescoes on the ceiling.

The exact date of the automaton's debut is uncertain. Dr. Alice Reininger gives the year as 1769 (*Wolfgang von Kempelen: A Biography* 231) and states that von Kempelen was traveling in Banat from August 1769 to early June of 1770 (39–40), though Tom Standage says that the automaton first appeared in spring of 1770 (22). The deciding factor for me was a passage in Reininger's book stating that a newspaper made mention of the automaton's appearance in court in August of 1769 (231).

PAGE 19

In the panel where von Kempelen illuminates the interior with the candle, there should be a second panel of gears behind the ones in front, but I wasn't able to add them and still leave enough room to show the candle.

Dr. Emrah Sahin, my cultural consultant, notes that the automaton's turban is not correct if it's meant to be a Turkish kavuk, which should have white fabric wrapped around the fez with its ends tucked up inside the rolls. My representation of the turban was taken from Windisch's original engravings, which did show the ends sticking out; more evidence, I suppose, of the automaton's cultural inaccuracies.

PAGE 20

It's easy to forget just how intimidating a machine like this would have been to an eighteenth century audience, especially considering that such a machine must have seemed entirely plausible, given the rudimentary scientific discoveries of that era. The Industrial Revolution was still in its infancy: James Watt's steam engine wouldn't enter production for another six years ("Watt, James"). From the standpoint of the nobility gathered at Schönbrunn Palace, this automaton—which von Kempelen claimed could think just like a human being—constituted a breakthrough of unimaginable proportion and consequence.

PAGE 21

The earliest drawings of the automaton were featured in *Inanimate Reason* by Karl Gottlieb von Windisch, and seem to show that the paired doors were actually one big door, which hinged on the viewer's right. I based my design (with permission, of course) on the replica built by John Gaughan, which includes a vertical strut between the paired front doors.

From a design standpoint, it adds to the claustrophobic feel of the larger chamber.

I should also mention a bit of the automaton's history that I had to omit due to story considerations: After its main chessplaying performance, von Kempelen would place an alphabet board over the chessboard and allow the audience to ask questions, which the automaton answered by pointing to each letter in sequence, like a self-driven Ouija board, and responded in French, German and English. Bradley Ewart, in *Chess: Man vs. Machine*, lists some of the questions and answers, as recorded by an author who attended a performance (38).

PAGE 22

The historical texts I studied didn't mention how closely von Kempelen permitted his audience to inspect the automaton, but Windisch, a friend of von Kempelen, wrote:

> I was not, as you may imagine, one of the most backward in my scrutinizing inspection. I did not neglect the least corner: and nevertheless, finding no possibility of its concealing anything the size of my hat, my self-love was terribly hurt at seeing a conjecture vanish, which at first appeared to me so ingenious.

The quotes from the audience–and their costumes–reflect Europe's growing fascination with all things Turkish. From clothing to coffee to opera, Vienna couldn't seem to get enough Turqueric, and the automaton would have represented the absolute height of contemporary fashion and culture (Standage 23).

PAGE 23

Almost every part of the automaton appeared to have clockwork inside, though its legs past the knees were just stuffed trousers with slippers sewn on the ends.

"One of Handel's Operas" refers to *Tamerlano*, which is about the defeat of Ottoman Sultan Bayezid (r. 1389-1402).

PAGE 24

The courtier finding himself volunteered is Count Philipp von Cobenzl, a nobleman (Standage 27).

PAGE 27

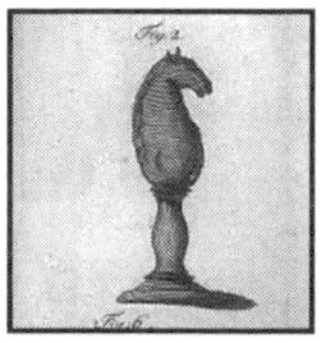

If the chess set looks a little odd, it's because the design most associated with modern chess, the Staunton Set, wouldn't exist for another eighty years. The only existing image of the automaton's chess pieces comes from an engraving by Racknitz from 1789. I took my primary design from Racknitz's image, but blended it slightly with the Staunton set to make the individual pieces more immediately recognizable to modern readers.

PAGE 30

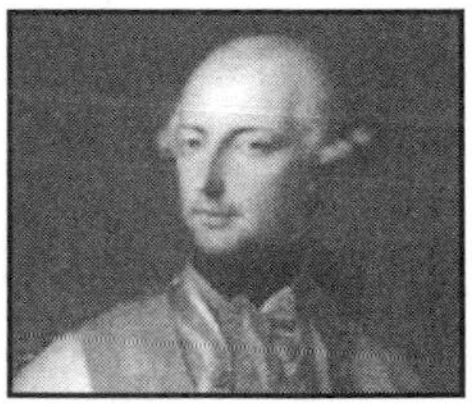

Sitting next to the empress is her son Emperor Joseph II. In theory, they were co-regents after the death of Maria Theresia's husband Franz I, but in reality, the empress had the upper hand until her passing ("Joseph II").

PAGE 32

Chessgames.com provided the game I used for this scene, though I altered it a bit because of the forfeited move.

PAGE 33

The Banat is a region in Central Europe that spans present-day Romania, Serbia, and Hungary. The empress first assigned von Kempelen there in his capacity as Director of Salt Mining, then to oversee a failing fabric factory, and later as a commissioner in charge of overseeing the settlement of German citizens in the territories which Austria recaptured from the Ottoman Empire in the late seventeenth and early eighteenth centuries (Reininger, *Wolfgang von Kempelen: A Biography* 17–186).

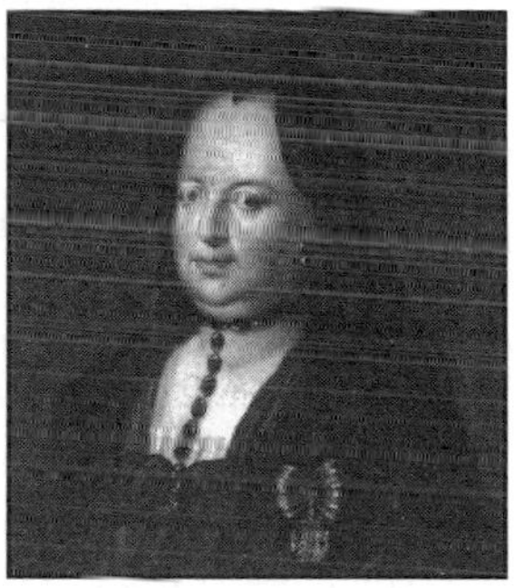

Regarding Maria Theresia's use of the word "heathen," the empress was a religious conservative, and showed little tolerance towards any religion other than her own Catholicism. Only after her death did her son, Emperor Joseph II, ratify edicts that allowed Protestants and Jews to practice their religions more freely ("Joseph II").

I'm stretching the truth when I have the empress say that she wouldn't waste von Kempelen's talents "in the settlements"– in truth, von Kempelen would continue to travel all over the empire on his duties, and returned to the Banat in August 1769 (Reininger, *Wolfgang von Kempelen: A Biography* 39). Over the next several years, he proved himself a tireless and dedicated civil servant, with wide-ranging expertise that garnered him assignments in several different fields, from overseeing the repair of waterworks at Pressburg Castle, to negotiating worker relations in Upper Austria, to managing the conversion of the Carmelite Monastery in the Buda Castle into a theatre (17–186).

PAGE 34

Von Kempelen's shock was justified—the empress' allowance equaled a third of his salary, and would be annually renewed. Reininger states in *Wolfgang von Kempelen: A Biography* that the bonus was much more for his successful work as a civil servant than for the automaton (40).

PAGE 35

Panel three refers to the Battle of Vienna, which occurred in 1683.

Pelletier was the French illusionist whose visit sparked the invention of the automaton, and Franz Mesmer was the "physician" from whom we get the term "Mesmerized."

PAGE 36

I find it likely that von Kempelen was not only subject to the common prejudices of his era, but also willing to use his fellow courtiers' odd combination of fear and fascination to the automaton's benefit.

On von Kempelen's monologue, Dr. Emrah Sahin comments that:

> von Kempelen dates the origins of the Ottoman world of science to an early period. Strikingly, astronomers such as Ali Kushji, philosophers, poets, mathematicians, chemists, and other intellectuals continued leading in fields of education with little to no physical harm inflicted upon them by the Mongol invasion. Likewise, a widespread intellectual network functioned until the nineteenth century in a transcontinental cultural basin stretching from Anatolia through Iran and the Middle East into Turkestan. Though the Mongols left a crushing impact on the libraries by burning unique manuscripts, Ottoman men of knowledge, those who had the means and skills, were able to remain intact in pursuing their careers. Evidently, an inclusive education system that had integrated new generations of the bright and smart into intellectual niche lost dynamism in later centuries and ceased to be only claimed by rather exclusive circles across Ottoman cities. The elites in these circles monopolized knowledge, cast out prospective outsiders—typically poor yet inquisitive youngsters—by preferring over them their own children in a highly hierarchical system that they themselves created to minimize mobility. Losing ground was of their making perhaps more than of the Mongols.

PAGE 37

Pressburg (or more accurately, Preßburg) is the old German name of modern-day Bratislava, the capitol of Slovakia, and was also known as Poszony in Hungarian. It is located a few miles to the east of Vienna.

The plans on von Kempelen's desk show a mobile bed he invented and built for the Empress. No blueprints for it survive, so its design is my own (Reininger, *Wolfgang von Kempelen: A Biography* 225).

The engravings which decorate von Kempelen's office are his own, drawn from reproductions in Reininger's *Wolfgang von Kempelen: Eine Biografie* (422–3).

PAGE 38

In a bit of artistic license on my part, all the Scotsmen except the Ambassador are in violation of the Dress Act—which forbade the wearing of any tartan or traditional Scottish dress by civilians on pain of transportation—by arriving in their best Highland attire (Browne 413–416).

Since the Act was only really enforceable on British soil, they probably would not have suffered any consequences.

PAGE 39

The text for this, while abridged, comes from *The Memoirs and Correspondence (Official and Familiar) of Sir Robert Murray Keith* (19–20).

PAGE 40

For men of von Kempelen's status, wigs were compulsory dress, worn daily except during the most casual moments. Since wigs were inexorably linked to the aristocracy, as the French Revolution approached and nobles fell out of favor, so did the fashion. Anthon's hair is his own, though he wears a powdered wig during court appearances.

The device on the door represents another of von Kempelen's many inventions. No such design of his exists—but I liked the idea of him outfitting his house with labor-saving devices, like this counterweight to keep the front door's crossbar from slamming down.

PAGE 41

Anna is actually von Kempelen's second wife; his first marriage, to a noblewoman named Francziska Piani, ended tragically after only two months, when she died of a stomach obstruction.

Five years after Francziska's death, he married Anna Maria Gobelius. Despite their best efforts, their first three children didn't survive infancy, so Theresia and Karl must have been especially well-loved (Reininger, *Wolfgang von Kempelen: A Biography* 7–8).

No images exist of the rest of his family, but I based von Kempelen's character design on his own self-portrait.

PAGE 43

Von Kempelen accomplished many tasks in the seven years between this page and the last (though none of it related to the automaton): he helped move a university to its new location in Buda Castle, built a printing press for a blind musician, and wrote a play, *Andromeda and Perseus*, which was presented in the National Theatre in Vienna (Reininger, *Wolfgang von Kempelen: A Biography* 17–186).

PAGE 44

After Maria Theresia's death in 1780, her son Joseph II began making budgetary cuts to his civil servants' accommodations, pensions, and salaries. Unfortunately for von Kempelen, this included the annual pension of 1,000 Gulden that the Empress had granted him. Some histories claim that the retraction was punitive due to von Kempelen's political views, but Reininger makes it clear that all civil servants were affected by this cut, not just von Kempelen (*Wolfgang von Kempelen: A Biography* 44).

PAGE 45

I've placed this scene in the Mirror Room at Schönbrunn Palace. According to the palace's website, it's the same room where a young Mozart debuted his talents before Empress Maria Theresia twenty years earlier. The gentleman asking von Kempelen to visit his mother is Grand Duke Paul, the future Emperor of Russia.

Many stories about the automaton include reference to a meeting between the automaton and Catherine the Great, but according to Standage, it never actually happened (95).

PAGE 46

Emperor Joseph's sister Antoine is better known as Marie Antoinette.

PAGE 47

This scene takes place in the Café de la Régence, the premier chess club in Paris and, by extension, the world. "André" is André Danican Philidor, who in addition to being the top-ranked chess player in Paris (Standage 43), was also a noted composer (Allen, *The Life of Philidor* 37).

PAGE 50

Franklin's cane and suit are drawn from surviving examples in the Smithsonian Museum.

Despite the fact that it's summertime in Paris, Franklin still wears his trademark marten-fur hat (I always assumed it was made from beaver fur until I read Walter Isaacson's biography of Franklin). He apparently wore it regardless of weather or season, and it quickly became fashionable—in Nantes, ladies wore their wigs styled in a "*coiffure à la Franklin*" (Isaacson 325).

One of Franklin's many inventions was a carriage-wheel odometer, which did indeed employ cogs and gears, but none such as (apparently) complex as the inner workings of von Kempelen's automaton.

While von Kempelen could speak French (Reininger, *Wolfgang von Kempelen: A Biography* 7), Franklin had only a rough (and sometimes self-invented) command of the language (Isaacson 370–71). I decided, for the sake of the story, to do away with the stumblings and grammatical errors that must certainly have occurred during their conversations.

PAGE 51

The overlay text, while edited, comes directly from Franklin's *Morals of Chess*. Franklin's obsession with chess was well-known; he sometimes played till dawn, put off important messages until a game was finished, and once played against a mutual friend in Madame de Brillion's chambers while the lady watched from her bathtub (Isaacson 362).

PAGE 52

Thomas Jefferson tells this anecdote in his memoirs:

> When Dr. Franklin went to France, on his revolutionary mission, his eminence as a philosopher, his venerable appearance, and the cause on which he was sent, rendered

him extremely popular. For all ranks and conditions of men there, entered warmly into the American interest. He was, therefore, feasted and invited to all the court parties. At these he sometimes met the old Duchess of Bourbon, who, being a chess player of about his force, they very generally played together. Happening once to put her king into prize, the Doctor took it. 'Ah,' says she, 'we do not take kings so.' 'We do in America,' said the Doctor (Jefferson 500).

Franklin's grandson Temple (who accompanied him in Paris as his secretary) reported that Franklin did enjoy the game, and that he had a pamphlet about the automaton in his library. So why did I decide to show Franklin storming out at the end of the game? Standage says that Franklin had a reputation as a sore loser. Having him leave in a huff seemed to encapsulate this aspect of his personality, though this scene is probably not entirely true to history (Standage 48).

PAGE 54

Von Kempelen's dialogue was provided by Standage (52).

During his two year trip, Emperor Joseph only granted von Kempelen half his salary, because he was "undertaking it solely for his own purposes," so although it may sound like a fib, von Kempelen was speaking honestly about his lack of funds, especially considering he may have had to maintain his household during his absence (Reininger, *Wolfgang von Kempelen: A Biography* 46, 11).

Standage indicates that von Kempelen was reluctant to leave Pressburg, and did so at the insistence of the emperor (41), but Reininger makes it clear that he made the best of the opportunity, especially during his trip to England. He used his time to contact other engineers and scientists working on steam engine designs of their own, including James Watt and Matthew Boulton, though he was discouraged by their unwillingness to share their knowledge with him (214–222).

PAGE 55

According to Bradley Ewart's *Chess: Man vs. Machine*:

> Philidor, with his usual benevolence and lack of vanity, replied, 'Sir, I would be glad to do it.'
>
> Then, after a moment's reflection, he added, 'But you must admit that, in your own interest, we must not appear to conspire. I must defend myself and it must not seem that I am demonstrating any negligence, but I shall do all I can, I promise you, to be beaten by your automaton' (Ewart 30).

The 'Defence' that Philidor mentions is a famous chess opening, named for him.

PAGE 56

The gentlemen with the badges on their coats are members of the Académie des Sciences.

PAGE 58

In *The Life of Philidor*, George Allen asserts that "[Philidor] told André [his eldest son], who was with him at the time, that he had never played so fatiguing a game" (41), and Standage reports that he believed the chess-player was real (52).

The quotation at the bottom of the page comes from the September 1783 edition of *The Journal des Sçavans*, the earliest scientific journal published in Europe, as translated by Standage (53).

PAGE 59

Savile Row, now a legendary center of bespoke men's clothing, was then upscale, newly-built houses (Shephard). Mrs. Salmon's waxworks were a popular London attraction at the time, similar to Madame Tussaud's (Altick 52–4).

PAGE 60

Theresia's involvement in this scene stems from Windisch's speculation about a child acting as the driving force inside the automaton. Karl would have been too young to play against Paris' greatest chess masters, but a small, clever girl of fifteen would have seemed an entirely plausible director.

PAGE 61

Anna's given name was "Maria Anna," but she was known to her family as "Anna Maria." Theresia's given name was "Maria Theresia," but she was also called by her middle name (Standage 20). The Hungarian version of von Kempelen's first name is "Farkas," which translates to "Wolf."

PAGE 64

The apoplectic audience member is Philip Thicknesse, nicknamed "Dr. Viper." He was once the patron of Thomas Gainsborough, until a "wretched squabble" ended their friendship. Gainsborough did a splendid portrait of Thicknesse's third wife, Anne Ford, whom you can see here in the last panel. He was also the subject of a scathing political cartoon by James Gillray, entitled *Lieutenant Governor Gall-Stone, inspired by Alecto*, which you can see on The British Museum's website.

PAGE 66

This is an abridged version of Thicknesse's exposé; the full-length version is full of even more bile, hyperbole, and incorrect assumptions.

PAGE 67

Von Kempelen made several other stops on the tour between London and Leipzig. The Leipzig Trade Fair, or Leipziger Messe, still takes place today, as it has for nearly a thousand years. The device von Kempelen displays is his speaking machine.

Panel 1: The Castle Theatre still stands today, and is currently the home of Budapest's National Dance Theatre. Also, by this time, von Kempelen had seen two of his own plays, *The Magic Book* (1767) and *Andromeda and Perseus* (1781), performed in Pressburg and Vienna, respectively (Reininger, *Wolfgang von Kempelen: A Biography* 251–256).

Panel 2: Von Kempelen spent an enormous amount of his own money and time developing his steam engines, and despite some initial failures, persevered until Joseph II granted him a privilege on his designs in 1788 (206–221).

Panel 3: von Kempelen's book on the synthesis of human speech, published in German and French, collected nineteen years of his research into phonetics, speech formation, and the construction of his speaking machine.

PAGE 70

Theresia von Kempelen was twenty-nine years old and still unmarried in 1797 (Reininger, *Wolfgang von Kempelen: A Biography* 8), though the idea that she was checking her father's work is my own speculation. Von Kempelen did, however, invent a tobacco-cutting machine in 1798 (226).

I had to invent Joszef von Bittó out of whole cloth. All I had was his name; I could find no other information about him.

PAGE 71

The model you see here is von Kempelen's third attempt at building a speech synthesizer. As Joszef mentions, the first wasn't much more than a bagpipe reed and a kitchen bellows, and the second was more like an organ, with an individual pipe and key for each phoneme. The third design was an attempt to more closely emulate the human mouth, nose, and throat.

Because the machine had difficulty with harsh consonants, von Kempelen usually made it pronounce words and short phrases in Latin, Italian, or French rather than German. Despite

nearly twenty years of work and continual adjustments to improve its inflection and pitch control, its voice remained very crude. Still, it was an amazing effort given the technology available at the time, and von Kempelen's contributions to the field are still noted today.

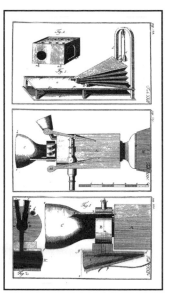

A version of the speaking machine still exists in the Musical Instruments section of the The Deutsches Museum in Munich, and you can see photos of it on the museum's website (Standage 76–80).

PAGE 72

The concept that von Kempelen might enclose his speaking machine inside a mannequin and his trick of covering the machine with a sheet are taken from anecdotes in Windisch's *Inanimate Reason*.

In the original draft of the script, this scene, with its discussion of art and its relationship to science, took place between von Kempelen and Goethe. Goethe did see von Kempelen demonstrate the speaking machine; he wrote to his patron that it "is not very loquacious, but it can pronounce certain childish words nicely" (Standage 75). Unfortunately, my research suggested that Goethe never traveled to Vienna, let alone Pressburg, so it's much more likely that he was one of the thousands of anonymous viewers who filed past it during von Kempelen's tour of 1783–84.

PAGE 73

Von Kempelen's creations inspired many other inventors through both their form and function. After the automaton's tour through London, a former clergyman named Edmund Cartwright wrote this account of a meeting with some fellow inventors:

> ... in the summer of 1784, I fell in company with some gentlemen of Manchester, when the conversation turned on Arkwright's spinning machinery. One of the company observed, that as soon as Arkwright's patent expired, so many mills would be erected, and so much cotton spun, that hands never could be found to weave it. To this observation I replied that Arkwright must then set his wits to work to invent a weaving mill. This brought on a conversation on the subject, in which the Manchester gentlemen unanimously

agreed that the thing was impracticable... I controverted, however, the impracticability of the thing, by remarking that there had lately been exhibited in London, an automaton figure, which played at chess. Now you will not assert, gentlemen, said I, that it is more difficult to construct a machine that shall weave, than one which shall make all the variety of moves which are required in that complicated game ("Cotton Manufacture" 450).

The following year, he patented the power loom.

A British scientist named Charles Wheatstone (who also invented the concertina) built a reconstruction of von Kempelen's speaking machine, made a few improvements of his own, and exhibited it in London. In 1863, Alexander Graham Bell saw a demonstration of Wheatstone's machine while visiting London with his parents. Inspired by the machine's abilities, the young Bell returned home and built his own version. Though he never developed von Kempelen's design further than his early experiments, he did go on to make a speaking machine of his own (Standage 80).

PAGE 74

The current emperor is Francis II, von Kempelen's fourth head of state since arriving at court in 1755, and the last ruler of the Holy Roman Empire (Standage 99).

Over the years, there has been much confusion over von Kempelen's title; some sources claim he was a Baron, others a knight. Reininger states that this is due to confusion with his elder brother, Johannes Nepomuk, a decorated general who earned the rank of knight ("Ritter"), received an estate, and was granted a title from Maria Theresia (von Pázmánd, sometimes also incorrectly attributed to Wolfgang von Kempelen) (Reininger, *Wolfgang von Kempelen: A Biography* 8–11).

PAGE 75

Count Cobenzl did offer von Kempelen a teaching position at the Academy of Fine Arts Vienna, but not until 1801. Von Kempelen declined due to ill health (Reininger, *Wolfgang von Kempelen: A Biography* 238).

I realize that I've shown von Kempelen and Maelzel shaking hands left-handed; it's less a mistake and more to imply that von Kempelen can't release his grip on his cane.

PAGE 77

Reininger lists his cause of death as "debilitation" (*Wolfgang von Kempelen: A Biography* 13).

I am taking a bit of artistic license with history on this page: after his retirement, von Kempelen did petition Emperor Franz II, asking for 20,000 Gulden in compensation for the annual pension that Maria Theresia had granted him, but that Joseph II had rescinded. However, his request was denied in 1802, not 1804 (54–55).

PAGE 78

In my retelling, Karl has redecorated his father's study to fit his Neoclassic taste. As a dedicated and canny civil servant, von Kempelen probably wouldn't have owned much artwork that sympathized so heavily with the French Revolution. However, by 1806, Napoleon had defeated the Austrians and occupied Vienna, and the Holy Roman Empire was months away from dissolution. Karl's choice of decor reflects more than just the changes of his home life; it's a political move as well.

Von Kempelen moved his family to several different apartments during his long and busy career, including residences in Vienna and Pressburg, and a private apartment for von Kempelen during his work on the theatre in Buda. Von Kempelen also inherited a farm in Gomba-Hubice from his father (Reininger, *Wolfgang von Kempelen: A Biography* 11–13). In an effort to simplify my storytelling, I used one single Pressburg apartment to represent them all.

I'm compressing history a bit as well—according to *Grove's Dictionary of Music and Musicians*, Maelzel didn't actually become Court Mechanician until 1808 (194).

PAGE 79

Von Kempelen's gravestone design is speculation on my part, because it no longer exists. He was buried in the Währing cemetary, which was converted into Schubert Park in 1925. Beethoven and Schubert were both originally interred in the Währing cemetary, but were moved to the Vienna Central Cemetary, their original tombs preserved (Reininger, *Wolfgang von Kempelen: A Biography* 14).

Did Maelzel know the automaton was a trick? My guess is that he did, but I've no conclusive proof one way or the other. By 1806, he had built several of his own very impressive automata—including a statue of a boy that actually played the trumpet, its fingers, lips, and breath all driven by the same studded drum—so he surely knew the limits of technology at the time. Additionally, von Kempelen always made it a point to let the audience know that the chess-player was a trick, referring to it as a "trifle" and a "bagatelle."

Von Kempelen kept his secrets close; I could find no record of the directors he hired for any of the automaton's games.

In reality, Karl did present the automaton after his father's death, donating the proceeds to charity, so he probably knew how it functioned (Reininger, *Wolfgang von Kempelen: A Biography* 235).

PAGE 80

This gentleman in the work apron is Dr. John Kearsley Mitchell, whom Mrs. bin Ibrahim mentioned back on page 15.

PAGE 83

Dr. bin Ibrahim refers to Sultan Mahmud II, who ruled from 1808–39 ("Mahmud II (Ottoman Sultan)").

PAGE 85

Dr. bin Ibrahim's character is based on Ibrahim Ben Ali—including his medicines. The inspiration for this scene came from a passage in Dr. James Harvey Young's *The Toadstool Millionaires*:

> In the meantime, however, Americans continued to be fascinated by the remote. While excitement was high over the depredations of the Barbary pirates, Ibraham Adam Ben Ali, a Turk or (as an editor thought more likely) 'some crafty native, who has assumed a Turkish name' went about selling the Incomparable Algerine Medicine for the scurvy.

PAGE 86

The General seated at the table is Louis Alexandre Berthier, and Napoleon's manservant is Louis Constant Wairy.

PAGE 87

I based my retelling of this scene and the next on the account written by Wairy in his book *Recollections of the Private Life of Napoleon* (220–2). Based on his notes, it seems that Maelzel did try to pass the automaton off as his own invention (220).

PAGE 88

Marshall Berthier is referring to the Siege of Acre, where the Ottoman Empire put an end to Napoleon's invasion of Egypt and Syria (Cole 243–4).

PAGE 94

This is Napoleon's stepson Eugène de Beauharnais, son of Joséphine de Beauharnais and her late husband Alexandre.

PAGE 96

Maelzel's mechanical trumpeter has been lost to time, but a similar automaton built at about the same time by Friedrich Kaufmann still exists.

PAGE 97

The Conflagration of Moscow was an enormous mechanical diorama that Maelzel created to capitalize on Napoleon's Pyrrhic victory in 1812.

The woman in the last panel is Nannette Streicher. Maelzel rented his shop space in the piano factory she owned with her husband (Thayer 233). According to Barry Cooper's *Beethoven*, the composer was very close to Streicher, and favored her pianos for many years, even going so far as to help advertise them (74).

PAGE 98

Maelzel created a number of ear trumpets for Beethoven, some of which still exist, and may be seen at the Beethoven Museum in Bonn. You can also see a photograph of them on the museum's website.

PAGE 99

In reality, the Panharmonicon was probably much bigger than this, but I had to simplify the design so that I could draw it multiple times.

The music is the second movement from Haydn's Military Symphony (Allegretto, Symphony No. 100 in G Major). Haydn was once Beethoven's teacher, and was also one of the few composers he respected. Maelzel's original design for the metronome is described as "a lever, striking upon a little anvil" (Grove 320), but I couldn't find any images of it, so I did my best with the design.

PAGE 100

"Ta ta lieber lieber Maelzel"—there is a longstanding anecdote that claims Beethoven made this "musical joke" first into a lighthearted little canon, (Canon WoO 162, also known as the Mälzelkanon), and then into the second movement of his Eighth Symphony. According to the Beethoven Haus Bonn website, the story has been debunked and the canon attributed to Anton Schindler, but I kept the idea of it as a storytelling device to represent the often-antagonistic relationship between Maelzel and Beethoven.

PAGE 101

The history surrounding this incident was rather more complicated than I'm portraying here. In *The Life of Ludwig van Beethoven*, Thayer states that Maelzel and Beethoven originally planned to take the Panharmonicon on tour to London (254), but their legal fight sent Maelzel out on his own to keep ahead of Beethoven's lawyers, first to Munich, then Amsterdam (Standage 117). The legal fight was messy, and only Beethoven's side of the argument still exists. Beethoven did repay the fifty ducats Maelzel loaned him, as soon as the fight began (271).

It's worth noting that Thayer cites both the composer Moscheles and one of the Stein family (Nannette Streicher's maiden name was Stein, and Thayer refers to him as the son of the factory owner, so he was presumably related to her) as siding with Maelzel (253).

PAGE 103

The gentleman on his way out is Dietrich Nikolaus Winkel, and he did invent the first real metronome (Standage 117).

PAGE 105

By this point, Beethoven was almost entirely deaf, and used conversation books as a means of communication. Some of them still survive, though many have been lost or destroyed. Cooper reports that Beethoven did not begin using these books until 1818, so I hope readers will forgive me a bit of artistic license (280).

Thayer states that Maelzel and Beethoven did finally make up, each paying half the legal expenses (231). Though Beethoven was at first skeptical of the instrument, calling it "silly stuff," he did eventually see the utility of the metronome, and used its tempos in his later works (386).

PAGE 106

After his stepfather's final exile to the island of St. Helena, Eugène de Beauharnais became the Duke of Leuchtenberg and resided in Munich (Standage 118).

True to his statement, de Beuharnais did lead the remains of Napoleon's army back from Moscow after Murat defected, and Napoleon credited his leadership with keeping the horrendous conditions of the retreat from becoming even more tragic (Montagu 273–8).

PAGE 107

That 15% rate required Maelzel had to clear 4500 francs per month—no small amount—just to keep up with the interest.

PAGE 108

In the three years since the last scene, Maelzel toured his mechanical menagerie through Paris, London, Liverpool, Manchester, Edinburgh, and eventually back to London (Standage 119, 124).

During his public performances, Maelzel had the automaton's opponent sit at a separate table "... in order... not to intercept the view of the audience." (Allen, "The History of the Automaton Chess Player in America" 430).

PAGE 109

Babbage did indeed play against the automaton. The text on this page comes from Babbage's own notes, found inside his copy of Windisch's book, as quoted by Standage (140).

PAGE 110

It's true: von Kempelen's box was nothing more than a clever distraction technique. Maelzel's quotation was provided by Standage (123).

Though Babbage wasn't fooled by Maelzel's show, he did believe that it was possible to build a machine capable of playing games of skill, including chess, and devoted a chapter to the subject in his book *Passages from the Life of a Philosopher*.

Babbage's dislike of music in general, and street musicians in specific, is well (and hilariously) documented in Sydney Padua's lovely webcomic *2-D Goggles*.

PAGE 111

Maelzel is working on one of his "funambulists"—a pair of rope-dancing dolls he added to the touring exhibition somewhere during his European tours. I couldn't find any evidence determining whether he built them himself or purchased them from another inventor.

PAGE 112

In the first panel, Constance is using a powder measure and flask to fill the smoke pots in *The Conflagration of Moscow*.

PAGE 114

As the conversation suggests, Eugène de Beauharnais died in 1824, but his family still held Maelzel to their financial arrangement (Standage 146).

PAGE 115

Packet ships were vessels that made frequent, scheduled trips back and forth across the Atlantic, usually carrying mail and passengers.

PAGE 118

I admit I've drawn Maelzel's cabin as rather roomy for a packet ship (even the first-class cabins were tiny), but I did have to make enough space for the automaton. As you'll see, though, even this cramped space was far preferable to the accommodations in steerage.

Normally, the automaton would stand a few inches off the floor, but Maelzel has removed its casters, to keep it from sliding around with the motion of the ship. It's unknown whether Maelzel actually assembled the automaton during the voyage, but it wouldn't be impossible for him to have done so.

PAGE 121

If you remember von Kempelen's version of the performance, you now understand why his long-winded descriptive patter was so important.

PAGE 126

It bears repeating that no definitive plans or photographs of the automaton exist. Though several books have been written on the subject, the remaining evidence consists only of guesses by educated people of its day and a few letters or articles written by people who directed the automaton, but even those sometimes contradict one another. This scene represents my own best guess as to how the illusion worked.

PAGE 127

When I designed the first-class cabins and steerage, I used the interior of the immigrant ship *Dunbrody*, though she was a bit more modern than the *Howard*. For the exterior, I referenced a model of the packet ship *Shenandoah*, which you can see on the Smithsonian National Museum of American History's website.

PAGE 128

Maelzel's book of endgames contains hand-selected series of games that were essentially guaranteed wins for the automaton, provided that the director memorized them correctly. It still exists today, held by the Library Company of Philadelphia.

The switch from complete games to endgames caused a bit of consternation amongst the American audiences, but using them not only allowed Maelzel to challenge more opponents and put on more performances a day, but also afforded Constance—who was probably the weakest player to ever direct the automaton—a real chance of winning.

PAGE 129

Henry's father is William Coleman, who wrote the editorial excerpted on the previous page (Standage 208).

PAGE 130

These are, of course, Eugène de Beauharnais' lawyers, come to collect on the debt (Standage 115).

PAGE 133

In case it's hard to tell what he's doing, Jean-Marc is emptying the performance hall's cuspidors.

PAGE 134

Constance and Jean-Marc, whose real names were lost to history, seemingly disappeared just after Schlumberger arrived. I've no basis in fact for their departure, so I had to invent a reason, though Allen describes Maelzel as having "been deserted... by his female assistant" (Allen, "The History of the Automaton Chess Player in America" 433).

PAGE 135

By this point in history, enough had been written about the automaton that it was generally known to be von Kempelen's invention, as opposed to Maelzel's.

Guillaume Schlumberger was born in Alsace, and like Maelzel, spoke a half-dozen languages with ease. Allen suggests that they spoke French or German to each other when not around other Americans ("The History of the Automaton Chess Player in America" 445).

PAGE 136

Schlumberger was described by different writers as "handsome, his nose well-formed and prominent... dark brown hair... beautiful chestnut eyes... muscular and well-proportioned... tall—full six feet high" (Allen, "The History of the Automaton Chess Player in America" 440), having "a remarkable stoop in the shoulders" (Poe 325), and "with little or no dignity in his personal appearance" (Blitz 169). For the purpose of the story, I attributed his symptoms to kyphosis, and did my best to portray its effects accordingly.

Maelzel was described as "stout and florid" (Allen 473), and as "... a large, phlegmatic man, extremely irritable, yet very kind," who "displayed great taste and refinement in all his arrangements without regard to cost" (Blitz 168).

Despite all my research, I could find no surviving images of either Schlumberger or Maelzel.

PAGE 137

As an example of the Philhellenism Maelzel mentions, the city where I attended college, founded in 1825, was named after Demetrius Ypsilantis, a hero in the Greek War of Independence—the same in which Lord Byron died. Childe Harold's Pilgrimage is one of Byron's poems.

PAGE 138

The original Greco was a famous seventeenth century Italian chess-player.

PAGE 140

Long before the Yankees and the Red Sox, there was indeed a chess rivalry between New York and Boston (Standage 150–159).

PAGE 142

Allen reports that:

> ... Maelzel was always angry with Schlumberger for losing a game, and that whenever this happened... in consequence of an innocent cup too much, he used to swear horribly at his meek and penitent director in the terrible German, which he reserved for such occasions ("The History of the Automaton Chess Player in America" 451).

PAGE 143

"Pawn and two moves..." comes from Allen's "The History of the Automaton Chess Player in America" (438–40).

PAGE 145

Greco's letter to the New-York American and the description of the scene come from Standage (158–9), however, it was my own decision to have Schlumberger come up with the plan.

PAGE 146

The story of the boys on the rooftop, and the exchanges between newspapers, comes from Ewart (102–3).

PAGE 148

In actuality, Maelzel left for Europe in late 1828 and returned to the U.S. in early 1829 with a new assortment of automata he had presumably purchased. According to Ewart, they included the Cathedral of Rheims, the French Oyster Woman, the Old French Gentleman, the Little Troubador, and the Grand Carrousel or Grand Tournament, a display of automaton horses and riders. It seems that Schlumberger stayed behind, manning an exhibition of Maelzel's smaller automata with a man named Kummer (Ewart 109–10).

For the sake of brevity, I omitted this trip and showed Maelzel sending for the automata—which he had in fact done, in 1827 (Standage 166). The Conflagration of Moscow was part of that shipment, but I've omitted it in order to keep the focus on the automaton.

Other events that I regretfully had to leave out of the script, and which happened around this same time period, were the creation of—and Maelzel's $1,000 failed bribe to close down—a rival chess-playing automaton by the Walker brothers; the chess match "lost" to an elderly signator of the Declaration of Independence, Charles Caroll; and Maelzel's decision to sell off several of his other automata, dividing some into separate traveling shows (Ewart 101–11).

PAGE 149

The exchange between Maelzel and Schlumberger can be found in Allen's "The History of the Automaton Chess Player in America" (445).

PAGE 150

Schlumberger was known as "Mulhouse" to his peers at the Café de la Régence (Allen, "The History of the Automaton Chess Player in America" 437).

PAGE 151

Mr. Vaton was indeed a Swiss watchmaker in the city of Philadelphia, and while he was Schlumberger's friend (Allen, "The History of the Automaton Chess Player in America" 465), the story that they knew one another back in Europe is fiction on my part. Schlumberger's misfortune in business, tutelage at the Café de la Régence, and chess obsession are also described by Allen (437–9).

PAGE 156

In The Showman and the Slave, Benjamin Reiss reports that Barnum's biographers have disagreed on whether or not Heth was technically Barnum's slave when he exhibited her (23).

Barnum purchased the 'exhibition' from R.W. Lindsay, with a bill of sale containing the words "the possession of the person of the African woman JOICE HETH and the sole right of exhibiting her" (24). That alone is enough evidence for me to personally conclude that for all intents and purposes, she was his legal property and therefore his slave. Barnum later purchased two more slaves during a trip to Mississippi, and wrote of whipping them and selling them at auction (26).

Most of Barnum's dialogue comes from the pamphlet *The Life of Joice Heth.*

PAGE 158

There's no record of how Maelzel and Schlumberger reacted to Heth's exhibition; this scene is entirely my own conjecture.

PAGE 159

This conversation is taken in part from Barnum's own biography (139). Barnum continued to take notes from Maelzel, whom he saw as "the great father of caterers for public amusement":

> When the audiences began to decrease in numbers, a short communication appeared in one of the newspapers, signed 'A Visitor,' in which the writer claimed to have made an important discovery. He stated that Joice Heth, as at present exhibited, was a humbug... 'The fact is,' said the communication, 'Joice Heth is not a human being. What purports to be a remarkably old woman is simply a curiously constructed automaton, made up of whalebone, india-rubber, and numberless springs ingeniously put together, and made to move at the slightest touch, according to the will of the operator. The exhibitor is a ventriloquist, and all the conversations apparently held with the ancient lady are purely imaginary, so far as she is concerned, for the answers and incidents purporting to be given and related by her, are merely the ventriloquial voice of the exhibitor.'

> Maelzel's ingenious mechanism somewhat prepared the way for this announcement, and hundreds who had not visited Joice Heth were now anxious to see the curious automaton; while many who had seen her were equally desirous of a second look, in order to determine whether or not they had been deceived. The consequence was, our audiences again largely increased (139–40).

The hoax played on the Providence abolitionists is also mentioned by Reiss (74–6).

PAGE 160

The origin of Heth's story is the source of debate, and Barnum's duplicity only makes the issue more difficult; he alternately claimed to have fabricated the entire story himself, and to have been duped by Heth (Reiss 21–2).

On the subject of Heth's own willingness to perform, Reiss also makes an excellent point with regards to her agency:

> "Because she was a slave, therefore, Heth's 'consent' could only be a matter of seeming; whether she 'wanted' to perform for her master was a question that could never truthfully be answered because, as slaves knew too well, to say 'no' was impermissible" (100).

Though it's almost impossible to know the origin of her story with any certainty due to the lack of accurate records, Heth's inability to speak freely for herself, and Barnum's constantly shifting stories, Reiss speculates that Heth invented the narrative as a way to lampoon her master, William Heth, for his constant bragging about his minor connection to George Washington, and that she may have suffered from dementia, eventually coming to believe her own story out of sheer repetition (211–24). In my own retelling, I chose to have Heth create the story for her own purposes, and to give her enough competency and strength of will to drive her own Faustian bargain.

I created Margaret's character based on the fact that Barnum hired a free Black woman as a nurse for Heth in Boston (103–4).

PAGE 161

True to her word, Joice Heth did not receive a Christian burial. After her death in February 1836, she was publicly autopsied at a New York saloon, and Barnum charged his audience 50¢ admission to watch. She was found to be entirely human, with an estimated age of between seventy-five and eighty years. Still not content to let the story die, Barnum went on to claim that Heth was alive and well, living in Connecticut.

Such treatment of Black people—during and after life—was heartbreakingly common during this time; Sartje Baartman, a South African woman, had been exhibited all over Europe, and after her death she was dissected, her genitals removed, and her skin stuffed and put on display in England. Nat Turner, a rebel slave from Virginia, also met a similarly grotesque fate (Reiss 126–40).

I elected not to illustrate any of these scenes in *Clockwork Game* because of a point that Reiss made, working from the writings of Saidiya Hartman:

> Hartman's suggestion is that such scenes can too easily amount to either pornography or a self-serving 'empathy' for the victims, an empathy that is so facile as to block an understanding of the real differences between observer and victim. Her solution is to avoid the spectacular altogether and to focus instead on the terror inherent in those routine aspects of slavery that are not physically brutalizing... 'the diffusion of terror and the violence perpetrated under the rubric of pleasure, paternalism, and property' (137).

Barnum had a change of heart later in life and became strongly anti-slavery during the Civil War, even going so far as to say that his decision to enter politics was so that he could vote for a Constitutional amendment to abolish slavery. After his election to the Connecticut General Assembly, he also gave a speech before the legislature in favor of male African-American suffrage (196).

Ironically, Barnum requested a closed-casket funeral, to prevent himself from becoming a public spectacle (203).

PAGE 166

You may have noticed Señor Alvarez in the background of page 110.

PAGE 168

The "bank panic" on Maelzel's copy of the *Philadelphia Courier* refers to the market crash of 1837. Unfortunately for my storytelling requirements, newspaper headlines weren't usually set in such large type until the days of yellow journalism later in the century, so this panel contains some artistic license.

PAGE 169

Maelzel and Schlumberger mentioned Mouret in their very first conversation. He was indeed a notorious drunk—an article published in *Fraser's Magazine* in 1839 said he had "burnt out his brain with brandy"—and sold the story for money.

PAGE 172

Maelzel and Schlumberger arrived in Havana right around Easter 1837, and so missed Lent altogether. The following year, Easter fell much later in the year.

PAGE 175

Yellow fever is a particularly nasty way to die (the accompanying "black vomit" is partially-digested blood that collects in the victim's stomach, and is said to resemble coffee grounds), and in the nineteenth century, people were terrified of it, more so than many other, more lethal diseases. A virulent outbreak in 1878 caused more than 20,000 deaths in Memphis, TN, and over half the residents fled for their lives (Historic-Memphis.com). Contemporary reports of the disease are chilling, especially considering that doctors of the time could only guess at its causes. It would take until 1900, when Walter Reed, working from the papers of Carlos Finlay, finally attributed its spread to mosquitoes.

It may not seem so, but the doctor is being merciful—contemporary "treatments" for yellow fever often included enemas, mustard applied to the feet, and hot bricks placed on the arms and legs (Chérot).

PAGE 177

George Allen had this to say about Maelzel's relationship with Schlumberger:

> Their connexion had lasted so long, they were always so much together, their manner towards each other was such, that an opinion grew up, among our German citizens [in Philadelphia], at least, that Schlumberger was a near relation, or an adopted son, of Maelzel's; nay, some thought him to be actually his son (465).

Though I've omitted them from the story for the sake of brevity, Maelzel also employed an assistant named Fischer and his wife to help with the show in Havana, and they both deserted him immediately upon Schlumberger's death (472).

The design for the *Otis*, described by Ewart as a brig (117), was taken from the modern replica brig, the *Lady Washington*.

PAGE 178

Allen described Maelzel's return to Philadelphia as rather grim:

> When Maelzel came on board, with the other passengers, Capt. Nobre was struck by the remarkable change, which had taken place in his appearance, since he had seen him with Schlumberger only three months before, in April. At that time not the slightest sign of wearing disease or natural decay could be seen: he was as stout and florid, as active and as lively, as he had been twelve years before, when he landed at New York, still a young man at the age of fifty-three. But now it was evident that he was 'breaking up'—that all the powers of mind and body were rapidly sinking, as though the source from which they had derived their strength had been suddenly withdrawn ("The History of the Automaton Chess-Player in America" 473).

PAGE 184

When Dr. Mitchell began to reassemble the automaton, he found that Maelzel had mixed the parts of his automata together across many different crates, presumably to deter thieves and secret-hunters, though I suspect it may also have been due to his condition when he packed up the show for the last time.

Dr. Mitchell found himself searching through not only the crates he'd purchased, but others still in Mr. Ohl's warehouse, and it took him several months to find all the parts, reconstruct the ones that had gone missing, and figure out how it all went together (Standage 189).

Dr. Mitchell was also the Poe family's physician, and reportedly loaned them money (Standage 188).

PAGE 190

Silas Weir Mitchell, the son of John Kearsley Mitchell first seen on page 15, went on to become a famous physician and author of both fiction and nonfiction. His research with Civil War amputees led him to coin the term "phantom limb" (Cervetti 78), and he also became known for advocating a

"rest cure" (108–122)–frequently used on "hysterical" women–which earned him an appearance in Charlotte Perkins Gilman's *The Yellow Wall-Paper*.

Nathan Dunn opened his Chinese Museum in 1838, and it shared a building with the Philadelphia Museum, which also housed Charles Willson Peale's collection of Chinese artifacts (Caplan).

In *Orientals: Asian Americans in Popular Culture*, Robert G. Lee states that:

> Peale particularly wanted to use his collection of memorabilia to refute negative portrayals of the Chinese as barbaric heathens—being circulated by frustrated Christian missionaries—and instead to promote a positive image of the Chinese as potential trading partners.

Though some or all of Dunn's collection may have been auctioned off at the time of the fire (Caplan), Dr. Weir Mitchell still referred to the building as "The Chinese Museum" in his article "Last of a Veteran Chess-Player."

PAGE 192

Dr. Weir Mitchell claimed to have heard the automaton speak as he fled the burning building. He may have added this flourish for effect, but it did make for a fitting ending.

SELECTED BIBLIOGRAPHY

Al-Hassani, Salim T. S. "Al-Jazari: The Mechanical Genius." The Foundation for
    Science Technology and Civilisation. 9 February 2001. Web. 21 Aug. 2013.
    <http://muslimheritage.com/topics/default.cfm?ArticleID=188>.

Al-Jazari. *The Elephant Clock: Leaf from The Book of Knowledge of Ingenious Mechanical Devices by al-Jazari.*
    N.d. The Metropolitan Museum of Art. Web. 21 Aug. 2013.
    <http://www.metmuseum.org/toah/works-of-art/57.51.23>.

Allen, George. "The History of the Automaton Chess Player in America." In *The Book of the First American
    Chess Congress.* New York: Rudd and Carleton, 1859, 420–84. *Google Book Search.* Web. 21 Aug. 2013.

___. *The Life of Philidor: Musician and Chess-Player.* New York: P. Miller & Son, 1858. *Google Book Search.*
    Web. 21 Aug. 2013.

Altick, Richard D. *The Shows of London.* Cambridge, MA: Belknap, 1978. Print.

Arrington, Joseph Earl. "John Maelzel, Master Showman of Automata and Panoramas."
    Pennsylvania Magazine of History and Biography 84 (Jan. 1960) 56–92. Print.

Babbage, Charles. *Passages from the Life of a Philosopher.* London: Longman, Green,
    Longman, Roberts, & Green, 1864. *Google Book Search.* Web. 21 Aug. 2013.

Barnum, Phineas Taylor. *The Life of P.T. Barnum, By Himself.* London: Sampson Low, Son and Co., 1855.
    Google Book Search. Web. 21 Aug. 2013.

"Ben Ali Stakes." *Wikipedia: The Free Encyclopedia.* Wikimedia Foundation, Inc., 21 Apr. 2013.
    Web. 26 Aug. 2013.

"Biography of James Ben Ali Haggin." Haggin Histories. 20 Jan. 2006. Web. 21 Aug. 2013.
    <http://haggin.org/JBAH_Biography.html>.

Blitz, Antonio. *Fifty Years in the Magic Circle: Being an Account of the Author's Professional Life, His
    Wonderful Tricks and Feats: With Laughable Incidents and Adventures as a Magician, Necromancer,
    and Ventriloquist.* Hartford, CT: Belknap & Bliss, 1871. *Google Book Search.* Web. 21 Aug. 2013.

Browne, James. *A History of the Highlands and of the Highland Clans.* London:
    A. Fullerton and Co., 1849. *Google Book Search.* Web. 21 Aug. 2013.

Caplan, Aaron. "Nathan Dunn's Chinese Museum." *American Philosophical Society.* N.p., n.d. Web.
    31 Aug. 2013. <http://www.amphilsoc.org/mole/view?docId=ead/Mss.069.C17n-ead.xml>.

Cervetti, Nancy. *S. Weir Mitchell, 1829–1914: Philadelphia's Literary Physician.* University
    Park, PA: Pennsylvania State UP, 2012. *Google Book Search.* Web. 6 Sept. 2013.

Chérot, Lassalinière. "Treatment of Yellow Fever" *Official Report of the Deaths from Yellow Fever.* New Orleans:
    W. L. Murray's Publishing House. 87–95. *Google Book Search.* Web. 21 Aug. 2013.

Clarke, Adam, and Clarke, Joseph Butterworth Bulmer. *An Account of the Infancy, Religious and Literary Life
    of Adam Clarke.* New York: B. Waugh and T. Mason, 1833. *Google Book Search.* Web. 21 Aug. 2013.

Cole, Juan Ricardo. *Napoleon's Egypt: Invading the Middle East.* New York: Palgrave Macmillan, 2007. Print.

Cooper, Barry. *Beethoven.* Oxford: Oxford UP, 2000. *Google Book Search.* Web. 21 Aug. 2013.

"Cotton Manufacture." *Encyclopaedia Brittanica*. 8[th]ed. Vol. 7:450. Edinburgh: Adam
    and Charles Black, 1854. *Google Book Search*. Web. 21 Aug. 2013.

"Diyarbakir (Turkey)." *Encyclopaedia Britannica Online*. Encyclopaedia Britannica, n.d. Web. 16 Nov. 2013.

Ewart, Bradley. *Chess: Man vs. Machine*. London: A.S. Barnes and Co., 1980. Print.

Franklin, Benjamin. "The Morals of Chess." *The Chess Player*. George Walker. Boston:
    Nathaniel Dearborn, 1841. 7–11. *Google Book Search*. Web. 21 Aug. 2013.

Fuller-Maitland, J. A., and George Grove. *Grove's Dictionary of Music and Musicians*. Vol. 2,
    8. London: Macmillan, 1907. Print. *Google Book Search*. Web. 21 Aug. 2013.

Gillray, James. *Lieutenant Governor Gall-Stone, inspired by Alecto*. The British Museum.
    N.d. Web. 26 Aug. 2013.

Gilman, Charlotte Perkins. *The Yellow Wall-Paper*. Boston: Small, Maynard and Company, 1901.
    Google Book Search. Web. 21 Aug. 2013.

Grove, George, J. A. Fuller-Maitland, and Edmond R. Wodehouse. *A Dictionary of Music and Musicians
    (A.D. 1450–1889) by Eminent Writers, English and Foreign. With Illustrations and Woodcuts*.
    London and New York: Macmillan, 1879. *Google Book Search*. Web. 21 Aug. 2013.

Isaacson, Walter. *Benjamin Franklin: An American Life*. New York: Simon and Schuster, 2004.
    Google Book Search. Web. 16 Nov. 2013.

Jefferson, Thomas. *The Writings of Thomas Jefferson*. York: H.W. Derby, 1861. *Google Book Search*.
    Web. 21 Aug. 2013.

"Joseph II." *Encyclopaedia Brittanica*. 8[th]ed. Vol 13:8. Edinburgh: Adam and Charles Black, 1854.
    Google Book Search. Web. 21 Aug. 2013.

Keith, Sir Robert Murray. *Memoirs and Correspondence (Official and Familiar) of Sir Robert
    Murray Keith*. London: Henry Colburn, 1849. *Google Book Search*. Web. 21 Aug. 2013.

Kempelen, Wolfgang von. "Kempelen-charcoal.jpg." *Wikimedia Commons*. Wikimedia Foundation, Inc., 29
    May 2013. Web. 21 Aug. 2013. <http://commons.wikimedia.org/wiki/File:Kempelen-charcoal.jpg>.

Lee, Robert G. *Orientals: Asian Americans in Popular Culture*. Philadelphia: Temple UP, 1999.
    Google Book Search. Web. 21 Aug. 2013.

"Lettres de M. Charles Gottlieb de Windisch, sur le jouer d'échecs de M. de Kempelen" (review). *Journal des
    Sçavans* (September 1783): 629–630. *Gallica, Bibliothèque Nationale de France*. Web. 21 Aug. 2013.
    <http://gallica.bnf.fr/ark:/12148/bpt6k57214x/f631.table>.

"Maelzel's Automatons." Editorial. *New York Daily Post*, 14 April 1826: 2. Old Fulton NY Post
    Card Website. N.p., n.d. Web. 26 Aug. 2013. <http://www.fultonhistory.com>.

"Mahmud II (Ottoman Sultan)." *Encyclopaedia Britannica Online*. Encyclopaedia Britannica, n.d.
    Web. 16 Nov. 2013.

Mitchell, Silas Weir. "Last of a Veteran Chess Player." *The Chess World*. 4.1 (1868) 3–7 and 4.2 40–45.
    Google Book Search. Web. 21 Aug. 2013.

"Maria Theresa." *Encyclopaedia Brittanica*. 11ᵗʰed., American reprint. New York: The
    Encyclopaedia Brittanica Company, 1911. *Google Book Search*. Web. 21 Aug. 2013.

Montagu, Violette M. *Eugène De Beauharnais; the Adopted Son of Napoleon*. London:
    John Long, 1913. *Google Book Search*. Web. 29 Aug. 2013.

Marr, Timothy. *The Cultural Roots of American Islamicism*. Cambridge: Cambridge UP, 2006. Print.

Padua, Sydney. "Dangerous Experiments in Comics." *2D Goggles*. N.p., n.d. Web. 31 Aug. 2013.
    <http://www.sydneypadua.com/2dgoggles>.

Poe, Edgar Allen. "Maelzel's Chess-Player." *Southern Literary Messenger*, 2.5 1836): 318–26.
    Google Book Search. Web. 21 Aug. 2013.

Racknitz, Joseph Friedrich, Freyherr zo. Kupferstich, Racknitz, Tafel 7. *Hermann von Helmholtz-Zentrum für
    Kulturtechnik*. N.d. Web. 26 Aug. 2013. <http://www.sammlungen.hu-berlin.de/dokumente/23234>.

Reininger, Alice. *Wolfgang von Kempelen: A Biography*. York: Columbia University Press,
    East European Monographs, 2011. Print.

___. *Wolfgang Von Kempelen: Eine Biografie*. Vienna: Praesens Verlag, 2007. Print.

Reiss, Benjamin. *The Showman and the Slave: Race, Death, and Memory in
    Barnum's America*. Cambridge, MA: Harvard UP, 2001. Print.

"Rigged Model, Philadelphia Packet Ship Shenandoah." *On the Water*. Smithsonian
    National Museum of American History. N.p., n.d. Web. 29 Aug. 2013. <http://
    amhistory.si.edu/onthewater/collection/TR_322426.html>.

Sahin, Emrah. "Re: Response #2!" Message to the author. 4 April 2011. E-mail.

___. "I am sending my comments this week," Message to the author. 1 Nov. 2013. E-mail.

Said, Edward W. *Orientalism*. New York: Vintage, 1979. Print.

Schloß Schönbrunn, *Schönbrunn Palace*. N.p., n.d. Web. 29 Aug. 2013. <http://www.schoenbrunn.at>.

Schindler, Anton, and MacArdle, Donald W. *Beethoven as I Knew Him*; a Biography. Chapel
    Hill: University of North Carolina, 1966. *Google Book Search*. Web. 21 Aug. 2013.

Sheppard, F. H. W. (General Editor). "Cork Street and Savile Row Area: Savile Row." Survey of
    London: Vols, 31 and 32: St. James Westminster, Part 2 (1963): 517-545. British History Online.
    Web. 31 Aug. 2013. <http://www.british-history.ac.uk/report.aspx?compid=41492>.

Standage, Tom. *The Turk: The Life and Times of the Famous Eighteenth Century Chess-Playing Machine*.
    New York: Walker and Co, 2002. Print.

"Staunton Chess Set." *Wikipedia: The Free Encyclopedia*. Wikimedia Foundation, Inc., 18 Aug. 2013.
    Web. 29 Aug. 2013.

Summers, Thomas Osmond. Yellow Fever. Nashville: Brothers, 1879. *Google Book Search*.
    Web. 21 Aug. 2013.

"'Ta ta ta ...' vierstimmiger Kanon WoO 162." Beethoven-Haus Bonn. Web. 21 Aug. 2013. <http://www.beethoven-haus-bonn.de/sixcms/detail. php?template=werkseite_digitales_archiv_de&_werkid=305>.

Thayer, Alexander Wheelock, Henry Edward Krehbiel, Hermann Deiters, and Hugo Riemann. *The Life of Ludwig Van Beethoven, Volume 2*. New York: Beethoven Association, 1921. *Google Book Search.* 21 Aug. 2013.

"The Elephant Clock by Al-Jazari." 1001Inventions. *YouTube,* 03 Nov. 2009. Web. 26 Aug. 2013.

The Life of Joice Heth, the Nurse of Gen. George Washington, (the Father of Our Country,) Now Living at the Astonishing Age of 161 Years, and Weighs Only 46 Pounds. Documenting the American South. University Library, The University of North Carolina at Chapel Hill. 31 Aug. 2013, Web. 31 Aug. 2013. <http://docsouth.unc.edu/neh/heth/heth.html>.

"The Turk (Automaton) vs. NN." Chessgames.com. Web. 21 Aug. 2013. <http://www.chessgames.com/perl/chessgame?gid=1305753>.

"There Were Giant Quacks in Those Days of Seventy-Six," *The Alienist and Neurologist,* 23.3 (Aug, 1902): 384. *Google Book Search.* Web. 21 Aug. 2013.

Thicknesse, Philip. *The Speaking Figure, and the Automaton Chess-Player Exposed and Detected.* London: Stockdale, 1784. Electronic Educational Environment, UCIrvine. Web. 21 Aug. 2013. <https://eee.uci.edu/clients/bjbecker/NatureandArtifice/week5g.html>.

Wairy, Louis Constant. *Recollections of the Private Life of Napoleon.* Trans. Walter Clark. New York, Boston: H. M. Caldwell Company, 1895. *Google Book Search.* Web. 21 Aug. 2013.

Walker, George, "Anatomy of the Chess Automaton." *Fraser's Magazine* 19 (Jun. 1839): 717–731. *Google Book Search.* Web. 21 Aug. 2013.

"Watt, James." *Encyclopaedia Brittanica.* 9th ed., American reprint. Vol 24, 412–14. Philadelphia: Maxwell Somerville, 1894. *Google Book Search.* Web. 21 Aug. 2013.

Windisch, Karl Gottlieb von. *Inanimate Reason.* London: S. Bladon, 1784. John Rampling. Web. 26 Aug. 2013. <http://web.onetel.net.uk/~johnrampling>.

"Yellow Fever: The Plague of Memphis." Historic-Memphis. Web. 21 Aug. 2013. <http://historic-memphis.com/memphis/yellow-fever/yellow-fever.html>.

Young, James Harvey. *The Toadstool Millionaires: A Social History of Patent Medicines in America Before Federal Regulation.* Princeton, NJ: Princeton UP, 1961. Quackwatch. Web. 26 Aug. 2013. <http://www.quackwatch.com/13Hx/TM/11.html>.

All images appearing in the Notes section are in the public domain and are taken from Wikimedia Commons.

ACKNOWLEDGEMENTS

When I started *Clockwork Game* on a lark back in 2007, I had no idea it would become such an all-encompassing project, or that it would span six years of my life. Along the way, I have been blessed with the help of many people who have all believed in the story and wanted to see it succeed, even when I wasn't sure how it could. I owe deep gratitude to:

Nisi Shawl, for being my primary editor and for including an essay of mine in *The WisCon Chronicles, Vol.5: Writing and Racial Identity*.

Dr. Emrah Sahin, for acting as cultural consultant on the script.

Woodrow Jarvis Hill, for his patience, and solid, correct advice as my original editor, and for pricking my conscience with his own writing.

All the other editors and beta readers who so generously gave their time and advice: **Dr. Timothy Marr**, **Ron West**, **Shveta Thakrar**, Karen Williams, **Haddayr Copley-Woods**, **Pam Bliss**, **Eric Braun** and **Allison Frame**, **Kathy Ha**, **Trevor Bennett**, **Mark Bernstein**, **Madison Clell**, **Mike Zawacki**, **Dagny Hanner**, **Solomon and Jennifer Foster**, **Emily Peterson** and **Dirk Tiede**, **Becky Cooper**, **Jeff Berndt**, and **Matthew Messana**.

The people who modeled for characters in the book: **Tamsey Glaser**, **Katherine Gilbert**, **Dave Glide**, **Logan Kelly**, **Neil Breyer**, and my most frequent subject, **Paul Sizer**.

David MacMillan for explaining to me how an eighteenth century printing press works.

Beth Huffington, who let me photograph all over the Lady Washington and climb the mainmast rigging, even though I couldn't make it past the first top.

Cordelia King at the Library Company of Philadelphia, for photocopies of important documents, and for helping me with obscure trivia about Philadelphian landmarks.

Tom Standage, for vetting the original draft of the script, answering questions based on his own research, and for photos of one of the automaton's performance locations, which I unfortunately could not work into the final version.

John Gaughan for the copy of Ewart's *Chess: Man vs. Machine*, for conversations which led me to work out my own solution to the automaton's inner workings, and for his encouragement and interest along the way.

Jim Ottaviani, for helping me find papers I needed for my research, including a public domain version of Gillray's political cartoon depicting Thicknesse, and for continual ear-bending.

Pam Bliss, for story suggestions, and for thinking a biography of an automaton was a good idea in the first place.

Layla Lawlor, for reading the script more times than anyone, for her kindness and continued faith in both the book and me as an author.

Carla Speed McNeil, for being a daily mentor and teacher, for her art lessons and confidence in me, and for andouille and bacon.

And more than anyone else, my greatest thanks are owed to **Paul Sizer**.

KICKSTARTER SUPPORTERS

$10-$75 Backer Levels

Alex Woolfson
Alexandra Yost
Almut Berenike Ruso
Alvaro Rivera-Rei
Amanda Penrose
Amanda Schwarz
Andrew Monk
Anika Page
Anne K Gray
Backer Name
Balazs Kosaras
Ben Harvey
Bill Brieger
Bill Gimbel
Brenda Haas
Brian Gan
Brian M. Gray
Brian Sebby
Bruce Woolley
Caitlin Pasqualone
Calvin Heighton
Cara Lieurance
Carey Wallace
Carolyn Bea
Catherine Fraas
Cecelia and Thor Thomas
Chad Burns
Chad Hoverter
Charlotte Anne Churchill
Chris Scholtens
Chris Tracy
Christina Gietzen
Christopher Willett
Christopolis Tiberius Markus
Clara Loveny
Colleen Cubbin
Cynthia Ward
D-Rock
Damian Gordon
Daniel Athearn
Daniele Sabatini
Dave Carter

Dave Jordan
Dave Sizer
Dave Zucker
Dawn Oshima
Deb Fuller
Denis MacDougall
Dennis Strasburg
Diana M.
Dirk Lapere
Dug North
Ellen McMicking
Emily Carc Boss
Emily Peterson amd Dirk Tiede
Erica J. Dedo
Erica Marotzke
Erin Snyder
For Good Measure
Günther Ottendorferk
Gary Bratzel
Gary Gaines
Greg McElhatton
Gus Grosch
Guy Thomas
Haddayr Copley-Woods
Happy Killmore and
    Crashive Aggressive
Harald Niesche
Haroun Khan
Harris O'Malley
Helen Taylor
horizonfactory
Ian Millington
Imhotep
J. Kevin Carrier
Jack Posont
Jake E. Fitch
James Heirman
James Sacchetti
Jane Carnall
J. Okanishi
Janine Lawton
Jay Quigley

Jay V. Schindler
Jed Hartman
Jeff Dickerson
Jeff Hadfield
Jenn Manley Lee
Jeremy Levett
Jesus Delgado
Jason Fortier
Jim Kosmicki
Joe Saul
Joan Flintoft
Johanna Draper Carlson
John Bintz
John Wimmer
Jonathan Cohn
Joseph Brennan
Joseph Leven
Josh Buschbacher
Josh Rosenbaum
Josh Thomson
Joshua King
Juan Diego Ramirez
Karen Lakkides
Karen Oettel
Karen Riggin
Kat Kan
Katharine Beach
Kathleen Smith
Kathryn W. Nilsen
Keith Lewis
Kelli Pax Phillips
Kerin Schiesser
Kevin A. R. King
Kevin D Freeman
Kevin Hogan
Kevin J. Maroney
Kimberly M. Lowe
Kirk Lund
Larry Thorson
Laura Hedges
Layla Lawlor
Leah and Stewart Tame

KICKSTARTER SUPPORTERS

$10-$75 Backer Levels

Lin Lang
Lisa Wishinsky
Logan Kelly
Lord Mercanden and
    Lady Kyrielle
ManicMarauder
Marc Specter
Marco Barnig
Margaret Bumby
Mark Bernstein
Mark Smith
Martha Bissell
Marvin L Thomas
Mary Ellen Wessels
Matt Commins
Matt Farstad
Matt Yuill
Matthew D. Miller
Matthew Messana
Megan
Michael Brewer
Michael Richey
Michael & Kathy Neufeld Dunn
Michael Chiasson
Michael Maroon
Michael Tisserand
Mike Hainsworth
Mike Welham
Mike Zawacki
Mikkel Sebastian Keilhau
Moti Lieberman
Naomi Kritzer
Nathan Seabolt
Nathan Stapleton
Nathaniel Allard
Neil Bryer
Nicholas Harman
Nikki Jeffries Sørensen

Nora Proni
Ozwell
Pat Wozniak
Patrick Rennie
Peggy Daub
Peter Westlake
Petra Mayer
Pierre LeBlanc
R l artwork
Randy Belanger
Raptor
Rasmus Viking Lømand R.
    Christiansen
Rebecca Boensch
Rebecca Rocha Siwicki
Rich Vander Klok
Rika Smith
Rob Steinberger
Robert Dahlen
Robyn Moore
Rowena Mante-Rumpf
Russ Herschler
S. Mouse Bowden
Sachin Nithyan
Sally Lou Thompson
Sally Mittler
Sam Hanes
Samuel Hansen
Sara Forss
Scott Davis
Scott Harriman
Sean Bieri
Sean Kinlin
Sean Kleefeld
Sentiashinou
Sequential Imagery
    Consortium
Serina Patterson

Shaun Gilroy
Sir Otis Kaiser Doyle
SkunkBoy
Solomon and Jennifer Foster
Sotiris Tseles
Staci Lowman Ainsworth
Stefan Einarsson
Stephanie Benson
Stephanie C.
Stephanie Wagner
Steve Simmons
Steven desJardins
Steven Goldman
Steven Mollison
Steven Ransel Mills
Sue Vasquez
Susan Connolly
Susan R Grossman
Svend Andersen
Tanika S. Perryman
Thomas Jansen
Tiff Hudson
Tiffany Middleton
Tim and Kathy Broderick
Tisha and Matt O'Malley
Tom Deater and Becky Cooper
Tom 'Filkertom' Smith
Trisha L. Renken-Sebastian
Turner Dehn
Victor Raymond
Victoria Jones-Avie
Virginia Watson
Vyasar Ganesan
Winefred Washington
Yin Yin Leong

KICKSTARTER SUPPORTERS

$100+ Backer Levels

Adam Smith

Allison Frame and Eric Braun

Alex Tang

Allan Harvey

Amy Beth Russell

Andrea Angott

Anna-Katharina Niederberger

Ben Nichols

Carol 'klio' Burrell

Catboy

Chris Dangerfield

Christopher Smith

Craig Jarvis

D. A. Gordon

Dan Sugalski

Dennis M. Wenzel

Earl Cook

Falling Down Beer Company

Galia Appel

Gregory Kane

Hugo Huggett

Jürgen Pünter

James Barron

James Galvin

Jason Aaron Wong

Jeff Berndt

Jim Ottaviani and Kat Hagedorn

Joel Derrough

John J. Walsh IV

Judith A. Irwin

Kevin Nolan

Kimberly Pudliner

Mark 'Disco' Troyer

Melissa Aho

Michael Ball

Michelangelo Cicerone

Nicholas Diak

Patricia Shipman

Rollande Krandall and
   David MacMillan

Timothy David Elrod

Wendy L. and Steven J. Benedict

William Greentower

Wim Keppens

Zach Murray